PERIL
AND
PROMISE

PERIL
AND
PROMISE

COLLEGE LEADERSHIP
IN TURBULENT TIMES

Beverly Daniel Tatum, PhD

BASIC BOOKS
NEW YORK

Basic Books
Hachette Book Group
1290 Avenue of the Americas, New York, NY 10104
www.basicbooks.com

Printed in Canada

First Edition: September 2025

Published by Basic Books, an imprint of Hachette Book Group, Inc. The Basic Books
name and logo is a registered trademark of the Hachette Book Group.

The Hachette Speakers Bureau provides a wide range of authors for speaking events.
To find out more, go to hachettespeakersbureau.com
or email HachetteSpeakers@hbgusa.com.

Basic books may be purchased in bulk for business, educational, or promotional use.
For more information, please contact your local bookseller or the Hachette Book Group
Special Markets Department at special.markets@hbgusa.com.

The publisher is not responsible for websites (or their content)
that are not owned by the publisher.

Print book interior design by Sheryl Kober.

Library of Congress Cataloging-in-Publication Data

Names: Tatum, Beverly Daniel, author
Title: Peril and promise : college leadership in turbulent times / Beverly Daniel Tatum, PhD.
Other titles: College leadership in turbulent times
Description: First Edition. | New York : Basic Books, 2025. | Includes bibliographical
references and index.
Identifiers: LCCN 2024061867 | ISBN 9781541606616 hardcover |
ISBN 9781541606623 ebook
Subjects: LCSH: Universities and colleges—United States—Administration
Classification: LCC LB2341 .T28 2025 | DDC 378.1/07—dc23/eng/20250616
LC record available at https://lccn.loc.gov/2024061867

ISBNs: 9781541606616 (hardcover), 9781541606623 (ebook)

MRQ

1 2025

To Travis, with love and gratitude for so many reasons for joy

CONTENTS

INTRODUCTION: For Such a Time as This   1

CHAPTER ONE: The Dean with the ABC Agenda   19

CHAPTER TWO: Who's Afraid of DEI—and Why?   47

CHAPTER THREE: Free Speech in the Time of War   79

CHAPTER FOUR: Who's in Charge, Really? Understanding Shared Governance   103

CHAPTER FIVE: Presidents, Protests, Police, and Politics   119

CHAPTER SIX: Managing Risks: Campus Safety and Mental Health   155

CHAPTER SEVEN: Walking on the Edge of a Cliff   189

CHAPTER EIGHT: College Finances 101   211

CHAPTER NINE: "The Time Has Now Come": The End of Affirmative Action   243

CHAPTER TEN: Disruption at the Door?   267

CHAPTER ELEVEN: Reasons for Joy   299

Acknowledgments   315

Notes   319

Index   353

INTRODUCTION

FOR SUCH A TIME AS THIS

W hen I told a friend, a man who happens to be the CEO of a large financial institution, that I was writing a book about contemporary higher education and its challenges, he replied with great sincerity, "I think being a college president has to be the hardest job in America." I was surprised to hear him say so, given the difficulty of his own job. But he was not alone in his assessment. Throughout the 2023–2024 academic year, the headlines in national newspapers and higher education publications echoed his sentiment. Articles with titles such as "You Could Not Pay Me Enough to Be a College President," or "Anyone Want to Be a College President? There Are (Many) Openings," and "Campus Protests Prompt the Question: Who Wants to Be a College President?"[1] turned up with regularity that year.

Admittedly, the 2023–2024 academic year was especially difficult for college leaders, particularly in the wake of the Israel-Hamas war and the campus protests that followed. To quote the editors of the *Chronicle of Higher Education*, 2024 was "an annus horribilis for college presidents.

Budget shortfalls, enrollment declines, protest encampments, congressional interrogations, high-profile resignations."[2] The cascading problems of 2023–2024 on campuses still recovering from the toll of the COVID-19 pandemic surely felt like a very heavy weight on presidential shoulders. But the pronouncements about the difficulties of college leadership did not begin with the war in the Middle East.

Just a few years before, in 2019, the *Atlantic* featured an article titled "Who Wants to Be a College President? Probably Not Many Qualified Candidates."[3] In March 2023, the *Chronicle of Higher Education* did a special feature issue titled "Trouble at the Top: Meeting the Daunting Challenges of Today's College Presidency." The cover illustration captured the essence of the issue's message as it depicted a man looking out his office window while the seat of his desk chair was aflame. Figuratively, if not literally, college leaders were on the hot seat.

I was one of the presidents interviewed for that special issue. Among the interview questions I responded to via email were "Has it become harder than ever to be a college president?" and "Is it an impossible job?" At the time, I was serving as the interim president of Mount Holyoke College, a position I held for one year (2022–2023). Previously, I had served for thirteen years as president of Spelman College (2002–2015). My experience at both those institutions, and my knowledge of their histories, informed the response I gave in the fall of 2022. I wrote,

> The role of a college president today is undoubtedly very challenging. Is it harder now than ever? I imagine that depends on your point of comparison. Mary Lyon, the founder of Mount Holyoke College, was creating an institution for women in 1837 at a time when the very idea of higher education for women was revolutionary. The founders of Spelman College, Sophia Packard and Harriet Giles, were two White women from Massachusetts building an institution for Black women in Atlanta in 1881, less than 20 years after

the end of the Civil War. In both cases, resources were scarce, nay-sayers were many. Difficult does not mean impossible.

Were my on-the-job challenges really so much harder than what those women faced? I don't think so. My intention in this book is to give the reader an insider's view of higher education today, an understanding of the context in which its most pressing concerns have arisen, and the tools that will allow us to address them. Based on forty-plus years of experience in higher education, I can attest that wise, creative, and courageous leadership can mitigate even the most challenging problems of our time.

This book has transformed considerably over the course of the past decade. When I retired in 2015 from my position as the president of Spelman College, I planned to spend my time working on two books—the first was a twentieth-anniversary revision of my 1997 book, *Why Are All the Black Kids Sitting Together in the Cafeteria? And Other Conversations About Race*, with the goal of having it ready for publication in 2017. The second book I imagined writing was a memoir of some kind, an opportunity to reflect on my thirteen years as a college president and the lessons learned. I envisioned a small book with very short chapters, quickly read and easily digested, a book perhaps for would-be college presidents. But that second project was delayed, first by a two-year stint of speaking engagements following the 2017 release of the updated *Why Are All the Black Kids…* book, the distraction of the COVID-19 pandemic in the spring of 2020, and most especially, the 2020 murder of George Floyd, which sparked renewed interest in books and dialogue about racism, catapulting my book to the *New York Times* bestseller list for weeks that summer. The so-called racial reckoning that followed George Floyd's death became an intense eighteen-month period of public engagement for me, even if often mediated by Zoom. By the start of 2022, I felt a need for a respite from such personally draining work. I knew it was time to pause and do something different.

Fortunately, something different was on the horizon. I was heading back to Mount Holyoke College to serve as the interim president for the 2022–2023 academic year. I spent thirteen years at Mount Holyoke earlier in my career (1989–2002)—first as a professor of psychology, then as a dean, and for six months as acting president—before I left in July 2002 to become the president of Spelman College. In March 2022, the chair of the Mount Holyoke Board of Trustees contacted me to discuss the presidential transition underway at the college. President Sonya Stephens had just announced her intention to accept a new position as president of the American University of Paris. She would be stepping down as president of Mount Holyoke College at the end of June. The chair asked if I would be willing to serve as interim president for the coming 2022–2023 school year while the search for the next permanent president was underway. I was intrigued by the possibility.

Soon to be sixty-eight, I was not interested in the job on a long-term basis, but the idea of returning to Mount Holyoke for just one year was appealing to me. Finding the right person to serve as college president is a daunting and time-consuming task. I knew that having an experienced president in the role as interim would make the process easier for everyone. The college had given me so many career-transforming opportunities at a pivotal time in my life, it seemed only right that, during its time of need, I should return and give something back to the institution that had given so much to me. On July 1, 2022, I returned to the campus of Mount Holyoke as the interim president, exactly twenty years from the day I had left it to head to Atlanta. It felt like a homecoming, a full-circle moment.

To paraphrase the Greek philosopher Heraclitus, "You can never step in the same river twice." The college had grown and changed during those twenty years, as had I, and the world was rapidly changing around us. For example, just a week before, on June 24, 2022, the US Supreme Court had delivered its ruling in the *Dobbs v. Jackson Women's Health* case, overturning the 1973 *Roe v. Wade* decision, in a major setback for reproductive rights.[4] My return to the campus as interim president coincided with this and other global inflection points that impacted everyone. We had all come through two long years of a global pandemic. We could see the escalation of global conflict as wars raged in Ukraine and elsewhere. We recognized the backlash against racial progress and the rise of White nationalist movements at home and abroad. We witnessed the pushback against LGBTQ+ rights and the increase of transphobic legislation. We could see evidence of the impact of climate change locally and globally. The mental health crisis and the growing threat of gun violence challenged our collective sense of safety. Budgetary pressures, and resulting increases in tuition, were continuing to fuel the crisis of college affordability. The public questioning of the value of higher education was troubling, and the pool of college-going students was predicted to shrink. In short, the world, as we had known it, seemed to be unraveling.

Yet it is in just such a time as this that colleges and universities— institutions that encourage us to think critically about important social issues and exercise our capacity for leadership—become beacons of hope and sources of inspiration. Colleges and universities are communities of problem-solvers, communities that attract creative thinkers. They are places where leaders can see the impact of the work they do every day, where effective leadership can be transformational. Despite the challenges, a college campus is a wonderful place to be. It was energizing to be back on the campus in a leadership role.

Twelve months later, together with the Mount Holyoke community, we had navigated the end of COVID protocols (and managed a COVID-related campus building takeover), galvanized trustee support for the transition from gas-powered heating and cooling to a carbon-neutral geothermal heat exchange system, gained approval of a new, more concise and impactful mission statement as part of the strategic planning process, and most importantly, helped to rebuild the spirit of community and campus optimism about the college's future. The campus was ready to welcome its new leader.

On September 21, 2023, Danielle R. Holley was inaugurated as the twentieth president of Mount Holyoke College, the first Black woman to serve as the permanent president in its 186-year history. As President Holley gave her inaugural speech, I watched the dynamic leader at the start of her presidency, still in her forties, and I was reminded of the moment I stood before the Spelman College community pledging to offer my best in the service of that powerful educational mission. I was excited for Danielle and for Mount Holyoke as she made a similar promise. Truly it was a moment to celebrate!

Finally, back in Atlanta, just as I was ready to start that next book, I realized something else was needed, something that would address the contemporary challenges that confront higher education leaders today. In my year at Mount Holyoke, I could see that over the last two decades many things had become more complicated—gender fluidity and the use of preferred pronouns, as just one small example. The question of creating a diverse and inclusive community had grown more complex, particularly in the context of an increasingly polarized society. Concerns about free speech and academic freedom, perennial on college campuses, had become more intense in the face of that polarization. Budgetary pressures in an inflationary economy were mounting, amplified by the potential enrollment challenges created by declining US birth rates. Questions of campus safety in an era of increasingly common school shootings and other threats of violence were terrifying. Mental health concerns in a post-COVID world were rising, too. When on June 29, 2023, the Supreme Court ruled in *Students for Fair Admissions, Inc. v. President and Fellows of Harvard College* that race-conscious admission practices violated the Constitution, race-based affirmative action programs were eliminated across the higher education landscape in one fell swoop.[5] A whole new set of questions about how colleges and universities could maintain their commitments to campus diversity without running afoul of the law was added to the list of presidential concerns. If that were not enough, the growing loss of confidence in higher education as a public good posed an existential threat in an age where technology offered new education solutions beyond the traditional in-person campus experience.

Throughout my year at Mount Holyoke, people I knew—friends, acquaintances, even strangers sitting next to me on planes—asked about these concerns. They wondered why presidents said X or didn't say Y, why institutions operated the way they did, why college wasn't the way they remembered it decades ago. Those comments and questions shifted my thinking about what kind of book this should be. While it is rooted in my higher education experience, particularly as informed by my life as a college president, this book is not a memoir in the traditional sense. It is my reflection on the challenging higher education landscape at a pivotal moment in American social history, and on the role that effective leaders can play in shaping our future through the power of education.

Over the course of my life, I have been involved with lots of different higher education institutions—as a student, a professor, a dean, a college president, and a trustee. I attended a small, highly selective liberal arts college (Wesleyan University) and then earned my master's and doctorate in clinical psychology at the University of Michigan (a leading research university with close to fifty thousand students, undergraduates and graduate students combined). At the start of my career, I spent four years working as a part-time lecturer at the University of California, Santa Barbara, a public land grant university. My first full-time tenure-track teaching position was at Westfield State College (now University) in Massachusetts, a teaching-centered, small public institution (approximately five thousand undergraduates) with a unionized faculty, serving many first-generation college students. After achieving tenure at Westfield, I left to accept a teaching position at Mount Holyoke College, the oldest of the prestigious women's colleges once known as the Seven Sisters.[6] Thirteen years later I went on to serve as president of Spelman College, a historically Black liberal arts college for women in Atlanta, my first experience working at an

HBCU (historically Black college or university) and living in a southern city. In 2017, I spent a trimester as a visiting scholar at the Haas Center for Civic Engagement at Stanford University, a leading research university and one of the most selective undergraduate institutions in the nation. As a trustee, I served on the board of Morehouse College (the only HBCU men's college) when they launched their innovative online program targeted for older Black men who want to get a Morehouse education. Other higher education boards have included Smith College (another of the Seven Sisters); my alma mater, Wesleyan University; and the boards of the Association of American Colleges & Universities and the Council of Independent Colleges. Along the way I have coordinated with two-year community college leaders in developing transfer articulation agreements to smooth the transitions from those two-year schools to bachelor's-degree-granting institutions like Spelman and Mount Holyoke. Traveling on book tours and speaking circuits, I have visited literally hundreds of colleges and universities and engaged with senior campus leaders.

Throughout these experiences I have learned that each institution—regardless of type—has its unique qualities and dilemmas, but the twenty-first-century challenges I have identified transcend these categorical boundaries. Whether it is the enrollment challenge of a declining birth rate, the rising threats to campus safety, the growing demand for mental health services, or the advance of artificial intelligence, every institution and its leaders are affected (or will be) by some, if not all, of the challenges discussed in the following chapters. I know that most of the readers of this book will never lead a college—or may never even work at one. It is my hope that those readers will not only gain an understanding of the complexities of the challenges facing higher education as we enter the second quarter of the twenty-first century, but also gain insight into how and why institutional leaders make the decisions they do to navigate those challenges.

In addition to those general-interest readers, this book is for anyone who has a particular interest in leadership and higher education—personal or professional—or for anyone who has been to college or is thinking about going or sending a child, for anyone who wants a better understanding of why colleges and universities function the way they do, and why they matter so much to all of us. I hope it will raise some questions, answer others, and just perhaps convince a few that, yes, someone in their right mind might indeed want the job of being a college president.

Good leaders are needed for just such a time as this.

SETTING THE CONTEXT: A FEW FACTS AND SOME DEFINITIONS

To set the context for the chapters that follow, let's start with the basics. Who are today's students? What college options do they have? And who is leading those institutions?

In 2022, who were those undergraduate students?[7] Most students who enroll in college in the US do so immediately following their high school graduation. In the fall of 2022, 62 percent of new high school graduates were joining in college their peers from previous high school graduating classes. Women outpaced men, with 66 percent of women immediately enrolled at a two- or four-year school as compared to 57 percent of young men.[8] The student population in the US was approximately 52 percent White, 22 percent Hispanic, 13 percent Black, 7 percent Asian, 4 percent two or more races, 1 percent American Indian / Alaska Native, and less than one-half of 1 percent Pacific Islander.[9] The average age of those students attending full-time was twenty-two; for those attending part-time, it was twenty-seven. Roughly one-quarter of current undergraduates were twenty-five or older.[10] Collectively they represented 15.4 million undergraduate students, with a broad range of educational options to consider.

The US higher education system is unique in its size, diversity of type, and array of choices within and across categories of institutions. According to the *Report on the Condition of Education 2024*, an annual report prepared by the National Center for Education Statistics (NCES), in the 2022–2023 academic year there were 3,633 degree-granting postsecondary institutions in the United States. A "degree-granting institution" is defined by NCES as an institution that awards associate or higher degrees and participates in Title IV federal financial aid programs. (Institutions that award only graduate degrees are not included in this count.) Sixty-five percent (2,365) were four-year institutions, more than half of those private nonprofit colleges or universities (1,319). Only one-third of the four-year institutions (769) were public institutions, and fewer than 10 percent (277) were private for-profit institutions. Two-year institutions, often referred to as community colleges or technical schools, represented 35 percent (1,268) of the total number of higher education institutions in 2022–2023. Of that number, 817 of them were public (64 percent), 78 were private nonprofits (6 percent), and 373 were private for-profit institutions (29 percent).[11]

Ninety-five percent of the 15.4 million undergrads attended either a public four-year institution (48 percent), a public two-year institution (29 percent), or a private nonprofit four-year institution (17 percent). Five percent of them attended either a private nonprofit two-year institution or a private for-profit four-year institution. When the news is full of stories about higher education, the examples are often taken from well-known private colleges and universities. In that context it is worth remembering that fewer than one in five college students is attending a private four-year college. Fewer than 1 percent are attending one of the Ivy League schools in the Northeast. We not only want to keep track of the demographic diversity of today's students—we also need to understand the diversity represented by the different kinds of institutions.

When considering "who goes where," it should be noted that the racial/ethnic distribution of students varies across types of institutions. The NCES 2023 report indicated that public four-year institutions had enrollments that were the most representative of the undergraduate population overall in terms of race and ethnicity. Public two-year schools and private four-year institutions were less evenly balanced. At 27 percent, Hispanic students were overrepresented in public two-year schools and underrepresented in private four-year institutions (15 percent). White students were overrepresented in private four-year nonprofit institutions (61 percent) and less likely to enroll at private for-profit institutions (43 percent). Asians were also less likely to enroll at private for-profit schools (just 4 percent). Black students had a much higher representation at private for-profits, making up 27 percent of their student population as compared to 12 percent at the private nonprofit schools. Overall, the enrollment at for-profit institutions is disproportionately older (65 percent of students are twenty-five or older), African American as noted, and female (65 percent), many of whom are single parents.

As will be discussed in Chapter 8, the distinctions of "private nonprofit," "public," and "private for-profit" tell you something about how the institutions are funded and who controls them. Public institutions are controlled by state governments and are partially funded by state revenues. Private nonprofit institutions operate independently, with little or no state funding, relying on student tuition payments, fundraising, and endowment earnings for their revenue. For both public and private nonprofit institutions, delivering on the educational mission of the institution is their primary concern.

The private "for-profit" institutions are independent businesses intended to earn a profit for their investors while offering educational opportunities to students. Sometimes referred to as "proprietary institutions" or "career colleges," they often offer programs to match high-demand labor needs, for example in health care, business, and information technology. Their funding comes primarily from the federal financial aid (Pell Grants and student loans) that their students use to pay the cost of attending. They advertise heavily, typically targeting students who want to jump-start a career. Unfortunately, their track records of high costs, low graduation rates, and high levels of indebtedness among the students who enrolled have cast a long shadow on this segment of postsecondary institutions.[12] Researchers have found repeatedly that "students *pay more and benefit less* from for-profit education than from education in other sectors."[13] The adult learners who choose the for-profit option typically learn about it through advertising, without the benefit of guidance counselors who might caution them about the poor outcomes most students experience.[14] Over the decade from 2012 to 2022, the number of private for-profit institutions dropped nearly 50 percent, from 1,388 to 650 (including both two-year and four-year schools).[15] Except when specifically noted, throughout this book I will only be referring to public and private *nonprofit* institutions.

Beyond the differences of public and private, nonprofit or for-profit, are factors like size (ranging from a few hundred students or fewer, to fifty thousand or more), location (urban, suburban, or rural), in-person or online instruction, secular or religiously affiliated, research-intensive or teaching-centered, and those that serve special interests (music conservatories, art schools, engineering schools, for example) and specific populations (e.g., women's colleges, men's colleges, HBCUs, and tribal colleges or universities, or TCUs). The diversity of institutions that make up the US higher education landscape is clearly one of its strengths.

The diversity of the leadership in higher education is much less robust. According to the 2023 American College Presidents Study conducted by the American Council on Education (ACE), most college presidents were older White men. The average age of presidents was sixty, and only 33 percent were women. In the ACE survey, presidents of color accounted for approximately 25 percent of the respondents, and women of color accounted for approximately 10 percent. Significantly, 58 percent of current college and university presidents reported that they plan to step down within the next five years.[16] The number of anticipated vacancies provides a unique opportunity to expand the presidential ranks beyond the traditional White male profile that has been the norm throughout the history of higher education. It seems particularly appropriate to do so when we consider that the college-going student population has never been more diverse, and that diversity is increasing in the US with each passing year.

Not only are we facing new twenty-first-century challenges, we are also in the midst of the changing of the guard across higher education. Such a change presents an opportunity to think creatively about the mounting problems, as well as about what kind of problem-solvers are most needed in this moment. In her book *Leading from the Margins: College Leadership from Unexpected Places*, Mary Dana Hinton, an experienced college president, lifts up the value that diverse voices can bring to the task of leadership. As someone born on the margins of society, "poor, Black and a woman," Hinton asserts that "perspectives formed by life in the margins give us new ways of viewing the world, a readiness to question inherited assumptions, and the tools to give witness to the harm these assumptions cause....Because this leadership starts from a different point, it will, by design, manifest itself differently."[17] Like Hinton, I am a Black woman, though one who grew up in a middle-class family of educators— my mother was a public school teacher and my father a college professor. I grew up in a small town in Massachusetts, where I was often the only Black student in my class. My perspectives on leadership are undoubtedly shaped by that starting point. I have the dual perspective of an industry "insider" and a societal "outsider." My long-standing commitment to creating inclusive learning communities is undoubtedly rooted in that duality.

However, just as there is a changing of the guard among higher education leaders, so has there been a change in national leadership that promises to impact higher education and its leadership in significant ways. On January 20, 2025, as this book was being completed, Donald J. Trump was inaugurated as the forty-seventh president of the United States. President Trump launched his second term by immediately issuing a slew of executive orders, including one titled "Ending Illegal Discrimination and

Restoring Merit-Based Opportunity," which rescinded the long-standing 1965 executive Equal Employment Opportunity order issued by President Lyndon Johnson. Johnson's order prohibited discriminatory hiring practices and established federal affirmative action programs. In revoking it, Trump's sweeping executive order not only removed the existing federal obligation to ensure fair and equitable hiring practices but also ordered all federal agencies "to combat illegal private sector DEI preferences, mandates, policies, programs and activities."[18] While such activities were not defined or delineated in the order, "it was the latest indication that the Trump administration is determined to eliminate diversity, equity and inclusion and affirmative-action practices not only across the federal government, but higher education as well."[19]

In relation to gender diversity, the president issued "Defending Women from Gender Ideology Extremism and Restoring Biological Truth to the Federal Government," an executive order intended to codify two sexes, "male" and "female," described as immutably determined by biological reproductive markers, as the only ones recognized by the federal government. Any reference to gender identity (as indicated by gender identity choice options on forms) would be removed from federal documents, and any existing federal protections for transgender people were to be revoked.[20] This executive order was the first of several that specifically targeted transgender and nonbinary people, increasing their vulnerability on college campuses.[21]

In a related action, Trump categorically rejected the Biden administration's proposed expansion of Title IX protections. Title IX is the gender-equity law that "requires colleges to ensure that sex-based discrimination doesn't prevent students from accessing their education." Title IX regulations determine how colleges handle complaints of sexual harassment, sexual assault, or other sex-based mistreatment.[22] The Biden administration interpreted Title IX to include protection against gender-identity-based discrimination and consequently updated the regulations to provide protections for

LGBTQ+ students, including guaranteed access to facilities that match their gender identities. It also added new protections for pregnant and parenting students, removed live-hearing and cross-examination requirements for sexual misconduct cases, and expanded the definition of sexual harassment from behavior that is "severe, pervasive, and objectively offensive" to "unwelcome sex-based conduct." However, Biden's Title IX rule changes were challenged in federal court by six Republican-led states that objected to the transgender protections. On January 9, 2025, with less than two weeks of the Biden administration remaining, Chief Judge Danny C. Reeves of the Eastern District of Kentucky ruled that Title IX only applied to sex-based discrimination, and including gender identity exceeded the authority of the Department of Education, thereby violating the Constitution. Consequently, all the Biden changes were thrown out, and the Title IX rules established in 2019 during the first Trump administration were restored.[23]

While President Trump had been expected to revoke the Biden changes, the court decision made doing so unnecessary. Trump began his second term with a narrowed definition of sexual harassment in place and no federal antidiscrimination protection based on sexual orientation or gender identity.[24] In fact, on February 4, 2025, the Education Department's Office of Civil Rights issued a "Dear Colleague" letter to college administrators, reminding them that "President Trump ordered all agencies and departments within the Executive Branch to 'enforce all sex-protective laws to promote [the] reality' that there are 'two sexes, male and female,' and that '[t]hese sexes are not changeable and are grounded in fundamental and incontrovertible reality.'...ED and OCR must enforce Title IX consistent with President Trump's Order."[25] While many institutions are expected to maintain campus policies that, apart from Title IX, recognize and support transgender students, some wonder if there will be federal consequences for doing so.[26]

As promised throughout his campaign, Trump took immediate action to begin deporting undocumented immigrants and to further restrict legal immigration, by barring new asylum seekers at the southern border and suspending the Refugee Admissions Program.[27] The frightening impact of these actions on the four hundred thousand undocumented students attending colleges across the nation, and the many more who have undocumented family members who might be deported without notice, cannot be underestimated. At Trump's direction, policies that had protected colleges from Immigration and Customs Enforcement raids were rescinded, allowing ICE arrests to take place on campuses without advance notice.[28] Would ICE really target campuses? What could leaders do to support students and preserve the learning environment in the face of such threats?

The anti-immigrant federal policies were creating an unwelcoming climate for international students, a group that makes up almost 5 percent of US college enrollment. International students are an important source of tuition revenue for many colleges, each paying on average $30,000 per year to attend a college or university in the United States. But their numbers fell by fifty thousand during the first Trump term. If the number of international students dropped by fifty thousand again during this Trump administration, the loss of much-needed revenue to US colleges would be about $1.5 billion.[29]

The president also used his first few days in office to impose new restrictions within the research community. The Department of Health and Human Services told employees of several health agencies, including the National Institutes of Health (NIH), to suspend all public communications, as well as travel, meetings, and hiring.[30] The NIH is the largest federal research funding source for colleges and universities, awarding nearly $33 billion in research grants to colleges and universities in 2023. The January meetings when grant proposals are reviewed and funding awards recommended were among the meetings that were suspended, leaving researchers across the nation in a state of confusion, if not panic. With the distribution of billions of research dollars on hold, it was feared that the interruption would "have long-term effects on medicine & short-term effects on state, higher education & hospital budgets," with negative implications for everyone.[31]

At the time of this writing, it was too early to know the full effect of these orders or potential future actions such as eliminating the Department of Education or taxing college endowments, ideas discussed during Trump's presidential campaign.[32] Would there indeed be legal attacks on colleges committed to principles of diversity, equity, and inclusion? Would institutions see significant reductions in research funding or unanticipated changes in how such awards were made? Would there be new disruptions to federal financial aid programs or a sharp decline in international students? One thing was certain—the launch of the second Trump administration further complicated the preexisting challenges facing campus leaders.

As you read the following chapters, I invite you to consider the national context and how it may have changed from the time of this writing, as well as what perspective educators may bring to their understanding of the current challenges, and the ways that leaders can address them, for better or worse, because the solutions matter to all of us. The long-term success of higher education as a public benefit depends not just on the institutional leaders—and their boards, their faculty, staff, administrators, and alumni—but also on the broader communities that support them and believe in the transformational power of their educational mission.

CHAPTER ONE

THE DEAN WITH THE ABC AGENDA

I loved being a college professor. I appreciated the freedom and autonomy that came with the role. Most of the time I could choose which courses I taught, when they would be offered, how the courses would be organized, and what texts to assign. I enjoyed the intellectual stimulation that came from teaching my psychology courses, advising my students, doing my research, and publishing my work. My favorite class to teach was Psychology of Racism, a subject I first began teaching in 1980. By the time I joined the faculty at Mount Holyoke College in 1989, I had made Psychology of Racism my signature course, and my professional writing was centered on helping fellow educators as well as students understand the complex dynamics that can emerge in multiracial classrooms when engaging in cross-racial conversations about race and racism. An article I wrote in 1992, "Talking about Race, Learning about Racism: The Application of Racial Identity Development Theory in the Classroom," published in the *Harvard Educational Review*, was well received and widely circulated, giving my work new visibility within the community of educational researchers.[1]

Other articles followed, and in 1996 I signed a book contract with Basic Books for the publication of my book *Why Are All the Black Kids Sitting Together in the Cafeteria? And Other Conversations About Race.*[2]

Inspired and informed by my years of experience teaching about the psychology of racism, the book was intended to help a general audience of readers understand what racism is; how it operates in our society; the impact it has on how we think about ourselves, our racial/ethnic identities, as well as the identities of other people; and ultimately what we can do at home, at school, and in the workplace to counteract racism's toxic effects. With that book contract in hand and a strong record of successful teaching as well as significant service on campus committees, I was promoted that year from associate professor to full professor, the top rank among professors.

When I received that promotion at Mount Holyoke College in 1996, I was thrilled to hit the career milestone that I had been aiming to achieve. Promotion to full professor was validation of my years of hard work, and it was not lost on me that I was one of few Black women to reach that goal, not just on my campus, but nationally. In fact, as of 2022, still fewer than 2 percent of full professors in the United States were Black women.[3] Though my promotion was cause for celebration, I soon discovered its downside. As the newest full professor in my department, my colleagues informed me that I would be next in line to become department chair. It was not a role I wanted, but it was the practice in the department to rotate the responsibility of department chair among the senior members of the faculty. Now as a full professor, I was one of them. My colleagues agreed among themselves that it was my turn to serve. The term of service was expected to be three years. I reluctantly accepted the assignment.

Why was I reluctant? Just like me, my colleagues enjoyed their freedom and autonomy. They liked to be able to select their own courses, set their own schedules, and teach their classes with little interference by the "administration." As the chair of the department, it would be my responsibility to make sure that courses were scheduled without conflicting with one another, that the required courses needed to complete a psychology major were offered with regularity, that student concerns involving faculty members or departmental policies were addressed, and that interdepartmental conflicts were resolved, amicably if possible. Administrative management of the departmental budget, curricular reviews, and faculty evaluations were all part of the job. The responsibilities of department chairs are considerable, but the actual authority of the chairs is quite limited among their peers. Leadership must be exercised by persuasion rather than coercion. As chair, your freedom and autonomy become subsumed to the administrative needs of the department, while your colleagues continue to insist on their freedom and autonomy. In my view, being the department chair was likely to be a thankless and tedious job. But the other full professors in the department had done it. It was indeed my turn.

In the fall of 1997, I became chair of the Psychology and Education Department. Prior to assuming the chair position, I had never *ever* considered college administration as a desirable career choice. Chairing the department did not change my mind. When a friend asked me what I thought about being the chair, I replied, "I think it is a good reason to look for another job." And, in fact, I did begin to consider new opportunities.

Why Are All the Black Kids Sitting Together in the Cafeteria? had just been published that September and was getting a lot of positive publicity. Its timing was perfect. In the summer of 1997 President Bill Clinton had announced his initiative "One America in the 21st Century: The President's Initiative on Race," with an advisory panel chaired by the distinguished historian John Hope Franklin. The panel's task, as described by Clinton, was "to help educate Americans about the facts surrounding issues of race, to promote a dialogue in every community of the land to confront and work through these issues, to recruit and encourage leadership at all levels to help breach racial divides, and to find, develop and recommend how to implement concrete solutions to our problems—solutions that will involve all of us in government, business, communities, and as individual citizens."[4] That was exactly what my book was designed to do! Suddenly my book was in the national spotlight. When Clinton hosted the initiative's first public forum at the University of Akron on December 1, 1997, I was one of three authors of books on US race relations invited to be part of the conversation.[5] I was especially thrilled when my book was named by the National Association of Multicultural Education as Book of the Year, affirmation that it was reaching an audience of educators as I had intended. As the visibility of my work increased, I began to be actively courted by research universities for professorships. As the mother of two sons, then eleven and fifteen, and the wife of a fellow college professor tenured at a nearby university, I really did not want to disrupt my family situation by moving to a new institution. Still, I recognized my readiness for a change.

Unsure of my next steps, I sought out a senior colleague in my department for some career advice. She suggested that I consider applying for the position of dean of the college, the chief student affairs position at Mount Holyoke, which at the time included oversight of undergraduate academic curricular concerns as well as all co-curricular areas of student life, including academic and career advising, residential life, student activities, health and counseling centers, athletics, pastoral care, study abroad programs, honor code enforcement, and campus safety. It was a broad and varied portfolio of responsibilities. The current dean had already announced his intention to step down from the role at the end of that academic year. My immediate response to my colleague's suggestion was *"Who in her right mind would want that job?"* I imagined endless days of boring meetings. As the department chair, I was already attending a lot of meetings that I found boring. I didn't want more. She said, "You are not using your imagination. If you were dean of the college, you could take the ideas that you have been writing about and put them into practice. You could really impact the student experience here. And what you do here will influence practice at other schools, too."

I was intrigued by that possibility. I had been writing about how to create inclusive learning communities where all felt welcome and the importance of educating the next generation of leaders, to be able to overcome the legacies of segregation and engage effectively across lines of difference. What if I could indeed help increase the college's ability to be that kind of learning environment? What if we could provide best-in-class examples that other institutions might learn from? In *Why Are All the Black Kids Sitting Together in the Cafeteria?* I wrote about the spheres of influence we all have and how we might use those social networks of influence to bring about positive social change. Was being the dean an opportunity to expand my sphere of influence in just the way that I had been writing about? I decided to give that idea some thought.

Not long after that conversation, I traveled to the University of Michigan to attend a conference on intergroup dialogue. The University of Michigan is widely acknowledged as the intellectual home of intergroup dialogue programs on college campuses. The first program of its kind in the nation, the Program on Intergroup Relations (IGR) is a social-justice education program founded in 1988. Unique in its partnership between the university's Student Life division and the College of Literature, Science, and the Arts, IGR blends theory and experiential learning to facilitate students' learning about social group identity, social inequality, and intergroup relations. The dialogues are an essential pedagogical part of the program—facilitated face-to-face encounters, sustained over several weeks, that foster meaningful engagement between members of two or more social groups with a history of conflict (e.g., Whites and people of color, Arabs and Jews).[6] By 1997 the University of Michigan architects of the IGR program had almost a decade of experience to share. I was excited to attend the conference and learn more about this new pedagogy. The more I learned about intergroup dialogue, the more I thought it would be a great program to launch at Mount Holyoke, a wonderful tool for developing the leadership capacity of the students within a very diverse campus community. It occurred to me that if I were the dean of the college, I might have the opportunity to make it happen.

With my perspective considerably broadened by these conversations, campus leadership began to have greater appeal. I applied and was selected for the position of dean of the college. My colleague had been right. I immediately found it to be a job full of creative possibility and opportunity for positive impact, both on campus and off. The learning curve was just the challenge I needed. My days were indeed full of meetings, but to my delight, they were not boring. I discovered quickly that meetings are much more interesting when you can set the agenda. As the dean, I could do that.

The agenda I set became known as the ABCs—*affirming* identity, *building* community, and *cultivating* leadership for the twenty-first century. The abbreviation was taken from the first public speech I gave in my new role as dean of the college. It was my first divisional staff meeting, and I told the gathering that our shared intention should be to *affirm the identities of all our students*, particularly those at risk of marginalization; to *build a shared sense of community* where all felt included; and to *cultivate the leadership capacity of our students* so that they might be ready with the tools of twenty-first-century leadership, able to engage effectively across lines of difference. Those three goals—affirm identity, build community, cultivate leadership—became the cornerstone of our work together, foundational to our efforts to support student academic and social success and well-being. Working with a talented team of administrators, I was able to introduce new programs and policies, all designed to create a more inclusive learning environment for all students. The ABCs I championed as the dean became the foundation of my leadership as a college president in the years that followed, and these ABCs have informed every leadership role I have held since then.

Why would anyone want to be a college or university leader today? One reason might be that, like me, they want to ensure that students are benefiting from the ABCs in action.

AFFIRMING IDENTITY

Imagine this scenario: You are in a room full of people, and a photographer has arrived to capture the gathering with a group photo. The photographer has carefully arranged everyone so no one's face is blocked. All are visible, smiling on cue. The photographer takes the shot. Later everyone in the room will get a copy of the photograph. When handed the photo, what is the first thing each person will do? Look for themselves in the picture! That is the only honest answer to that question. We would all look at the photo and try to find our own face in the crowd before we look for anyone or anything else.

But imagine if for reasons unknown to you, your image was digitally removed from the photo. You would feel quite puzzled to discover you are not in the picture. Recalling the scene, you remember exactly where you were positioned at the time the photo was taken. You see in the photo the faces of the people who were standing all around you that day. Yet, for some unexplained reason, your face is no longer visible. There is no evidence that you were even there. Your immediate response might be to ask, "What's wrong with this picture? Why am I missing from it?"

Let's imagine that this experience has happened, not just this one time, but repeatedly. Whenever there is an occasion for a group photograph, you gather up with the other people, but again and again, your face is missing from the final photo. Your response is likely to become not "What's wrong with this picture?" but instead "What's wrong with me? Am I invisible? Why am I always being left out?" You might find that eventually you stop participating. When the photographer invites everyone to gather up, you choose instead to head for the door. Why participate if you are never included?

We all have a need for affirmation—to be seen, heard, and understood.[7] We want to be seen in our full personhood, including those aspects of our identity that are most salient for us as the result of our life experiences. We all have multiple dimensions of our identity. If asked to describe yourself, what would you say? Would you mention your race or ethnicity? Your gender identity or expression? Religious affiliation? Sexual orientation? Age? Disability of any kind? Socioeconomic status? Geographic place of origin? Profession or career? Family relationships? Dietary restrictions? Favorite hobbies? How you answer the question of your self-description is socially determined in large part by your interactions with others. Our identities are shaped through our social interactions with others, who become like mirrors, reflecting images back to us about who we are or are supposed to be.[8]

Today the collective reflection in that mirror of social interaction is a multihued, multicultural collage. In the 1950s the total US population was nearly 90 percent White. At the time of the 2020 US Census, the White (non-Hispanic) percentage had dropped to approximately 58 percent, the Latinx/Hispanic population had grown to approximately 19 percent, and the Black/African American population was the third-largest group, representing approximately 12 percent of the population. Less than 1 percent in 1965, in 2020 Asian Americans represented approximately 6 percent of the population; Alaska Natives, American Indians, and Pacific Islanders together made up slightly more than 2 percent. In 2020, approximately 10 percent of the US population self-identified in the census as multiracial (representing two or more racial groups) as compared to only 2 percent in the year 2000.[9] The Census Bureau recognizes more than 350 languages, 177 of which are indigenous to the US or its territories, with 68 million people in the US—almost 20 percent—speaking a language other than English at home.[10]

The religious landscape has shifted as well. According to the 2020 Public Religion Research Institute (PRRI) Survey of American Religions, while 70 percent of Americans identify as Christian, that number drops to 54 percent among younger Americans. Those between the ages of eighteen and twenty-nine represent the most religiously diverse age group. As noted, a majority (54 percent) are Christian, yet only 28 percent are White Christians (including 12 percent who are White mainline Protestants, 8 percent who are White Catholics, and 7 percent who are White evangelical Protestants), while 26 percent are Christians of color (including 9 percent who are Hispanic Catholics, 5 percent who are Hispanic Protestants, 5 percent who are Black Protestants, 2 percent who are multiracial Christians, 2 percent who are Asian American / Pacific Islander Christians, and 1 percent who are Native American Christians). The religiously unaffiliated are growing in number, with more than one-third of young Americans (36 percent) so identified. The remainder are Jewish (2 percent), Muslim (2 percent), Buddhist (1 percent), Hindu (1 percent), or another religion (1 percent).[11] What is required in this new context? Affirmation!

Everyone wants to feel included, to find themselves in the photograph. That is especially true if some aspect of your identity has been marginalized or even stigmatized because of social norms rooted in a hierarchy of human value, where some people are seen as more worthy of inclusion than others. Affirmation of that devalued dimension of identity can be hard to find, but it is sorely needed.

Invisibility is the opposite of affirmation. If an important psychological need goes unmet, energy must be invested to correct the situation. Fighting against invisibility is exhausting. Leaders who want people to function at their best in their organizations must think about how they can make them feel seen, heard, and understood. How can we affirm the identities of everyone? I learned to start by asking this fundamental question: Who is missing from our picture? That is, who steps onto this campus or into this organization and sees themselves (or people like them) reflected, and who does not? I learned to then ask, "What can I do about it?"

I came to understand that not only do we want to see ourselves in the picture, but we want to be in the picture *looking good*. If the picture is always an unflattering one, the result is not much better than being left out altogether. Years ago, when I was a young psychology professor teaching child development, I was bothered that so many textbooks featured lots of pictures of White children but very few of Black, Indigenous, or other people of color (BIPOC). Too often when there was a photo of a child of color it was in the section of the textbook that dealt with deviance of some kind, such as fetal alcohol syndrome, mental illness, or juvenile delinquency. While today that textbook situation may have improved, it is still the case that BIPOC youth are too often invisible in the curriculum and BIPOC adults too often missing from the workplace and the boardrooms. I learned that paying attention to who is in the picture as you plan programs, as you consider hiring—as you do *anything*—can make a meaningful shift in how or whether people feel like they belong. A sense of belonging is an important dimension of emotional well-being and one of the best predictors of whether someone will remain in an organization. In an academic context, educational researchers have shown that students who report a strong sense of belonging are likely to be more engaged academically, resulting in better attendance, less misconduct, higher self-esteem, better mental health, and improved academic performance.[12]

The most fundamental affirmation of identity is in the respectful use of someone's chosen name. When someone has a name that is linguistically unfamiliar to you, it may take some effort for you to learn how to pronounce it correctly. But in my experience, the effort is always appreciated. It might seem that this is so obvious it is hardly worth mentioning. Yet in my professional development work with teachers, I found sometimes that teachers would impose a nickname on a student to avoid having to learn the correct pronunciation or might avoid using the name simply by not addressing the student at all, not out of malice but out of fear of making a mistake. I recall working with a very experienced White male high school teacher who stood at the door of his classroom as students entered. He greeted some, but not all, of his students by name. The students whose names felt unfamiliar to him were most often students of color. They were also the students who performed less well in his class. After learning more about the importance of affirmation, he made the effort to greet each student by their chosen name as they entered. To his surprise, the achievement level of his lowest-performing students began to improve.

The small step of learning to say their names conveyed an important message: "I see you, and you belong here." A sense of belonging is a critical ingredient in a productive learning environment. In his classic essay, "I Won't Learn from You," Herbert Kohl describes what happens in the absence of affirmation of one's personhood. "To agree to learn from a stranger who does not respect your integrity causes a major loss of self. The only alternative is to not-learn and reject their world."[13] When the teacher acknowledged each student's humanity by learning to say their name, an important connection was made that facilitated learning in his classroom.

The same might be said of using someone's preferred pronouns. I am of the generation that studied grammar and diagrammed sentences in middle school and high school English classes, and long-ingrained habits make it hard for me to get used to using what I learned to be plural pronouns such as "they" and "them" to refer to a single individual, but I make the effort when asked, because I know it demonstrates respect to the person who made the request. Affirmation matters.

The creation of affinity groups—in the form of cultural centers on a campus or employee resource groups (ERGs) in a company—is one structural way organizations can affirm the identities of their members. When people who have meaningful shared experiences—whether as the result of a common marginalized identity related to race, gender, or culture, for example—are able to gather together for mutual support, their sense of belonging and well-being is enhanced. Throughout my career I have seen and heard administrators across industry sectors question the wisdom of endorsing such efforts, sometimes referring to affinity groupings as "self-segregation," a term that is itself problematic.[14] Yet I have seen the benefit of creating such spaces, particularly for those who are underrepresented in their organizations, allowing the opportunity for them to connect and refuel with the support of others with whom they have a shared identity.

Indeed, research has shown that participation in affinity groups, particularly for Black and Latinx students, is associated with not only a greater sense of belonging at the institution *but also* higher rates of cross-racial interaction during other times of the day.[15] When you have refueled, you have the energy you need to take on the often-taxing social challenge of cross-group interaction. Not every student from a marginalized or underrepresented group will choose to affiliate with an affinity group or cultural center, and not every employee will want to be part of an employee resource group, but the existence of these programs signals to all that the institution sees them. They are not invisible.

The positional authority of the leader gives additional symbolic meaning to whatever the leader does. It matters if the president attends the Diwali celebration hosted by the Hindu students or attends the LGBTQ+ student-sponsored panel. It is not possible to be everywhere all the time, but the leader's visibility matters. People notice when and where you invest your time. While serving as president of Spelman College, I regularly hosted an iftar, the traditional meal that celebrates the end of fasting during the season of Ramadan, for our Muslim students, faculty and staff, and their invited friends. On a campus founded by two Christian missionaries, and culturally dominated by students and employees who identify as Christian, members of the Muslim community represented a significant but often invisible minority. Hosting the iftar was seen as an important gesture of hospitality that gave visibility to this portion of our community in a way that was very meaningful to them.

When I returned to Mount Holyoke College as interim president in the summer of 2022, I was aware that incidents of antisemitism were on the rise nationally, and the college had also experienced some antisemitic acts on campus during the previous year, leaving the Jewish community feeling increasingly vulnerable. Since September marks the start of the Jewish New Year, and Yom Kippur (the day of atonement) is a day of fasting, I had an early opportunity to affirm the presence of Jewish students by hosting a break-the-fast meal at the president's residence. In a spirit of gratitude, Jewish student leaders remarked that such an event had never happened on campus before, but they were wrong. More than twenty years before, when I was the dean and Joanne Creighton was the president, she regularly hosted a break-the-fast meal. But subsequent presidents apparently had not continued the practice, campus staffing had changed, and those who had experienced that hospitality had long since graduated. My conversation with the students in 2022 reminded me that our affirmation efforts, once established, need to be institutionalized if we want to maintain our progress toward building inclusive communities. Otherwise, we are always starting over.

How can we make progress? Asking the question "Who is missing from this picture?" should become a habit of mind for all of us, not just the institutional leaders. But don't ask yourself in solitude. We all have gaps in our awareness. We don't always know or recognize what it is that we might be overlooking. The input of others around the table who are also asking "Who's missing?" is likely to result in a more complete picture. We all benefit when *everyone* can feel seen, heard, and understood. Affirmation matters.

BUILDING COMMUNITY

Every leader I know talks about building community in some way. Whether leading a small college or a large corporation, we understand that bringing people together with a sense of shared purpose contributes to a greater sense of well-being and a desire to support the organization and its goals. Creating community is a cumulative process—fostering connection through shared activities over time. My desire as a leader is always to help everyone see that we are all in this shared enterprise together, a community in which everyone has an important contribution to make, a place in which everyone belongs and can thrive. Intentionality is required.

Every institution has community-building rituals—orientation activities, community celebrations, holiday parties, to name just a few. These activities can bring community members together in a spirit of joie de vivre, but they can also result in marginalization and feelings of alienation, particularly if in the planning process we forget to ask ourselves, "Who's missing?" Those who repeatedly feel left out will eventually disengage from the community, contributing to low morale and/or retention concerns. It is very difficult to do the B—building community—successfully without simultaneously attending to the A—affirming identity. They must go together.

I have two examples to illustrate this point. The first occurred in the early days of my presidency at Spelman College. A member of the special events team at Spelman came to my office in the early fall and let me know that it was time to plan the campus Christmas party, an event sponsored by the Office of the President. To his chagrin, I said I could not sponsor a Christmas party. I explained that I knew that not everyone on our campus celebrated Christmas. There were Jewish, Hindu, Muslim, Baha'i, and perhaps other religious traditions represented in our community, and I did not want to host a party that by its very name excluded them. I proposed that we have a party at the end of the fall semester that included recognition of the Christmas season and the other seasonal celebrations such as Hanukkah and Kwanzaa but was also welcoming by design to everyone, including those who didn't celebrate any of those holidays. "How would we do that?" he asked. "We need a committee," I replied.

I asked my chief of staff, Sherry Turner, to lead the planning committee, and populated it with a multifaith group of faculty and staff willing to help. Sherry and I had worked together at Mount Holyoke College, and we knew each other well. I had confidence that she understood my inclusive intent. Sherry was also an ordained Baptist minister with southern roots, who understood the cultural context of our campus. We both knew I had given her a tough assignment.

Just a few weeks before, at our opening convocation, the gathering of students, faculty, and staff that marks the start of the school year, I had given my first public speech on the campus and shared my views about the importance of creating an inclusive environment that was welcoming to all. I wanted to honor the history of Spelman College, an institution founded in 1881 by two White women from Massachusetts, inspired by their Christian faith to travel to post–Civil War Atlanta to start a school for formerly enslaved Black women, and whose missionary zeal was captured in the school's motto, "Our whole school for Christ." Nevertheless, in the twenty-first century it was also important to acknowledge and appreciate the reality of our multifaith community. I had already been asked by some alumnae if I planned to try to change the school motto. I did not. But I did want to invite our campus community to think about how we might use our motto to include others, rather than exclude them. I reminded the audience that at the core of Christian teachings is the principle of "hospitality"—welcoming the stranger, treating others the way you want to be treated. Every great world faith tradition has some version of that Golden Rule as part of its teaching. To be at our best, and live up to our motto, I said, we should embody that principle in all that we do. It was in that spirit that the planning for our year-end celebration began.

As the planning proceeded, Sherry would update me on the committee's progress. She told me that one of the most contentious meetings was about the color scheme for the party. When the decision was made not to use the traditional Christmas colors of red and green, at least one committee member told her with great distress that she was taking away his religion. The committee eventually settled on white and gold. Despite the struggles, the result was inspirational. The theme of the party was "the Best of the Season," and the venue was decorated with large banners that said, "Love, Hope, Joy, Peace." In the Spelman tradition, the dean of the chapel (a Protestant Christian) would have offered a blessing at the start of the event, before the food was served. For this occasion, the planning committee had asked each member of the multifaith committee to share a blessing from their own tradition—Hindu, Jewish, Muslim, Baha'i, Buddhist, indigenous African, Catholic, and Protestant offerings were shared. The committee members beamed with pride at what they had accomplished together, and the party was a great success—in terms of both attendance and the awareness of the religious diversity within our community that had not previously been visible.

The experience of being part of the planning committee was so affirming that a Hindu faculty member came to my office the following year and asked if she might organize a campus Diwali celebration to which the whole campus would be invited. Known as the "Festival of Lights," Diwali is the biggest Hindu festival, taking place in October or November, depending on the Hindu lunar calendar. The faculty member had been at Spelman for decades but had never felt the permission to bring that aspect of herself into full view in our Christian-centric community—but being part of the holiday planning committee had empowered her in a new way. She felt fully seen, and our community was enriched as a result.

Years later, back at Mount Holyoke College as interim president in the fall of 2022, I was again confronted with the need for inclusive community building. As we were slowly emerging from the two years of social isolation imposed by the COVID pandemic, many people experienced a yearning to reconnect with colleagues and friends across campus. Some employees, hired during the pandemic, had never met some of their colleagues in person, only knowing them as faces on a Zoom screen. Community building was sorely needed.

In this context, the fault line in the community was not determined by faith tradition but by employment status, with faculty in the favored position relative to staff. Such distinctions are common in higher education institutions, but on this campus, past institutional practices had exacerbated the "us-them" positionality. For example, it was routine for the president to host events at the president's residence for faculty (retirement celebrations, for example) to which staff were not invited. Conversely, those special events that were designed specifically for staff were rarely attended by faculty. Both faculty and staff commented on the sense of separation they felt from each other, but staff, in particular, articulated feeling overlooked and invisible when they were not included or when faculty chose not to attend staff-centered events. This pattern was particularly noticeable at the year-end celebrations, with one celebration hosted by the president for faculty and another organized by the Staff Council for staff.

Because of the COVID pandemic, none of the celebrations had taken place during the previous year. When we were able to gather again, it seemed to me to be a good opportunity to change the pattern and have one campus-wide celebration that would engage both faculty and staff. To that end, I announced that there would not be a special holiday reception for faculty, and the Staff Council decided not to host the special staff party. Once again, I needed a committee and invited both faculty and staff influencers to serve on it. I knew I would need the faculty influencers especially to get faculty to attend what might otherwise be dismissed as a "staff" party. The party was set to occur on the last day of exams, just after the exam period ended, so faculty would still be on campus, and just after the 7:00 a.m. to 3:00 p.m. shift ended, so hourly facilities workers could enjoy the festivities before heading home. The location was the campus community center, a neutral space that would be inviting to both faculty and staff. Its multilevel design would accommodate both loud activities—a live band—and quiet corners for conversation. The pub space was designated to be a karaoke room. The party needed a name—one of the committee members coined the perfect one: *The Bright Lights Celebration—Let Us Shine Together!*

I repeatedly reminded everyone about the party with campus-wide invitations, and the committee "influencers" leaned in to encourage their colleagues to attend. Despite these efforts, longtime staff members expressed considerable skepticism about whether any faculty would attend, as did some faculty. But on that December afternoon, at the end of the semester, in a campus center beautifully decorated with bright lights, great food, and fabulous music, the whole community was there—faculty, staff, and administrators, literally hundreds of people having fun together. It was amazing!

When the celebration was over, a staff member, a leader among her peers, sent me this email summarizing comments she received:

What a party! The smiles and excitement were just what this community needed! What you helped us to imagine brought people together in a way that I have never seen since I arrived on the campus in 2017! I want to share a few comments that I will summarize to the best of my ability:

- I have worked here for a year and haven't met a lot of people. I wasn't sure that I made the right choice to come to work here. And this party made me realize that I am in the right place and I'm really happy to be here!
- I have only met people on zoom screens and I don't even recognize some people without their masks on, so I feel like I'm meeting people for the first time.
- I finally feel like I found joy at work!

Another wrote: *Today was, as one faculty member told me, exactly what the community needed—and she didn't even know how much until she saw and felt it.*

We all want to feel that we belong to a larger, shared community. Out of many, we want to become one. We want to feel that mutually supportive connection with others. Hierarchical differences—whether defined by race, class, religion, employment status, or other social identities—can and often do impede community-building efforts, but with intentionality such impediments can be reduced. Long ago, Gordon Allport, a prominent social psychologist, argued that bringing disparate groups together under conditions of equal status (as when all are contributing members of an appointed committee), working together cooperatively toward a common goal, with the endorsement of an authority figure such as the organizational leader, results in improved intergroup relations.[16] An "us-them" dynamic, whatever the source, that can undermine community well-being and collective progress needs to be mitigated whenever possible. A great campus-wide party is not the only solution, but it can certainly be a good place to start.

CULTIVATING LEADERSHIP

Every institution of higher education sees itself as preparing the next generation for leadership and effective civic participation. But are we truly providing the tools needed for democratic participation and leadership in the twenty-first century? The multiracial, multiethnic, multilingual, multireligious America in which today's students have come of age is very different from the one that shaped my early years or those of most senior leaders.

Ironically, despite the changing demographics of the United States, most students in the US today still live in relatively homogeneous residential communities and, as a result, attend racially segregated schools. As documented by a July 2022 report on K–12 education by the US Government Accountability Office, many schools remain divided along racial, ethnic, and economic lines.[17] Yet to be an effective twenty-first-century leader, each of us must be able to interact effectively with people different from ourselves. Where will the next generation of leaders get the practice to do that, if not in their learning environments? For many, the college experience is likely to be the most diverse learning environment they have experienced and perhaps their best chance to develop that capacity for leadership. In diverse environments, there is much to learn about people with different ideas and experiences. There is also often unanticipated awkwardness. Fear of making mistakes (and perhaps being blasted on social media) too often leads individuals to retreat from important learning opportunities. What is needed are structured opportunities to practice.

Our efforts to affirm identity and build community inevitably create situations that allow students to engage in what Henry Giroux called "border studies, the points of intersection, where different histories, languages, experiences and voices intermingle amidst diverse relations of power and privilege."[18] When we encourage students to become "border crossers," we are cultivating their capacity for leadership in the twenty-first century.

Some border crossing happens socially as students enter unfamiliar spaces on campus. For example, when "minority" students organize programming at their cultural centers and invite "majority" students to participate, a unique learning opportunity is created in that the invited students are required to shift their cultural lens "from the center to the margin."[19] As one White student at Mount Holyoke told me, she was initially hesitant to attend campus events hosted at the Betty Shabazz Cultural Center (established to serve the needs of students of African descent) because she was not a woman of color. But when she did attend a party there, she had a great time, and returned to attend other events, slowly shedding her sense of discomfort. She observed, "Cultural centers represent an important educational site for White students. All students should take advantage of the excellent opportunity cultural houses provide to rid them of fear." Creating opportunities for such border-crossing experiences is essential for developing the skills required to interact effectively in the increasingly pluralistic world of the twenty-first century.

One of my favorite examples of just such a learning opportunity took place during my years as dean of the college at Mount Holyoke—a powerful example of the ABCs in action. At that time, there were nine active faith groups on campus—Baha'i, Buddhist, Hindu, Jewish, Muslim, Unitarian Universalist, Wiccan, and Christian—both Catholic and Protestant. In her effort to apply the ABCs, the dean of religious life and Protestant chaplain Andrea Ayvazian recognized that some faith groups had privileges (funding, chaplains, worship space, institutionally observed holidays) while others did not. In this context some groups were affirmed, while others did not see themselves reflected in the environment at all.

To address this situation, Andrea started having conversations about resources with the Religious Life Advisory Board, a group made up of faculty, staff, and the Multi-faith Council, a group of thirty student representatives, three representatives for each of the nine groups, plus three students representing "unaffiliated seekers." It was very evident that the

Christians had the most (a large and a small chapel, plus Protestant and Catholic chaplains). The Jews had a part-time rabbi and no space, the Muslims had a chaplain and a small prayer room they were rapidly outgrowing, and everybody else had nothing. The advisory groups talked about what it meant to be a religiously pluralistic campus, what it meant to share power and resources, what that might look like and feel like.

We decided there were two things we could do right away—one was to find religious advisers for all those groups who were without one. Andrea successfully identified members of the faculty and the wider community who might be willing to serve as a religious adviser for those groups who didn't have one. These advisers agreed to meet with their groups for a weekly gathering, prayer, or sharing service, and to meet regularly with the religious life staff—all on a volunteer basis.

The second was to find worship space. The campus has a big, beautiful Gothic-cathedral-styled chapel which seats one thousand, and an adjoining small chapel that could accommodate about one hundred, both clearly designed for Christian worship. Most of the other faith groups were relegated to an overused lounge in the Office of Religious Life that offered little quiet or privacy for devotional activity. The advisory groups concluded that the obvious thing to do was to convert the small chapel into an interfaith sanctuary—a project that Andrea had estimated could be accomplished quickly and at relatively little expense during the week of spring break when most students would be away from campus. As planned, the pews, which had been bolted to the floor, were removed and replaced with eighty lovely, easily moved chairs, all the hanging crosses were taken down, and the stone floor was covered with a beautifully patterned rug rescued from college storage. These changes, along with fresh paint and increased lighting, transformed a traditional chapel into an attractive interfaith sanctuary, newly decorated with symbols and signs of every faith, displayed in ways that could acceptably accommodate the rules for each.

For example, Muslim students needed space to pray prostrate on the floor (movable chairs made that possible) in a space free of visual representations of religious figures. Hindu students used religious figurines called *murtis* in their worship practice, which once installed by a Hindu priest were not supposed to be moved. How to accommodate both? A handsome wooden cabinet was built to hold the installed *murtis*, with doors that when closed removed them from view. Similarly, a student Torah was stored in a beautiful wooden ark, visible only when in use by Jewish students. Christian students still had access to the large chapel, but when the smaller space was desired, a pulpit with the image of a cross could be easily wheeled out from a storage closet when needed. The interfaith chapel, a space once used only on Sunday afternoons by Protestant students, became available for daily use by students from every faith group.

While this was a very creative solution, it was also a controversial one. Many Protestant students, the largest faith group on campus, felt betrayed by their chaplain. Why was she "ruining" *their* chapel? For some, this "diversity stuff" had gone too far! Posted in the online student chat group were many angry messages from Christian students who did not see the need for this change. But in response there were very thoughtful messages from students who had been active in the multifaith council, explaining why the change was necessary. In fact, the student representatives on the council met on their own to discuss the problem, and then asked the dean of religious life not to address the posted criticisms herself but to let the students on the council take the lead in responding. It was an inspiring example of cultivating effective leadership in a pluralistic context. For one student to be able to explain to another about why it was necessary to share resources, why it was necessary to think about the needs of people different from yourself, was a very exciting thing to see.

Clearly it was then, and still can be, a very hard task to help people who have enjoyed the privilege of the dominant group to recognize how we all gain when we share and are more inclusive—what author Heather McGee calls the "solidarity dividend."[20] Yet it is a necessary lesson if one is to learn to live peacefully in today's multiracial, multiethnic, multireligious world. It was a joy to see the students in action doing just that. Not long after the interfaith space had been activated, there was a day where in the morning Hindu *murtis* were consecrated, and everyone gathered on the beautiful carpet covering the stone floor. Then the Hindus departed the space, and the sanctuary was set up for Yom Kippur service. When the Jewish service was over and their worship elements were put away, the hymnals and the cross were brought out for Sunday afternoon worship with the Protestants. In one day, there were three complete services—Hindu, Jewish, and Protestant—the interfaith worship space full for each one.

What happened is that the different faith groups each felt very affirmed. Each group was able to be deeply connected with its own faith tradition and was also in dialogue with others.

The Protestant students shifted their perspective and took pride in the new interfaith chapel. They learned it was not too hard to come early to set the chairs in rows like pews, bring the crosses and the kneeler out, and turn the sanctuary into a little church again. It was a powerful example of both holding individual identities and asking a campus, a community, to be in dialogue about the pluralistic nature of who we were and could be as a community.

Of course, it is not just students who need practice. All of us have gaps in our understanding about those whose life experiences are different from our own. To the extent that campus leaders have also lived, and perhaps worked, in homogeneous settings, we too may struggle with discomfort with difference and need professional development opportunities of various kinds to grow our own leadership capacity and foster the leadership capacity of those with whom we work. Even when resources are scarce, choosing to invest in those opportunities—inviting speakers, supporting faculty and staff workshops, seminars, and reading groups, encouraging conference attendance—makes a meaningful difference in building leadership capacity within diverse communities, not just in schools but in other organizational settings.

WHAT ABOUT DEI?

Some readers may be asking themselves—aren't those ABCs just another way of saying DEI—diversity, equity, and inclusion? Certainly there is some overlap; the difference is in the details. Many people use the term "diversity" as code language for issues of race and ethnicity, though of course the diversity of our communities extends to other significant dimensions of identity—religion, language, ability, sexual orientation, gender identity, age, veteran status, and more. People whose identities are considered "normative"—White, male, heterosexual, Christian, for example—sometimes feel that references to "diversity" do not include them. But, of course, in a pluralistic society, the term "diversity" should include everyone. We each bring something unique and important into the room. The notion of affirming identities that matter to people should include everyone in an equitable way.

As I have discussed, building community requires equitable inclusion. We know that historic inequities denied many people the freedom of choice as to when and where they could be educated. In today's higher education context, where all but the most selective institutions are strenuously competing for students to meet their enrollment goals amid a shrinking population of eighteen-year-olds, students of all backgrounds have options. Why would students voluntarily decide to be in environments that did not strive to include them in an equitable way, places where they did not feel meaningfully included in the classroom or on the campus? Most would not choose to do so. Institutions ignore the needs of what demographers are calling "the new majority" at their enrollment peril. Even at the most selective institutions, the demographic realities of US society have dramatically changed the racial and ethnic composition of the student body from what it was a decade or two ago. True success lies in creating a community that works for all.

The goals of my ABCs and the intent of DEI programs are similar— to create an environment where everyone can thrive and perform at their best. Why would anyone *not* want historically marginalized groups to find the support they need to achieve their personal best—unless the goal is to maintain the status quo of a society that has routinely benefited some groups over others? When I was growing up in Bridgewater, Massachusetts, Harvard was an all-male, predominantly White institution. In contrast, the Harvard class of 2027 is majority female (53.6 percent) and of color (59.2 percent).[21] Some people will read that last sentence and see it as a sign of a world turned upside down. And yet it is simply a reflection of the new majority of the twenty-first century.

In that context, it is important to recognize that "affirming identity" is important for everyone. As Nolan Cabrera documents in his book *White Guys on Campus*, straight White cisgender Christian able-bodied men want to be seen, heard, and understood, too.[22] The challenge is that if you are used to being seen, heard, and understood a lot, and others want to share some of that attention and affirmation, you may experience the need to share as a loss, much as some Christian students initially did when the idea to turn the small chapel into an interfaith space was first proposed. If a classroom instructor or meeting facilitator is trying to make sure that everyone is participating, some people may get called on less than they are accustomed to, and that might not feel so good to them. The flip side of that change, however, is there will be new voices and new insights added to the conversation. The change enriches the learning for everyone, including those who are learning to listen more and talk a little less. *All of us* need to learn how to do that.

WHY LEADERSHIP MATTERS

Decades of research by social scientists have taught us that there are certain very predictable things about us as human beings and the way we behave in groups that can help us create more inclusive school and work environments where *everyone* feels welcome and accepted, environments where everyone is able to perform at their best, and consequently where the organization is able to thrive and excel.[23] Ultimately that is the goal of any good leader—to foster an organization that can thrive and excel. You can't do one without the other, because where people feel disconnected, disengaged, and disempowered, you have higher turnover and lower productivity, resulting in lost creative energy, time, and talent.

Fundamentally, we know that human beings are not that different from other social animals. We follow the leader. Yes, we have an innate tendency to think in "us" and "them" categories, but we look to the leader to help us know who the "us" is and who the "them" is. The leader can define who is in and who is out. The leader can draw the circle narrowly or widely. When the leader draws the circle in an exclusionary way, with the rhetoric of hostility, the sense of threat among the followers is heightened. As our society grows more polarized, we see the toxic effect of such rhetoric. However, when the rhetoric is expansive and inclusionary, the threat is reduced. The leader sets the tone.

Even in the most collegial of work settings, leadership and authority matter. But it's not just formal authority; informal authority matters as well. Who is it that others admire in the organization? What skills do they have? What do they model? What example are they providing? It's not just the talk, but the walk, that matters. Leadership by example influences us because we as human beings are paying attention to what the leader says and does.

One of the best things that campus leaders can do is to model a willingness to talk about difficult issues. In October 2016, Dan Porterfield, then president of Franklin and Marshall College, invited me to participate in a campus-wide "Day of Dialogue." To launch the day's events, he and I held a public conversation, explaining the focus of the day. President Porterfield was engaged with me in this conversation about why dialogue is so important, why these conversations matter—in front of many hundreds of students and members of the campus community. He did a fabulous job, not only in talking about why it was important to the campus, but, as a White man, why it was important to him. He shared with the audience some of his early experiences growing up in segregated Baltimore and how those events helped inform his view of why the value of diversity was so important, and how to embrace it, as opposed to push it away. His willingness to share his own experiences was a powerful example for his students, the faculty and staff, and other campus leaders. It doesn't always have to be the president who provides the example, though it sends a powerful signal when it is. Leaders throughout any organization should model that kind of personal commitment and vulnerability and demonstrate how it is possible to have these conversations and to do so productively.[24]

In the context of my experience as president of Spelman College, a historically Black women's college, my most challenging conversations were not about diversity in terms of race, but more often about religious diversity and LGBTQ+ inclusion on what was then a predominantly Christian and religiously conservative campus. The campus community, including our alumnae, took note when in my first year as president I insisted that Muslim students should be allowed to read from the Qur'an, along with Christian students who traditionally read from the Hebrew Scriptures and the New Testament of the Bible at the opening of our baccalaureate service. It was important to me that all our graduating seniors see themselves represented in this final campus ritual before their commencement ceremony. (Yes, I did get a few letters of complaint that first year, but received many more expressions of appreciation from those who felt included.)

Attending a panel of students and alums who talked about the hurtful and isolating ways they had been treated by members of our community because of their sexual orientation or gender expression mattered not only because I was the president, thereby lending symbolic institutional importance to such events, but because I learned things I didn't know and deepened my own understanding of what needed to change on our campus. Throughout my tenure as president, I was reminded again and again how important it is just to show up, even if sometimes that is uncomfortable, modeling for others what it looks like to be a "border crosser."

Symbolic acts, large and small, make a difference. In 2005 Spelman College received a generous gift from the Arcus Foundation to help digitize the archived papers of the well-known Black feminist writer Audre Lorde so that scholars could have easier access to them.[25] Lorde was a lesbian who wrote openly about her sexual orientation. In acknowledging the gift as part of my opening convocation speech on campus that year, I talked about its significance and the importance of the Lorde papers in the Spelman archives. I referred to Lorde as an important figure in Black women's history, but also as a writer who was a lesbian. When I mentioned that aspect of her identity in my speech, I could hear some uncomfortable chatter in the audience in response. Decades later, it seems strange that my comment should have provoked any reaction at all. And yet, at that time in our community's development, it was important to signal to my campus audience that diversity in sexual orientation was something we could talk about, and Audre Lorde's legacy was something we could celebrate.

There is no question that leadership in the global economy of the twenty-first century not only requires the ability to think critically and communicate clearly, but also demands the ability to interact effectively with those different from oneself. Even if we did not acquire those skills in our youth, it is never too late. Growth can come through mentoring, developmental work experiences, and the expectation that each of us can move beyond our own comfort zone to bring about change in our organizations—to expand our circles and make our organizations work for everyone. Our collective responsibility is to promote mutual support and respect for one another by affirming identity, building community, and cultivating leadership—our own and that of our colleagues. Together it is possible to move beyond individual action to the policies and practices that make a difference for everyone, creating a climate of full engagement where everyone can thrive. The ABCs are the foundation on which inclusive communities can be built.

Chapter Two

Who's Afraid of DEI—and Why?

Whenever someone asks me what was the one thing I liked best about being a college president, I always say, "Graduation." The experience of greeting students onstage as they received their diplomas, knowing what obstacles many had to overcome to achieve that goal, was always a source of joy and inspiration. It was also a special privilege to be the person to deliver the commencement address. On May 17, 2019, I had that opportunity at the New College of Florida. It was an auspicious occasion not only because then President Donal O'Shea presented me with an honorary degree. It was also the sixty-fifth anniversary of the 1954 Supreme Court decision that we know as *Brown v. Board of Education*, the decision that outlawed the "separate but equal" doctrine of school segregation.

It was very meaningful to me to stand on the stage as the commencement speaker of one of the premier public institutions in Florida on the anniversary of the *Brown* decision because I am a *"Brown"* baby, born in Tallahassee, Florida, in 1954, just a few months after the landmark

Supreme Court decision. My family history and the segregationist history of the state of Florida are closely intertwined. When I was born, my father, Robert Daniel, was an art professor at Florida A&M University, a historically Black institution located in Tallahassee. Both of my parents came from educated families with a history of college attendance, all at historically Black colleges and universities—Morris College, Spelman College, Atlanta University, and Tuskegee University among them. My parents attended Howard University, where they both majored in art, graduating together in 1949. For financial reasons, my father had to interrupt his undergraduate education to serve in the army, but with the educational benefits of the GI Bill he was able to return to Howard to complete his undergraduate degree and then earn a master's degree from the University of Iowa. Upon his completion of that degree, my parents married in Washington, DC, and then moved to Tallahassee, where my father began his career as a college professor.

To advance in his chosen career, he knew he needed to earn a doctorate in art education and sought to do so at Florida State University (FSU), conveniently located just across town from Florida A&M. But even after the 1954 Supreme Court ruling, FSU remained a "Whites only" institution. It would be nearly a decade after the *Brown* decision before the state of Florida would open the doors of FSU to an African American graduate student. Instead, Florida met its legal requirement to provide equal educational access by paying the train fare of Black graduate students like my father to universities in the North. In his case, he traveled back and forth from Tallahassee to State College, Pennsylvania, eventually completing his doctorate at Pennsylvania State University in 1957.

By that time, my older brother was five, soon to begin school, and my parents decided they were done with the segregation policies of the state of Florida. A year later, we moved to Massachusetts, where my father became the first African American professor at Bridgewater State College (now Bridgewater State University). Our family had joined the "Great

Migration" of Black families out of the Jim Crow South. By the time I was the commencement speaker at the New College of Florida, my parents had both passed away. But I know they would have been both surprised and proud to see that the "moral arc of the universe" had indeed bent toward justice in the state of Florida.

It seemed fitting that the proud occasion was taking place at New College. Indeed, the New College of Florida had distinguished itself from other Florida institutions from its beginning. While Florida State University did not admit its first Black student until 1962, a *New York Times* article published in the summer of 1961 announced, "New College Due in Florida in '64; Privately Endowed School to Be Open to All Races." With the organizational assistance of the Board of Home Missions of the Congregational Christian Churches, a board of trustees hailing from across the country was established, and articles of incorporation specified that the college would serve "the education of men and women, irrespective of racial origin or religious belief in all branches of learning and education." The vision of the founders was that of a liberal arts college that "would stress freedom of inquiry and the responsibility of the individual student for his own education" and would be a "prestige college" in the quality of its faculty and student body, with academic standards at the "top level of excellence," not unlike Harvard University, another school established by the Congregationalists.[1] In fact, when the campus was dedicated in 1962, soil from the Harvard campus was mixed with soil from New College, a tangible representation of the "shared lofty ideals" of the two institutions.[2]

Facing financial difficulties in 1975, New College merged with Florida's State University System as part of the University of South Florida. However, in 2001, it became a freestanding institution, the eleventh member of the State University System and designated by the Florida Legislature as the "Honors College for the State of Florida." Known to be a learning environment that encouraged students to pursue their interests as independent scholars under the guidance of faculty members, with written faculty evaluations of student work submitted at the end of each semester rather than grades, New College attracted talented and self-directed students and earned a reputation as one of the top one hundred liberal arts colleges in the country.[3] Consistent with its progressive history of racial inclusivity, it became known as a learning community focused on social justice.

I offered my family story to the New College graduates that day because I knew for many young adults born in the twenty-first century, knowledge of the civil rights struggle of the 1950s and 1960s is often quite limited, and even when known is seen as a set of events in a far distant past. It is worth reminding them that it was not so long ago. As I have said to my own children, born in the 1980s, it was all in my lifetime, and I am not *that* old. I also wanted to remind the new graduates that change is possible. The painful history of which we are the inheritors should be acknowledged, as it had real consequences then for families like mine and many others, a legacy that for many persists into the present. And yet, the past does not have to determine the future. A new direction is possible.

We live in a time when some voices are calling for a silencing of historical truths and banning the teaching of so-called divisive concepts, ideas usually so labeled because they are linked to teaching about racism and other topics related to social justice. By 2024 under the leadership of Governor Ron DeSantis, among the most fervent of those voices, the state of Florida had become a symbol of the national tension between a desire among some to return to the comfort of a familiar past despite its exclusionary characteristics and the yearning among others to continue to forge a more diverse, equitable, and inclusive future. Known as DEI, the terms "diversity," "equity," and "inclusion" collectively became a lightning rod for attack, particularly in the context of higher education. But why? Perhaps there is no better explanation to be found than in the story of Derek Black at New College of Florida.

THE WHITE NATIONALIST'S SON

Among the community of New College graduates is Derek Black, class of 2013, whose presence at New College took his classmates by surprise. Derek is the son of Don Black, founder of the oldest and largest White nationalist website, Stormfront, and godson of former Klan leader David Duke. Derek's story was captured in Eli Saslow's 2018 book, *Rising Out of Hatred: The Awakening of a Former White Nationalist*.[4] Derek had grown up as a home-schooled student immersed in his family's White nationalist network, and by the age of nineteen he had developed a website for "white children of the globe," hosted his own online White nationalist radio program, and won a local election running as a Republican in Florida.[5] Given the progressive history of New College, it might seem like an odd choice for a White nationalist. However, as a transfer student from a community college, Derek was attracted to New College because of its strong program in medieval studies. His parents liked that the student population was overwhelmingly White, and they supported his decision to attend.[6] Upon enrolling at New College, Derek hid his White nationalist activities from his classmates, and to his own surprise he began to make friends with people he had been taught to denigrate—Jews and people of color. When Tom McKay, a New College student doing a senior thesis on domestic extremism, discovered evidence online of Derek Black's White nationalist activities—links to his daily radio show and his archive of Stormfront posts—Tom shared that information on the New College student email group called "the forum," asking "How do we as a community respond to this?"[7]

Some students responded by circulating a petition calling for Derek's expulsion. (He was not expelled.) Others called for his social ostracization. Some students felt Derek's presence was a threat to their own campus safety. James Birmingham, class of 2010, was working as a staff member on campus when these events took place. He reflected, "My biggest worry was... that Derek being ostracized or bullied would get out in public and someone who saw themselves as a loyal Stormfront soldier would come onto campus and do something." Birmingham also noted that while most students refrained from commenting, the dominant narrative on the forum was "We don't really know what Derek thinks. If he's here, there must be a reason. We can change his mind."[8]

As it turned out, those students were right. Matthew Stevenson, an observant Jew, invited a small group of friends, including Derek, to share Shabbat dinner with him on Friday evenings. Even after Derek's involvement with a daily radio program espousing antisemitic, White nationalist rhetoric was exposed on campus, Matthew continued to include him. Matthew's roommate, Allison Gornik, thought Matthew was wrong to keep inviting him, and she initially avoided interacting with Derek, but eventually befriended him. Allison, a White woman majoring in psychology, wanted to understand why Derek was so committed to his White nationalist beliefs, so completely contradictory to her own. As Derek spent more time with Matthew and Allison in particular, he began to question those beliefs himself and began to feel deep regret at the harm he had done spreading those ideas for so many years.

By the time of his graduation from New College, Derek had not only changed his thinking and ceased participating in Stormfront activities, but he had also concluded that he must atone for his past by publicly renouncing White nationalism, knowing full well it would rupture his relationship with his family and the community in which he had grown up. He wrote a long letter explaining how his views had changed and sent it to the Southern Poverty Law Center, the civil rights organization most visibly working in opposition to the growing White nationalist movement, requesting that they publish it in full.

In the letter, while he acknowledged his abiding respect for his parents, who were staunch advocates of White nationalist views, and his reluctance to injure his relationship with them, he described both his need to "be honest about my slow but steady disaffiliation from white nationalism" and his new understanding of the impact of his past actions. "The things I have said as well as my actions have been harmful to people of color, people of Jewish descent and all others affected. I will not contribute to any cause that perpetuates this harm in the future." Disavowing any further support of White nationalism, Black credited his college experiences—the new people he had met, the conversations he had had, and the books he had read—for helping him to grow "past my bubble."[9]

Later, in another statement, he elaborated on how essential the influence of his New College peers was to his awakening, particularly those who didn't abandon him when they learned of his affiliations but instead engaged him in dialogue. "They let me know when we talked about it that they thought my beliefs were wrong and took the time to provide evidence and civil arguments. I didn't always agree with their ideas, but I listened to them and they listened to me." Mutual respect led to cognitive dissonance that Derek could not reconcile. "It's a huge contradiction to share your summer plans with someone who you completely respect, only to then realize that your ideology doesn't consider them a full member of society. I couldn't resolve that."[10]

From my vantage point as a person born in the Jim Crow South, when White nationalist ideas of separation and segregation were the law of the land, I see Derek's transformation as a hopeful outcome and a dramatic *and positive* illustration of the power of a liberal arts education in a multicultural context to expand one's thinking. Educational researchers have long documented the beneficial outcomes of learning in diverse environments.[11] Research conducted by social psychologist Pat Gurin and her colleagues using data from colleges and universities across the country, as well as specifically from Gurin and her colleagues at the University of Michigan, highlighted the educational benefits of learning in a diverse community. They found that those students who experienced the most racial and ethnic diversity in and out of their classrooms benefited in terms of both "learning outcomes" and "democracy outcomes."[12] Among the learning outcomes were greater engagement in active thinking processes, growth in intellectual engagement and motivation, and growth in intellectual and academic skills. Students actively involved in a diverse campus community also showed the most engagement during college in various forms of citizenship, the most engagement with people from different races and cultures, and were the most likely to acknowledge that group differences are compatible with the interests of the broader community—the "democracy outcomes" consistent with Derek Black's experience at New College.

However, if your goal is to perpetuate a White nationalist agenda, as it was for Derek's parents, Derek's New College experience was a disaster, resulting in the undermining of his family's worldview. When Derek renounced the ideology of White nationalism, his parents and their friends speculated that Derek was suffering from Stockholm syndrome, a term used to describe a coping mechanism in which people being held captive develop positive feelings toward their captors.[13] But of course Derek was not being held captive. Nor was any faculty member or administrator requiring him to attend DEI training. What Derek experienced at New College was not indoctrination but rather the critical thinking that comes from exposure to new ideas and, most importantly, the impact of a diverse learning community. No one forced Derek to attend his friend Matthew's weekly Shabbat dinners or to engage in the deep conversations with his peers that took place over the time spent at New College. Yet those experiences were transformational.

Who should decide the value of what New College offered Derek? In 2023, ten years after Derek's graduation, Ron DeSantis, the conservative Republican governor of Florida, thought he should make the decision about the value of New College. His conclusion was that New College was too "woke." The slang term "woke" is defined in the Merriam-Webster dictionary as "aware of and actively attentive to important facts and issues (especially issues of racial and social justice)." The term is acknowledged as originating in the Black community, gaining popular usage in 2014 as part of the Black Lives Matter movement.[14] By the time it had become part of Governor DeSantis's vocabulary, it was being applied by him and other right-wing commentators as a general pejorative for anyone who is or appears to be aligned with progressive political positions.

According to DeSantis, New College was a prime example of what he called "woke activism," promoting "ideological conformity" at the expense of learning. Consequently, he placed it at the center of his "anti-woke" agenda for higher education. He declared his intention to defund and dismantle diversity, equity, and inclusion efforts at all of Florida's state colleges and universities, starting with New College of Florida.

On January 6, 2023, DeSantis appointed six new trustees: Christopher Rufo, Matthew Spalding, Charles R. Kesler, Mark Bauerlein, Debra Jenks, and Eddie Speir, all of them White, and the first four known to be conservative academics or activists from outside the state.[15] Of particular note was the appointment of Rufo, who rose to prominence in his media campaign to promulgate widespread fear and rejection of "critical race theory," loosely applying the term (which has its origin in legal theory) to any discussions of racism in schools, fueling parental opposition to such conversations as well as other diversity, equity, and inclusion efforts.[16] Following his appointment to the board, Rufo tweeted, "We are now over the walls and ready to transform higher education from within. Under the leadership of Gov. DeSantis, our all-star board will demonstrate that the public universities, which have been corrupted by woke nihilism, can be recaptured, restructured, and reformed."[17] They started by removing the president.

Following the nine-year tenure of President Donal O'Shea, Patricia Okker had become the first female president of the New College of Florida on July 1, 2021. Just eighteen months into her position, she responded with grace to the board takeover, saying, "I believe our new trustees will bring fresh ideas and new perspectives." But just a few weeks later, when the board had its first meeting on January 31, 2023, they fired Okker without cause and appointed Richard Corcoran, a Republican former state politician, as interim president. The goal, Governor DeSantis said, was to reshape New College of Florida into an institution modeled after Hillsdale College, a small, private Christian college in Michigan known for its conservative values and emphasis on a "classical liberal arts education."

By the summer of 2023, the New College chief diversity officer had been removed and the Office of Outreach and Inclusive Excellence dismantled, more than a third of the faculty had resigned, and an effort to increase enrollment and shift the student culture was well underway.[18] Many of the existing students left to take a pause or transfer to another institution, with approximately 10 percent of returning students accepting the invitation to continue their education at Hampshire College in Massachusetts, an institution similar in size, structure, and campus climate to the pre-DeSantis New College. The board was unfazed by their departure. "The student body will be recomposed over time: some current students will self-select out, others will graduate. . . . We'll recruit new students who are mission-aligned," Rufo commented. In the first incoming class under the new leadership, the recruiting emphasis was on student athletes, predominantly male, from conservative counties, religiously affiliated high schools, and transfers from Christian colleges or universities, who in the words of trustee Rufo "will begin to rebalance the hormones and the politics on campus."[19]

Interim New College president Corcoran began immediately focusing on building an athletics program where none had previously existed, hiring head coaches for six sports: baseball, softball, men's and women's basketball, and men's and women's soccer, with plans to hire coaches for lacrosse and volleyball, even though at that point New College did not have any athletic facilities or membership in any national athletic association. When school opened in the fall of 2023, with 300 new students—a record number for a school whose total population was about 700—140 of them were student-athletes.[20]

The New College I visited in 2019 is clearly not the New College of 2024—a change engineered by Ron DeSantis in his "anti-woke" crusade. But the power of the diverse learning environment that transformed Derek Black a decade before had not been completely erased. Having discovered belatedly that her desired major, marketing, was not offered at New College, one student athlete, Jayleigh Totten, decided she might study sociology. She told a *New York Times* reporter that her sociology classes were giving her a lot to consider, "like how once you change your community and your society, your perspectives and your ideas change." In particular, she noted her new understanding of the concerns of the LGBTQ+ community. She commented, "I just wasn't exposed to it—and now that I am, I realize where they're coming from and why they feel threatened in the world the way they do.... Just getting yourself out there and exploring, finding new things, is how you're going to learn and get along with more people."[21]

Perhaps it was that kind of new understanding, so well articulated by Jayleigh Totten, that prompted Governor DeSantis to add sociology to his list of things that should not be offered as a core course option in Florida's state institutions. On January 17, 2024, Florida's State Board of Education, appointed by the governor, voted to replace a Principles of Sociology course with an American History course, arguing that students could be radicalized by sociological content.[22] Florida Commissioner of Education Manny Diaz Jr. commended the action, saying, "Higher education must return to its essential foundations of academic integrity and the pursuit of knowledge instead of being corrupted by destructive ideologies.... We will not spend taxpayers' money supporting DEI and radical indoctrination that promotes division in our society."[23]

In response, the American Sociological Association issued a statement disputing the commissioner's claim that sociology as a field of study is "radical" or "woke" ideology, and asserting the value of sociology as "the scientific study of social life, social change, and the social causes and consequences of human behavior, which are at the core of civic literacy and are essential to a broad range of careers."[24] The association called on the Florida State Board of Education to reverse its decision, but as of this writing, it was to no avail.

Gender studies was another curricular target. The academic program at New College was dismantled, and the Gender and Diversity Center library that had been created by students over a period of more than thirty years was destroyed, the books literally thrown in a dumpster without notice. As horrified as many faculty and students were to see the books discarded so cavalierly, DeSantis-appointed trustee Rufo gleefully posted to X that "we abolished the gender studies program. Now we're throwing out the trash."[25]

Lest we think the story of New College, as dramatic as it is, merely an isolated example of a group of misguided Florida politicians run amok, former New College President Patricia Okker cogently summed up the significance of the situation in an essay she wrote after her removal. "Far more than a political shift in the governance of our small liberal-arts college, New College had become the epicenter of a debate about the future of academic freedom, shared governance, freedom of expression, and diversity, equity and inclusion." She rightly concluded that "the New College saga is part of a national phenomenon. State legislatures across the nation are considering sweeping academic reform."[26] Diversity, equity, and inclusion—DEI—offices and programs were the most visible targets of those legislative efforts.

Perhaps that "sweeping academic reform" was also part of an international phenomenon. Some scholars suggest that Viktor Orbán's remaking of higher education in Hungary was the model for the radical changes taking place at New College of Florida. In the spring of 2023, just as New College was being restructured, Christopher Rufo spent six weeks as a visiting fellow at the Danube Institute in Hungary, a think tank closely aligned with both Orbán and the Heritage Foundation, a conservative American think tank. Orbán's use of "muscular state policy to achieve conservative ends" was of interest to Rufo as Orbán's rhetoric and methods "succeeded in casting higher education as a dangerous foe in his largely successful prosecution of the culture wars. He has also imposed real change, banning gender and women's studies departments and overhauling university governance."[27] Both Donald Trump and J. D. Vance have praised Orbán's approach. In a February 2024 interview, Vance said, "The closest that conservatives have ever gotten to successfully dealing with left-wing domination of universities is Viktor Orbán's approach in Hungary....I think his way has to be the model for us: not to eliminate universities, but to give them a choice between survival or taking a much less biased approach to teaching."[28]

What light does the story of Derek Black shed on this reactionary movement? Though his example is an extreme one—most students are not the presumed heirs of a White nationalist media organization—his story has elements that are familiar to me, having taught a course on the psychology of racism to many students, most of them White, over the course of my now decades-long career. The students who took my course always did so voluntarily; it was always offered as an elective course, rather than a required one. It was a popular course, and I often had a waiting list of students hoping to enroll, as the course was limited in size to thirty students to better facilitate everyone's active participation in discussion. Even so, students eager to take the course would nevertheless express anxiety and hesitation about speaking openly about the topic of race, particularly in a racially mixed classroom.

Some of the information they learned about the history of racism in the United States—policies and practices of the past (like those that impacted my family in Florida, for example) and their continuing impact in the present—sometimes upset them. Often White students expressed a sense of anger or betrayal at the adults who had withheld this information from them earlier in their education. After seeing the first episode of *Eyes on the Prize*, the documentary series on the civil rights movement of the 1950s and '60s,[29] a White male student wrote in a reflection paper, "Why didn't I learn this in elementary or high school? Could it be that the White people of America want to forget this injustice?...I will never forget that movie for as long as I live. It was like a big slap in the face." That kind of anger and embarrassment at one's own ignorance was common. For example, in response to learning about the internment of Japanese Americans during World War II, another White student commented, "I feel so stupid....I never knew the Japanese were treated so poorly. I am becoming angry and upset about all of the things that I do not know....I am angry at [my parents] for not teaching me and exposing me to the complete picture of my country."

For their parents, such conversations may feel quite uncomfortable. "Is this what I am paying all this money for?" they might ask. Surely it is easier to just avoid such conversations, or so it might seem. But as my students learned more and gained more confidence from their class discussions, they didn't want to stop talking. They talked to their friends and family members about what they were learning and wanted to share their new insights and often did so during holiday visits. They started noticing the racial stereotypes embedded in family humor or the comments relatives made and would speak up about them, only to find sometimes that their efforts were unappreciated, perhaps dismissed as a "phase" or worse, greeted with open hostility.

One of my former students, a young White man from a very affluent family, described such a family dilemma. "So many people I know from home...have simply accepted what society has taught them with little, if any, question. My father is a prime example of this....It has caused much friction in our relationship, and he often tells me as a father he has failed in raising me correctly." Describing his own commitment to using his privileged social position to advocate for social justice, he lamented, "It is an unfortunate result often though that I feel alienated from friends and family. It's often played off as a mere stage that I'm going through. I obviously can't tell if it's merely a stage, but I know that they say this to take the attention off of the truth of what I'm saying."[30]

I can't help but wonder if the politicians who are trying to silence discussions of racism and other social justice issues in schools and eliminate the curricular and co-curricular programs that make space for such discussions on college campuses have children at home like my former students, who are asking questions their parents don't want or don't know how to answer. Or, as was the case with Derek Black, their children are rejecting assumed human hierarchies of worth that no longer make sense to them, thereby threatening the societal status quo. Undoubtedly *something* has spurred the flurry of anti-DEI legislation.

The *Chronicle of Higher Education* began tracking anti-DEI legislation in early 2023, and by August 2024 it reported that eighty-six bills had been introduced across twenty-eight states. By that time, twelve states had passed such legislation: Alabama, Florida, Idaho, Indiana, Iowa, Kansas, North Carolina, North Dakota, Tennessee, Texas, Utah, and Wyoming—but momentum was building for even more anti-DEI legislative activity in the coming months.[31] The impact of the legislation was immediate. For example, in Texas, where legislators banned diversity, equity, and inclusion programs based on race, gender identity, and sexual orientation, the University of Texas at Austin closed its Gender and Sexuality Center to comply with the law (SB 17). A new Women's Community Center opened in its place, with a mission to "be a place for Longhorns of all genders to connect, find resources, and get support around experiences of intersectionality, community, and gender solidarity." With a new name believed to be compliant with the law, the center still intends to provide support to LGBTQ+ students, but several of its previous programs specific to the LGBTQ+ community had to be discontinued because the new law bars public-college employees from offering programs that reference race, sexual orientation, or gender identity. "One program that is definitely discontinued is ally training, a workshop where faculty, staff, and students could learn about identity formation, pronoun use, and other issues important to their LGBTQ+ students and peers." On a campus where 16 percent of the hate crimes reported in 2020 were related to sexual orientation, second only to race, the inability to promote specifically tailored programs for targeted students or related diversity education for the broader campus is highly problematic.[32]

Names were changing all over Texas. At Texas Tech University, the Black Cultural Center became the Student Enrichment Center. At Texas A&M University, the Pride Center became a Student Life Center. At the University of Houston, the LGBTQ+ Resource Center became the Center for Student Advocacy and Community.[33] Institutional leaders were scrambling to stay within the law and still meet the needs of their students. Unsatisfied, conservative legislators and activists claimed that the spirit of the new legislation was not being upheld. Consequently, new laws, much more specific about what can and cannot be done, have been offered for consideration. For example, in 2024 in Nebraska, legislators proposed a bill that would prohibit administrators from advancing "any theory of unconscious or implicit bias, cultural appropriation, allyship, transgenderism, microaggressions, microinvalidation, group marginalization, anti-racism, systemic oppression, ethnocentrism, structural racism or inequity, social justice, intersectionality, neopronouns, inclusive language, heteronormativity, disparate impact, gender identity or theory, racial or sexual privilege, or any related theory."[34] Though the legislation failed to pass, the very idea of such bills poses a direct threat to higher education, public and private, as they represent a frontal assault on free speech and academic freedom.

Though the focus here is on higher education, similar activity has been focused on K–12 education, including the banning of books in classrooms and school libraries. In 2022, PEN America, an organization dedicated to the protection of free expression worldwide, issued a report titled *Educational Gag Orders: Legislative Restrictions on the Freedom to Read, Learn, and Teach*, chronicling the evolution of these legislative efforts at censorship.[35] Cutting through the fog of vague political rhetoric, the report editors wrote, "We refer to these bills not by incomplete or misleading terms like 'anti-critical race theory,' or 'divisive concepts'—as their proponents prefer—but rather by a more accurate description: educational gag orders." The lawmakers' intent is clear: "to stop educators from introducing specific subjects, ideas, or arguments in classroom or training sessions." The report connected this legislative activity to both the 2019 release of the *New York Times*'s 1619 Project, a special issue documenting the centrality of chattel slavery in the founding of and development of the United States, and the public reckoning with racism that followed the 2020 murder of George Floyd, the Black man whose brutal and callous killing by a White police officer in Minneapolis was captured on cellphone video for the world to see.

Floyd's murder triggered mass multiracial protests across the country and around the world, amplifying the Black Lives Matter movement and focusing national attention on the persistent problem of racism in American society. "This public reckoning with racism led many American institutions in various fields to adopt new curricula, training, and commitments to confront and dismantle racism. These have in turn become the focus of pointed ideological disagreement…'a post–George Floyd backlash.'"[36]

On September 22, 2020, President Donald Trump set the tone of this backlash response when he issued an "Executive Order on Combating Race and Sex Stereotypes," prohibiting the discussion of "divisive concepts" related to race and sex in training or workshops offered by federal agencies and federally funded organizations, including most colleges and universities. A few days later, the term "divisive concepts" was clarified by the Office of Management and Budget to include such terms as "White privilege," "unconscious bias," or "critical race theory." The executive order triggered resistance, not just from the higher education sector. Ironically, as Trump was working to limit discussions about racism in the United States, approximately two hundred CEOs from global companies like Microsoft, Walmart, and JPMorgan, recognizing their responsibility to provide societal leadership, were unveiling a new plan to address racism in America.[37] One hundred and sixty business organizations, including the US Chamber of Commerce, lobbied Trump in an open letter to rescind the order because it would impede their efforts to "promote diversity and combat discrimination in the workplace." They asserted in the letter that the executive order was "already having a broadly chilling effect on legitimate and valuable D&I training companies use to foster inclusive workplaces, help with talent recruitment, and remain competitive in a country with a wide range of different cultures."[38] Though Trump's executive order was short-lived, revoked by President Joe Biden as soon as he took office in January 2021, it nevertheless inspired Republican-led state legislatures across the nation to make similar efforts to limit discussions of race, racism, and gender by restricting the teaching of ideas Trump had labeled as divisive.[39]

In further consideration of why anti-DEI legislation has taken hold and is proliferating so rapidly in some parts of the country, we might ask if this is part of a predictable pattern of pushback against changing social norms. Every period of progress seems to be followed by pushback against that progress. In fact, in his last book, *Where Do We Go from Here: Chaos or Community?*, published in 1968, Dr. Martin Luther King Jr. wrote about just that. At that moment of history, at the height of protests against the Vietnam War and the push for economic justice, he wrote, "The line of progress is never straight....The inevitable counterrevolution that succeeds every period of progress is taking place."[40] We are undoubtedly living through such a period of "counterrevolution" today, a response to a period of advancement in civil and human rights stretching across more than fifty years from the milestone of the 1954 *Brown v. Board of Education* Supreme Court decision to the historic 2008 election of President Barack Obama, the first African American president of the United States.

If there had been no advancement in women's rights, there would be no pushback against that advancement.[41] If there had been no change in voter participation—like the surge in participation of young people and people of color in US elections in 2008 and again in 2012—the rush to block access to the ballot that began in earnest in 2013 and has accelerated after the election of 2020 would not be occurring.[42] If there had been no expansion of civil rights in the LGBTQ+ community, there would be no pushback against that change.[43] If there had been no expansion of anti-racist social justice education in the schools, there would be no pushback against it today.[44] If there had been no improvement in employment statistics, slow as that improvement has been, there would be no pushback against that progress. As troubling as the pushback is to me, I find it helpful to acknowledge it is a reaction to and evidence of the meaningful social change that precedes it.

But are there legitimate concerns that are not simply rooted in a resistance to change? For example, are DEI programs "stigmatizing" or "demeaning" groups of people on the basis of race and sex, as Trump's executive order suggested? Are students who learn about the legacy of racism being taught to "hate our country," as President Trump asserted?[45] Are some White students being made to feel guilty about the history of enslavement and the genocidal removal of Indigenous peoples, while students of color are being defined as victims? Are some DEI programs poorly conceived and ineptly delivered? These are among the arguments DEI critics and state legislators have made.

Hasan Kwame Jeffries, associate professor of history at Ohio State University, responded to some of these concerns in a 2021 NPR interview. Acknowledging the power of historical knowledge to inform the present, he said, "That's the project of history—not to create patriotism, but to create understanding. And if you teach it right, even the hard stuff will not cause you to dislike the country, to hate the country. It will cause you to take pride in the fact that there were always people who were willing to fight to make it better."[46]

My own teaching experience mirrors Jeffries's comments. As noted earlier, for many students, talking about racism, particularly in racially mixed company, was a new experience that sometimes generated uncomfortable emotions, especially at the beginning of the learning journey. I found it helpful (and ethically necessary) to let students know at the beginning of our time together that feelings of guilt, shame, embarrassment, or anger in response to the new information they would be learning were common, and that there might be a point in the semester when they might want to disengage from the material by not coming to class or doing the reading. But I made clear that we would have time in class to talk about why it was so hard sometimes to learn about this material.

I described what I call the arc of discomfort. It peaks and then subsides. If the learners stuck with it, it would get easier, even enjoyable, to have new understandings. Naming the problem in advance helped students to remain engaged when they experienced those common feelings of discomfort. As Alice, a White woman, wrote at the end of a semester, "You were so right in saying in the beginning how we would grow tired of racism (I did in October) but then it would get so good! I have *loved* the class once I passed that point."[47]

Yes, sometimes new ideas cause discomfort. Having one's assumptions challenged can be unnerving. I call such responses growing pains. What I know from having taught about racism since 1980 is that once students get past the initial discomfort, they revel in the opportunity to learn more. Just like my students who expressed frustration about the history/information that had been kept from them, I fear we are creating another generation of students who will ask in frustration, "Why didn't I learn about this before?!"

THE POWER OF DIALOGUE

Banning books, removing courses, and purging anything that looks like "critical race theory" will not solve the myriad problems we face. What would happen if instead of managing student discomfort with enforced silence, we helped students grow through their discomfort? What if we encouraged professional development for faculty and staff when needed to enhance their facilitation skills, improving the quality of their DEI offerings? What if, instead of attempting to squelch conversation legislatively, we encouraged campuses to double down on dialogue? The impact could be game-changing for the deep divisions currently at work in our society.

It's not hard to imagine what that might look like in practice, as there are already examples of institutions leaning into dialogue as an educational tool. On November 17, 2023, I sat with Ximena Zúñiga in a conversation moderated by Barbara Love at the opening of the Intergroup Dialogue (IGD) Symposium at Mount Holyoke College. We were in the company of 175 symposium registrants from thirty colleges and universities from across the Northeast and beyond eager to engage in the conference IGD theme, "Learning from Its Past and Mapping Its Future." Thirty-five years after the launch of the first Intergroup Dialogue program at the University of Michigan, known as the Program on Intergroup Relations (IGR), we had gathered to reflect on the past, present, and future power of the IGD pedagogy to transform lives and serve as a catalyst for social change. The conference planning team had spent nine months preparing, but for me it was a moment many years in the making.

As mentioned in Chapter 1, the University of Michigan's Program on Intergroup Relations was founded in 1988 as a social justice education program, unique in its partnership between the division of Student Life and the College of Literature, Science, and the Arts. Blending theory and experiential learning to facilitate students' understanding of social group identities, social inequality, and intergroup relations, from its beginnings the program was designed to prepare students to live and work in a diverse world and educate them in making choices that advance equity, justice, and peace, using dialogue as the primary pedagogical method. As defined by Zúñiga, Nagda, Chesler, and Cytron-Walker (2007), an intergroup dialogue is a facilitated, face-to-face encounter that seeks to foster meaningful engagement between members of two or more social identity groups that have a history of conflict (e.g., Whites and people of color, Arabs and Jews).[48] According to the Michigan website, each dialogue involves identity groups defined by race, ethnicity, religion, socioeconomic class, gender, sexual orientation, (dis)ability status, or national origin. The course structure emphasizes both process and content, using a four-stage model that provides a developmental sequence for the dialogue, including creating a shared meaning of what dialogue is as group relationships are formed, trust building through personal narratives about social identities, navigating conflict through the collective exploration of difficult issues known as "hot topics," then eventually coming together to build alliances and empower participants to work toward the social changes they want to see, making explicit the connection between dialogue and action.[49]

When I became dean of the college at Mount Holyoke in 1998, I was eager to introduce intergroup dialogue as a curricular option to our students. With the expert assistance of Ximena Zúñiga, one of the founders of the Michigan IGR program and subsequently a professor of social justice education at the University of Massachusetts's Amherst campus (nearby to Mount Holyoke), in 2000 we launched our first IGD course at Mount Holyoke. After I left the college in 2002, the effort to develop a truly robust Intergroup Dialogue program at Mount Holyoke waxed and waned with the changes in staffing and institutional leadership that inevitably occurred over the years, but was reinvigorated in 2016 with the arrival of a new dean of students, Marcella Runell, who had been trained in intergroup dialogue in her doctoral program at the University of Massachusetts. When I returned to Mount Holyoke as interim president in the summer of 2022, I was delighted to hear a new generation of student leaders talking about the transformational impact of intergroup dialogue in their Mount Holyoke experience.

It was a stroke of good luck that during my year as interim president I was able to invite Kristie Ford, a sociologist nationally known for her expertise in IGD curricular development and pedagogy as well as her research on its educational outcomes, to spend the 2022–2023 year as a Presidential Fellow, leading IGD workshops for faculty and staff interested in learning more about its pedagogy.[50] With rising student demand for dialogue opportunities, it was essential to build the capacity of those faculty willing to consider incorporating dialogic methods in their classrooms. I was elated when Kristie agreed to remain at the college as a tenured member of the faculty and the founding director of what we envisioned to be a Center for Intergroup Dialogue, allowing us not only to expand opportunities for students, faculty, and staff to experience IGD and build their own facilitation skills, but also to serve as a regional resource for other institutions interested in building their own capacity for intergroup dialogue. With the support of my successor, President Danielle Holley, inaugurated in September 2023, the November 2023 IGD Symposium was the first public manifestation of that vision.

At the opening session of the symposium, Barbara Love asked why I was so passionate about the pedagogical power of dialogue. I explained that as a professor of psychology I had taught many courses—child development, theories of personality, the psychology of the family, qualitative research methods, in addition to psychology of racism and its follow-up course on intergroup dialogue. Yet, decades later, when I met former students at alumnae gatherings, the only courses of mine they mentioned as "life-changing" were my Psychology of Racism class and Intergroup Dialogue. As useful as the other courses I taught may have been, no one has ever said to me, "Theories of Personality changed my life." Instead, they tell me the ways they use what they learned through intergroup dialogue in their workplaces, in their communities, and at home with their family members.

Their experience is echoed more contemporaneously in the words of Lasya Priya Rao Jarugumilli. The student speaker at the 2022 Fall Convocation at Mount Holyoke, Lasya told an audience of two thousand students: "An experience that has significantly shaped my time here...is the Intergroup Dialogue Program. I could talk for a long time about the impact of that class. You should take it." She highlighted the key ideas she had internalized from the experience—to treat every person she talked to with respect; to listen carefully, resisting the temptation to interrupt; to be authentic in her interactions without the self-censoring that comes from fear; to be willing to speak up for herself but also to make space for other voices as well. She wisely added, "For all of us, learning takes time.... You will need to show yourself compassion. You are doing your best, but you cannot possibly know everything. You, like everyone else, are in college to learn.... [This] is the perfect place for this journey to begin."[51]

Lasya's testimony is powerful, but it is not necessary to rely on anecdotal evidence about the effectiveness of IGD. Multiple research studies have documented learning outcomes that persist beyond the life of the course itself. Both White students and students of color demonstrate attitudinal and behavioral changes, including increased self-awareness about issues of power and privilege, greater awareness of the institutionalization of race and racism in the US, better cross-racial interaction, less fear of race-related conflict, and greater participation in social-change actions during and after college.[52] In a multi-university study comparing students in IGD courses with those in other social science courses covering similar content about race/ethnicity and gender, researchers found greater positive effects among the students in the dialogue courses. Specifically, "students in dialogue courses learned, as predicted, not only from content but also from a distinctive pedagogy and set of communication processes. Social science classes had positive effects, as they should. It is simply that on a large majority of these measures, IGD courses had larger effects."[53] Notably, the multi-university study had a longitudinal component, following up with students a year after their courses had ended. They found the greater effect of IGD was still evident a year later. In addition, a year later, the IGD students showed gains in their comfort in communicating across difference, complex thinking, and skills in dealing with conflict, suggesting time to practice what had been learned allowed for continued growth beyond the classroom experience.[54]

Why is the experience of intergroup dialogue so impactful? In a presentation at the IGD symposium, Rani Varghese, professor of social work at Adelphi University, identified intergroup dialogue as a high-impact educational practice consistent with those practices identified by George Kuh (2008) in his influential AAC&U publication, *High-Impact Educational Practices: What They Are, Who Has Access to Them, and Why They Matter*.[55] Kuh's research named practices such as first-year seminars, learning communities, writing-intensive courses, undergraduate research opportunities, study abroad programs, service learning, internships, and capstone projects as having high educational impact for students. According to Kuh, what these practices have in common are opportunities for student investment in purposeful tasks, for meaningful interactions with faculty and peers over an extended time, for engagement with peers across lines of difference, to receive frequent feedback, to see how their learning works in settings inside and outside the classroom, as well as on and off campus, and ultimately to increase their own understanding of themselves in relation to others. What Varghese astutely observed was that IGD provides all those opportunities simultaneously over the course of the IGD experience. It packs a powerful punch.

What intergroup dialogue is *not* is instant. Trust building takes time. The commitment to listen deeply to someone else whose life experiences and viewpoints are different from your own is necessary, and that kind of listening takes practice. As trust builds, dialogue deepens. Conflict, sometimes referred to as "hot topics," can be discussed in productive ways. The goal is not agreement, but understanding and respect—and, as is often possible, finding common ground that can lead to shared commitments and productive action for positive social change.

Yet, sometimes in a crisis, when emotions are running high and there are polarized positions demanding institutional action, as was the case in the fall of 2023 in response to the Israel-Hamas war, for example, there is a temptation to invoke dialogue as the preferred response. But what I call "dialogue on demand" is not effective, and in fact can be detrimental when attempted without the prerequisite of initial trust-building. Difficult conversations, sometimes in the form of a town hall gathering, can be facilitated, and often are, by individuals who have acquired the skills of dialogue and are able to use those skills to good effect during conflict. But such conversations—often onetime occurrences—should not be confused with the experience of extended engagement with a commitment to return week after week, even when those weekly sessions feel uncomfortable.

As was the case with my Psychology of Racism class, those who facilitated structured dialogue know that there is indeed an arc of discomfort that comes with new knowledge and understanding. Yet those who persist in the endeavor learn that, over time, discomfort can shift to excitement and joy. I am reminded of the professional development work I did in the 1990s with teachers in a course called Antiracist Classroom Practices for All Students, an adaptation of my Psychology of Racism course designed specifically for preK–12 educators. In the evaluation of the course experience, the teachers, like my former undergraduate students, talked about the life-changing nature of the work they had done after their course participation. Describing a dialogue group in which participants met to talk about racial issues, a White teacher said, "It was such a rich conversation, and it just flowed the whole time. It was exciting to be a part of it. Everybody contributed and everybody felt the energy and the desire." Another participant described the process of sharing the new information she was learning with her adult son and said, "There's a lot of energy that's going on in all sorts of ways. It feels wonderful."[56]

Do you have to be a student or a teacher to experience this kind of dialogue? No, you don't. What if community leaders, such as state legislators, made the commitment to participate in structured dialogues? There are community organizations that bring people together for just that purpose, some of which I have described in earlier writings.[57] Two powerful examples are Everyday Democracy (formerly known as Study Circles) and Essential Partners (until 2014 known as the Public Conversations Project). Everyday Democracy is a nonpartisan, nonprofit organization that for more than thirty years has worked with hundreds of communities across the nation through its "Dialogue to Change" program. As described on its website, "the Dialogue to Change process begins with inclusive community **organizing** that draws people from all parts of the community to work on a shared issue. Next, several small, facilitated **dialogue** groups meet to consider the issue from multiple perspectives and explore practical solutions. Then, moving to **action**, participants connect the ideas from the dialogue to actionable outcomes, ranging from new projects and collaborations to institutional and policy change."[58] Since 1989 Essential Partners has been using a method it calls reflective structured dialogue to help communities engage with each other around such challenging issues as partisan polarization and political dysfunction, interfaith conflicts, and abortion rights—without compromising their deepest values or identities—working with civic groups, schools, faith communities, colleges, and other organizations to foster mutual understanding and trust across differences of values, beliefs, and identities.[59] Both organizations offer community resources on their websites.

The Program on Intergroup Relations at the University of Michigan began its intergroup dialogues with a focus on race relations, but as we have seen in some of these examples, dialogues need not be limited to that. Patricia Gurin, an early IGD leader and the Nancy Cantor Distinguished University Professor Emerita at the University of Michigan, reflecting on future directions for IGD, observed the need to create opportunities for dialogue along differences of political ideology as well as rural/urban identities.[60] Dialogues can be built around other markers of difference, always recognizing that we all have multiple identities. We can experience ourselves with multiple marginalized identities and also simultaneously experience privileged identities. For example, a heterosexual Christian who is Black and has a physical disability might experience marginalization because of racism and ableism but still experience privilege that comes from membership in a Christian-dominant, heteronormative society. We all have something to learn when in dialogue with others.

As David Schoem, retired director of the Michigan Community Scholars Program and another one of the founders of the Michigan IGR Program, advocates, "Every organization ought to be teaching young people in K–12 and universities, in businesses, this is how we're going to engage with one another, and how we're going to create a better world."[61] If we are preparing the next generation of leaders, it is necessary to cultivate their problem-solving capacity. You can't solve problems without talking about them. Learning how to have true dialogue is a necessary part of moving forward as a healthy society. We owe it to our students and one another to develop this transformational practice as a foundational educational experience, an important step toward achieving a more just world where everyone can thrive.

WHAT CAN LEADERS DO?

I became a dean because I wanted to launch a dialogue program at my institution. Presidents have even more opportunity, with institutional resources and a positional platform, in partnership with faculty, to encourage the development of similar learning opportunities for students on their campuses. If developing skills for the twenty-first century is an important part of the institution's educational mandate, making sure there are programs in place to deliver on that promise is essential. But you don't have to be a president or a dean to advocate for these essential learning opportunities. Faculty, staff, and especially students and parents have a role to play as well. They should ask institutional leaders what steps they are taking to ensure students have dialogue opportunities and make it an expectation that colleges need to meet.

Coalition building can and should go beyond the campus gates. In her essay reflecting on her experience as the ousted president of New College of Florida, Patricia Okker wrote, "Building powerful alliances among faculty, staff, and students is also possible on a national level.... Faculty voices are essential. The combined voices of faculty, students, and staff are even more powerful."[62] In 2023 a new organization, Education for All, was formed by a group of presidents seeking mutual aid and support in finding effective ways to respond to the attacks on their diversity efforts. In its initial stages of formation, the group had no formal or legal structure but was intended to give presidents a place to share openly and problem-solve with their peers. Most of the early participants were presidents of community colleges, perhaps not surprisingly, as community colleges enroll the most diverse student body of any sector in higher education. The attack on DEI is perceived by them as "an attack on the students that community colleges serve."[63] While the anti-DEI crusade has focused primarily on issues of race, community college advocates know that campus diversity extends well beyond racial categories—including military veterans, working adults or parents, rural and low-income backgrounds. "We take everybody, we want everybody, and we have a responsibility to do our very best to make sure all those students are successful.... My community cares about my students, but they may not necessarily always understand my students," explained Stephanie J. Fujii, president of Arapahoe Community College in Colorado. The DEI programs she is advocating for are the tools she needs to help her community understand its students and support their academic success.[64]

When leaders of public institutions speak up, there is always political risk because of the potential loss of state funding. Unlike public colleges and universities, private colleges receive very little of their funding, if any, from state governments. Consequently, private college presidents typically are less constrained by the actions of state legislatures than are presidents of public institutions. They can speak up against misguided policies without fear of removal by an unhappy governor, though there may be a risk of other kinds of penalties inflicted by vindictive legislators. For example, when Delta Airlines CEO Ed Bastien spoke up in 2021 about new voting restrictions enacted in Georgia that would disproportionately impact voters of color, the Republican-led Georgia House of Representatives passed a bill to repeal a tax break on jet fuel, openly acknowledging that the action was in retaliation for the CEO's comments.[65] While this example does not involve a higher ed institution (and the action failed to become law), it does illustrate the possibility of retaliation if institutional leaders draw legislators' ire. As I will describe in the next chapter, even the US Congress can get in on the act, as they did in the fall of 2023, dramatically leading to the resignations of the presidents of both Harvard University and the University of Pennsylvania.[66]

For leaders in every sector, within education and beyond it, there may be safety in numbers. When corporate CEOs spoke up against anti-DEI legislation, they did so as a group. When University of Kentucky President Eli Capilouto issued a public statement in opposition to proposed anti-DEI legislation in Kentucky, he said the bills would undermine university efforts "to build a community where everyone feels as though they belong as we pursue our mission to advance this state in everything that we do.... We should value and support that work, not diminish it." Not long after, his presidential colleague at the University of Louisville, Kim Schatzel, expressed similar sentiments, emphasizing the need to cultivate students' capacity for twenty-first-century leadership. "I strongly believe that you cannot deliver a high-quality university education without a diverse classroom and campus—inclusive of all demographics, identities and ideologies.... Only in such circumstances and with such experiences will our students be prepared to foster their own and others' excellence in a diverse global economy. In short, a diverse and inclusive campus better prepares our students to lead."[67] As of this writing, the proposed anti-DEI legislation in Kentucky had not passed.

There is no question that the executive order issued by President Trump raised the stakes in this situation. In his executive order, he called upon the attorney general, in consultation with the heads of relevant federal agencies, to seek out "the most egregious and discriminatory DEI practitioners" and identify as many as nine "potential civil-compliance investigations" in each sector of concern, with particular attention to those higher education institutions with endowments of $1 billion or more. There are 130 institutions who meet that endowment criteria.[68]

The Trump administration's assault on DEI escalated on February 14, 2025, with the issuing of a "Dear Colleague" letter advising all educational institutions to eliminate any vestiges of race-conscious student programming, resources, and financial aid, declaring as illegal a wide range of common practices such as ethnically based cultural centers, race-based scholarships, and even culturally specific celebrations such as special graduation ceremonies. Issued by the Department of Education's Office for Civil Rights, the letter imposed a fourteen-day deadline to respond, threatening an investigation and the loss of federal funding for any institution that failed to comply.[69] The letter shocked and dismayed campus leaders. Its enforcement threatened to "upend decades of established programs and initiatives to improve success and access for marginalized students."[70] Legal scholars quickly asserted that the "Dear Colleague" letter represented federal overreach, "effectively demanding new obligations of institutions without the proper legal authority to do so," infringing on the constitutional rights of academic freedom and institutional autonomy under the First Amendment.[71]

Yet, even those institutions that are confident in their ability to defend their policies and their educational programming against charges of "illegal DEI" may blanch at the legal expense of doing so. Still, the cause is worthy and those well-resourced institutions may be willing and able to take a stand in support of their educational missions and the higher education sector as a whole.

The significance of these and other leaders' voices pushing back against anti-DEI efforts was illustrated by President Capilouto's earlier 2024 comment: "We don't speak as an institution on public policy unless the issues will impact our entire community in potentially significant ways. This is one of those moments."[72] College presidents as well as other community leaders can be a force for good at this moment in history if they are willing to speak up about an issue so central to the educational mission of colleges and universities.

Whether in the private or public sector, campus leaders can rally support for their institutional commitments to diversity, equity, and inclusion among their constituents. Their trustees, typically selected because they are people with resources and influence, can be asked to wield that influence in support of those commitments. Students who are the firsthand beneficiaries of DEI programs can speak up about why those programs are so important. The faculty, particularly those who have the job security that comes with tenure and the status that comes from promotion to full professor, can mobilize to speak out in ways that may be more difficult for the president—writing op-eds, posting on social media, and perhaps even in-person visits to legislative offices to discuss the issue with their representatives.

Ultimately, though, an institution's graduates are the best messengers for the education they received. Sharing their personal experience of the benefits of listening and learning in a diverse context, as Derek Black did, and the power of dialogue to build leadership capacity, as Lasya did, along with many others, may in the end be the best cure for the anti-DEI fever sweeping the nation.

CHAPTER THREE

FREE SPEECH IN THE TIME OF WAR

Controversies over freedom of speech on college campuses have existed as long as there have been college campuses. But the specific issues vary with each generation." So wrote Erwin Chemerinsky and Howard Gillman, two constitutional law scholars and university leaders (dean and chancellor, respectively) in their book, *Free Speech on Campus*.[1] For those of my generation who came of age in the late 1960s and early 1970s, free-speech struggles revolved around protesting the Vietnam War and the struggle for civil rights. While students pressed for the right to speak out against the status quo and to challenge local, state, or federal policies at a time of state-sponsored discrimination at home and military action overseas, campus administrators often tried to limit their protests. Today, Chemerinsky and Gillman observed, it is students who insist on limiting speech they find offensive.

The generation of students who have grown up with social media are highly sensitized to the power of unregulated speech on the internet to cause serious psychological harm. Perhaps because they have limited knowledge, if any, of the importance of free speech to the social movements of the 1960s and 1970s, polls show that they tend to express a preference for limiting speech, particularly in educational settings, rather than demanding free speech protections. Their frame of reference is different from that of earlier generations of students. Chemerinsky and Gillman note, "Many students associate free speech with bullying and shaming. Their sense of speech is not sit-ins at segregated lunch counters to bring about positive change.... Social media make students think immediately of the harms, not the benefits, of speech."[2] In that context, they look to college administrators to protect them and their classmates from that harm. "Their instinct is to trust the government, including the public university, to regulate speech to protect students and prevent disruptions of the educational environment."[3]

This changing social context has focused contemporary conversations about free speech on the tension between fostering an inclusive learning environment that is welcoming to all (i.e., no speech that might create a hostile learning environment) and protecting freedom of expression. Is it possible to do both—create inclusive learning environments *and* protect freedom of speech? I believe the answer must be yes if we are to fulfill our educational mission. Chemerinsky and Gillman agree. "To achieve both of these goals, campuses may do many things, but they must not treat the expression of ideas as a threat to the learning environment. Freedom of expression and academic freedom are at the very core of the mission of colleges and universities, and limiting the expression of ideas would undermine the very learning environment that is central to higher education."[4]

Doing both is not easy. While acts of targeted harassment such as name-calling, bullying, and physical violence are universally condemned by campus leaders, sometimes the principle of free speech requires one to defend even very offensive language that can be quite upsetting to students. I understand why. As someone who writes and speaks about racism, I know that there are people who may not like what I have to say. I always seek to be respectful of others in my presentations, and yet I know that my ideas sometimes cause discomfort, even offense. I don't want anyone to tell me that I can't express those ideas, as some of the anti-DEI legislation discussed in Chapter 2 would threaten to do in some states. The challenge of creating an inclusive learning environment for all and protecting freedom of speech was at the heart of the campus conflicts that erupted in the fall of 2023.

Just a few weeks after the start of the school year, the October 7 Hamas attack on Israelis sent shock waves across college campuses in the US. The brutal attack left twelve hundred Israelis dead and more than two hundred taken hostage. Many campus leaders quickly issued statements condemning the October 7 violence. Two days later, on October 9, Israel formally declared war, vowing to destroy Hamas. The bombing of Gaza that ensued resulted in the deaths of tens of thousands of Palestinian civilians, many of them women and children. Campus leaders were suddenly caught in a political struggle between campus supporters of Israel and those who expressed solidarity with the plight of the Palestinians. The unfolding humanitarian crisis in Gaza was hard to ignore, as hundreds of thousands of Gaza residents were displaced, trying to escape the bombs, and soon were at risk of starvation and disease as access to food and clean water grew increasingly scarce. Yet leaders who expressed sorrow and concern for the loss of life on both sides of the conflict found themselves vulnerable to criticism for their "both sides" language, accused of a lack of moral clarity by those on either side of the issue. Those presidents who chose not to comment at all were challenged by their constituents to take a stand.[5] Surely for many presidents, the early days of the conflagration in the Middle East presented them with a no-win situation.

Unconstrained by presidential concerns, student protesters were making their voices heard, most often in support of the Palestinians. Their passionate chanting of phrases like "From the river to the sea!" quickly became a source of controversy. When pro-Palestinian campus protesters used that language, their chants were heard by some as a call for violence, perhaps even threatening Jewish genocide. The phrase, which refers to Israel's stretch of land between the Jordan River and the Mediterranean Sea, is for Palestinians like US Rep. Rashida Tlaib a call for Palestinian freedom from Israeli control. However, Tlaib—like campus protesters— was rebuked by Congress when she used the phrase, which many consider antisemitic because it is heard as a call to destroy the state of Israel.[6] College presidents were expected by many—powerful donors among them— to condemn such language. Surely, they argued, it was creating a hostile learning environment for Jewish students to have to listen to such chants.

When some presidents did indeed respond by banning such rhetoric and the pro-Palestinian groups who had used it, others questioned such actions as a violation of principles of free speech.[7] When pro-Palestinian students were doxed, assaulted, and even shot and wounded, questions were raised about whether those students received the same concerns about safety and rising Islamophobia as their Jewish peers did about antisemitism.[8] At the same time, Jewish students complained of actions that were personally threatening, such as swastikas written on walls, mezuzahs ripped from doors, and physical assaults.

To add more drama to a difficult situation, congressional leaders seized the opportunity to insert themselves into the campus controversies by calling a select group of college presidents to testify in a series of live-streamed hearings. Held by the House Committee on Education and the Workforce, the hearings were focused on antisemitism on campuses in the wake of the October 7 Hamas attack in Israel and the subsequent Israeli-Hamas war in Gaza. The first of those hearings was held on December 5.

Four presidents—all women—were invited, but only three attended. The fourth, the newly installed president of Columbia University, Nemat "Minouche" Shafik, was scheduled to speak at an international conference and consequently declined the congressional invitation. The three who attended, all of whom were still relatively new to their positions, represented three of the most elite American universities: Claudine Gay of Harvard (five months in her position), Sally Kornbluth of MIT (eleven months), and Elizabeth Magill of the University of Pennsylvania (seventeen months). Of the three women, Gay is Black and Kornbluth is Jewish. Their questioners wanted to know what the leaders were doing to contain the speech of the pro-Palestinian protesters. Specifically, Rep. Elise Stefanik (R-NY) asked each if they would discipline students calling for the genocide of Jews. It would seem easy enough to say yes, of course they would. But it was a trick question. The chants of the pro-Palestinian students are interpreted by some as calling for violence against Jews, but that understanding is contested. In response to the congressional questioners, they each gave legalistic responses, essentially saying it depended on the context. For example, Kornbluth of MIT said, "I have not heard calling for genocide of Jews on our campus." Stefanik interjected, "But you've heard chants for intifada"— an Arabic word that means uprising. Kornbluth replied, "I've heard chants which can be antisemitic depending on the context when calling for the elimination of the Jewish people." Legal scholars would later say that the presidents' responses were technically correct from a legal perspective; but the nuance was lost on their audience. The response from the congressional leaders was outrage. That the presidents could not speak plainly against what had been described as expressions of antisemitism was seen as a failure of their leadership.[9]

The three women had "walked into a trap" baited by Rep. Stefanik with the competing understandings of the language of campus protest. As Michelle Goldberg described in her *New York Times* opinion piece,

When Stefanik again started [her] questioning...about whether it was permissible for students to call for the genocide of the Jews, she was referring, it seemed clear, to common pro-Palestinian rhetoric and trying to get the university presidents to commit to disciplining those who use it. Doing so would be an egregious violation of free speech. After all, even if you're disgusted by slogans like "From the river to the sea, Palestine will be free," their meaning is contested in a way that, say, "Gas the Jews" is not. Finding themselves in a no-win situation, the university presidents resorted to bloodless bureaucratic contortions, and walked into a public relations disaster.[10]

The public relations disaster resulted in the forced resignation of the University of Pennsylvania president, Liz Magill, just four days after her congressional testimony, and calls for both Kornbluth and Gay to be removed from office as well. The assertions of continuing support for their respective presidents from the boards of MIT and Harvard were quickly forthcoming, and Kornbluth of MIT survived the incident.[11]

However, the storm intensified for Claudine Gay when, in addition to widespread criticism of her legalistic responses in the hearing, allegations of plagiarism were leveled against her and amplified by her most vocal critics, eventually placing her in an untenable position as an academic leader. On January 2, 2024, she resigned, her historic tenure as the first Black female president of Harvard coming to an end just six months after it began.

In a guest essay published in the *New York Times* the day after her resignation, Gay chronicled the venomous attacks on her character and intelligence to which she had been subjected in the weeks after her congressional testimony, her inbox flooded with racist hate mail and death threats. She said, "My hope is that by stepping down I will deny the demagogues the opportunity to further weaponize my presidency in their campaign to undermine the ideals animating Harvard since its founding: excellence, openness, independence, truth."[12] Her essay continued by making a larger point about the attack on her as "a single skirmish in a broader war to unravel public faith in pillars of American society." One of her most outspoken critics, conservative activist Christopher Rufo, who had helped publicize the plagiarism allegations, seemed to underscore her point when he celebrated her downfall as a victory, saying, "This is the beginning of the end for D[iversity], E[quity], I[nclusion] in America's institutions," echoing the thrust of the attack on New College of Florida, discussed in Chapter 2.[13] Clearly the pursuit of Gay's removal was not just about her.

While of course concerns about issues of academic integrity are important, attention should also be paid to the role that the intersection of racism and sexism played in this unfolding drama. As I read social media commentary on Gay's demise, I saw an array of hostile remarks posted by those who questioned her selection as president as an "affirmative action" appointment based on her race and gender, simultaneously dismissing the role of "isms" in her departure because, after all, she was a "plagiarist." Her critics declined to acknowledge her merit as an academic leader who was well-known to the Harvard community as a tenured faculty member who had achieved the rank of full professor and later served with distinction as the dean of the Harvard Faculty of Arts and Sciences, widely respected for her skill as an administrator prior to her selection as president. She was well-known inside the Harvard community, and her appointment was greeted with "exuberance" by her Harvard colleagues, a piece of her story that should not be erased.[14]

In this context, I thought about the former Stanford University president, Marc Tessier-Lavigne, a White man, who resigned from the Stanford presidency in July 2023, just a few months before the Harvard debacle, because of allegations of fraudulent research claims made earlier in his career. Though Tessier-Lavigne was ultimately cleared of any intentional wrongdoing by an independent panel of research scientists, the panel did conclude that the work under review had "multiple problems" and "fell below customary standards of scientific rigor."[15] Like Gay, when Tessier-Lavigne resigned, he acknowledged that doing so was in the best interest of the university, "because Stanford 'needs a president whose leadership is not hampered' by discussions of problems with his own research."[16]

Unlike in the case of Gay, however, I am not aware of public discussions of the Stanford controversy as evidence of Tessier-Lavigne's fundamental unworthiness as a scholar or that he was the target of racial invective because of it.

If it seems that Black women in high places are subject to more scrutiny and more vitriol than their White peers, male or female, it is not just your imagination.[17] In fact, only a few months after President Gay's resignation, three other Black women at Harvard were targeted by anonymous accusations of plagiarism, along with several scholars at other institutions. Almost all of those initially targeted in the spring of 2024 are Black and are either leaders associated with DEI programs or scholars writing about issues related to race and equity. Anti-DEI activist Rufo, who has publicly declared the "plagiarism hunt" the focus of his work, asserted, "We will keep exposing them, one by one, until the university [Harvard] restores truth, rather than racialist ideology, as its mission." In the case of one of Rufo's targets, Harvard assistant sociology professor Christina J. Cross, the two scholars whom she was accused of plagiarizing have publicly defended her against what they have called "false allegations," as have more than a dozen other prominent scholars in her field. Georgetown University public policy professor Donald Moynihan described Rufo and his colleagues' efforts to discredit Cross and others as "open season on scholars of race. . . . They're not taking on the idea, they're not taking on the analysis. . . . They're just trying to invalidate the work using other means."[18] As these examples make clear, the Israel-Hamas conflict and the struggle for freedom of speech are not the only wars that have come to campus.

Away from the limelight of congressional hearings, many campus leaders struggled to find the balance between protecting students from a potentially hostile learning environment and protecting free speech. The power of speech to impact campus climate is undeniable. In the month between mid-December 2023 and mid-January 2024, the Chicago Project on Security and Threats at the University of Chicago (CPOST), a nonpartisan research center with particular expertise in studying American attitudes toward political violence, did an extensive study of college students involving two national surveys of five thousand college students from more than six hundred colleges and universities across the United States "to better understand how the [Israel-Hamas] conflict is contributing to antisemitism, Islamophobia, and fears on college campuses and communities."

Among several important findings in the CPOST study was the observation that many students (19 percent of all surveyed) expressed fear for their physical safety, regardless of which side of the conflict they supported. When the data were disaggregated, the researchers found that 56 percent of Jewish students, 52 percent of Muslim students, and 16 percent of other college students felt in personal danger because of their support for either Israelis or Palestinians, fears escalated to some degree by campus speech. Robert Pape, the author of the CPOST report, wrote, "Different perceptions of intent are likely contributing to these fears. 66% of Jewish college students understand the pro-Palestinian protest chant 'From the River to the Sea, Palestine Will Be Free' to mean the expulsion and genocide of Israeli Jews, while only 14% of Muslim students understand the chant that way; of Jewish students who understand the phrase this way, 62% report feeling afraid."[19] As Pape points out, "speech is not action," but the use of speech that is perceived as implying violence normalizes the possibility of political violence and lowers the threshold for such action, reducing "norms of restraint."[20] And indeed it seemed that on some campuses restraint was in short supply.

Jewish students reported experiencing or witnessing acts of violence and intimidation targeting Jews, Jewish cultural institutions, or symbols of Israel. For example, at Cornell University a student posted messages threatening to kill Jewish students and "shoot up" a university dining hall that caters to Kosher diets and is located next to the Cornell Jewish Center on campus.[21] Muslim students also reported experiencing or witnessing acts of violence and intimidation targeting Muslims, symbols of

Palestinian culture such as the keffiyeh, or symbols of Islam. The shooting of three Palestinian college students while they were taking a walk on a Thanksgiving weekend visit with relatives in Vermont was especially frightening. Two of the young men were wearing keffiyehs at the time of the attack. Indeed, both the Anti-Defamation League (ADL) and the Council on American-Islamic Relations (CAIR) reported increases in bias incidents in the three months following October 7. The ADL documented 3,283 anti-Jewish incidents in that period, more than 500 of them on college campuses, an increase of 300 percent over the previous year. CAIR reported an increase in bias incidents of more than 200 percent during the same three-month period, with 3,578 incidents reported, almost 600 of them involving students (K–12 as well as college).[22] Fear was real for both groups.

For students who are not Jewish or Muslim, their sense of danger reportedly came from the ripple effect of campus environments described as "generally hostile and tumultuous for any student holding any opinion at all about the current Israel-Palestinian conflict.... In essence, the non-Jewish and non-Muslim students fear being caught in the crossfire, unable to avoid the hostility.... Even silence or neutrality are punished." Said one such student, "I think having an opinion at all is dangerous."[23]

Students also expressed concerns about being discriminated against academically and in terms of professional opportunities because of their political positions relative to the conflict. For example, pro-Palestinian students protesting at Harvard and Columbia were targeted for doxing and threatened with the loss of internship or other employment opportunities by influential pro-Israel alumni.[24] In this context, it is notable that the CPOST study found that college students were almost twice as likely to participate in protest activities in support of Palestinians (11 percent) as they were for Israel (6 percent), reflecting a strong generational difference from American adults forty-five and over who report much higher pro-Israel activism (11 percent) than pro-Palestinian (2 percent).[25]

A unique and useful dimension of the CPOST study is its effort to distinguish between different meanings of antisemitism (e.g., prejudicial antisemitism, violent antisemitism, and antizionism) and measure the attitudes represented by each concept separately. The CPOST researchers defined prejudicial antisemitism as "holding negative stereotypes about Jews as a people, culture, or religious group," violent antisemitism as "holding the belief that violent attacks against Jews as a people, culture or religious group are justified," and antizionism as "holding negative views about the state of Israel, not Jews as a people, culture or religious group."[26] These new data were benchmarked against a previous survey conducted in the spring of 2023 among a nationally representative sample of adults on feelings of antisemitism and support for political violence.[27] This disentanglement of the three concepts was clarifying, yielding the insight that the level of prejudicial antisemitism among college students is about the same as that of the general adult population and has remained stable at relatively low levels even after October 7. However, "college students as a group have more negative attitudes toward the state of Israel than the general population of American adults."[28]

Adding fuel to the fears for personal safety is the CPOST finding that a significant percentage—10 percent—of the college students surveyed would permit student groups to call for genocide, and 13 percent would say that when a group was attacked, it was because group members deserved it. Whether the question was asked about Jews or Muslims, the percentages of students ready to support calls for genocide and a willingness to blame the victims were the same—10 percent and 13 percent, respectively. Though clearly it was a minority of students who expressed an acceptance of violence toward Jews or Muslims, the percentages shown above are disturbing, as violent behavior among even a small number of people can have a chilling effect on many students' feelings of security, and at worst can threaten everyone's safety. Pape rightly concluded, "Widespread personal fears for physical safety, academic discrimination, and economic livelihood among students are severely at odds with the mission of the university to foster scholarship and intellectual achievement in an environment where students and all members of the university community will grow and thrive."[29] Can the educational mission of the university be fulfilled when so many students are afraid to even express an opinion about important political and social issues?

In this context of widespread campus fear, should protest speech be constrained? How should contested language be addressed? At Columbia University, President Shafik responded to campus climate concerns in the fall of 2023 by announcing a new initiative called Values in Action, intended to foster compassion and respect and make space for civil and informed debate in an environment "free of bigotry, intimidation, and harassment."[30] Simultaneously, two pro-Palestinian student groups— Students for Justice in Palestine and Jewish Voice for Peace—were temporarily suspended for violating a campus protest policy, an action Shafik's critics saw as an attempt to shut down pro-Palestinian speech.[31] In support of the president's Values in Action initiative, eighteen deans at Columbia collectively issued a letter that both asked students to acknowledge the pain of pro-Palestinian students in the face of so much death and destruction in Gaza and asked pro-Palestinian student groups to refrain from using chants and phrases like "intifada" because they are heard by many as "antisemitic and deeply hurtful."[32]

In response, Rashid Khalidi, a prominent Palestinian American historian of the Middle East and the Edward Said Professor of Modern Arab Studies at Columbia, wrote, "This statement amounts to a new norm that prohibits using or learning about these terms and their histories, in favor of the privileging of a politics of feeling. While perhaps appropriate to a kindergarten, it is hard to imagine an approach more contrary to the most basic idea of a university." Mohsen Mahdawi, a cofounder of Columbia's Palestinian student union, described the request to "self-police protest chants" as a "double standard," a trap, rather than free speech.[33]

Yet "free speech and academic freedom are the lifeblood of any great university and any healthy democracy"—so stated Princeton President Christopher Eisgruber in his annual State of the University Letter 2024, titled "Excellence, Inclusivity, and Free Speech."[34] His letter directly and eloquently addressed the debate about free speech that was fueled by campus protests and made clear the central importance of the principle of free speech to the educational mission of the university, providing students, faculty, and staff with "the broadest possible latitude to speak, write, listen, challenge, and learn." Even speech that is regarded by many as "offensive, unwise, immoral, or wrong-headed" must be protected, he explained, first because listening to and rebutting arguments with which we disagree strengthen our ability to articulate and defend our own positions. Most importantly, "while we recognize that speech can sometimes cause real injury, great universities do not trust any official—their presidents included—to decide which ideas, opinions, or slogans should be suppressed and which should not. Censorship has a lousy track record."

Honoring the principle of free speech, he elaborated, means that "punishing student speech is and should be exceedingly rare." Only when speech is personally targeted or harassing—such as writing slurs on someone's door or yelling slurs directly at a particular individual—is such speech prohibited. But just because you *can* say something doesn't mean you *should* say it. Advising students to use restraint and avoid offensive speech is part of the educational enterprise as well. Eisgruber offered as an example the advice of Amaney Jamal, dean of the School of Public and International Affairs and a leading expert on Palestinian politics, who cautioned against the use of contested slogans such as "From the river to the sea" because they might be construed as "endorsing Hamas's terroristic methods and aims." But Eisgruber emphasized, "Advising students to avoid offensive speech, however, is very different from suppressing or punishing that speech." He concluded the portion of his letter that addressed the topic of free speech by reaffirming the educational role the university should play, writing, "Universities must protect even offensive speech, but that does not mean we must remain silent in the face of it. On the contrary, we must speak up for our values if we are to make this campus a place where free speech flourishes *and* where all our students can feel that they are 'hosts' not 'guests.' We must model and teach constructive forms of dialogue if we are to enable our students to build and inhabit a society more inclusive than the one that exists today."[35]

That kind of modeling and teaching is exactly what students say they need. Many students (52 percent) surveyed by CPOST wanted campus leaders to take action to help de-escalate campus tensions, agreeing that "the leaders of America's largest universities and colleges should make a statement condemning violence and intimidation against students for their political views." But notably, even more (63 percent) wanted opportunities to learn in dialogue with each other, agreeing with the statement, "We should encourage students to talk with one another and with their professors to learn about the history of the Israeli/Palestinian conflict in an effort to create empathy and understanding."[36]

IS CIVIL DISCOURSE POSSIBLE?

Of course, college and university presidents across the nation spent much of the 2023–2024 academic year trying to do just that—de-escalate tensions and foster dialogue—with varying degrees of success. The use of the "heckler's veto" to interrupt speakers and shut down campus events that protesters find offensive has become an increasingly common impediment to civil discourse.[37] What can campus leaders do to "lower the temperature" and allay the widespread climate of fear?

Writing for the *Chronicle of Higher Education*, Erin Gretzinger investigated this question in her article titled "Can Colleges Foster Civil Discourse?" In a review of more than sixty institutional programs intended to provide information or opportunities to discuss the conflict in the Middle East, the *Chronicle* identified which strategies supported the goal of civil discourse and which tended to generate more conflict. Perhaps the most significant finding was that civil discourse was indeed happening. As Gretzinger pointed out, "While much of the public and media attention has focused on protests led by students and faculty, and by speakers being shouted down, colleges *are* hosting events that aim to promote education and discussion around the Israeli-Palestinian conflict.... A majority of the events proceeded without major incident."[38]

The *Chronicle* analysis found that events that featured subject-matter experts representing multiple disciplinary perspectives in a panel discussion format were particularly useful, since many people lack knowledge about the conflict's history and context. Campus pushback was most often triggered by events that featured just one speaker, opening the door to criticism about "lack of viewpoint balance" or "perceived bias." Yet even when multiple perspectives were represented, the assessment of balance still remained in the eye of the beholder. "The complexity of the conflict and the life-or-death stakes for those experiencing it mean that emotions run high and consensus about what counts as neutral information diverges quickly along ideological lines."[39]

For that reason, perhaps one of the best strategies was that offered by the Marlboro Institute of Liberal Arts and Interdisciplinary Studies at Emerson University, a campus-wide event called "Reclaiming Nuance: Polarization and Framing Post October 7th—a Conversational Approach," to be followed by several small-group discussions. The organizers indicated the event would not be "about the history of the conflict" but instead about "what makes it so challenging to productively discuss this issue." I know from my own experience of teaching about racism that beginning the conversation by *naming the problem* of why so many people find the topic hard to talk about provides a common point of entry to difficult conversations that is often helpful.[40]

Timothy J. Shaffer, the Stavros Niarchos Foundation Chair of Civil Discourse in the Joseph R. Biden Jr. School of Public Policy & Administration at the University of Delaware, also warned against the dangers of oversimplification, which can be one unintended consequence of trying to create "equally matched point-counterpoint sessions." Shaffer noted, "There are not two camps. There's not the Palestinian view, and then there's the Israeli view. There's a lot more nuance. There are these significant gradations." Again, the answer lies in naming the problem. "Avoiding oversimplification can be as easy as acknowledging how complex the conflict is."[41]

In the highly politicized environment in which college presidents now operate, certainly conflict is unavoidable. The circumstances may not always be as externally focused as the Israel-Hamas campus conflicts of 2023 were, but conflict is inevitable. Whether focused on internal campus politics related to faculty-administration disputes, student concerns, or alumni dissatisfactions, working through conflict is a perennial dimension of presidential leadership. It helps if you can at least choose your battles.

In a message to the Williams College campus issued on October 12, 2023, President Maud Mandel articulated with great clarity how she was choosing her conflicts. She explained why she was not issuing a statement on the situation in the Middle East, or any other global calamity. It was a statement I found quite compelling. In essence, she said there are just too many of them! To speak of some and remain silent on others is to create, however inadvertently, attentional inequities. Giving some issues "great visibility while leaving others unseen" ultimately does more harm than good, she explained.[42]

I came to a similar conclusion during my 2022–2023 year as interim president at Mount Holyoke. The school year began with news of massive floods in Pakistan, and I was prompted by a faculty member's request to issue a statement of concern and support for Pakistani students and their families, which I willingly did. Our international students had just arrived on campus, and students from the affected region needed our institutional support. Later that semester, late in the night of November 19, 2022, the eve of Transgender Day of Remembrance, there was a mass shooting at

Club Q, a gay bar in Colorado Springs, Colorado, violence clearly directed at the LGBTQ+ community,[43] and I posted a message of solidarity and support of our own LGBTQ+ members in response. On Monday, February 13, 2023, there was a campus shooting at Michigan State University (MSU), and I issued a statement about the epidemic of gun violence as well as condolences for the MSU community and support for those on our campus experiencing distress triggered by the incident.[44] Not long after that, another tragedy was in the news, and the College Communications team asked if I wanted to prepare a statement. I replied, "No, I'm not issuing any more statements. There are just too many—it will become meaningless unless it is something directly relevant to our campus and our educational mission." Of course, we care about what is happening in the world, and we must prepare our students to be educated global citizens who can think critically about contemporary issues. Yes, our institutions should have a role to play in advocating for issues core to our mission, but routinely issuing statements in response to the headlines of the day was not the path I wanted to stay on. Neither did President Mandel. In particular, she highlighted the tension between representing the community and preempting the community's voice. She said,

> When I speak as president of Williams, I am speaking on behalf of thousands of people who together make up "the Williams community." I feel it is both right and necessary for me to do so on topics related to our core educational mission. But when the topics are national and world events—even events that affect us personally, and on which we feel great moral clarity—I do not believe it is the president's job to speak for the whole community, or even that it is possible to do so. In those moments, my job is to help ensure that the educational opportunities and personal support are in place so that we can reflect, study and decide what we think and believe, individually and collectively.[45]

The hope for any positive outcome in moments of conflict lies in effective communication. Communicate, communicate, communicate—as directly and transparently as possible. Mandel's explanation of her position is a model of both. It also represents an enactment of the 1967 recommendations of the University of Chicago *Report on the University's Role in Political and Social Action*, widely known as the Kalven Report.[46] In response to the campus turmoil of the Vietnam War era, a faculty committee at the University of Chicago led by legal scholar Harry Kalven Jr. was convened, and it recommended that the university should not take institutional positions on public issues but rather maintain a position of neutrality in order not to constrain the free expression of ideas:

> The neutrality of the university as an institution arises then not from a lack of courage nor out of indifference and insensitivity. It arises out of respect for free inquiry and the obligation to cherish a diversity of viewpoints. And this neutrality as an institution has its complement in the fullest freedom for its faculty and students as individuals to participate in political action and social protest. It finds its complement, too, in the obligation of the university to provide a forum for the most searching and candid discussion of public issues.[47]

When there is conflict on campus of the scale provoked by the Israel-Hamas war, it is evident that, even in the context of institutional neutrality, clear, constant, and *consistent* communication rejecting violence and condemning intimidation by students and against students is critical. The CPOST finding that a small but significant percentage of students consider political violence acceptable underscores the importance of consistent messaging rejecting such violence and its precursors of harassment and intimidation. In the CPOST report recommendations, the point is made emphatically that "every leader in a position of power should find ways to send this message repeatedly and convincingly."[48] The educational mission of the institution cannot be achieved in a climate of fear.

Sally Kornbluth, president of MIT, the only one of the three presidents at that difficult December 7 congressional hearing to keep her job in the weeks that followed, said in a statement a month later, "The hardest, most important work—for the administration and for everyone at MIT—is the challenge of listening seriously, rebuilding trust, and caring for our community.... I'm working to use every lever available to address conflict on our campus, enhance the tenor of our discourse and help us find improved ways to live and work together." The steps she outlined for MIT are examples of best practice:

- We continue to join with faculty and staff experts to work directly with the students most affected by the conflict in the Middle East.
- The faculty-led Unity Across Difference group and the Third Way lunch series are finding ways—person to person—to foster respectful, informed dialogue.
- Standing Together Against Hate, the community-led effort we announced in November, is offering a suite of lectures, discussions, classes and community-building efforts. . . .
- And the Center for Constructive Communication is launching discussions in student residences to foster appreciation for each other's humanity, even across deep differences.[49]

Colleges and universities are one of the few places where people from diverse backgrounds and life experiences can come together to learn from one another in meaningful interaction. Through such interaction, they can begin to see the world from another's perspective, expanding their understanding of the world's complexities. Such learning rarely happens without some level of discomfort. Neither does it happen in an atmosphere of intimidation or harassment.

The skills of dialogue are necessary, and conflict expressed within the scaffolding of community standards for civility makes it possible. Academic freedom is a critical ingredient in that mix, recognizing that the response to discomfiting free speech is most often *more speech*, more engagement with the offending ideas and those who articulate them. The "cancel culture" that seeks to expunge those who are "in the wrong" needs to shift to what social justice educator Loretta Ross calls the "call-in" culture, defined as "initiating difficult dialogues with those you disagree with while respecting their human rights and differences."[50] We need more visible examples of that approach. Building the infrastructure for dialogue by providing opportunities for students, faculty, and staff to develop skill and confidence in how to facilitate difficult conversations before the crisis hits can help.

One thing is for certain—conflict cannot be avoided. It comes with the job. In her inaugural speech at Harvard, Claudine Gay spoke of the importance and need for courage to do the work we are called to do.[51] She undoubtedly was right about that.

On April 17, 2024, the US House Committee on Education and the Workforce again convened to discuss the problem of antisemitism on college campuses in the wake of the tumultuous campus protests in response to the Israel-Hamas war. This time the proceeding was titled "Columbia in Crisis: Columbia University's Response to Antisemitism," and Columbia University President Nemat "Minouche" Shafik was on the hot seat. Like the presidents of Harvard, Penn, and MIT who appeared before the committee a few months before, she was a woman new to her role, arriving at Columbia as president in July 2023, and her campus had been rocked not only by pro-Palestinian protests and counterprotests but also by disturbing antisemitic attacks—both verbal and physical—on Jewish students. But unlike her peers at the earlier hearing, she did not appear alone. She was joined by the two cochairs of the Columbia Board of Trustees, Claire Shipman and David Greenwald, as well as Professor David Schitzer, cochair of Columbia's Task Force on Antisemitism.

Having had the benefit of seeing video of the previous congressional hearing, President Shafik was able to learn from the mistakes the first group of presidents made. When asked, "Does calling for the genocide of Jews violate Columbia's code of conduct?" she did *not* say, "It depends on the context," as the presidents of Harvard, Penn, and MIT had tried to explain. "Yes, it does," was Shafik's unhesitating reply, her response echoed by each of the other Columbia representatives.[52] They were praised for their directness.

Nevertheless, in a hearing that lasted more than three hours, the Columbia University representatives were challenged repeatedly to explain or defend the disciplinary actions that had been taken (or not taken) against students and faculty who had used language or expressed opinions that House committee members regarded as antisemitic and, in some instances, offensive because of expressed (or alleged) support of Hamas, the perpetrators of the brutal October 7 attack on Israeli civilians. The legislators were particularly concerned about how faculty were being disciplined, questioning why some had not been fired.[53]

Several placed the spotlight on Joseph Massad, a man of Palestinian Christian descent who is a tenured Columbia professor in Middle Eastern, South Asian, and African studies.[54] On October 8 Massad had published a pro-Palestinian essay titled "Just Another Battle or the Palestinian War of Liberation?," which opened with these lines: "What can motorized paragliders do in the face of one of the most formidable militaries in the world? Apparently much in the hands of an innovative Palestinian resistance, which early on Saturday morning launched a surprise attack on Israel by air, land and sea.... It came in retaliation for the ongoing Israeli pogroms in the West Bank town of Huwwara and Jerusalem, especially by settlers storming al-Aqsa mosque during the Jewish High Holy Days." Massad went on to describe the "jubilation and awe" of Palestinians on October 7 in response to "the stunning victory of the Palestinian resistance over the Israeli military."[55] Tim Walberg, a Republican representative from

Michigan, characterized Massad's viewpoint as that of a supporter of terrorism and demanded to know "why is he still in the classroom?"

As I watched the video of Shafik's testimony at that moment, I imagined what I might have said in response had I been in her seat. I am quite sure that none of the responses in my head would have satisfied the committee. They were looking for clear condemnations and promises of swift punishments. But that is not how it works in higher education. The organizational structure of higher education, with the president as the chief executive officer, a board of trustees providing oversight, *and* a faculty committee structure often referred to as *shared governance*, means that a college president cannot just unilaterally decide to fire tenured faculty members without following due process, not to mention observing the principle of academic freedom in determining whether such discipline is warranted.

I wanted the president to explain that to her questioners, but even if she had made that attempt, it is unlikely that she would have been allowed to finish her sentences. The legislators were quick to cut off her responses. Instead, she said, "I'm appalled by what he's said," and did not defend his right to say it. She was not alone in her opinion about his commentary. After the publication of his essay, a student circulated an online petition, which was boosted on social media by David Friedman, a 1978 graduate of Columbia and the former US ambassador to Israel, generating more than forty-five thousand signatures calling for Professor Massad's removal.[56] In response, however, hundreds of Columbia students, faculty, and alumni signed a letter of support, urging the university to provide protection for Massad in the face of the death threats he had received and to protect his academic freedom.[57]

The concept of academic freedom was noticeably absent from the discussion at the congressional hearing. "What happened to the idea of academic freedom? I don't think that phrase was used even once," commented Sheldon Pollock, a retired Columbia professor active in the Columbia University chapter of the American Association of University

Professors (AAUP).[58] The national president of AAUP, Irene Mulvey, was pointed in her criticism of Shafik's failure to defend Massad's right to express his viewpoint, however offensive she may have found it to be. Mulvey said, "When faculty speak as citizens, they should be free from institutional censorship or discipline. Shafik's public naming of professors under investigation sets a dangerous precedent [and] echoes McCarthy era cowardice."[59] An important opportunity to educate the public—or at least attempt to do so—about this core concept so central to the mission of the university was lost.

There is historical precedent in times of war for the protection of controversial speech, as highlighted in Len Gutkin's essay "The Antisemitism Hearing Forgot About Academic Freedom." He wrote, "Massad's essay, which appeared in *The Electronic Intifada*, is obviously protected extramural speech, no less than was the Rutgers University historian Eugene Genovese's proclamation, in 1965, that 'I do not fear or regret the impending Vietcong victory in Vietnam. I welcome it.'" Rutgers, in a watershed victory for academic freedom, refused to discipline Genovese—despite demands by politicians that he be fired.[60] Similarly, Gutkin pointed out that the failure to articulate clearly what academic freedom protects (protest rhetoric) and what it does not (targeted harassment of individuals) left room for legislators to call for the punishment of students whose protest chants such as "From the river to the sea" offend them. As discussed earlier, what you *can* say may not be what you *should* say, but protest speech is protected speech. Gutkin rightly concluded, "There is no real academic freedom—which includes the rights of students to associate for purposes of political expression—when a college president dictates which slogans protesters can or can't use."[61]

Of course, institutions can legitimately place parameters around protests, using time, place, and manner restrictions—setting basic rules about where, when, and how protest speeches and other activity can take place. Such parameters can help buffer students from uncomfortable encounters.

However, even when students call for protection from speech they don't like, it may be in their best interest as learners to push them toward developing counterstrategies that challenge rather than silence others. Professor Sigal Ben-Porath, chair since 2015 of the University of Pennsylvania's Committee on Open Expression, has helped students through her work on citizenship education to build their toolkit of responses, sometimes looking to history for examples of how to engage effectively with offensive ideas.

In this time of widespread political polarization, colleges and universities have an opportunity to not only help students engage in effective dialogue, but also educate them on why freedom of speech is so important. In the twentieth century, the exercise of free speech—freedom to protest—changed our society for the better. The civil rights heroes we celebrate today were the "radicals" of the past that so many tried to silence. Students should understand the connection between the freedom of speech and the everyday freedoms they enjoy today. As Chemerinsky and Gillman write, "Sturdy protection for the expression of ideas should be considered one of the past century's most important accomplishments."[62] We have to pass that understanding on if we want to preserve it.

Indeed, it is perhaps in the "sturdy protection for the expression of ideas" that college leaders may find it necessary to lead by example. Though the principle of institutional neutrality found in the Kalven Report can serve a useful purpose for college leaders caught in the crosshairs of campus conflict, there are times when neutrality becomes complicity. Kalven and his colleagues recognized this eventuality as well. They observed, "From time to time, instances will arise in which the society, or segments of it, threaten the very mission of the university and its values of free inquiry. In such a crisis, it becomes the obligation of the university as an institution to oppose such measures and actively defend its interests and its values."[63] It is clear to me that we are living in such a time today, a time when leaders must actively defend institutional values. Our silence will not protect us.[64]

CHAPTER FOUR

WHO'S IN CHARGE, REALLY?

Understanding Shared Governance

"Presidents come, and presidents go. It's the faculty that remains."
When the newly elected chair of the Faculty Council said that to me
during our first meeting, I thought it was a snarky thing to say and bris-
tled at the comment. Still, she was factually accurate. Though I served
thirteen years (twice the average tenure of contemporary college presidents), when I retired from my role, she was still on the faculty. Indeed,
many faculty members who were at the college when I arrived were still
there when I left. That kind of longevity is one reason that shared governance as an organizing principle of colleges and universities is so central
to how they operate. It is, however, a principle that is not well understood
by those who live and work outside the academy.

That lack of understanding was on full display during the congressional hearings that dominated the higher education news cycle in the
2023–2024 school year. For example, in one such hearing, when one of
the legislators demanded to know why a particular professor whose

comments he found offensive had not been fired, his question implied that the hiring and firing of professors was something that the president does, or if not the president, then perhaps the trustees. After all, those are the people in charge, right? Well, not exactly. In fact, initial hiring decisions are usually determined by faculty within their disciplinary departments (i.e., the faculty members in a particular department are the people who decide who should be hired in their department) with input from the dean of the school in which the department is housed, or from the provost (the chief academic officer). At most institutions, the president is not likely to participate in that hiring process until the very end, if at all.

Similarly, the decisions about promotion and tenure—the granting of permanent employment—are largely determined by faculty through a well-defined review process that includes members of the tenure candidate's department who evaluate the quality and quantity of the teaching, scholarship, and institutional service of the candidate. Teaching evaluations submitted by students are reviewed, scholarly publications or other creative works are evaluated, and the candidate's self-assessment about the teaching, research, and service is considered. External reviewers who are experts in the candidate's subject matter are also asked to provide written commentary about the person's scholarship and other relevant contributions to the profession. Once the department members have completed their evaluation, they make a recommendation (positive or negative) to a multidisciplinary faculty committee whose responsibility it is to review all the candidates being considered for tenure and to make an independent assessment of the worthiness of each candidate. The tenure committee's recommendation and the recommendation of the department are shared with the provost and eventually sent to the president. If all parties are in favor of granting tenure, it's easy—the president makes the recommendation to the board of trustees, and the board finalizes the decision with a vote to approve. If all parties agree that tenure should be denied, that information is also shared with the board, but no board vote is needed.

When there is disagreement (a split vote among the tenure review committee, for example), the provost or president might become the tiebreaker. In any case, once the president makes the recommendation to the board, the board is very likely to accept it.

In my experience, both as a president and as a board member, I have never seen a board overturn a president's tenure recommendation, and why would they? Board members are rarely experts in the faculty member's area of study. They must rely on the academic expertise of the department members, the faculty leaders who sit on the tenure review committee, the chief academic officer of the institution, and the judgment of the president they hired to guide them. If all those people have concluded that the candidate is worthy of tenure, how can the board say they know better?

Can a faculty member who has been awarded tenure be removed from the faculty? Yes, and as a president, I have been a party to disciplinary processes that resulted in termination of employment. But again, the process begins with a faculty review committee. When a faculty member is subject to disciplinary action, the process, typically detailed in the faculty handbook, must include faculty input. To hear personnel matters regarding faculty—usually treated as highly confidential—discussed openly as they were in that previously mentioned televised congressional hearing was quite disturbing to higher education observers. For example, Marianne Hirsch, a Columbia Professor Emerita of English and comparative literature and of the Institute for the Study of Sexuality and Gender, commented, "This is shocking, I've never experienced it before and I've been in academia for 50 years."[1] Her colleague Helen Benedict, professor at the Columbia School of Journalism, agreed and raised concerns about the specter of congressional interference in the governance process. She asserted, "In the American democracy, Congress isn't supposed to tell campuses who they must fire, who they can hire—it's none of their business, we do this for ourselves."[2]

So, does this mean the faculty are in charge? Well, not exactly. Newcomers to higher education are often mystified by the governing process of colleges and universities. The organizational structure is unique to higher education. What *does* the president do? And what about the board? Exactly what is the role of the board in relationship to the president? And what about the faculty? What do people mean when they talk about "shared governance"? *Who is in charge, really?*

It all starts with the board. Governing boards "hold ultimate authority for an institution, as defined in bylaws and other foundational documents as well as state fiduciary principles. There is very little debate on this point. However, through longstanding academic practice, this authority is delegated to—or 'shared with'—institutional leaders and faculty."[3] Given this delegation of authority, among a governing board's most important responsibilities is the selection of the president. The board is responsible for appointing, evaluating, supporting, and if necessary removing the president. Typically, presidents are charged with, and held responsible for, institutional leadership, strategic planning, and daily management. Responsibility for the academic program—curriculum development and delivery— is traditionally delegated to the faculty. However, the board also provides collective oversight of educational and fiscal policy, approves the promotion and tenure of faculty based on the recommendation of the president (made in consultation with a faculty committee), as well as the granting of all degrees. The details of how a board functions might vary from institution to institution, as defined in the institution's bylaws, but fundamentally the role of board members "is not managerial or operational in nature."[4]

This governance structure—with authority held by the board and shared with the president, and to a lesser extent the faculty—can be traced to the earliest days of American universities. According to educational historian John R. Thelin, the vesting of ultimate legal authority in an external lay board of trustees, "which in turn worked closely and almost exclusively with the president, who was the head of a strong administrative structure," was a distinctive and innovative feature of the first colonial colleges, dating back to the founding of Harvard College in 1636 and the College of William and Mary in 1692. Thelin explained, "The driving force for this innovation was distrust of and disgust with faculty governance at Oxford and Cambridge universities. Reliance on the external board plus a powerful president was designed to promote a 'tight ship' character to the colleges in the New World. Indeed, the model was immediately effective and enduring."[5] From the seventeenth to twenty-first centuries, this governing model of "a strong presidency joined at the hip with an ultimately powerful board of trustees" has been the model of choice in American higher education.[6]

Who are these powerful board members? Thelin observed that "a peculiar consequence" of this American governing model is the relative anonymity that is typical of boards of trustees and their "negligible accountability."[7] Relative to the college president and the campus community, board members usually keep a low profile. In public institutions, board members are often politically appointed by a state authority, typically the governor. In private colleges and universities, boards are self-perpetuating, meaning that current board members collectively choose the new ones, often with the president's input, but not necessarily. Members are selected for their industry expertise (e.g., legal, financial, technological, academic), their history with the institution (graduates often preferred), and/or their demonstrated ability and willingness to support the institution with their treasure as well as their time and talent. Though often rewarded with special invitations to campus events (including perhaps highly coveted tickets to athletic events), they are otherwise unpaid volunteers. Most are not higher education experts. They are people with busy lives and careers of their own, which means they must rely on the president and the senior leadership team to give them the information they need to fulfill their oversight responsibilities.

Their role is to govern, not manage—their task is to ask strategic questions but not "get in the weeds." Though their role is governance, not management, trustees sometimes blur the line between the two, meddling in decisions that are managerial in nature. In the best of circumstances, the board chair will provide guidance and remind the members of their appropriate roles. If the chair is the one who oversteps the line, trouble is not far behind.

Particularly when a president is new to the role, anxiety about the transition and the desire to make sure that it goes well can lead trustees to insert themselves into daily operations in a way that is inappropriate. For example, in the early days of my presidency, the person who served as my first board chair asked my chief of staff, who also served as secretary to the board, to send her the weekly agendas for my staff meetings, a particularly intrusive request. The staff member was appropriately hesitant and asked me for help in managing the relationship with the chair. I interpreted the chair's request as an expression of anxiety and a desire for more information. I explained to the chair my need to test ideas with my team before making them visible to the board in the way that she had requested, but offered instead to have a weekly phone call in advance of my staff meeting where I could alert her to any concerns that might be important for her to know about, drawing a boundary that protected the privacy of my staff meeting and yet helped her feel "in the loop" of information. That solution was satisfactory, but it was just the first instance of boundary-setting I was required to do.

Later that year I made a hiring decision that the chair did not like. I knew that she was not in favor of a particular candidate, but based on my best assessment of the choices available and the recommendation of the faculty-led search committee, I proceeded with the hire. The college by-laws were clear—personnel decisions were the chief executive's responsibility. Nevertheless, in making this choice, I provoked the ire of the chair. When the board met in executive session without me, the chair instructed three members of the board, all of whom were employed as faculty or administrators from other educational institutions, to serve as "advisers" to me to help me undo my "hiring mistake." When I was informed of their task, I was livid. As a new president, I felt that I was in an untenable position. Either I was "in charge" or I wasn't. There is certainly value in seeking trustee feedback in the process of hiring a senior leader, but in this instance, I felt like my legitimate authority was being undermined. I will always be grateful to an influential board member who in a private moment encouraged me to stand up for myself. I did, and the appointment proceeded as planned. It was the first time that I really had to draw a clear line between the board's role and mine. It was an important test.

Every president needs the support and confidence of the board to be successful. In particular, the relationship between the board chair and the president should be a supportive partnership. Happily, by year three of my presidency, the board had elected a new chair, with whom I had that kind of partnership, a pattern that continued for the rest of my presidency, even when board leadership changed again in the later years of my tenure. This new chair served for the next seven years of my time as president and brought to the role a clear understanding of the distinction between governance and management. I especially appreciated her leadership in keeping the rules of engagement clear. She often reminded me of two things: "The trustees are all volunteers, and they lead busy lives. If you feel they don't understand what is happening at the college, it is your responsibility to explain it." But she wisely cautioned me, "Keep your communications at the strategic level. If you take the board into the weeds, bogging them down with too many details, they will stay there"—an important reminder for me.

The shared governance roles between boards and presidents are more easily delineated perhaps than the shared governance roles between presidents (and other senior administrators) and faculty, and to a lesser extent, staff and students. Broadly defined, shared governance means giving faculty as well as other constituent groups a role in key decision-making processes.[8] In the case of faculty and the curriculum, for example, faculty typically hold primary responsibility for decision-making, usually with active participation from the provost, who is the chief academic officer. In the case of hiring senior administrators, faculty and staff might give input as members of a search committee and recommend candidates, but the final decision-making authority rests with the president, who ultimately will be held accountable for the success or failure of the new administrator. Scott Cowen, who served as president of Tulane University for sixteen years, succinctly stated, "A first step [in effective shared governance] is to make sure that everyone understands that the sharing in 'shared governance' isn't equally distributed, nor does it imply decision-making authority. That authority is held by the president and the board, the ones who are accountable for both results and shortcomings."[9]

In a study of effective academic governance across a wide cross-section of four-year colleges and universities, the research team at the Collaborative on Academic Careers in Higher Education observed, "Without a clearly defined 'jurisdiction,' some faculty members expect to 'be involved in everything' while others interpret the lack of a specified role as a sign that the faculty are powerless. Similarly, administrators expecting a faster 'pace of change' may assume broad decision-making authority, provoking conflicts with faculty—and other administrators—who expect more deliberation and collaboration."[10] When the expectations for shared governance are not clearly aligned, conflict is likely the result, which is exactly what happened to me in the fall of 2007.

SIGNED, THE FACULTY

When I arrived at Spelman in the summer of 2002, I quickly identified five challenges that needed immediate attention. *Challenge #1* was inadequate cross-campus communication. In my initial conversations with key campus constituents, it became apparent that there were no well-developed mechanisms for communicating information across the campus in a timely way. In the absence of needed information, faculty and staff sometimes engaged in overlapping or even competing activities and were unable to maximize the benefit of their efforts. The administrative divisions were operating as independent silos. My goal was to establish cross-functional collaboration and problem-solving as the norm for doing business at Spelman. *Challenge #2* was the lack of stable leadership in the division of Academic Affairs. Prior to my arrival, there had been five provosts in as many years. During this time of revolving-door leadership in the division, many faculty needs had gone unaddressed. Stabilizing the leadership in the Office of the Provost was imperative. *Challenge #3* was the very low level of alumnae financial support and a weak fundraising infrastructure in terms of both staff and technology. *Challenge #4* was the decentralized structure of our student recruiting effort, with the Office of Financial Aid and the Admissions Office reporting to two different vice presidents, with insufficient coordination between them. In an increasingly competitive enrollment landscape, disconnection between the two offices was a self-imposed disadvantage. *Challenge #5* was the widespread frustration with the state of technology on campus, with intermittent loss of internet connectivity a common complaint. The transition from twentieth-century manual processes to twenty-first-century technological solutions was stalled. When I shared my initial assessment of these challenges with the executive committee of the board of trustees at our first meeting together, one of the trustees offered this wisdom: "How do you eat an elephant? One bite at a time." And so our work began.

I had a sense of urgency about what needed to be done and moved quickly to initiate action in each of the challenge areas. The CFO gave me the nickname "Speedy." By the end of year four (2006), significant progress on all five challenges had been made. The *Spelman Connection*, a weekly electronic newsletter, was instituted to be the venue for communicating important campus information internally, and we revamped our website for better external messaging. Stable leadership had returned to the Office of the Provost with a successful hire, and we had reallocated the budget to fully fund the existing sabbatical program for tenured faculty and launch a pre-tenure sabbatical program for junior faculty. The initially low percentage of annual alum support (13 percent) had more than doubled to

28 percent and was still rising. I created a new Enrollment Management division (bringing together the Office of Admission, the Office of Financial Aid, and the Registrar's Office) and hired a new vice president to lead it. Under the new structure, applications had increased from 3,000 annually to 4,500, a 50 percent increase, a number that grew steadily in each subsequent year. A new chief information officer was making the operational changes necessary to improve the reliability of our systems and was developing a road map for improving our IT capability. The physical campus was also undergoing a transformation. Two historic buildings had been completely renovated (both garnering architectural awards for historic preservation), a third renovation project was underway, and we were preparing to break ground on newly acquired land adjacent to the existing campus for what would become a three-hundred-bed residence hall and dining commons. Signs everywhere on our construction-weary campus read, "Building a Better Spelman for You!"

It seemed that wonderful things were happening at Spelman *every* day. I was surrounded by bright and energetic students and dedicated faculty and staff who accomplished amazing things. We had a great story to tell, and once we began to tell it more energetically, the results were fantastic. Our media presence grew exponentially. Our media impressions (the number of times information about Spelman was presented to the public—online, over the airwaves, or in print) grew from seventy million in 2003 to over *one billion* in 2005. Perhaps the most tangible result of our increased visibility was our rise in the *US News & World Report* rankings. Peer ratings are an important dimension of how the rankings are calculated. The positive "buzz" about Spelman was growing. In August 2003, we made our first appearance on the *US News & World Report* top one hundred National Liberal Arts Colleges list, ranked at number 81. Twelve months later, we had an amazing fifteen-point rise to number 66, an upward trajectory that continued in the years that followed, eventually placing Spelman among the top fifty national liberal arts colleges.[11]

A lot was happening quickly. From my vantage point, shared governance was working well. I regularly invited faculty to serve on search committees and join problem-solving task forces, and created formal and informal opportunities for faculty to participate in dialogue about the future of the college. The flow of communication was improving. In addition to my weekly meetings with the senior leadership team and monthly convenings with faculty representatives (Faculty Council), meetings with a newly organized representative group of mid-level managers (Leadership Council) and hourly wage staff representatives (Staff Council) were established for the purpose of information exchange and shared problem-solving. A campus-wide end-of-year "State of the College" address became a vehicle for sharing important budgetary information with transparency as well as highlighting our annual progress toward our strategic goals.

Then, while I was still in my fourth year as president, the board commissioned an external review of both president and board performance, led by two consultants from the Association of Governing Boards of Universities and Colleges (AGB). As stated in their report summary, "The ongoing assessment of performance, one element of continuous improvement, allows the board and the president to view each other's work more objectively as well as through the lenses of various campus constituencies." Their conclusions were, I thought, quite positive. They wrote, "The relationship between the Spelman board and president is strong. The College has undergone tremendous changes and made great strides during the past four years under President Tatum's leadership, and she is seen as the driving force behind the progress. Things are going well from the perspective of all constituencies—administrators, faculty, staff, students, and board members." I took the phrase "she is seen as the driving force" as affirmation. In retrospect, I can imagine that others might have seen that statement as a sign of insufficient faculty engagement.

In any case, I was surprised when in the fall of my sixth year, the newly elected Faculty Council president, just two days before Thanksgiving, delivered to me a long and highly critical letter, signed "The Faculty." The six-page, single-spaced missive began with this sentence: "On September 17, 2007, the Faculty convened for its first general meeting of the year to address our deepening concern for the deteriorating functionality of the campus" and continued, "The sense of urgency that characterized the Faculty meeting was prompted by our fresh frustration with the chaotic circumstances surrounding the opening of the Fall 2007 semester. During the meeting we named and listed the specific system failures that marked an unprecedented low in the Spelman College advising and registration process for incoming and returning students. It was clear to us that these recent events reflected larger systemic problems that have become characteristic of the entire campus." It continued in that tone.

Yes, our student enrollment that fall was higher than originally anticipated, and an administrative glitch in the Registrar's Office had impacted advising and student assignments to course sections for heavily enrolled classes in the first few days of the semester, the source of faculty frustration. Still, what I perceived as the letter's "nothing's any good" tone was in such contrast to the positive energy I felt when I walked across the campus each day and the campus-wide progress I and others could document. Was "deteriorating functionality" really what the faculty was seeing and thinking? And if there was so much distress, why did the Faculty Council president wait two full months to share the information?

The challenge of responding nondefensively to this important letter surely was a growth opportunity for me. I started by reaching out to a faculty member I trusted to ask what she thought about the letter. I learned she had not seen it. While it was true that the faculty had given input in September to the myriad issues covered in the document, it was clear to me that the letter I received that November had been drafted by the Faculty Council president herself, perhaps with the assistance of one or two other writers, and most faculty had not seen the letter prior to its delivery to me. But because the letter was signed "The Faculty," I intended to send my reply to the entire faculty via email as soon as we all returned from the Thanksgiving break. Before responding, I reread the letter several times. I could see that the core of the letter was about concern with shared governance. This excerpt was quite telling:

> The greater part of any solution is the difficult process of acknowledging the nature and source of the problem. Within our historical and present culture there is a great reluctance to trace the source of a problem to our President-centered organizational hierarchy. While this leadership style was surely necessary and successful at our founding, it is now insufficient and detrimental to our current needs and goals.... We would all be better served if we could envision and transition to a system modeled on shared governance which values a culture of cooperation, generosity, respect, and intellection. We do not yet enjoy this culture at Spelman, and in this lack lies the source of our most intractable problems.

After detailing specific concerns about limited faculty involvement in organizational decisions I had made about administrative departments and frustrations with related hiring decisions, the faculty letter concluded with a set of recommendations. I had a lot to say in response and struggled to keep my letter to an appropriate length. My faculty colleague had advised that I not try to address every issue but instead invite the Faculty Council to have in-person conversations with me about their concerns and the recommendations that had been put forward. It was good advice. Here's a portion of my response:

> I share your hope for a better and "future" Spelman and am grateful for your willingness to be fully participatory in creating it. I completely agree that the College would be "better served if we could envision and transition to a system modeled on shared

governance which values a culture of cooperation, generosity, respect, and intellection" and that we do not yet enjoy this culture at Spelman. Culture is the hardest thing to change about an institution and clearly no President can change it alone. . . .

As most of you know, I was a member of the teaching faculty for more than twenty years, and I deeply appreciate the investment of self that teaching faculty make not only in their students, but in the institution they serve. The dedication of Spelman faculty is clear, and I am encouraged by the commitment to active engagement in shaping the future of the institution that this letter represents. . . . I hope we will work to achieve a climate where we all feel like we are on the same team working toward the same goal—a community characterized by trust and transparency, rather than suspicion and secrecy—a place where together we can truly say Spelman College is "nothing less than the best."

I look forward to further discussion. Thank you again for your commitment to excellence and your courage in initiating this dialogue.

Though I can't say that the "President-centered organizational hierarchy" and the "faculty culture of silence" described in the original letter to me were interrupted by our exchange of letters, it did lead to a productive dialogue with the Faculty Council and its president. We met several times specifically to discuss the faculty letter, and I also used the letter as a case study for discussion with my senior leadership team. There was a lot to unpack in the letter, creating an important opportunity for feedback within the group, and an opportunity to examine the pattern of their interactions with faculty as well as my own.

Looking back now, I see the conflict highlighted by the letter as a misalignment of expectations. Clearly the pace of change, which was undoubtedly benefiting the college in significant ways, had been fueled by my action-oriented personality and my exercise of "broad decision-making authority." The faculty author(s) of the letter apparently expected more deliberation and collaboration. Was it possible to have both? That is, both time-sensitive change *and* extensive faculty deliberation? The tension between action and deliberation is an ever-present one on college campuses. That tension did not go away over the course of my thirteen years as president, but I tried to stay attuned to it and find the right balance. Happily, I never received another letter like that one.

How shared governance is enacted—among board, president, and faculty—will vary from campus to campus, shaped by the institution's unique history and culture. Coming to shared understanding may not be easy, but it is necessary. Just as presidents cannot be successful for long without board support, neither can they succeed over the long term without widespread faculty support. In the words of Susan Resneck Pierce, author of *On Being Presidential*, "No matter how campuses practice shared governance, what is important is that the president not only communicate regularly with the faculty but also actively engage and listen to those faculty selected by their peers to be in leadership positions during conversations about matters of academic importance."[12]

As the campus events following the October 7 attack on Israel and the Israel-Hamas war in Gaza made apparent, conversations about free speech, academic freedom, *and* student physical and psychological safety in the face of both rising antisemitism and Islamophobia could not be more important to the educational mission of the institution. Shared governance demands that faculty must be engaged in these important conversations in a meaningful way, ideally providing essential leadership for them. In times of crisis, faculty leadership is critically needed as students look to their faculty, perhaps more than anyone else on campus, for advice and guidance.

Failure to fully engage with faculty through the process of shared governance places a president at risk for a "no confidence" vote by the faculty.

The number of such votes has increased over the last decade, perhaps an expression of the increased stress within the higher education ecosystem. Among the reasons usually identified for no-confidence votes, a president's failure to participate in shared governance is among the most common, along with financial mismanagement and interpersonal friction. Since only boards hire and fire presidents, a no-confidence vote by the faculty is largely symbolic, a formal expression of their disapproval of a president's performance. However, according to an analysis done by the *Chronicle of Higher Education*, more than half (51 percent) of presidents who receive a no-confidence vote leave office within the year.[13] If the board of trustees continues to express support for its president despite such a vote, a president can remain in place and slowly work to rebuild the faculty's confidence, difficult as that might be.

One thing is for certain: in good times, and especially in bad, institutional leaders need faculty support to succeed. There will always be diverging points of view in academic communities—unanimity of opinion is not required, nor should it ever be expected. Yet a recognition of the community's shared future and the interdependence and need for mutual trust and respect among the various campus constituent groups is essential for the institution to thrive. For faculty especially, trustworthiness, mutual respect, and a commitment to shared governance are qualities foundational to an effective partnership with the president. Presidents do come, and presidents do go. If faculty have been actively engaged in the shared governance process, the core mission of the institution can be sustained and nurtured even during times of leadership transition and challenge. Without faculty confidence in shared governance, there is little hope for long-term success.

CHAPTER FIVE

PRESIDENTS, PROTESTS, POLICE, AND POLITICS

S tudents like to say that shared governance includes them. And indeed, at some institutions, students have an elected seat on the board, and representation on college committees. On many campuses, elected student government representatives are invited to speak at faculty meetings and regularly meet with the president and other senior administrators. But even when those institutional structures are not in place, students will tell you that there would be no institution without them, and they are right about that. They are the largest constituent group on campus. No students, no college. So, when they are passionate about something they think needs to change, they want institutional leaders to listen and respond. When the leaders don't respond in the way that students hoped or expected, a student protest is a likely outcome.

According to Angus Johnston, a historian of student activism, "There has never been an American higher-education environment where student protest wasn't a major part of the student experience."[1] The history of student protests goes back to the earliest days of higher education, but the baby boomers in higher education will likely remember the twentieth-century student protests that defined our own coming-of-age student experiences. Among the most memorable are the student protests of the 1960s at the University of California, Berkeley, advocating for the right of free speech; the activism nationwide in support of the civil rights movement and against the Vietnam War, including the reactions to the deadly National Guard shootings of student antiwar protesters at Kent State University in 1970 and the fatal police shootings of racial justice protesters at Jackson State University just a few days later; and later, the 1985 student push for divestment from all entities whose operations supported South African apartheid.[2]

My own career as a college administrator was in some ways launched when a group of student protesters at Mount Holyoke College took over the main administration building and occupied President Joanne Creighton's office in the spring of 1997. As Creighton described in her 2018 memoir, *The Educational Odyssey of a Woman College President*, her first few years at the college were rocky ones.[3] She started her position in January 1996, and by the fall of that year students were starting to complain about the new president, particularly as it related to her resistance to their advocacy for two new cultural centers on campus. The campus was already home to the Betty Shabazz Cultural Center (a gathering place for students of African descent established in 1969), the Eliana Ortega Cultural Center (opened in 1995 to serve the needs of Latinx students), and the Zowey Banteah Cultural Center (originally called Native Spirit, opened in 1995 to support Indigenous students). Student activists, some of whom were in my Psychology of Racism class, were advocating for a cultural center focused on the needs of students of Asian descent, as well as a cultural center for students who identified as members of the LGBTQ+ community.

President Creighton had framed her opposition to further expansion of cultural centers on campus as a concern about the "balkanization" of the campus, a point of view I had often heard expressed by college administrators on campuses across the country. My research on the adolescent development of racial and ethnic identity during the college years had given me another perspective on this question, which I was in the process of writing about in my then-forthcoming book, *Why Are All the Black Kids Sitting Together in the Cafeteria? And Other Conversations About Race.* I was keenly aware of the psychological benefits that marginalized students often get from the opportunities to gather in supportive environments like cultural centers. In March 1997, I wrote a long letter to the president about the importance of cultural centers, and subsequently a version of the letter was published as an op-ed in the campus newspaper.

Meanwhile, as President Creighton pursued a new strategic plan for the campus that included the need to shift away from a fiscally unsustainable "need blind" financial aid policy to one that was "need sensitive," some students worried this change would disproportionately impact prospective students of color. Student concerns about financial aid policy, the cultural centers, perceived lack of support for campus religious life programs, and other diversity-related concerns had led to a broad coalition of students united in their opposition to the Creighton administration. The tension erupted in April 1997 when student activists staged a takeover of key administration buildings—first the Office of Admission, and then a few days later the main administration building, Mary Lyon Hall.

On that Monday in April, a group of about fifty students entered Mary Lyon Hall and seized control of the president's office, evicting the office staff in the process. That afternoon President Creighton came to my office in the Psychology and Education Building to talk with me about the situation. The student protesters, many of whom had been in one or more of my psychology classes, had asked that I serve as one of the mediators in their discussions with the president and her staff. I agreed to help. Over the next twenty-four hours, the situation began to de-escalate, and by Tuesday evening the students had left the building.

In the process, I could see how difficult the situation had been for the president. She held her ground on the change in financial aid policies—the only fiscally responsible position she could take—but she very reluctantly agreed to the establishment of the two new cultural centers, what became the Asian Center for Empowerment (known as the ACE House) and the Lesbian, Bisexual, and Transgender Community Center, later named the Jeannette Marks House. It was clear to me she still thought the creation of more cultural centers was a bad idea and that she felt coerced into that decision. I thought perhaps I could help her take a more positive view of the commitment she had made by illustrating for her the positive impact cultural centers can have. After the takeover crisis had ended, the president and I met to talk about it. As I sat with her discussing the protest outcomes, I did not imagine that just a few months later I would be appointed the next dean of the college, with responsibility for all aspects of student life on campus, in and out of the classroom, but that is what happened. Looking back on it now, I see that my role as a trusted faculty member during what the president called "the troubles" helped open the door to that new and unanticipated phase of my academic career.

Unlike the campus protests of earlier times, the Mount Holyoke protest of 1997 was not specifically connected to national events but rather was a response to campus-based decisions to which students were objecting. Their takeover action, which occurred at the height of the admissions acceptance season, was highly disruptive. The occupation of the president's office symbolized the seizing of power as nothing else could. The adrenaline among the student protesters was running high, and the president's temperature was also rising. Turning to faculty that students trusted to help de-escalate the situation was exactly the right thing to do at that moment, a much better alternative than turning to law enforcement.

LESSONS LEARNED: THEN AND NOW

Fast forward twenty-five years, I was again confronted with a student takeover of the main administration building at Mount Holyoke. This time it was the fall of 2022, and I had agreed to serve as the interim president for the 2022–2023 academic year. As a nation, we were still working our way through the global COVID-19 pandemic. The availability of vaccines and treatment options had reduced the risks of COVID enough to allow a return to campus life in residence halls and in-person classroom instruction without all the health and safety protocols such as weekly mandatory COVID testing and mandatory mask wearing that had been in place during the previous academic year. Yet, since many of our students would be coming back to campus from countries outside the United States, the campus Health and Safety Committee recommended that we require indoor mask-wearing for at least the first few weeks of school to prevent the potential spread of any new COVID strains that might be circulating around the globe. In early October, with low COVID case counts at the campus health center, and in keeping with Center for Disease Control guidelines, I announced that our "mask indoors" mandate would end on October 14. We would remain a "masks welcome" community so that anyone who wanted to continue wearing a mask to reduce their exposure would feel free to do so. The announcement was greeted with relief by many, but some members of the campus community were still worried about potential infection. On October 19 a group of immunocompromised students, calling themselves the MHC COVID Safety Now Collective, entered Mary Lyon Hall at the end of the business day and announced on social media their intention to occupy the building until their demands—a list of eight—had been met. Equipped with sleeping bags and snacks, they took up residence in the hallways of the building, including sitting outside the doors of the president's office.

Their list of demands was largely based on policies and procedures that had been put in place the year before, during the height of the pandemic. The students were upset that, a year later, the campus protocols had become less restrictive—or in their view, less protective. The first demand on their list was clearly a nonstarter: maintain the mask mandate *indefinitely.* The remaining items were a reinstatement of mandatory PCR laboratory testing twice a week; a return to a public COVID dashboard of positive cases on campus (made possible by mandatory PCR testing); reinstatement of isolation housing of six to ten days of quarantine for those who tested positive; delivery of food (and improvement of its quality) for those in quarantine; reinstatement of contact tracing; establishment of mandatory flexibility in attendance policies, with hybrid support for all classes; and student representation (at least two students) on the campus health and safety committee.

I knew from my previous work with students that the most important first step is to listen to the concerns, and when possible, respond positively. I reached out immediately to the Safety Now Collective and set up a meeting with them for the next day. After hearing their concerns, deeply rooted in worries about their own health and that of their peers, I promised to consider the list of demands and provide a written response within twenty-four hours. Some of their requests (PCR testing, contact tracing, indefinite mandatory masking) far exceeded CDC guidelines at that waning stage in the pandemic and were not reasonable in my view. But I could agree with the request for isolation housing (we had some vacant housing space available). I also thought student representation on the health and safety committee was important and probably should have been there all along. I could say yes to those two demands right away. I wrote to the collective, as well as the entire campus community, to share my response.

The "campers," as I referred to them, were never large in number—a maximum of twenty students stayed in the building overnight at the beginning, sleeping on the floor in the hallways. That number eventually dwindled to eight or ten, but that core group was persistent. They vowed not to leave until all eight demands had been met. Fortunately, their protest remained in the hallways, never attempting to take over office space. They were a sullen presence but not an obstructive one. The building remained open for business during the day, and students took turns holding their protest space, allowing one another to continue attending their classes. They never left their protest space unattended.

I worked from the president's residence and held my regularly scheduled office hours with students in a room in the Campus Center rather than using the office in Mary Lyon Hall, as I didn't want to create an opportunity for protesting students to come inside the president's office. Meanwhile, they issued daily social media posts urging other students to join them and for alums to take up their cause, but without much success. At the start of the protest, the student government association (SGA) president, with whom I had established a good relationship, advised me to do two things: (1) educate students about the most current knowledge about COVID to allay fears, and (2) let students know how the decision to go "masks optional" had been made. The health center director took care of the first item, giving a presentation at the next SGA meeting about COVID, the availability of vaccines, the CDC recommendations, and the state of COVID cases on our campus. At the next SGA meeting, two weeks later, I addressed the student body, transparently laying out the steps I had taken in my decision-making, sharing the emails I had received from people asking me to remove the mask mandate sooner, and from those who wanted me to prolong it. I also explained the process of making required accommodations in classrooms for immunocompromised students who registered with the Office of Disability Services when that help was needed. Students could see that there was no decision about COVID policies that would satisfy everyone, yet it helped to demonstrate that there was a thoughtful process involved in arriving at the ultimate policy decision. At the end of that meeting, a representative of the collective tried to rally students to join the protest, but she was largely ignored by her peers. And yet the collective persisted, remaining in the building night after night. The protesters framed their demands as a matter of disability justice, and they continually repeated the pledge to continue their protest until all eight demands had been met. Two weeks after our initial meeting,

I met with the students again, the meeting arranged and facilitated by the chief diversity officer, who had worked with students on issues of disability justice. We were even joined by a parent who had flown in to support her daughter. Still, little progress was made; the students were determined to get all eight of their demands met.

I was worried about the fact that students, self-described as immunocompromised, were sleeping on the floor in the building every night, a situation that seemed to me inherently unhealthy. An unarmed member of the college public safety department walked through the building every night to do safety checks, a practice the students complained was intended to intimidate them but in my view was a reasonable precaution. The two concessions I had made on the second day of the protest were the only two on the list of demands that were ever going to be granted. With each posting announcing their "all eight demands" position, the students were painting themselves into a corner they could not get out of gracefully. We had several email exchanges, and in each of my communications I reminded them of the success they had achieved in getting two of their demands met. I started every communication with a message of this sort: "I appreciate your dedication to the well-being of the Mount Holyoke community. Though we are not in agreement about the methods to be used, we share a commitment to everyone's health and safety. I want you to know that your activism has resulted in positive outcomes."

Did we consider a forced removal? My team and I only discussed police involvement as something to be avoided. I knew that a photo or video of students being forcibly carried from the building would only galvanize other students to support them, not for their original cause, but because the administration was denying their right to protest. I had nothing to gain by escalating the situation. I was prepared to wait. My goal became to help the students find a face-saving exit. I called upon the faculty, who served as their advisers and instructors, to help students see that they could claim a partial victory and then go home. Perhaps the faculty members did indeed do that—or maybe it was because Thanksgiving was approaching—for finally we had a breakthrough.

On November 13, the twenty-fifth day of their occupation, the students wrote to let me know their goals had shifted. They wanted to focus on *working with* the administration to make certain that disabled and high-risk students on campus had equal access to a safe education. They requested another meeting with me. I expressed my gratitude for their desire to work with my administration and offered a date to meet, contingent on everyone discontinuing the camping out in the building. On November 18, a month after the protest started, on the Friday before the Thanksgiving break, the students declared victory and cleared the building. They issued an email statement, saying, "We started the occupation of Mary Lyon Hall so we could be taken seriously.... We are leaving Mary Lyon Hall with the understanding that administration will work with us to meet the health needs of the community, but we want to stress that if administration does not meaningfully engage, we have agreed as a collective to return to the sit-in. We look forward to continuing dialogue on creating a safer and more equitable community at Mount Holyoke College."

I learned three things from the Mount Holyoke protests of 1997 and 2022: (1) listen carefully to what students are seeking to accomplish and, if possible, find common ground; (2) engage trusted faculty to help mediate conflicts with students whenever you can; and (3) unless there is imminent danger, avoid the escalation that will come from involving law enforcement. While neither of the situations I experienced at Mount Holyoke approached the complexity posed by the student protests that spread so rapidly across the nation in the spring of 2024 in response to the Israel-Hamas war, leaders whose responses aligned with these three rules—*listen and seek common ground, ask faculty for help, and don't call the police*—seemed to fare much better than those who chose a different path.

Consider, for example, the twin cases of Smith College and Pomona College—one in Massachusetts, the other in California, both small, private, elite, well-resourced liberal arts colleges, coincidentally both led at the time by Black women. Though the circumstances were similarly problematic, the choices the leaders made differed, as did the outcomes. On March 27, 2024, three weeks before the protests at Columbia University erupted, approximately fifty students at Smith College took over the main administration building, vowing to remain until the college divested from all weapons manufacturers supplying the Israeli-Hamas war in Gaza. The protest was triggered by the rejection by the college's Advisory Committee on Investor Responsibility of just such a divestment proposal, presented by students to the committee in October 2023. The Advisory Committee had concluded that there was little to divest from, since "the endowment's investment in military contractors and weapons manufacturers is negligible and entirely indirect." Still, in response to the occupation of the building, President Sarah Willie-LeBreton met with the students to hear their concerns. The initial meeting did not lead to resolution, but it was the beginning of a dialogue.[4]

Twelve days later, following further discussion with the president along with three trustees, as well as an opportunity for faculty consultation and engagement, the students left the building, with a commitment from the president for continuing dialogue, yet still without the promise of divestment. Vowing to continue their efforts, the student protesters read a statement on the steps of College Hall as they left: "We are choosing to relocate to Seelye Lawn, and the wider campus space, so that we may join together as a full Smith community to expand the occupation until our goal of divestment has been achieved." They pledged to run "constant educational programming and [ask] the community to have face-to-face conversations with us on how we can work towards divestment as a collective." According to a statement issued by the administration, "Smith is committed to continuing this dialogue across campus so that the understanding that began during the protests can be further enhanced and as a community we can think in new ways about the challenges of conflict."[5]

The détente held, allowing the spring semester to close with relative calm and commencement to proceed as planned. No police required.

As at Smith, Pomona student protesters were calling for Pomona to divest—in this case from Israel and weapons manufacturers—and escalated their demands by staging a takeover of the administration building, including occupying the president's office. Pomona's president, Gabrielle Starr, described their action as "part of an escalating series of incidents on our campus, which has included persistent harassment of visitors for admission tours." Prior to the building takeover, the protest action had included an encampment on a portion of the main quad, set up alongside a thirty-two-foot-long art installation known as the Apartheid Wall, intended to represent the Palestinian struggle under Israeli control. Though against school policies, the students had been allowed to maintain the encampment in recognition of their right to protest, "unless that protest impedes the rights of others." On the morning of Friday, April 5, students had voluntarily packed up the encampment. But when college employees began to dismantle the art installation in preparation for a campus weekend event, some protesters objected and verbally harassed the staff. By the end of the afternoon, the protesters had taken over the president's office, with many more outside the office in the building's hallways.[6]

Was there an opportunity that afternoon to slow the action down and discuss the dismantling of the art installation? Had there already been conversations with student leaders during the encampment that had allowed for deep listening and the search for common ground? Perhaps. But on the afternoon of the building takeover, events unfolded rapidly, without the speed bumps that efforts at dialogue might have provided. Once the students were in the office, President Starr promptly issued a directive, ordering the protesters to disperse without delay, warning of immediate suspension for those who did not comply.[7] Not long after issuing her warning, she called the police. A swarm of police from four surrounding towns arrived, some in riot gear, and ordered the protesters to clear the building. About half of them left voluntarily, but the twenty who refused to leave were arrested.

The speed with which the president acted did not allow much time for faculty consultation. Could such consultation have led to de-escalation? It did at Smith. At Pomona, the situation continued to deteriorate. Six days later, on April 11, more than two-thirds of the Pomona faculty voted to condemn "the present and future militarization and use of police on the campus" and directed the administration "to immediately drop criminal charges and reverse the suspensions and all related consequences against student protesters for their actions of civil disobedience."[8] Student leaders also denounced the president's decision to call the police as "a direct call for violence and dangerous confrontation," an "unacceptable and shameful" choice that endangered students.[9]

In the face of what faculty observers described as a peaceful protest, calling for armed police officers to remove students forcibly was experienced by many students and faculty as a breach of trust. As one professor observed, "This is a peaceful act of civil disobedience and it does not warrant such a strong police response. It's actually extraordinarily difficult to imagine why anybody would think that would be an appropriate response."[10]

Trust once broken is hard to get back. The escalation that occurs when police arrive is difficult to undo. Typically, the protesters' response in such circumstances is to dig in, and other students, angered by the administration's actions, decide to join them. Indeed, at Pomona, the protests resumed, the calls for divestment continued, and the encampment returned, this time on the stage that had been erected on campus for the May 12 commencement ceremony. Did the president call the police again? She did not. Instead, the commencement ceremony was moved from the campus to a venue in Los Angeles thirty miles away, with tight security, in hopes of avoiding further confrontations with student protesters.[11]

At Smith it took longer—thirteen days—to empty the occupied building, but the end result was less damaging to the community. Listening to students and finding common ground, asking for help from the faculty, and choosing not to escalate by involving police worked for President Willie-LeBreton. In particular, she recalled, "partnering with faculty and talking with a staff member trained in mediation was a great help. Leaning in to shared governance is crucial, particularly when there is not an immediate health or safety issue."[12] The Smith commencement proceeded as scheduled on May 19 without disruption.

HISTORY REPEATING ITSELF?

Though the building takeovers at Smith and Pomona preceded the encampment set up on Columbia's campus, it was the protest at Columbia University that will be remembered as the match that lit the flame of student protest encampments across the country in the spring of 2024. As Columbia University President Minouche Shafik was testifying on April 17 before a congressional hearing on campus antisemitism, Columbia student protesters were building their encampment. Likely feeling the pressure of congressional scrutiny and the weight of her own declarations before Congress to stand up against protests that had been characterized by the Republican leadership as inherently antisemitic, on April 18 Shafik called the New York Police Department for help. It was a decision she would regret.

Fifty-six years before, in the spring of 1968, Columbia University was engulfed by a wave of student activism protesting US involvement in the Vietnam War. Students had taken over five campus buildings, occupied President Grayson Kirk's office, and taken Dean Henry Coleman hostage, holding him in his office for more than twenty-four hours. President Kirk was advised by representatives of Mayor John Lindsay's office not to call in the police. Jay Kriegel, one of Lindsay's aides, explained, "We tried to make clear that we didn't think anything would be normal the day after a thousand angry students confronted a thousand angry cops." Kirk called in the police anyway, "resulting in hundreds of student arrests, injuries, next-level mayhem, a strike and Mr. Kirk's resignation that summer."[13]

Still new to Columbia, was President Shafik aware of that history? Thomas Sugrue, professor of social and cultural analysis and history at New York University, thought she should have been. In an essay titled "College Presidents Behaving Badly," he wrote, "We are living through the most intense period of student protest since the 1960s, and college presidents seem intent on repeating the mistakes of their predecessors. Had they consulted any respectable scholar of politics and social movements, they would likely have heard one overriding piece of advice: inviting law enforcement to put down student protest is a big mistake."[14]

If history tells us that calling the police should be avoided, what about listening to students and seeking common ground? Or engaging faculty to help de-escalate? A legacy of the 1968 debacle, a Columbia University policy required the president to consult with the executive committee of the faculty senate prior to allowing police on the campus, and indeed, Shafik met with the thirteen-member faculty committee the day before the police were called. The committee unanimously rejected the idea of involving the police and recommended that she negotiate with the students. Her decision the next day to use the police to clear the encampment despite the opposition of the faculty was, according to the campus chapter of the American Association of University Professors, a direct violation of university policy. Shafik defended her decision as necessary because the encampment was "unsafe," but when asked if she had visited the encampment, she acknowledged that she had not. By contrast, many of the faculty in attendance at the meeting had done so.[15] By all reports, the students in the encampment were engaged in a peaceful protest and did not seem "unsafe."

On April 18, when Shafik called on the New York Police Department to arrest student protesters, even the police seemed surprised. The NYPD chief of patrol, John Chell, told reporters that the protesters were peaceful and responded to the police arrests with "no resistance whatsoever and were saying what they wanted to say in a peaceful manner."[16] Still, more than one hundred people were arrested. Said one of the arrested students, "They can threaten us all they want with the police, but at the end of the day, it's only going to lead to more mobilization."[17] She was right. The Columbia arrests set off a chain reaction of events. In solidarity with the Columbia protesters, students across the nation set up similar pro-Palestinian encampments. A professor and historian of student activism, Angus Johnston, described the speed with which the protests spread across the country as "extraordinary.... I think that is a reflection of the initial government and administrative response.... Once Columbia cracked down, we saw an immediate and I think, predictable, outpouring of response on the part of students at other campuses and it snowballed from there."[18] By mid-May, protests had spread to more than ninety campuses, representing a wide spectrum of institutions—small and large, public and private—in all regions of the country.[19] As the protests intensified, with the number of occupations of buildings and campus encampments growing, arrests grew exponentially as well. The *New York Times* reported that more than twenty-eight hundred people had been arrested or detained in campus protests across the country in the three-week period following April 18, the day of the first round of Columbia arrests.[20]

Meanwhile back at Columbia, on April 26 the faculty approved a resolution that called for an investigation into the president's leadership, stopping just short of a vote to censure her.[21] The student protest also intensified at Columbia, culminating in the April 30 takeover of Hamilton Hall (the same hall taken over by students in 1968, and during the 1985 protests against South African apartheid). Coincidentally, on the evening of April 30, I was talking on the phone to a Jewish friend whose daughter was in her second year at Barnard College, the women's college affiliated with Columbia. My friend had reached out to me to get my perspective as a former college president about the campus protests. By then, Columbia had canceled all in-person classes, and her daughter was doing her schoolwork from her apartment near campus and attending her classes remotely. The mother said her daughter was fine and did not feel afraid of the protesters on campus, some of whom she knew as friends and some of whom are also Jewish, but she told her mother that sometimes she felt nervous passing by the non-university protesters who gathered outside the gates of Columbia. As we were talking, each of us with a television news channel on the screen in the background, we were suddenly riveted to our televisions as we saw a massive mobilization of police preparing to cross a ladder bridge into Hamilton Hall. Looking like storm troopers, the officers streamed at a quick pace across the bridge through a window into the building. I told my friend that as a president I had never seen anything like it. Few of this generation of campus leaders have.

In the words of Evan Goldstein, the managing editor of the *Chronicle of Higher Education*, "While colleges have been here before, or close to here, *there is no playbook* for confronting a persistent and organized protest movement. And no decision is more fraught than whether to call the police."[22] On May 1, Columbia's president issued a statement explaining her decision to call in the NYPD to remove protesters from Hamilton Hall and all the encampments that remained on the campus. She described days of what was ultimately a failed attempt at negotiation, thanking the faculty who had been engaged in that effort, and reiterated her concerns for the safety of the campus community as protests escalated. Describing the forcible entry of "students and outside activists breaking Hamilton Hall doors, mistreating our Public Safety officers and maintenance staff, and damaging property" as acts of destruction that were "raising safety risks to an intolerable level," she both explained her decision and called on the Columbia community to "continue with urgency our ongoing dialogue on the important issues that have been raised in recent months, especially the balance between free speech and discrimination and the role of a university in contributing to better outcomes in the Middle East....

I hope Columbia can lead the way in new thinking that will make us the epicenter, not just of protests, but of solutions to the world's problems."[23]

At the president's request, police maintained a presence at Columbia through commencement weekend two weeks later. Despite their presence, however, the president decided to cancel the main university-wide graduation ceremony, citing security concerns. Instead, a host of smaller ceremonies took place without disruption, allowing students to share the celebration with their classmates within their schools of study. Still, as the school year ended, the faculty of arts and sciences at Columbia passed a resolution of "no confidence," explaining that President Shafik had violated the "fundamental requirements of academic freedom and shared governance" and engaged in an "unprecedented assault on students' rights."[24]

Could this situation have unfolded differently? It could have been worse. Emory University in Atlanta was an example of what "worse" could look like. When pro-Palestinian protesters set up camp on the Emory quad on April 25, just a week after the first wave of Columbia arrests, the response of Emory President Greg Fenves was swift. By that afternoon, a heavy presence of Atlanta police and Georgia state troopers had descended on the campus, and twenty-eight people had been arrested. No president had called on the police more quickly, and the show of force was among the most aggressive. At the time, it was the only campus where pepper balls, stun guns, and rubber bullets were used against the protesters.[25] Even nonprotesting passersby were caught up in the violence, which was described as being like a war zone. Noëlle McAfee, the chair of Emory's philosophy department, was captured on video being taken away in handcuffs, even as she called to a student to let her department secretary know that she had been arrested.[26] Another video captured a female professor being thrown to the ground, her chest and face pushed down on the concrete sidewalk. These and other videos went viral immediately. Local Republican politicians, from the governor to local city council representatives, quickly lent their support to President Fenves, while state Democratic legislators questioned the use of violence. Many faculty members were horrified by the infliction of so much force on what had been a peaceful protest. The response was so quick that there had been no time for faculty consultation. Several days later, the faculty of the Emory University College of Arts and Sciences passed a motion indicating "no confidence" in Fenves's ability as president by a vote of 358–119. "This decision reflects the faculty's support for the right to peaceful protests on campus, even amidst internal divisions regarding the protest's themes," said Emory professor of history Clifton Crais.[27]

ANOTHER WAY

What could have made the outcome on these campuses better? What would a negotiated peace have looked like? We saw one example at Smith College, navigated before the catalytic effect of Columbia's arrests. In the post-Columbia context, there were other examples of negotiated agreements—Brown University, Northwestern University, and Rutgers University among them.

At Northwestern University, on April 25, student protesters launched an encampment with about two hundred protesters and a dozen tents. When campus police made an early attempt to prevent the encampment from taking hold, organizers used social media to rally more supporters. By the end of the day, many more tents had been set up, and over five hundred people had gathered, with their chanting ringing out long into the night. Recognizing the dangers of escalation associated with police involvement, President Michael Schill made a different choice. Four days later, he and his team had worked out a deal with the students. The agreement included creating an advisory committee made up of faculty, students, and staff to engage with the university's investment committee; making information available about school investments; providing funding to support two visiting Palestinian faculty members impacted by the war, and scholarships for five Palestinian undergraduates; creating community space designated for use by Middle Eastern and North African and Muslim students; and providing additional support for both Jewish and Muslim students through the division of Student Affairs / Religious and Spiritual Life.[28] The three key elements I identified earlier—*listening, engaging faculty, and refraining from calling the police*—seemed to have been core components of the resolution at Northwestern. A statement released by the university described the agreement as "forged by the hard work of students and faculty working closely with school administrators to help ensure that the violence and escalation we have seen elsewhere does not happen here at Northwestern.... This agreement represents a sustainable and de-escalated path forward, and enhances the safety of all... while providing space for free expression that complies with University rules and policies."[29] In exchange, the students agreed to maintain just one tent on the campus lawn until the end of the academic year and abide by all other university protest policies.

At Brown University in Providence, Rhode Island, it was a similar story. The students at Brown began building their encampment with pitched tents on April 24, vowing to stay until they were forced out. They were calling on the university to end its investments in weapons manufacturers whose products fueled the Israel-Hamas war. However, by April 30, an agreement had been reached for how students might bring their demands for Brown's divestment from such companies to its board, the Corporation of Brown University, for consideration and potential vote at the board's October meeting, in exchange for the removal of the encampment and a promise to refrain from further conduct violations through the end of the academic year, thereby paving the way for a peaceful commencement and reunion weekend.[30] The student protesters, represented by the Brown Divest Coalition and other pro-Palestinian organizations, including Jewish Voice for Peace, acknowledged the momentum and solidarity they felt from the protests on other campuses. Posting the news of their agreement on social media, they said it "would not have been possible without the hard work of university encampments across the country, whose collective power has forced university administrators to acknowledge the overwhelming support for Palestine on their campuses."

The eventual outcome of the divestment discussion was not guaranteed, yet students felt heard. President Christina Paxson had managed to find some common ground. On the day the encampment began, she issued a statement clearly articulating the possibility and necessity of both "supporting freedom of expression, including the right to protest and preventing and addressing harassment and discrimination," and importantly, acknowledged both the shared pain and shared desire to be seen, heard, and understood amid that pain. She concluded, "Although we may not all agree on the best path forward, I think we can all appreciate the desire to build understanding across differences."[31]

A week later, after reaching an agreement with students, who were still subject to disciplinary proceedings for their conduct violations, she found a way to affirm their best intentions, saying in a statement, "Brown has always prided itself on resolving differences through dialog, debate and listening to each other. I cannot condone the encampment, which was in violation of University policies.... I appreciate the sincere efforts on the part of our students to take steps to prevent further escalation."[32]

Still, not everyone agreed that conflict resolution through negotiation was the right idea. At Northwestern, President Schill, who is himself Jewish, was accused by Jewish organizations on campus and beyond for "giving in" to antisemitism.[33] The Midwest chapter of the Anti-Defamation League, an organization dedicated to fighting antisemitism, called for his resignation. Christina Paxson at Brown found herself on a collision course with some of her largest donors, including the billionaire real estate mogul Barry Sterlicht, who called the agreement "unconscionable." Credited with more than $20 million of philanthropic support to

Brown University, in protest he announced he would pause his giving until further notice.[34]

And once again, Congress weighed in with another congressional hearing on campus antisemitism—this time focused on three male college leaders: Schill of Northwestern University, Jonathan Holloway, president of Rutgers University, and Gene Block, chancellor of the University of California, Los Angeles (UCLA). Like Schill and Paxson, Holloway had negotiated a peaceful end to protest encampments at his university. While several Democrats participating in the hearing praised Schill and Holloway for their success in resolving the encampments without police escalation, Republican legislators repeatedly berated both men for their negotiation efforts with the protesters, who were often derogatorily characterized as "terrorists" or "supporters of terrorism."[35]

What happened at UCLA was in stark contrast to Rutgers and Northwestern. There was no settlement with encamped protesters, and police were eventually called to clear the encampment. Yet unlike at other universities, on April 30 the pro-Palestinian encampment, widely described as peaceful, was attacked by violent pro-Israel counterprotesters, who appeared not to be affiliated with the university. The counterprotesters threw fireworks into the encampment, sprayed chemical irritants, and used poles and wooden planks to beat protesters. Law enforcement stood by for hours as the counterprotesters attacked, resulting in the worst violence stemming from any of the campus protests. As reported by CNN, "video footage shows that some counterprotesters instigated the fighting, while others did little to intervene. Then police did little as a large group of counterprotesters calmly walked away, leaving behind bloody, bruised students and other protesters.... At least 25 protesters ended up being transported to local emergency rooms to receive treatment for injuries including fractures, severe lacerations and chemical-induced injuries.... 'I actually thought someone would get killed,' said Rabbi Chaim Seidler-Feller, UCLA Hillel's director emeritus, who called 911 around midnight as he watched the violence on live TV. 'They came to beat people up.' "[36] Why didn't police intervene to stop the violence before so many students were hurt?

Rep. Ilhan Omar, a Democrat from Minnesota, asked precisely that question. "This happened in front of your eyes, on your campus, and it was live streamed for the whole world to see. If you are truly committed to keeping your students safe, how did you fail these students at many critical points where you could have intervened?" Though he tried to challenge her characterization, Chancellor Block had no satisfactory response in the face of the live-streamed video evidence of uninterrupted attacks.

A man whose leadership of UCLA spanned seventeen years, Block had announced his plan to retire at the end of the school year, well before the eruption of the protests and the violence of the counterprotests. Surely he was relieved to be able to say to his congressional questioners that he would not be returning to campus in the fall.

THEY ARE OUR STUDENTS

Presidents Holloway and Schill spoke of their summer plans to revisit campus policies and disciplinary procedures in preparation for the potential return of student protests in the fall. Both spoke of the importance of using this time of global and campus conflict as an educational opportunity to deepen understanding of both antisemitism and the complexities of the conflict in the Middle East. In a particularly noteworthy exchange, when Rep. Lloyd Kenneth Smucker, Republican of Pennsylvania, criticized Holloway for wrongly "negotiating with a mob," the Rutgers president challenged his characterization, replying, "The first thing I'll say, I was not negotiating with a mob, I was talking with students." For the most part, the protesters were not "outside agitators," as some initially claimed; they were indeed *students*, a point not to be forgotten.[37]

Many of the professors, administrators, and legislators of today were once the student activists of the sixties, seventies, and eighties. Said one such faculty colleague, "It's imperative that the state not treat this generation of student protesters as 'enemies of the state.'"[38] And yet some politicians seemed to be doing just that. Following the arrests of hundreds of protesters at Columbia and New York University, New York City Councilwoman Vickie Paladino posted on social media, "The NYPD confirms that 99% of arrests at NYU were indeed students, not 'outside agitators.' The sad reality is that our schools are producing monsters, and it's now our job to slay them." House Speaker Mike Johnson called on President Biden to activate military force to quell student protests that Johnson described as "violent and antisemitic," suggesting use of the National Guard.[39] When I heard Speaker Johnson make that suggestion, I thought to myself, "He must be too young to remember Kent State," and I looked up his birth date. Sure enough, he was born in 1972, not yet alive when the Ohio National Guard opened fire on student antiwar protesters at Kent State University in 1970, killing four students and wounding nine others. Did he not know that history? Certainly it is history that should never be repeated. Holloway, Schill, Paxson, and Willie-LeBreton at Smith College were not the only presidents who managed to resolve student protests through dialogue rather than law enforcement. While they and their like-minded colleagues received praise from some constituents, and enjoyed commencement ceremonies with little disruption, they were also criticized by some donors, legislators, and other constituents for "caving" in the face of student demands. But is that what they did? Perhaps they were creating space to listen to another point of view.

In the 1980s, student calls for divestment from South Africa were initially rejected, then subsequently adopted. There was a point of view that students brought forward to administrators, and their activism ultimately made an impact. In 1985, student protesters at Columbia pushed for the university to sever its ties to South Africa because of its system of apartheid, with thousands protesting over a three-week period, including launching a hunger strike. Eventually the students achieved their goal.

Within six months of the protests, Columbia University led the way as the first large American university to completely divest, with 155 universities eventually taking similar action.[40] In 1986 the federal government followed suit when Congress passed the Comprehensive Apartheid Act, intended to prevent new trade and investment between the US and South Africa.[41] Only time will tell how history will treat the protests of the spring of 2024.

In the congressional hearings on campus antisemitism, each of the leaders was asked who was behind these protests, and each president replied in essence, "I don't know." In her May 8, 2024, essay in the *New Yorker*, Princeton Professor Keeanga-Yamahtta Taylor offered an answer to that question. "What explains this growing student movement? Sometimes the correct answer is the one right in front of you. The students want an end to a war that has been executed with breathtaking violence and killed more than thirty-four thousand Palestinians, most of them women and children." The collateral damage of war—displacement, starvation, and disease impacting hundreds of thousands of Palestinian civilians who survived the bombing—was being broadcast directly to college students through their cell phones in an unprecedented and unmediated way, Taylor explained. The power of the images was undeniable. She wrote, "In the course of Israel's military campaign in Gaza, the endless images of dead civilians have shaped young Americans' understanding of the war.... Every smartphone has become a portal into Gaza. The obliteration of civil society, pictures of dead children, and the wails of their mothers are no longer mediated by the press. They come to you directly."[42]

Who is behind it? The students are—including some Jewish student leaders among them. Though the protests were broadly characterized in the congressional hearings and elsewhere as inherently antisemitic, doing so often represented a conflation of antisemitism and antiwar criticism of an Israeli policy led by Prime Minister Benjamin Netanyahu. In her essay, Taylor pointed out the routine failure to acknowledge the leadership role played by Jewish students opposed to the war. Indeed, just a few days after the first crackdown at Columbia, hundreds were arrested at a Passover celebration organized by antiwar Jewish groups near the Brooklyn home of Senate Majority Leader Chuck Schumer.[43] Reflecting on her experience at Columbia in an op-ed in the *Financial Times*, Minouche Shafik underscored the diversity among the protesters: "It would be a mistake to think that a small group of students with connections to the Arab world drove these protests. What I saw was a broad representation of young people of every ethnic and religious background—passionate, intelligent and committed."[44] The facts of the protests were more complex than any of the congressional characterizations.

As the school year ended, there was undoubtedly relief on those residential campuses where most students packed up and prepared to go home for the summer. But even as their departure created a respite for beleaguered administrators, there was a sense that the year-end pause was only that—a pause. Professor Taylor wrote, "The school year is wrapping up, but it feels like this movement is just beginning." Her words were echoed by Anwar Karim, a rising junior at Morehouse College, the historically Black college for men in Atlanta, who was protesting along with a few Morehouse classmates and students from neighboring Spelman College outside the Morehouse commencement ceremony, where President Joe Biden was the featured speaker. Disappointed by Biden's stance in support of Israel, Karim held a sign that read, "Black voices will never be silenced. #Free Palestine." He explained to journalist Alecia Taylor, "You have to understand that this is a movement and not a moment.... We're not just protesting today because of our displeasure with Joe Biden. It's bigger than that.... It goes back to humanity."[45]

President Biden's appearance at Morehouse highlighted the political importance of courting African American voters for their support, and the genuine risk of losing support from young voters like Karim during the 2024 presidential election year. While the Republican-led congressional hearings portrayed the student protesters as extremists, in fact their activism was a harbinger of changing American attitudes toward the war in Gaza. According to Gallup polls, American support for Israel's military action dropped dramatically from November 2023, when 50 percent indicated approval, to March 2024, when only 36 percent approved. Among Democrats, the number had dropped to only 18 percent. Princeton's Taylor observed, "Even the College Democrats of America, the student wing of the Democratic Party, which is certainly not known for its radical politics, has exalted students for enduring 'arrests, suspension, and threats of expulsion to stand up for the rights and dignity of the Palestinian people.'"[46]

In the calm of a post-commencement campus, as many students headed home, college and university presidents were surely asking themselves, "What if the Israel-Hamas war drags on?" If summer offered a respite, what about the fall? On those campuses where students would have a chance to make their case for divestment to their board of trustees, the outcome was not guaranteed. Would there be another round of protests if those cases were denied? And what would be the institutional consequences if that happened? More congressional hearings? Legal action on the part of the federal government?

On May 7, 2024, the US Department of Education Office of Civil Rights sent a "Dear Colleague" letter advising college administrators of the federal civil rights obligations of schools who are the recipients of federal financial assistance "to ensure nondiscrimination based on race, color or national origin, including shared ancestry or ethnic characteristics, under Title VI of the Civil Rights Act of 1964." The letter made clear that these protections "extend to students and school community members who are or are perceived because of their shared ancestry or ethnic characteristics to be Jewish, Israeli, Muslim, Arab, Sikh, South Asian, Hindu, Palestinian, or any other faith or ancestry," and that it was being sent in response to public reports of such discrimination. It underscored that Title VI protections extended to antisemitism as well as other forms of discrimination based on shared ancestry or ethnic characteristics, and that the Office of Civil Rights "vigorously enforces these protections." Offering examples of when free speech and protest behaviors crossed the line to become violations of Title VI, the letter provided clarity about what the institutional responsibility is to prevent or quickly remediate such incidents if they occur.[47] College administrators and their legal counsel would undoubtedly also spend the summer pause assessing the risk for Title VI violations.

CAN WE TALK?

What *can* be done? What opportunity is there to educate students and build the capacity for dialogue? Irene Mulvey, president of the American Association of University Professors, asserted, "The way forward is through education—to talk to each other, to understand each other, even in disagreement.... I think [the campus agreements are] modeling what should be done everywhere."[48] When asked for an example of a campus that was navigating this moment especially well, she mentioned Wesleyan University.[49] As a graduate of Wesleyan, I had been receiving President Michael Roth's communications to alumni about a pro-Palestinian encampment that appeared on the campus on April 29. In his letter, he explained his decision to let the encampment remain as long as the protesters remained peaceful and didn't disrupt campus operations. I especially appreciated Roth's emphasis in his message about the learning potential in the midst of the protest. He wrote, "There will be many on campus who cheer on the protesters, and many who are offended or even frightened by their rallies and messages. But as long as we all reject violence, we have opportunities to listen and to learn from one another."[50]

Three weeks later, he announced the resolution of the encampment with an agreement similar to those of Brown and Northwestern, including making a commitment to facilitate a meeting of representatives from the pro-Palestinian protest with the Investment Committee and to propose changes to the Environmental, Social, and Governance framework for investment/divestment consideration by the board of trustees at its fall meeting, as well as creating opportunities for displaced Palestinian scholars and students, and other programmatic initiatives.

His closing message to the community, including the alumni, was, from beginning to end, one of finding common ground. It began, "Over the course of the past three weeks, the Administration has been in meaningful engagement with the group of pro-Palestinian protesters on campus. Our conversations have been rooted in a shared affection for Wesleyan and a desire that the institution be aligned as fully as possible with its community's values." In its conclusion, he reinforced the opportunity for shared learning that the protests represented, writing, "It is always important that we maintain a safe enough environment on campus for people who disagree with one another and who embrace opportunities to learn from people with various points of view. Yes, protests are demanding for all constituencies of a university. At their best, they help turn our attention to issues that really matter."[51]

The Wesleyan example makes clear the value of respectful dialogue between students and administrators. But what about dialogue between students? Johns Hopkins University has a course that stands as a model of in-classroom learning rooted in dialogue. In the spring of 2024, sixteen students and one professor of international relations, Steven David, gathered each week for a two-hour seminar titled "Does Israel Have a Future?" Offered since 2016, David's course has attracted a wide range of students— Muslims, Jews, Christians, Hindus, and the nonreligious—whom he "expects to engage with ideas they may find repugnant and wrestle with the consequences of opinions they hold close." The course is taught chronologically, starting with the ancient history of Israel to its 1948 creation as a modern state, the impact on the hundreds of thousands of Palestinians who were displaced in the process, the two-state solution, the US-Israel alliance, the Iranian nuclear threat, and other existential threats facing

Israel today. Each class begins with two students debating a provocative statement, such as "The primary responsibility for the Palestinian refugee problem rests with the creation of Israel," or "International efforts to delegitimize Israel are unfair and antisemitic." Students are asked to debate from a perspective different from their own and back up their arguments with material from the readings and class discussions.[52]

Always challenging, teaching the course in the spring of 2024 as the Israel-Hamas war in Gaza raged was especially intense. Asked how he maintained civil discourse in the class, Professor David replied, "It's actually easier than you might think. The students who attend the class know that we encourage debate and dissent from each other and from me, but also in a very civil and respectful way. And all the students respected that." Even though emotions ran high, particularly with students who had family members in Israel or Gaza, they read powerful and opposing viewpoints as part of the class and learned the history of the conflict from multiple perspectives. David noted that when the students debated, they did so "in the context of knowledge.... When they came to their own viewpoints, they did it from a place where they knew a lot about what they were talking about."[53] David's goal is not to bring students to a particular answer to the title question of the course, it is to give students the tools to form educated opinions and engage in respectful dialogue. Ultimately, the process of engaging with multiple arguments helps students become "less polemical and in some ways less intense, recognizing that there are many sides to these problems."[54]

His students agree. Said one young woman who is Jewish, describing her learning process, "I was confused and I asked questions and I left certain classes a little upset about some things that my peers were saying. But every single week we would come back together.... I might disagree with a certain student about something, and the next week I might agree with them on something else.... It's not a black or white situation."[55] One might argue that in a university like Johns Hopkins, with more than six thousand undergraduate students and approximately twenty-three thousand graduate students, one course with fewer than twenty students enrolled at a time can have only minimal impact on the larger campus environment. Still, it is a model for the kind of powerful education colleges can and should provide. The course requires deep listening, which leads to deep learning, facilitated by a skilled and knowledgeable guide.

Students are hungry for such opportunities, and when unable to find them, some have created them themselves. That is what Elijah Kahlenberg did. A Jewish student at the University of Texas at Austin, Kahlenberg spent a summer in Israel working with Palestinians in the West Bank under the auspices of an organization called Roots, which works to create "trust and partnership" between Israelis and Palestinians. That summer he facilitated conversations between Jews and Arabs and led youth groups with Palestinian and Israeli children. When he returned home to Texas, he wanted more such opportunities and lamented that there was no mechanism in place at UT Austin for Jewish and Palestinian students to come together to "simply talk, to understand."[56] In 2022 at the end of his freshman year, he founded Atidna, now known as Atidna International. The name Atidna combines the Hebrew word for "future" with the Arabic suffix for "our," to mean "our future." It began with student-organized meetings between Jewish/Israeli and Arab/Palestinian students, the first campus effort to bring the two communities together for dialogue. Kahlenberg's hope was "to freely and openly speak with 'the other' to understand their identity, culture and history and begin to see the 'other' as part of their family." As described on the website, Atidna International is now "a grassroots, campus-based peace and open dialogue initiative which seeks to solidify Arabs and Jews as cousins, one unified family, and not enemies," working to "enshrine our founding values of peace, unity and freedom of speech/expression for Arab/Palestinian and Jewish/Israeli students on each campus that hosts an Atidna chapter."[57]

Fellow UT student Jadd Hashem, now vice president of Atidna International, is a Palestinian American from Dallas who was drawn to Atidna because he wanted to hear Israeli and Jewish perspectives, and he wanted them to hear his. Though born and raised in Texas, he has relatives who fled from Gaza to Egypt and the West Bank because of the war. In the aftermath of October 7, he struggled with his own questions about what it meant to be a "good" Palestinian. "How do we stand up for our people without also looking like we are appealing to terrorism? If we come out and we say something against terrorism, do we get called traitors? Should we defend the sort of resistance that happened, even though it resulted in terrorism?"[58] These questions were not his alone, but questions other Palestinian students were thinking about, and he wanted to be able to share them.

Atidna was a newly launched student organization at UT Austin in the fall of 2023, but when the Hamas attack of October 7 happened, some students—both Jewish and Palestinian—left the group, their emotions too raw to participate. Jadd Hashem and Elijah Kahlenberg leaned in and committed to continuing dialogue with each other. They organized the first vigil on campus intentionally designed to mourn the deaths of people killed in both Israel and Gaza, with prayers led by a Muslim imam, a Christian pastor, and a Jewish rabbi, with an Atidna banner displaying the message "one family mourning together." Held on November 7, 2023, it was reportedly one of few such joint campus vigils in the country.[59] "That evening as Hashem and Kahlenberg watched Jewish and Arab students gather and mourn together, the duo felt certain they were filling a crucial need on campus. If students don't organize and model unity for themselves, they realized, who will?"[60]

Now on a mission to spread their model of dialogue to other campuses, Hashem and Kahlenberg have received national coverage, such as being featured in an episode of *ABC News Nightline*, and held many meetings with students from other campuses interested in starting chapters.[61] As of May 2024, new chapters had been founded at Columbia, Harvard, the University of Chicago, the University of Pennsylvania, and Williams College, and by a group representing several colleges in New York City.

Though the highly charged nature of campus protests made the idea of creating space for dialogue more challenging, Atidna organizers were not daunted. One Atidna organizer at the University of Pennsylvania, Tova Tachau, explained that strong emotions indicate that people care deeply about the issue, and that passion can be channeled into meaningful conversation. "This is the way forward, even if it will take time." College leaders should take note and lend vigorous support to such efforts. Educational institutions are uniquely positioned to do so.

Antisemitism and Islamophobia are real and dangerous. As a reminder, the CPOST national survey, discussed at length in Chapter 3, found that 10 percent of the college students surveyed would permit student groups to call for genocide, and 13 percent would say that when a group was attacked, it was because they deserved it. Whether the question was asked about Jews or Muslims, the percentages of students ready to support calls for genocide and showing a willingness to blame the victims was the same—10 percent and 13 percent, respectively. While it was clearly a minority of students who expressed an acceptance of violence toward Jews or Muslims, the percentages are still disturbing, as violent behavior among even a small number of people can have a disastrous effect and put many people's safety at risk.[62]

The data underscore the importance of using the educational platform that higher education provides to interrupt this cycle of hatred and potential violence. It can be done without resorting to the censorship and authoritarian response advocated by some politicians. As AAUP leader Irene Mulvey said, "The way to balance safety and protest, on a college campus, is through education. We need to model, teach, and promote civil discourse, respectful dialogue.... The goal on a college campus should be education and understanding each other even when we disagree."[63]

Fundamentally, the goal in these seasons of conflict is to resolve situations safely and preserve trust and respect within relationships—not just with students, but with faculty, staff, board members, alums, donors, parents, community members, and even politicians—knowing it will be impossible to satisfy everyone. *New York Times* journalist Ginia Bellafante captured the enormity of the challenge when she wrote, "If Nemat [Minouche] Shafik, the president of Columbia University, has convinced the world of anything during these...calamitous days, it is almost certainly that there is no position in American executive life as thankless, as depleting or less enviable than running a major academic institution in an age of chronic, reflexive agitation."[64] In the end, President Shafik decided she had had enough. On August 14, 2024, just weeks before the start of the fall semester, she resigned from her position as president of Columbia University, effective immediately.[65]

By the fall of 2024, media attention had shifted away from campus protests to the presidential campaigns of Kamala Harris and Donald Trump, and in January 2025, in the waning days of the Biden administration, a cease-fire between Israel and Hamas was finally negotiated. Still, anti-Israel and pro-Palestinian protests continued on some campuses. In response, just a few days after his inauguration, Trump signed an executive order intended to combat antisemitism and punish any campus that, in the government's view, failed to protect the civil rights of Jewish students. The order promised that "immediate action will be taken by the Department of Justice to protect law and order, quell pro-Hamas vandalism and intimidation, and investigate and punish anti-Jewish racism in leftist, anti-American colleges and universities."[66] Soon after the executive order was issued, the Department of Education launched civil rights investigations into five universities where complaints of antisemitic harassment had been reported: Columbia, Northwestern, Portland State, the University of California at Berkeley, and the University of Minnesota, Twin Cities.[67]

Just as attitudes toward the protests and their chants were divided, so too was the response to Trump's order and its threatened enforcements.

"Jewish advocates and some faculty members who have watched tensions over the Israel-Hamas war play out on college campuses...say the order is necessary. But for free speech groups and many other college and university leaders, the order raises...concerns about academic freedom, the safety of international students and scholars who support Palestine, and even potential financial penalties."[68]

The executive order left important terms like "antisemitism" undefined. However, during the first Trump administration, the definition of antisemitism used by the International Holocaust Remembrance Alliance (IHRA) was adopted by the federal government. It states, "Antisemitism is a certain perception of Jews, which may be expressed as hatred toward Jews. Rhetorical and physical manifestations of antisemitism are directed toward Jewish or non-Jewish individuals and/or their property, toward Jewish community institutions and religious facilities." While IHRA acknowledges that "criticism of Israel similar to that leveled against any other country cannot be regarded as antisemitic," to further clarify its definition it offers several examples of behaviors that would be considered antisemitic, including "denying the Jewish people their right to self-determination, e.g., by claiming that the existence of the State of Israel is a racist endeavor," or "drawing comparisons of contemporary Israeli policy to that of the Nazis."[69]

With the IHRA definition as the standard underlying the executive order, college administrators wondered if virtually all anti-Israel protests could be considered antisemitic. Would every pro-Palestinian protester be considered by default a "Hamas sympathizer"? Would any international student who participated in a pro-Palestinian protest, no matter how peaceful, be subject to deportation? Fundamentally, was the order a violation of the First Amendment's protection of free speech?

The Foundation for Individual Rights and Expression (FIRE), a nonpartisan First Amendment advocacy group, said it was. While acknowledging that those who engaged in criminal activity (e.g., threats, violence, vandalism) should face consequences, including the potential loss of a visa, FIRE asserted that expressing points of view in conflict with the Trump administration was not a crime, and that threatening to deport anti-Israel protesters was an unequivocal attack on free speech. Sarah McLaughlin, a FIRE senior scholar, wrote:

> The strength of our nation's system of higher education derives from the exchange of the widest range of views, even unpopular or dissenting ones. This openness, albeit unpleasant or controversial at times, is a defining strength of American higher education.... Freedom of speech was never meant to be easy. But it allows us the space we need to work through thorny social and political challenges, even when it's fraught with friction and discomfort. The United States should preserve this freedom on our campuses—spaces for free learning that set us apart from more authoritarian nations around the world—not make an "empty mockery" of it.[70]

The geopolitical conflict that animated campus protests during the 2023–2024 school year has not gone away. Looking back over that year of protests, it is easy to take the role of an observer second-guessing the decisions that were made under the pressure of congressional hearings designed to be political theater or in the face of seemingly relentless campus protests at the end of an exhausting year. Similarly, as campus leaders seek to walk the narrow line between compliance with executive orders and the defense of free speech, many people may take on the role of armchair quarterback, offering opinions about what campus leaders should have done—or should do. Over the years of my presidency, it was not unusual to get such unsolicited advice via letters, emails, or sometimes phone calls from donors, alums, community leaders, even from interested strangers with no particular connection to the institution—all eager to share their point of view. You don't have to be a higher ed leader to have an opinion about how student protests should be handled or to imagine what you might have done had you been at the helm—or what you might have said in the hot seat before Congress. One thing is for certain: The situation is almost always more complicated than it looks. For better or worse, in the spring of 2024, campus leaders were working very hard to get it right. They still are. It is easy at home to imagine that you would have done it differently, done it better. But think again, do you *really* want that job?

CHAPTER SIX

MANAGING RISKS

Campus Safety and Mental Health

When I became dean of the college at Mount Holyoke in 1998, I served as the chief student affairs officer. In that role I understood that not only was it my responsibility to keep the president informed about student issues and concerns, but it was also my job to find a way to solve them. Student concerns—ranging from housing issues and dining hall complaints to academic and behavioral misconduct, substance abuse, and sexual assault—could all become quite complicated. The president relied on me to manage those situations. If new programmatic interventions or other resources were needed to enhance campus safety and improve student outcomes, it was my job to investigate those options and make the appropriate recommendations and necessary budget requests to her. In many ways, I was expected to be the firewall between student concerns and the president's office, and I was. When I became a college president, I had a similar expectation for the chief student affairs officer on my team. Of course, I needed to be informed about ongoing concerns, but only those matters that she and the student affairs team could not solve on their own would come to my desk for action. If there was a late-night emergency, I was confident that they would handle it and brief me about it in the morning.

On Thursday, September 3, 2009, I got a phone call that woke me up. I was in Washington, DC, for a business meeting, and was heading from there to Boston to spend the upcoming Labor Day weekend with my family, celebrating my elderly father's birthday. It was close to three in the morning, and the Spelman College director of public safety had called my cell phone to inform me that a Spelman student had been killed. I was stunned. The death of a student is a president's worst nightmare, and suddenly I had awakened to just such a nightmare. As he explained, our student, JL, had been visiting friends in an apartment on the edge of a neighboring campus, Clark Atlanta University.[1] It was nearly one in the morning when she and her friend were leaving the apartment. Not far from the building were some young men, students and nonstudents, embroiled in an argument. Witnesses said JL moved toward them, wanting to help break up the fight, and indeed, the group started to disperse. But just as one young man was heading away from the group, he turned and randomly fired six shots into the crowd. One of those bullets struck JL's friend, causing a minor injury. The bullet that struck JL hit her in the chest, a fatal wound. At the start of her sophomore year, the first in her family to go to college, JL was suddenly lost to gun violence. As I received this information on the phone, my mind was racing. What did I need to do next? Had JL's family been informed? Our public safety director told me that the dean of students had already called JL's mother. "I know you're traveling. You don't need to come back to campus, we have it under control," he said. This was a situation I could not fix.

As soon as we hung up, I called the dean of students. I wanted to know about the phone call with the mother and to think about how we would communicate with the campus about what had happened. The dean assured me that she was doing what needed to be done and would work with her student affairs staff, including the campus chaplain, to support our student community. She too told me I did not need to return to campus. "We got this," she said. Indeed, the public safety team, our counseling services staff, and our housing personnel had quickly mobilized to support the students who had traveled to the hospital with JL and to reach out to JL's family. They had also comforted those in JL's residence hall coping with the news of her death. Everything I would have wanted them to do they had done.

Still, instinctively, I knew the dean and the public safety director were both wrong when they told me I could continue my trip as planned. My next call was to Delta Airlines to change my flight. I needed to be on the very next flight back to Atlanta. When disaster strikes, the campus looks to the campus leader for guidance, direction, and consolation. No substitutions allowed. In that moment, I knew I had to be the consoler-in-chief.

I too called JL's mother to express my condolences and offer any support I could possibly provide in the wake of that terrible news. What words could I possibly offer that grieving mother? Yet it was important that, however inadequate, she hear some words directly from me. My next call was to the board chair to let her know what had happened. I did not want her to read it in the newspaper or see it on social media without first hearing the news from me. I also needed some comfort, and I appreciated her listening ear. On the early morning flight back to campus, I quickly drafted an email to send to the campus community about the tragic loss of our student, knowing that even those who did not know JL would be grief-stricken by the news of her senseless death.

Later that morning, the head of our communications team worked with me to prepare a letter to send to all current Spelman parents, intending to reassure them that we were doing all we could to ensure that our students—their children—remained safe. I was in my eighth year as a college president, my twenty-ninth year as a college educator, and I had never had to face such a tragedy before. We all felt shaken by the random nature of the violence. Though the incident had occurred beyond the boundaries of our gated campus, the feeling of peace and security that so many of us felt as we moved about the campus had been ruptured.

We flew the Spelman College flag at half-mast in JL's honor, and the day after the shooting we held a campus assembly to share our collective grief and to remind students of the many resources available to them as they processed their feelings of sadness. We reminded them of the steps our campus public safety officers were taking in partnership with the Atlanta Police Department and the neighboring colleges to increase area patrols, as well as the steps they should take for their own personal safety as they moved about the surrounding neighborhoods. In the days that followed, a campus memorial service was planned, with JL's family members in attendance. Repeatedly I was asked to speak, to find words of comfort and reassurance. Consoler-in-chief was not in my job description, but it was my job.

Keeping the campus safe was my job, too—fundamentally the most important job I had, and yet the least within my control. That awareness is terrifying. What is a leader to do? You learn to manage risks. And what are those risks? What else will wake you up at night? What dangers are lurking when you least expect them? You can never know! The exercise of risk management is one of perverse imagination. What if the athletic coach is a pedophile? What if the college physician is sexually assaulting female patients? What if a hurricane comes and the levees break, flooding the low-lying campus? What if on the coldest day of the year the steam plant fails and there is no heat in the residence halls? What if a freight train derails near the campus, causing an environmental emergency? What if the aging water pipes in the city burst and there is no water supply to the campus for several days? What if there is a deadly and unknown virus causing a global pandemic and the campus must shut down completely? All these things have happened somewhere. Did anyone imagine scenarios like these? Was there a risk mitigation plan in place? Would a reasonable person expect that someone would have prepared for that possibility? It's hard to prepare for the disaster that hasn't happened yet, the scenario that is so outside your experience that you can't even imagine it. What lurking disaster haven't we had yet? What can we anticipate and prevent? What must we do to keep the campus and our students safe?

KEEPING OUR CAMPUS SAFE

Losing one student to gun violence is horrible. Losing many in a mass shooting should be unimaginable—and yet it isn't, because it has happened repeatedly on campuses across the country. Defining a mass shooting as one where four or more people are murdered in public, according to the Violence Project, half of the thirty-six deadliest mass shootings since the 1900s occurred between 2015–2024.[2] Most of those occurred at a workplace or business location, but as of 2023, there had been six mass shootings at a college or university since 2003. As disturbing as that statistic is, it overlooks those campuses where the death toll was three or less. According to the National Center for Education Statistics' 2022 Report on Indicators of School Crime and Safety, from 2000 to 2021 there were eighteen active-shooter incidents on college campuses, defined as "one or more individuals actively engaged in killing or attempting to kill people in a populated area."[3] As Professor William Pelfrey Jr., an expert on policing and public safety, succinctly stated, "A shooting on a university campus was an extraordinarily rare thing 20 years ago. Now it's a much more common thing."[4] Fear is contagious, and the news of an active-shooter incident at a university, no matter how far away, can send ripples of distress across other campuses.

I experienced that ripple effect while serving as the interim president at Mount Holyoke College during the 2022–2023 school year. On the evening of February 16, 2023, a shooting occurred at Michigan State

University in East Lansing. A lone gunman, armed with two legally purchased 9-millimeter handguns, walked across the campus and entered a classroom on the first floor of Berkey Hall and, without saying a word, began shooting at students, hitting seven before he turned and left. Professor Marco Díaz-Muñoz was there, giving a presentation, when the gunman opened fire. "It looked like a robot, not someone human, covered with a mask and a cap.... It seemed just unreal," Díaz-Muñoz recalled. The shocked professor froze in his spot, but one student yelled, "A shooter!" and his classmates, well trained in classroom shooting drills, knew what to do. They hit the floor, trying to hide under desks or run toward another door at the back of the classroom. After the gunman left the room, the professor barricaded the door to prevent his return, and some students broke classroom windows to escape the room, while others stayed behind to help their wounded classmates, trying to stop the bleeding. Within ten minutes, help—police and paramedics—had arrived.[5] Meanwhile the shooter had found his eighth victim, shooting a young man he encountered outside the student union. That student and two women who were shot in the classroom died; the remaining five were critically injured. Three hours after his shooting spree had begun, the assailant was found, dead from a self-inflicted gunshot wound, leaving behind a traumatized campus community.[6]

Two weeks later, a Mount Holyoke student came to see me during my regularly scheduled office hours. She observed that the campus was a wide-open space, and she wanted to know what I was doing to ensure campus safety. How could we prevent an incident like what happened at Michigan State? It was not a question I or any president could easily answer. Most college campuses have very porous borders, making it easy for anyone to stroll onto the grounds or roam between buildings. Residents of the local community might walk the paths for exercise or come onto campus to attend a campus lecture or other cultural event. All over the country alums return to their alma maters for campus celebrations, and family members and friends are welcome to visit. It's not easy to tell who "belongs" on a campus and who doesn't.

At Michigan State the shooter was an outsider, a forty-three-year-old man with no known ties to the university, who took public transportation to the campus and entered unlocked campus buildings with ease. Even if we could easily separate the insiders from the outsiders by visible ID tags, for example, that would not guarantee safety. At Virginia Tech, the site of the deadliest campus shooting to date, the perpetrator was an enrolled student, living on campus in a residence hall. In 2007, he killed thirty-two people and wounded seventeen before killing himself. How can anyone know where the danger will come from?

The student and I talked about the fact that all our campus buildings had limited access, requiring the swipe of an ID card to enter. There was no practical way to seal all entry points to the large and sprawling campus, but we could lock down building doors remotely. I reminded her that we also had a cell-phone text alert system in place so anyone on campus could be quickly notified with safety instructions such as "shelter in place." Rapid dissemination of safety information is a critical tool for keeping people safe. I told her about the campus emergency response team, made up of faculty and staff leaders from across the campus, as well as first responders from the town, who routinely engaged in tabletop drills to prepare for emergencies of all kinds, including active shooters. Even as I acknowledged the risk of racial profiling on that predominantly White campus, we discussed the importance of students being willing to "see something and say something" when they thought someone was behaving suspiciously, or perhaps seemed to be struggling with emotional difficulties, potentially threatening harm to themselves or others. I understood and shared the anxiety she was expressing and wished I had more solutions that day to offer in response.

After the Michigan State shooting, that university increased its building security by adding locks to individual classroom doors and installing more cameras inside academic buildings, strategies that other campuses adopted as well. At Morgan State University, a historically Black university in Baltimore where five people were wounded in a shooting during the 2023 fall homecoming festivities, President David Wilson explained his safety plan. He was seeking to fence the perimeter of the campus—a project that had already been underway at the time of the shooting—in addition to increasing patrols by campus police, hiring more security guards, installing more than 850 security cameras, equipping residence halls with metal detectors, and establishing a clear-bag policy for attendees at athletic events. He said, "The measures being put into place on the campus will only serve to enhance the safety of the campus, not to separate it from the surrounding community or keep law-abiding community members out. To the contrary, these measures are designed to dissuade or deter bad actors from targeting the campus by way of unfettered access."[7] The incident at Morgan State was the third time in as many years that homecoming week had been disrupted by a shooting. Bill Ferguson, the Democratic state legislator representing Baltimore, diagnosed the situation with a post on social media: "The repetition of these horrific events is about one thing: easy access to guns."[8]

What can be done about so many guns? At Eastern Michigan University, new technology—ZeroEyes—was being tested, an AI-enabled gun detection platform that is capable of spotting weapons on campus and sending images to a central operations center, with an alert to campus security if a credible threat is identified.[9] However, ZeroEyes might not help in some places. As of 2021, ten states—Arkansas, Colorado, Georgia, Idaho, Kansas, Mississippi, Oregon, Tennessee, Texas, and Utah—allow people to carry concealed weapons on college campuses, a fact that brings little comfort to any president concerned about gun violence.[10]

While some have argued that "bad guys" with guns can be stopped if enough "good guys" are armed, the idea of faculty and students carrying loaded weapons on campus is horrifying to many, particularly when students themselves can be the source of danger. As one professor wrote in an essay, using the pseudonym Thomas Benton, "Many professors live in the shadow of the possibility of retaliation from disgruntled students whose actions may range from minor vandalism to deadly violence." He calculated that "even if only one in 100 students is a potential problem... if you teach a couple hundred students a year—and thousands of students over a career—then it seems only a matter of time before you run into a student who might be dangerous."[11]

Workplaces are the most common location for mass-shooting incidents, and college campuses are not immune to work-related violence. Prior to the COVID pandemic, during the years from 2006 to 2020, there had been only thirteen mass-shooting incidents in a workplace by a current or former employee, approximately one such incident per year.[12] At the height of the pandemic, in 2020, many people were working from home. As more and more people returned to work on-site rather than at home, there was an incremental uptick in workplace shootings.

Though active-shooter incidents are still relatively rare, the overall increase in such incidents is noteworthy. The FBI reported that there were three active-shooter incidents in the year 2000. In 2021, there were sixty-one of them, more than one per week.[13] Some of those post-pandemic incidents took place on campuses. In October 2022, a graduate student who had been expelled from the University of Arizona came back to campus and shot and killed one of his former professors.[14] In August 2023, a graduate student at the University of North Carolina fatally shot one of his faculty advisers.[15] Then in December 2023, an unemployed professor who had been seeking a job at the University of Nevada Las Vegas (UNLV) business school came to campus armed with a 9-millimeter handgun and a lot of ammunition and proceeded to kill three business school professors before he was confronted and fatally wounded by a police officer. UNLV president Keith Whitfield described the incident as "the realization of our greatest fear."[16] That great fear is widely shared.

WHEN HATE COMES TO CAMPUS

A fear that is perhaps less widely shared or discussed across higher education is the threat of racially motivated or other hate-crime-related violence. Despite a nationwide decrease in violent crimes, hate crimes—defined by the FBI as "a committed criminal offense which is motivated, in whole or in part, by the offender's bias(es) against a race, religion, disability, sexual orientation, ethnicity, gender, or gender identity"—have risen steadily over the course of the twenty-first century and have spiked since 2020.[17] Researchers have identified several factors as contributing to the sharp rise in hate crimes: "rising economic disparity, deep racist resentment at an African-American president, the overall climate of political vilification in the Trump era, and, perhaps most importantly, the emergence of the internet as a uniquely effective disseminator of hate."[18]

In "Report to the Nation: 2020s—Dawn of a Decade of Rising Hate," the Center for the Study of Hate and Extremism (CSHE), housed at California State University San Bernardino, documented that anti-Black hate crimes were consistently the most frequent, rising 46 percent from 2020 to 2022. Anti-Jewish, anti-gay, and anti-Latinx crimes were the next most frequent in 2022. However, after the Israel-Hamas war began in October 2023, there was a sharp increase in both anti-Jewish and anti-Muslim attacks. Anti-transgender crimes, while described in the CSHE report as "very small in number," rose 6 percent in 2021 and appeared to be accelerating in 2022 as the legislative and social landscape grew increasingly hostile toward transgender people.[19] Consequently, leaders of campuses that serve significant numbers of students from one or more of these targeted populations are likely to experience another level of risk and anxiety. Presidents of historically Black colleges and universities already have.

It was August 26, 2023, the weekend of the sixtieth anniversary of the 1963 March on Washington, when students at Edward Waters University, a historically Black college in Jacksonville, Florida, spotted a young White man in a car on campus donning a bulletproof vest and wearing blue latex gloves. They were suspicious enough to report what they saw to a campus public-safety officer. When the officer approached the man, he drove away, leaving the campus. The campus officer noted the license plate and called in the information to the Jacksonville Police Department, but before anyone could intervene, the assailant had stopped at a nearby Dollar General store, where he shot and killed three Black people before shooting himself. He was twenty-one. His weapon, an AR-15 rifle, was covered in swastikas, and he left behind a hate-filled manifesto on his computer, indicating his desire to kill Black people. Though no one was hurt on the campus, the incident certainly felt like a "near miss" to the president of Edward Waters, Zachary Faison Jr. As he expressed his gratitude to those who helped thwart the assailant on campus, Faison acknowledged "what we believe were the original aims of this white supremacist domestic terrorist, to come to the state of Florida's first historically Black university and wreak murderous havoc."[20]

The incident was just one of many threatening episodes for historically Black colleges and universities in recent years. HBCUs are, by legal definition, institutions that were established prior to 1964 for the purpose of providing access to higher education for Black students during the era of legalized segregation. Today there are also predominantly Black institutions (PBIs), which have become majority Black in their enrollment, but unlike HBCUs they were not created as Black-serving institutions from their beginnings. As of 2022, 9 percent of all Black college students were attending an HBCU, a population of approximately three hundred thousand. Though founded to educate Black students, HBCUs have always been multiracial communities with racially diverse faculties, and, in recent years, a growing number of non-Black students, who by 2022 made up 24 percent of the total population of students attending HBCUs. As of 2022, there were ninety-nine HBCUs spread across nineteen states—primarily in the South, the Southeast, and the Mid-Atlantic region (including Washington, DC)—representing less than 3 percent of US higher education institutions.[21] Yet of the 353 bomb threats reported in 2022, 49 of them were directed at HBCUs and another 19 at PBIs.[22] Combined, 19 percent of the bomb threats were directed at institutions known for educating Black students.

Most of the threats occurred in early February 2022, coinciding with the start of Black History Month. The FBI Joint Terrorism Task Forces led the investigation, involving more than twenty field offices across the country, calling it "of the highest priority" and identifying the threats as "racially or ethnically motivated violent extremism and hate crimes."[23] Ultimately no explosive devices were found at any of the locations, but the threats were damaging nonetheless. For example, Spelman College received three bomb threats within the space of a few weeks, and students expressed frustration and anger about the toll the threats were taking. Said one, "A lot of us go to HBCUs for that sense of community and that sense of safety, so to be here and be concerned that because of our identity that people are out to attack us while we're just trying to get our education, it's beyond frightening."[24] At a meeting of HBCU presidents hosted by the Southern Poverty Law Center, a civil rights organization known for its monitoring of the activities of domestic hate groups and other extremists, the campus leaders put the threats in their political context, calling it "a tragic irony that just when racism and antisemitism are surging in the country, school boards are banning books that deal with the issue and are taking action against teachers and administrators who introduce the study of America's painful history because such education could make white children 'uncomfortable.'"[25]

Initially, the FBI identified six juveniles who were suspected of making the bomb threats, including one who, while calling in a threat, had declared his affiliation with the Atomwaffen Division, a neo-Nazi organization identified by the Southern Poverty Law Center as a hate group known for its violent ideology.[26] Months later, in November 2022, the FBI determined that just one tech-savvy minor was responsible for the threats.

Because of the perpetrator's age, no details were given about the person's identity or location, and federal prosecution was not allowed; but state prosecutors were able to bring other charges against the individual, which allowed the Department of Justice to "hold the minor accountable" and restrict the person's activities. The FBI also indicated that there was an ongoing investigation into two other clusters of threats targeting HBCUs and other institutions, which also appeared to be racially motivated but were linked to a foreign internet address.[27]

The results of the FBI investigation brought little relief to the communities impacted. The months of waiting and worrying had been exhausting. Carmen Walters, then president of Tougaloo College in Mississippi, expressing the strain she felt, said, "Getting a call at 4 o'clock in the morning saying that there's a bomb threat...on your campus when you are responsible for hundreds of students, you're responsible for facilities and technology and the community that's around you, it's a nerve-racking, heart-wrenching concern."[28]

And what would prevent these threats from coming again—and would they be just threats? The parent of a student at Morgan State University, one of the schools threatened, commented, "I can't help but wonder and worry what will happen [next year]. It's not like the rhetoric has died down or the tension has died down. In fact...we seem to be in a more agitated state...with politics and our culture wars. I'm not encouraged by the existing climate." Her fears were understandable, as she looked ahead to the 2024 election season on the horizon. Her worries were supported by the historical data. According to a report from the Leadership Conference Education Fund (LCEF), a national civil rights group, FBI data show an "unmistakable pattern" of reported hate crimes spiking during presidential elections, going as far back as the 1990s. LCEF warned "there are few—if any—signs that tensions will lessen."[29]

How could risks of this kind be managed? What could be done to protect vulnerable institutions? As a start, the Department of Homeland

Security developed resources to help universities respond to bomb threats, including a YouTube video, *Critical Resources for Handling Bomb Threats*,[30] and worked with HBCU representatives to develop and deliver training on preparing for and responding to bomb threats, as well as an active-shooter preparedness webinar for HBCUs. Homeland Security also established the HBCU K-9 Bomb Detection Adoption Program. Yet by August 2022, only three HBCUs had received bomb detection K-9s to support campus public safety officers during an active bomb threat incident.[31]

Speaking before the House Judiciary Subcommittee on Crime, Terrorism, and Homeland Security at its convening on "The Rise in Violence Against Minority Institutions," Margaret Huang, the president and CEO of the Southern Poverty Law Center, observed, "It is understandable that one instinct is to increase physical security...higher walls, more cameras, more bulletproof glass, and even armed guards. But this cannot be our only response." As important as these defensive actions are, none of them address the behavioral dimension of these threats, made more alarming by the fact that they involve young people. The Jacksonville shooter was twenty-one. The person making the bomb threats was under eighteen. Their actions "underscore the need for parents, educators, and communities to be attuned to signs of radicalization and help inoculate young people against being drawn into an extreme and hateful path."[32]

In her remarks, Huang highlighted the danger that has come from the mainstreaming of extremist ideas such as the "great replacement theory," which espouses the notion that groups such as Democrats, leftists, "multiculturalists," and Jews are conspiring to seize political power by replacing White people in the United States with immigrants of color. Once considered a fringe conspiracy theory, it has been amplified by some politicians and cable news pundits and circulated widely on social media and on Fox cable news, tragically inspiring deadly terror attacks in Charleston, Pittsburgh, and El Paso. As Huang explained, "When people come to believe they face an existential threat, extreme measures like violence can appear more justifiable, and even necessary.... Violence and intimidation are increasingly seen as legitimate political tools."[33]

Huang also pointed to the helpful work of Cynthia Miller-Idriss, director of the Polarization and Extremism Research and Innovation Lab at American University, for an analysis of why young people were increasingly vulnerable to radicalization. In her July 2020 article, "We're Living in a Perfect Storm for Extremist Recruitment. Here's What We Can Do to Stop It," Miller-Idriss observed that during the years of the COVID pandemic, children and teens were at an even greater risk for radicalization because many of them experienced higher rates of anxiety, depression, and isolation, and spent more unsupervised time online, while simultaneously they were cut off from the opportunity for interaction with peers and caring adults—like teachers, employers, and coaches—who might otherwise have spotted the warning signs of changes in attitudes or behavior. Miller-Idriss emphasized the importance of parents deepening their understanding of how their children spend time online, particularly if it includes encrypted platforms, anonymizing apps, or toxic online communities. Even online gaming can be a conduit for early radicalization, as surveys conducted by the Anti-Defamation League found that nearly 25 percent of online gamers reported exposure to discussions about White supremacist ideology while playing online.[34]

Miller-Idriss challenged the assumptions that parents have about their children's immunity to toxic ideas that run counter to their family's values. She wrote, "Many parents believe their own child is incapable of violence, or trust that their own family values will be enough to protect their child from extremist and hateful beliefs. Both assumptions are sadly wrong. Helping all parents and caregivers recognize youth vulnerabilities to persuasive extremist rhetoric—particularly online—is key to preventing further tragedies."[35] To help parents learn to recognize the warning signs of online radicalization and how best to intervene, she partnered with Susan Corke, director of the Intelligence Project of the Southern

Poverty Law Center, to create a resource guide for parents and caregivers, *Building Resilience and Confronting Risk*.[36] In a study of more than 750 parents and caregivers who read the guide, they found that a quick read—seven minutes—was enough to give adults the information they needed and, perhaps most importantly, the confidence to have a conversation with the youth in their lives about online radicalization. Miller-Idriss and Corke concluded, "The good news is that equipping parents isn't all that difficult. It doesn't take much to enable front-line adults—parents, care-givers, teachers, coaches, mental health counselors and others who work with youth—to better recognize and respond to extremism."[37]

Though their guide is aimed at parents, it could be a useful resource for college and university faculty and staff as part of threat assessment efforts. We know from the story of Derek Black, discussed in Chapter 2, that it is possible through dialogue and exposure to new people and diverse ideas for students to reevaluate and let go of extremist viewpoints. We also know that efforts to recruit White youth into White nationalist organizations are increasing on college campuses.[38] Identifying strategies to help White students resist the extremist messaging and recruitment that are targeting them is important. *Being White Today: A Roadmap for a Positive Antiracist Life*, by Shelly Tochluk and Christine Saxman, is an example of a helpful re-source specifically designed for that purpose and to offer support to White students on their learning journey toward a "positive antiracist life."[39]

If we understand bomb threats at HBCUs as just one manifestation of the larger problem of rising extremism, we can see that physical campus barriers or other defensive measures may be necessary but are not suffi-cient to address that larger threat—a threat that affects every college or university. While HBCUs have been the recent targets, the perpetrators of extremist violence—often young White men of college age—are most likely to be enrolled at predominantly White institutions. Higher educa-tion has an important role to play in countering the growth of White na-tionalism. In her congressional testimony, Margaret Huang's number one recommendation was for community leaders of all backgrounds to "speak out against hate, political violence, and extremism."[40]

Campus leaders need to embrace that responsibility, a critical step in reducing the risk of extremist violence. Michael Gavin, president of Delta College and author of *The New White Nationalism in Politics and Higher Education*, wrote eloquently about the urgency of acting now.

> There are moments when higher education leaders have a responsibility not only to defend but also to articulate the role of academe in the nation's journey toward a truly free and democratic society. One of those moments is now, when higher education is facing an existential threat wielded from what I've called the new white nationalism.…Underneath the bomb threats and white supremacist rallies are antieducation views that seek to delegitimize racial, ethnic and LGBTQ+ identities as being unequal to those of white, male, heterosexuals.…The active marginalization of specific identities from education is hateful and should be couched in only those terms.…When our curriculum is under attack, and our students are as well, we protect freedom of expression and academic freedom by speaking out, not staying on the sidelines.[41]

The voice of the institutional leader is critically important, but the classroom may offer the best opportunity to engage students in the kind of critical thinking that serves as inoculation against extremist rhetoric. In her essay "Countering the Rise of White Nationalism," Karen Gaffney, professor of English at Raritan Valley Community College in New Jersey, proposes three ways higher education can reduce the risk of extremist indoctrination: (1) debunk racist and antisemitic myths, challenging ideas like the "great replacement" theory, for example; (2) help students develop critical media literacy skills; and (3) create a culture of belonging.[42] The importance of a culture of belonging was discussed in Chapter 1 as part of the ABCs—affirming identity, building community, and cultivating leadership—but in the context of the threat of White nationalist recruitment, the importance of creating a sense of belonging is underscored.

Gaffney explained, "This is a critical step because those most vulnerable to indoctrination into extremism are often those who, as Hannah Arendt put it, feel 'loneliness...the experience of not belonging to the world at all.'" Extremist groups welcome them in, offering a place and a way to belong. Gaffney concluded her essay with this warning: "White nationalism is no longer a fringe movement, and higher education, as well as our students, are targets. We cannot afford to keep our heads in the sand."[43] The risk to students and institutions is real.

THE DANGERS OF LONELINESS

As Gaffney noted, loneliness can put a student at risk for radicalization. It can also lead to suicide. In 2023 Dr. Vivek Murthy, the US surgeon general, issued an advisory report, *Our Epidemic of Loneliness and Isolation*, to shine a spotlight on the increasing rates of loneliness and the "profound mental and physical health risks of social disconnection." "Loneliness," he wrote, "is far more than just a bad feeling—it harms both individual and societal health." According to the report, loneliness is worse for your health than smoking fifteen cigarettes a day or being obese or being sedentary.[44] It places you at greater risk for heart disease, dementia, stroke, depression, anxiety, substance abuse, and premature death. Social isolation and the loneliness associated with it are among the strongest predictors of suicidal ideation, suicide attempts, and lethal suicide behavior. To quote Jeremy Noble, public health expert and author of *Project UnLonely: Healing Our Crisis of Disconnection*, "Loneliness won't just make you miserable. It can kill you."[45]

Loneliness is increasing everywhere. Noble notes that in the first quarter of the twenty-first century, "most of the developed world has experienced loneliness as a relentlessly expanding public health calamity," which is particularly impacting young people. "Studies worldwide show that people between the ages of 18 and 28 are the loneliest demographic."[46] The first global study of loneliness, which included nationally representative survey data from 142 countries (not including China), found that 27 percent of young adults from nineteen to twenty-nine reported feeling "very" or "fairly" lonely, making them the loneliest demographic. By comparison, only 17 percent of people over the age of sixty-five reported that degree of loneliness.[47]

Why are so many young people so lonely? Noble describes three types of loneliness: psychological, societal, and existential. Psychological loneliness is "the experience of wishing someone else was there...a longing for an authentic connection to another person," someone you truly trust and can confide in. If this is the loneliness you are experiencing, you can be interacting with people all day and still feel very much alone. Societal loneliness is "the overwhelming sense of not fitting in or belonging, of being systematically excluded. It's the experience of being uninvited or rejected by a peer group, work colleagues, neighbors, or society at large." Anyone who is frequently marginalized because of race, gender, sexual orientation or expression, nationality, or disability, or because of one's own idiosyncratic lack of conformity to social norms, is at greater risk of experiencing societal loneliness. Noble notes that societal loneliness is common in the profiles of the loners who eventually perpetrated mass shootings. Existential loneliness, also referred to as spiritual loneliness, is "part of the human condition," involving our search for meaning and purpose in our lives. When we feel disconnected from ourselves, our own inner core, we are likely to experience existential loneliness. As our society has grown more secular, with less participation in traditional religious life, existential loneliness has grown.[48]

The typology matters because "it's important to differentiate between the lonely feelings that arise when we tell ourselves, 'I don't know who I am anymore or what matters to me,' versus 'I don't have a friend in the world,' versus 'I feel excluded at work,'" to know how best to address the problem.[49] However, in the case of young adults, it seems as though many are experiencing all three types. In addition to not having a "special someone" in their lives, they worry about the societal isolation that comes from being "canceled" or systematically excluded in the context of increasingly polarized social environments. But existential worries are a factor, too.

In a 2023 study conducted by researchers at the Making Caring Common Project of the Harvard Graduate School of Education, 58 percent of the young adults (ages eighteen to twenty-five) surveyed reported that they lacked "meaning or purpose" in their lives, and 44 percent reported a sense of not mattering to others. Financial worries (56 percent), achievement pressures (51 percent), a general sense that "things are falling apart" (45 percent), concerns about gun violence in schools (42 percent), climate change (34 percent), and corrupt or incompetent political leadership (30 percent) were all cited as negatively impacting their mental health.[50] In sum, "fear of a world coming unglued, of not being up to coping with it, of being threatened by fire, wind, flood, war, or a maniac's hail of bullets—if students' loneliness is not primarily existential, the broth in which it simmers surely is."[51]

So much uncertainty! The pandemic of loneliness, as Jeffrey Noble describes it, is likely the result of the overwhelming uncertainty we are experiencing in the post-2020 world. Dealing with uncertainty creates a sense of vulnerability, which in turn generates anxiety and the physiological response to "fight or flee." As he puts it, "In that physical state, anxiety directs our mental focus toward the priority of survival.... Anxious minds stuck in survival mode are more concerned with protecting than connecting.... Vulnerability, driven by uncertainty, breeds anxiety, and anxiety breeds loneliness as we go into a defensive crouch and back away from those around us."[52]

What does that "backing away" look like in daily life? Maybe like this description, offered by Rachel L. Koch, assistant director of training at the University of Richmond counseling center: "Everybody has AirPods in, hats on, not making eye contact. They're really trying to hide themselves. And then they come into my [counseling] office and wonder why they feel so lonely and haven't made connections."[53]

Though presidents (and students) worry about the danger of an active shooter with a gun, the more common danger is a gun in the hands of a lonely student. The most dangerous gun violence for college students is not from active shooters, it is gun death by suicide.[54] According to the Centers for Disease Control and Prevention, the rate of suicides involving guns in 2023 reached an all-time high, with more than half of all suicides involving a firearm.[55] With a fatality rate close to 90 percent, guns are much more lethal than other common suicide methods, most of which have a fatality rate below 5 percent. Attempters using other methods have time to change their minds mid-attempt or can be rescued by other people before it is too late. With guns, once the trigger is pulled, there is no chance to change one's mind. The mere presence of a gun in a household doubles the risk of gun-related suicide,[56] another reason access to guns is a major source of worry for presidents in those places that allow guns on campus.

Since 2007, the Healthy Minds Network, one of the leading research organizations focused on adolescent and young adult mental health, has administered the Healthy Minds Study to students at more than six hundred colleges and universities, receiving over 850,000 responses.[57] In 2007, 22 percent of respondents showed indications of depression; in 2023, 40.8 percent did. In a ten-year period, from 2013 to 2023, rates of anxiety doubled from 17.2 percent to 35.5 percent. As rates of anxiety and depression rise within the college student population, the percentage of students experiencing suicidal thoughts also rises. In 2007, 6 percent of students reported they had seriously thought about attempting suicide; in 2023 that number had risen to 14.4 percent. Only 2 percent reported that they had attempted suicide in the last year.

Transgender and gender-nonconforming students, however, were at an especially high risk for psychological, societal, and existential loneliness, a fact reflected in their higher rates of attempted suicide. About 5 percent of transgender students surveyed indicated they had made a suicide attempt in the last year. President Trump's 2025 executive order revoking recognition of transgender and nonbinary gender identities and rescinding federal protection against gender-identity-based discrimination has only served to increase the sense of vulnerability and isolation among these students on college campuses.[58]

Suicide is the second leading cause of death for people between the ages of ten and thirty-four.[59] Regardless of the method, the effect of a suicide on a campus is devastating. It is no wonder that when presidents cite their greatest fears or worst experiences, a student's suicide is often at the top of the list.[60]

Sadly, the nightmare of losing a student to suicide also became a reality for me. Two years after the death of JL, the Spelman community was again impacted by the death of a student, the result of a self-inflicted gunshot wound. BG was a new transfer student, entering Spelman as a sophomore. At the time of her death, it was still early in the fall semester, so she was not yet well-known to her teachers or classmates. Though she lived in a campus residence hall, she was in her family home when she died. The news of BG's death did not come in the middle of the night this time, yet it was no less upsetting.

When a student dies by suicide, one important decision is what to say about the cause of death. There is always concern that sharing that news publicly might trigger other students with suicidal thoughts, but in the age of social media, news (or rumors) can spread quickly, sometimes forcing a reactive response from campus leaders. The Higher Education Mental Health Alliance recommends that campus messages about a student death should only confirm it as a suicide if the family has given permission, or if the death was so public that many people knew it was a suicide.[61] In this case, the decision was clear. Her parents wanted us to share the cause of death. Once again, the student affairs team mobilized to support the campus community—the students, faculty, and staff who mourned her loss and who wondered what they might have done to prevent the tragedy, as well as students whose own feelings of anxiety or depression might be exacerbated by the news of her suicide. And of course, we wrapped our collective arms around the grieving parents.

When I called the devastated family to express our condolences and offer support, I asked, "How can we be helpful?" I was surprised when BG's mother replied by asking me to speak at her daughter's funeral. I had not known BG so could not speak from personal knowledge of her daughter. However, BG's mother anticipated that there would be young people at the funeral. Perhaps because she knew I was a psychologist, she wanted me to tell them that it was OK to ask for help, not to suffer in silence. She didn't want another family to lose a child to suicide. I agreed, and just as the mother had predicted, the church was full of young people—her daughter's high school friends, as well as some from Spelman. I hoped the thoughts I shared with them that day would make an impact.

Indeed, being able to ask for help is important. Most students who die by suicide are not in counseling. Among youth experiencing major depression, more than 60 percent do not receive any form of treatment.[62] Though the stigma around mental health issues is not as great as it once was, access to care may not always be readily available. When students do seek help, being able to *respond* with the appropriate resources is the challenge facing many higher education institutions today. As the statistics regarding rising rates of loneliness, anxiety, and depression indicate, the need to support emotional well-being on college campuses is rising.[63]

When I returned to Mount Holyoke College in the summer of 2022 as interim president, one of the people I met with early on was the director of the counseling center, a woman I had known during my earlier years at the college. I knew that many institutions were struggling to meet the demands for counseling, and I wanted to know how we were doing in that regard, how we were managing the mental health risks on the campus. I was not surprised when she told me that the COVID pandemic had taken a toll—there had been

COVID-related staff turnover, and there were counselor vacancies she was trying to fill. I asked if our salaries were competitive. I was surprised when she told me that money was not her biggest problem. The supply of therapists in the region was so limited that she was challenged to find people she could hire at any price. The local demand in the region far outpaced the supply, even for off-campus referrals. The people we needed just weren't there. She told me that we would have to find strategies other than more one-on-one counseling appointments to meet our students' needs. The problem she described was not ours alone—indeed, it was a problem everywhere. As one longtime counselor at the University of Virginia said, "Our counseling staff has almost tripled in size, but even if we continue hiring, I don't think we could ever staff our way out of this challenge."[64] What can colleges do?

The Jed Foundation is an organization dedicated to helping colleges answer that question. Founded by Donna and Phil Satow two years after the 1998 suicide of their son Jed, today the foundation works with colleges and universities in an advisory capacity, providing expert support, evidence-based best practices, and data-driven guidance to protect student mental health and prevent suicide.[65] What is known as "JED's Comprehensive Approach to Mental Health Promotion and Suicide Prevention for Colleges and Universities" is built around seven essential steps: help students develop life skills, promote social connectedness, identify students at risk, increase help-seeking behavior, provide mental health and substance misuse services, follow crisis management procedures, and promote means safety (i.e., restrict access to lethal means such as guns, toxic drugs, rooftops). Through the JED Campus program, the foundation "assesses the state of campus policy and practice relative to the seven-part framework, provides targeted technical assistance to priority areas of improvement, and gives coaching support through a campus advisor over the course of four years."[66] The foundation's approach is collaborative by design, involving interdisciplinary campus teams that have broad representation, including participation from senior leaders across the institution, making clear that "mental health is part of everyone's work on the campus." Also, in partnership with the Steve Fund, an organization specifically focused on supporting the mental health and emotional well-being of young people of color, the Jed Foundation works to ensure that there is equitable implementation of its programs so that marginalized students who are at heightened risk for emotional distress and suicidality have their needs met.[67]

The basic premise of the JED Campus program is that "when college systems comprehensively support students' mental health, student attitudes and behaviors related to mental health will improve. In turn, student life outcomes will improve, including increased access to care, greater retention and graduation rates, and reduced suicidal ideation and behaviors."[68] Even small, low-cost changes can make a big difference. For example, training academic advisers to ask students about loneliness and isolation, and providing them with referral information if concerned about a student, empowers them to be part of the early identification of students at risk.

At Mount Holyoke College, one of the strategies used to help build life skills and reduce social isolation was Project Connect. The brainchild of social worker Jessica Gifford, Project Connect has been implemented on campuses across the country. It brings together small groups of students (four to six) to spend time getting to know one another through structured conversations and group activities. Facilitated by a peer leader, Project Connect, just as the name implies, fosters a healthy sense of connectedness.[69] Not every problem requires an individual appointment with a therapist. Sometimes what is most needed is a sense of community and the knowledge that you are not alone.

Increasingly, faculty are becoming the "first line of defense." While many faculty may feel hesitant to talk to students about mental health concerns, institutions are helping build their comfort level with workshops and resources to "recognize, respond, and refer." At the University of North Carolina (UNC), approximately nine hundred faculty and staff received training in "Mental Health First Aid." They learned that sudden changes in behavior—like missing classes, failing to turn in assignments, or unusually disheveled appearance—could be signs of a struggling student in need of help. Noticing distress and then asking if a student is OK, and then helping with a referral, could be life-saving.[70] UNC law professor Katie Rose Guest Pryal found that holding group office hours (rather than individual office hours) helped foster a greater sense of community among classmates, which benefited all concerned. She wrote, "When you nurture a mental-health community among your students, you give them others to turn to besides you. And you create a new, more powerful front line, made up of fellow students who trust one another, forming an interlocking web of support."[71]

Some campuses have established a formal process of threat assessment, a team approach to evaluating the potential danger that students or employees pose to themselves or others; but the effectiveness of threat assessment teams depends on the willingness of community members to share their concerns when they notice something. "Folks should know that if they have a concern, they don't have to make a determination or a decision or a judgment.... They simply have to say here's something I'm concerned about. Then it's the responsibility of the threat-assessment team to gather more information."[72] Though referral systems like this are not foolproof, campus awareness of the threat assessment team as a referral resource increases the likelihood that a struggling individual can be identified and offered appropriate help before it is too late. Threat assessment teams are considered a "best practice," and nearly 95 percent of schools who complete the JED Campus program have such teams in place.[73] For campuses seeking assistance in developing threat assessment protocols, the National Association for Behavioral Intervention and Threat Assessment offers education, professional development, and support to campus teams.[74]

A ten-year evaluation of data (2013–2023) from participating JED Campuses showed positive student outcomes: greater awareness of mental health resources, less shame related to seeking help, and lower rates of anxiety, depression, suicidal ideation, and suicide attempts. Rather than any one change being the catalyst for progress, "it's the accumulated effect that changes the student body."[75] As of 2024, there were more than five hundred colleges and universities, across forty-four states, in the JED Campus program, benefiting close to six million students.[76]

PUT THE SMARTPHONE DOWN

What else can we do on college campuses to improve emotional well-being and reduce the risk of self-harm? One answer could be to help students step away from their phones. Psychologist Jean M. Twenge is widely credited with sounding the alarm about the negative impact of smartphones and social media on the mental health of young people who entered adolescence just as smartphone use became commonplace. In her 2017 book, *iGen*, she described the generation born in the mid-1990s to the mid-2000s (now commonly referred to as Gen Z) as the first generation to grow up in the age of the smartphone.[77] "The twin rise of the smartphone and social media has caused an earthquake.... There is compelling evidence that the devices we've placed in young people's hands are having profound effects on their lives—and making them seriously unhappy."[78]

In her 2017 article, "Have Smartphones Destroyed a Generation?," featured in the *Atlantic*, Twenge cited the findings of a nationally representative annual study of adolescents, funded by the National Institute on Drug Abuse, called *The Monitoring the Future Survey*. The survey asked teens about their degree of happiness and how they spend their leisure time—including both screen-based activities such as using social media, texting, and web browsing, and nonscreen activities such as in-person social interaction and exercise. The results were undeniably compelling.

> Teens who spend more time than average on screen activities are more
> likely to be unhappy, and those who spend more time than average

on nonscreen activities are more likely to be happy. *There's not a single exception.* All screen activities are linked to less happiness, and all nonscreen activities are linked to more happiness.... If you were going to give advice for a happy adolescence based on this survey, it would be straightforward: Put down the phone, turn off the laptop, and do something—anything—that does not involve a screen.[79]

The strong link between high rates of screen time and depression is quite disturbing when we recognize just how much time most young people spend on social media, bringing those online habits with them to college. According to data reported by the US surgeon general Vivek Murthy, "Adolescents who spend more than three hours a day on social media face double the risk of anxiety and depression symptoms, and the average daily use in this age group, as of the summer of 2023, was 4.8 hours."[80] The rapidly accumulating knowledge about the potentially harmful effects of excessive social media consumption led Surgeon General Murthy in 2024 to declare the mental health crisis among young people an emergency to which social media was an important contributor, and to call on Congress to require warning labels on social media apps. In a cautionary *New York Times* op-ed, he called on school leaders to make classrooms and social spaces phone-free zones.[81]

Middle school and high school principals are beginning to do just that—making school a phone-free zone by using a product like Yondr (a specialized rubber phone pouch that locks magnetically, making the phone unusable until it is unlocked at the end of the school day).[82] Though the benefits of phone-free spaces are clear (e.g., more attentive students, fewer interpersonal conflicts escalated by online posting), mandating cell phone restrictions like Yondr on college-age students would likely generate a firestorm of protest.

Still, it is possible to influence behavior by talking about the hazards of addictive screen time and to support with word, deed, and budget allocations the expansion of non-screen-based activities that help build human connection in real life—community-based volunteer opportunities, group recreational activities, and opportunities to learn about mindfulness practices like meditation and yoga. Helping students change screen behavior does make a difference. In a study conducted at the University of Pennsylvania, those participating students who limited their use of social media sites to a maximum of thirty minutes a day felt better, significantly less lonely and depressed, than those students who did not limit their use.[83]

Students are not the only ones whose mental health has been impacted by ubiquitous smartphone use. On average, adults in the US spend more than three hours per day on their smartphones, and 70 percent use social media, "too often scrolling mindlessly instead of connecting meaningfully."[84] And just as campus leaders must be concerned about students, we also must think about employees and their health and well-being. Less is known about the mental health of faculty and staff members, but anecdotally, most campus leaders are aware of instances of employees experiencing mental health crises, particularly in our post-pandemic era. "In a survey conducted in September 2022 by Uwill, a teletherapy company that works with colleges, and NASPA, Student Affairs Administrators in Higher Education, approximately 70 percent of student affairs professionals surveyed reported that staff mental health had worsened over the previous year. About 62 percent of participants said that faculty mental health had declined."[85]

TIME FOR RECOVERY

According to surveys conducted by the Pew Research Center from March 2020 to September 2022, at least 41 percent of US adults experienced significant psychological distress at some point during the pandemic. When I arrived at Mount Holyoke College in the summer of 2022, the stress of the pandemic on employees was apparent. Almost every employee I talked with in my first few weeks on campus told me about the number of vacant positions and how tired everyone was. Indeed, the widespread labor trend of workers leaving their jobs during the COVID pandemic, known as the "Great Resignation," had also impacted the college. The resulting unfilled vacancies had increased the workload for everyone. The combination of working in isolation, often remotely, with fewer colleagues to share the load, had understandably resulted in a deep sense of fatigue for many, as well as feelings of disconnection. Fatigue and disconnection are a troubling combination. Research has shown that lonely employees are "less efficient, less effective, less satisfied, and less committed.... Disconnected workers often think about quitting and are nearly twice as likely to be searching for a new job."[86]

It was clear to me that one important task for my year as interim president was to help rebuild connections among the employees even as we worked hard to fill the vacancies. A wise friend once told me, "If you make a lot of withdrawals, you better make a lot of deposits." In that spirit, I used some discretionary funds in the president's office budget to create "The Good Idea Fund" and issued this invitation to all faculty and staff:

> The Good Idea Fund (TGIF) is a new presidential initiative with the goal of creating community "deposits," replenishing and connecting our employee community and encouraging nourishing and impactful ideas from faculty and staff. Our community has continuously risen to the challenges we face in our world, and within our own community, and that effort has withdrawn energy from many. To deposit energy back into the community and each other, this is an invitation to bring forth your good ideas. The Good Idea Fund seeks proposals from current faculty and staff that help connect each of us back to our campus and community, recognizing that there are multiple ways to do that within the context of our

workplace. This is about feel-good ideas that nourish us as individuals and reinvigorate our sense of community and belonging. Ideas big and small are welcome. While there is no minimum, the maximum funding request for any idea is $3,000. Let's get creative in ways to energize and connect!

Coordinated by a staff member in my office, a small selection committee representing both faculty and staff was assembled, and good ideas poured in. Most were very low cost. Among my favorites was a faculty member's request for $700 to buy a karaoke machine for faculty and staff karaoke parties. I attended the first one—it was a lot of fun! Another person requested a small budget for art supplies to make "gratitude squares." She organized the square-making event, and then hung the squares on a clothesline along a walking trail on the edge of the campus, with the opportunity for others to add to the display with their expressions of gratitude. Someone else had the idea of a lunchtime walking club—no funds required. At the end of the year, she sent me happy pictures of the participants with this note: "I wanted to share some pictures from the Earth Day Hike.... Thank you so much for your support of The MHC Walking Club. It was The Good Idea Fund that inspired me to bring people together and enjoy our beautiful campus." It was a joy to see community ties being revitalized.

Executive coach Naz Beheshti wrote, "Leaders and executives are uniquely positioned to combat [workplace] loneliness and to replace it with connection. Connection—between a company and its purpose, a company and its employees, and a company and its customers—is treasure, and leaders are the guardians and stewards of that treasure.... Cultivating connection should be a core leadership mission."[87]

But what about the leader? Can you rally the community when you yourself are depleted? Students, faculty, and staff are not the only lonely ones. What about the president's mental health? Carrying the weight of the community's mental health, managing the communal anxiety about the threat of disaster, being *responsible* twenty-four hours a day, seven days a week, is exhausting. It is often said that it is "lonely at the top," and it is. Confidentiality is often required when dealing with sensitive and complex issues. Having a team the leader can trust is essential, but even the best team can itself be a source of stress when it becomes necessary to manage its internal conflicts and individual personnel concerns. I learned that having a support team that was mine alone—my spouse, wise friends away from campus, a coach, presidential peers who understand firsthand the demands of the job—helps prevent the danger of social isolation and loneliness.

When I retired from Spelman College after thirteen years of service, double the tenure of the average college president, I was asked how I managed to stay in the position so long. My immediate answer was "regularly scheduled vacations," and I was quite sincere in my response. After my fifth year on the job, I was exhausted and unsure whether I could or should accept the next five-year contract the board was offering me. Did I have the stamina to do what needed to be done? I was contemplating this question while on vacation at a wellness retreat in Mexico called Rancho La Puerta. The environment was so restorative, just what I needed—beautiful surroundings, great vegetarian-friendly food, daily hikes and other exercise, plus a "no cell phone" policy! At the end of the week, I felt ready to commit to the next five years, but I knew I would need to return to the ranch to recharge again before the year ended. I called my board chair and let her know that I would not use all my vacation time in the summer but would save a week to return to the ranch again in six months' time. And I did. My husband and I visited the ranch for a week every six months, without fail, for the next eight years of my presidency.

The work of the leader is endless, and the emails never stop coming, but it is not the stress of the job that will do you in—it is the failure to allow time for recovery. In their book, *The Power of Full Engagement*, authors

Jim Loehr and Tony Schwartz argue convincingly that the secret to lasting success as a leader is how we manage our energy. They write, "The richest, happiest and most productive lives are characterized by the ability to fully engage in the challenge at hand, but also to disengage periodically and seek renewal."[88] Energy expenditure must be balanced with "intermittent energy renewal" to avoid burnout and deteriorating performance. Those regularly scheduled trips were essential opportunities for energy renewal, but daily "renewing" rituals were important, too. Meditation, exercise, healthy eating, time alone with a cup of tea, a long phone call with a confidante—all these proved to be essential recovery strategies.

It is hard to take a pause. But as a friend once said to me, urging me to take care of myself, "If something happens to you, they will get another one." She was right. No leader is irreplaceable, but to your family and friends, you are irreplaceable. Self-care matters. And you never know when you will be called on to do something extra hard, something you may never have had to do before. You need an energy reserve to handle whatever that new source of stress might be, the result of a new risk that you did not anticipate.

We live in such an uncertain time. If there is *any* certainty, perhaps it is that there are disasters awaiting we just haven't had yet. In the absence of practice, institutions must rely on the quality and character of leadership to think clearly, communicate effectively, and make hard decisions in a timely manner, providing calm and reassurance amid communal anxiety. Being the holder of that anxiety, even as you manage your own, is exhausting. It can feel like the weight of the world is truly on your shoulders. But it is in those moments you are reminded just how much others are depending on your leadership—and on your institution.

Educational institutions like Spelman College, and so many others, have been anchors of their communities for decades, if not centuries. Through times of war, the Great Depression, periods of social unrest, and more, they have endured. In the midst of a campus crisis, whatever it might be, there is comfort in knowing that history and the legacy of resilience that these institutions have. In a time of social disconnection, colleges can create the inclusive communities of belonging needed to reduce the scourge of loneliness. The uncertainties of the future can be mitigated through research and teaching. By remaining focused on the educational mission, risks—known and unknown—can be faced collectively with creativity and courage.

CHAPTER SEVEN

WALKING ON THE
EDGE OF A CLIFF

A s resilient as higher education institutions have been and can be in the face of unanticipated crises, still there is one problem that looms large for many campus leaders: the specter of declining enrollment. Student enrollment is the lifeblood of any institution of higher education. Yet, for many, that vital source is drying up. In 2014, writing for the *Chronicle of Higher Education*, Sara Lipka reported on its analysis of Census Bureau data and sounded an alarm for those college leaders who were paying attention. She wrote, "Two decades of steady supply drove enrollment growth and let campuses be choosy, gathering freshmen with good test scores and parents who could pay. *But those days are over.* Peer into kindergarten classrooms across the country and you will see fewer students. For every 100 18-year-olds nationally, there are only 95 4-year-olds." Quoted in her article, William T. Conley, then vice president for enrollment management at Bucknell University, captured the problem succinctly: "If they weren't born, they're not going to go to college."[1] Is this a problem contemporary leaders can solve? Not easily.

Indeed, there are a lot fewer babies being born in the United States now than in the late twentieth century. The 2008 economic collapse known as the Great Recession triggered a marked drop in the birth rate. In 2007 the overall fertility rate, estimated by births per thousand women between the ages of fifteen and forty-four, was 69.6 per thousand, and the actual number of births that year hit a record high of 4.3 million.[2] But in 2008 that number dropped precipitously and continued to decline each year, with few exceptions. By 2023 the fertility rate had dropped to below 55 births per thousand, and the yearly number of births was hovering at about 3.6 million, the lowest number since 1979.[3] Fast forward seventeen years from 2008, the first year of the drop in births, to 2025, and predictably there is now and is likely to be for many years—at least until 2040—a correspondingly sharp drop in the number of high school seniors preparing to go to college.

The problem, widely referred to in higher education as the "enrollment cliff," poses a real threat to many colleges and universities. In his book *Demographics and the Demand for Higher Education*, published in 2018, economics professor Nathan Grawe created an analytical model he called the Higher Education Demand Index (HEDI) to forecast future college-going behavior by region, type of institution, and student demographic characteristics such as race/ethnicity, family income, and parental educational attainment. Using the HEDI analysis, in 2018 Grawe predicted that in 2025 there would be a "precipitous reduction of 15 percent or more" in the college-going population. He wrote, "In 2025, the HEDI predicts that the cohort size of 18-year-olds will shrink more than 650,000, while the number of first-time college-goers contracts by nearly 450,000. Since several cohorts attend college in any given year, the aggregate effect on enrollments will be several times as large."[4]

While there have been other periods in US educational history—the 1960s, for example—when birth rates dropped and first-time college enrollments declined as much as 18 percent, the enrollment impact was gradual, spreading over a period of more than a decade, starting in 1980. The 2018 HEDI projections indicated "a similarly deep contraction accomplished in only half a decade." The steepness and speed of the projected enrollment drop made clear why the image of a dangerous cliff was so appropriate. Grawe added, "Unless something unexpected intervenes, the confluence of current demographic changes foretells an *unprecedented reduction* in postsecondary education demand about a decade ahead."[5]

Just two years later, in 2020, something unexpected did indeed intervene. The COVID-19 global pandemic was unlike anything else in our lifetimes. The speed and lethality with which it spread across the globe were unprecedented, forcing most colleges and universities to shut down their in-person operations and quickly pivot to online instruction in the middle of the 2020 spring semester. In the fall of 2020, with the pandemic still raging, many institutions (44 percent) began the school year completely online, others (21 percent) used a combination of remote and in-person instruction (with social distancing, testing, and masking precautions in place), and 27 percent offered fully in-person instruction. Freshman enrollment that year dropped 13.1 percent. Public two-year colleges were especially hard hit, with a decline of first-time student enrollment of 21 percent. Enrollment at public four-year institutions dropped 8.1 percent overall. International student enrollment in the US, which was at an all-time high in 2019, was especially impacted because of pandemic-related limitations on travel, with a drop of first-time enrollments of 43 percent and falling 16 percent overall (including both new and returning students) in the fall of 2020.[6]

Financial hardship followed. NAFSA Association of International Educators estimated that the declining enrollment of so many international students alone represented at least $3 billion of lost revenue in 2020. The disruption of college athletics because of the cancellations of lucrative events like the NCAA men's and women's basketball tournaments cost NCAA Division I schools as much as $375 million in revenue, forcing cuts in athletics programs at some schools. Institutional budgets were strained not only because of lost revenue but also because the response to the pandemic required unanticipated expenses. Refunds for room and board had to be issued to students who had to leave campus midsemester, the transition to online courses required more investments in technology, and additional resources were needed to cover the costs of increased cleaning to reduce the risk of infection and for on-campus COVID testing and related supplies. The federal Coronavirus Aid, Relief, and Economic Security Act, which passed in December 2020, provided some funding assistance to institutions but not enough to replace all that was lost.[7]

Despite the arrival of COVID vaccines, the enrollment crisis continued. According to the National Student Clearinghouse Research Center (NSCRC), undergraduate enrollment in the fall of 2021 was 6.6 percent lower than it had been in the fall of 2019, before the pandemic started.[8] In sum, the total undergraduate enrollment between fall 2019 (pre-COVID) and fall 2021 dropped from approximately 16.4 million to 15.35 million— just shy of a million students gone.[9]

The impact in academic year 2021–2022, though largest at two-year community colleges, was being felt deeply at four-year institutions.[10] Institutions were hoping for a post-pandemic enrollment rebound that never came. Doug Shapiro, the executive director of the NSCRC, noted, "During the early months of the pandemic, four-year institutions dodged the bullet, but in 2022, they also experienced drops in enrollment similar to two-year institutions."[11] Movement toward the edge of the enrollment cliff was clearly accelerated by the pandemic. According to an analysis of federal data by the State Higher Education Executive Officers Association (SHEEO), twenty-three nonprofit colleges and universities closed in 2022. Prior to that, the largest number of nonprofit colleges that closed in a single year was only thirteen. "It's not corruption, it's not financial misappropriation of funds, it's just that they can't rebound enrollment," said SHEEO senior policy analyst Rachel Burns, quoted in the *Hechinger Report*.[12]

Lincoln College was one of the schools that slipped off the cliff's edge in 2022. Founded in 1865 in the small town of Lincoln, Illinois, and named for Abraham Lincoln, it closed permanently on May 13, 2022. A statement on its website read, "Lincoln College has survived many difficult and challenging times—the economic crisis of 1887, a major campus fire in 1912, the Spanish flu of 1918, the Great Depression, World War II, the 2008 global financial crisis, and more, but this is different."[13] Despite reaching record enrollment (approximately nine hundred students) in the fall of 2019, with residence halls fully occupied, the college saw that success unravel when the pandemic hit just a few months later, disrupting recruiting and fundraising efforts and forcing costly expenditures on technology as well as on health and safety measures. A significant drop in enrollment amid the pandemic left the college without the revenue it needed to continue. The college leadership "worked tirelessly to strengthen its financial position through fundraising campaigns, selling assets, consolidating employee positions, and exploring alternatives for the leased [college property]. Unfortunately, these efforts did not create long-term viability for Lincoln College in the face of the pandemic." On Saturday, May 7, 2022, Lincoln held its final commencement, conferring associate, bachelor's, or master's degrees on 235 students.[14] Said President David Gerlach in a statement on the website, "Lincoln College has been serving students from across the globe for more than 157 years. The loss of history, careers, and a community of students and alumni is immense." The longevity of small private colleges like Lincoln, the fight to survive, the sad demise, and the profound sense of loss when closure comes are familiar elements of a story that is being repeated across the country. In a higher ed landscape of nearly four thousand degree-granting public and private nonprofit colleges and universities, the closing of twenty or thirty small nonprofit colleges in a single year may seem relatively insignificant, but to the students, employees, and surrounding communities impacted it is devastating, and perhaps a harbinger of what awaits others.

What president wants to be the last one standing? The one who turns out the lights and shuts the door, rupturing the economic life of an entire community, not to mention the academic futures of many students? No one wants to be that president, and leaders will struggle mightily to prevent it from happening on their watch. And yet sometimes there are circumstances—a global pandemic, for instance—that leaders just can't work around. For some of the institutions and their leaders who survived the enrollment stresses of the COVID pandemic, the federal government's botched launch of the new FAFSA form in the 2023–2024 academic year might have been the last straw.

THE FAFSA FIASCO

According to the press release from the US Department of Education issued on November 15, 2023, the "simplified, streamlined, and redesigned 2024–25 Free Application for Federal Student Aid," commonly referred to as the "Better FAFSA," would be "the most ambitious and significant redesign of the processes to apply for federal student aid and the formulas used to determine aid eligibility" since the 1980s. The changes were mandated by the bipartisan FUTURE Act and FAFSA Simplification Act, and the deadline for the implementation was December 31, 2023.[15] The original FAFSA, in use for many years, was the much-dreaded, very long and complex form that prospective college students and their families had to fill out to determine their eligibility for federal grants and student loans. The Better FAFSA promised to be much shorter and less confusing to complete.

Even more encouraging was the news that under the new aid formula, more than six hundred thousand students would become eligible for Pell Grant funding for the first time. Pell Grants are awarded by the US Department of Education to help low-income students cover the cost of their education. Pell Grants can be used to pay for school-related expenses at eligible two-year community colleges, career schools, trade schools, online schools, and four-year colleges and universities. Unlike student loans, the grant money does not need to be repaid. To be eligible, a student must be a US citizen or eligible noncitizen and have not yet received a bachelor's, graduate, or professional degree, *and* must demonstrate a high level of financial need as documented on the FAFSA. Named after Sen. Claiborne Pell of Rhode Island, the Pell Grant program has been in operation since the 1973–1974 school year.[16] Between 30 and 40 percent of all undergraduates receive some level of Pell Grant funding each year. In 2021–2022, Pell recipients numbered more than 6 million. More than 212 million Americans have received Pell Grants since 1980.[17] The new aid formula, which determines how much grant money a student can receive, also meant that nearly 1.5 million more students would be eligible for the *maximum* Pell award ($7,395 in 2023–2024), bringing the total number of students eligible for maximum funding that year to more than 5.2 million.[18]

Based on the most recent data provided by the National Center for Education Statistics (NCES), students from every racial/ethnic background have benefited from the Pell Grant program—among students attending school full-time, approximately 58 percent of Black students, 51 percent of American Indian / Alaska Native students, 47 percent of Hispanic students, 36 percent of Pacific Islander students, 42 percent of multiracial students, 32 percent of White students, and 31 percent of Asian students received some Pell funding.[19] As quoted in the press release, Federal Student Aid chief operating officer Richard Cordray described Pell Grants as "a critical lifeline for millions" in pursuit of higher education and the American dream. He spoke reassuringly of his department's commitment to "making sure students from all backgrounds can easily apply for and receive the federal student aid they need through the better FAFSA form. In every state and the District of Columbia, more students than ever before will benefit from greater access to Pell Grants."[20] It sounded good.

In implementation, it was a disaster. Typically, the Federal Student Aid (FSA) office, a unit within the Department of Education, made the FAFSA available to potential applicants in early October. Any student seeking federal aid had to complete the form and send it back to the FSA. In past years, more than 50 percent of high school seniors would have completed the FAFSA by December 15.[21] The FSA staff would then calculate how much federal aid—loans, grants, and work-study programs—the student was eligible to receive. That information would be sent by the FSA to the colleges to which the student had applied. The colleges would use the FSA information to create an accepted student's financial aid award letter, including, if applicable, notification about any additional scholarships or other awards that were coming from the institution along with the federal aid awards. In this process, timing and coordination between the FSA and the institution was critical to be sure that students had the time to evaluate the financial aid offers (and perhaps compare multiple offers) before May 1, the traditional decision deadline for schools across the country.

In "The FAFSA Broke Me," an essay by "A Director of Financial Aid" who chose to remain anonymous and published June 24, 2024, in *Inside Higher Ed*, the author explained just how disastrously far from normal the aid process was in the 2023–2024 school year. Ordinarily the form becomes available in October, students begin completing and submitting it in November, and financial aid offers start being sent out in early December. But in 2024–2025, the FAFSA form did not become available for completion until late December and was plagued with technical glitches, making it impossible for many students to complete the form. The FAFSA helpline was so clogged with calls it became nonfunctional. The director wrote in frustration,

> We are now months into the FAFSA launch and many of our students are still not able to submit or update their FAFSA because the form is still not working properly.... The academic year begins in two months.... A vital part of the college-selection process is making an informed decision. The ongoing FAFSA issues mean there

are students who still do not know how they can finance their education.... How many students will make a poor financial decision because they could not understand the cost of their education? How many students gave up on the idea of college because they could not figure out a broken FAFSA?[22]

By mid-June 2024, the answer to the financial aid director's question was looking like the ever-looming cliff, especially for small schools that typically enrolled high numbers of low-income students, the group most negatively affected by the FAFSA debacle. FAFSA completions among high school graduates of the class of 2024 were down 12.4 percent compared to the same period in 2023. While the hope was that some students might still be able to complete the FAFSA process during the remaining weeks of summer 2024, the decrease in FAFSA completions was more than double the 4.8 percent drop experienced after the COVID-19 pandemic hit.[23] Justin Monk, director of student and institutional aid policy at the National Association of Independent Colleges and Universities, described the FAFSA fallout as a "force multiplier" bearing down on small colleges, causing budget cuts that could weaken them further. He said, "Enrollment declines aren't just a one-year problem; those rippled effects follow you for four years. So there's quite a bit of worry now, but also certainly for the future."[24]

The University of Lynchburg was one example of a worried campus. Founded in 1903 in Lynchburg, Virginia, as noted on the website in July 2024, the university described itself as having evolved from a small private liberal arts college to a nationally recognized comprehensive university "where students gain a greater heart for humanity and a mindset of individual growth. Here, thought-provoking learning ignites change in each individual, and the world."[25] Situated on a picturesque campus of 264 acres with more than forty buildings, the university offered "small classes, easy access to professors, a student-to-faculty ratio of 10 to 1," and a surprisingly large number of academic and social choices. The Lynchburg website indicated fifty-two undergraduate majors, fifty minors, and fourteen preprofessional programs, as well as twenty-five intercollegiate sports teams (twelve men's and thirteen women's).[26]

Lynchburg provided this wide array of offerings at a deeply discounted price, presenting itself to be as affordable as attending a public state university. Lynchburg's published cost of attendance for the 2024–2025 school year (including tuition, fees, and room and board for a full-time student living in a traditional residence hall) was $50,450. However, Lynchburg guaranteed *every* entering student a merit scholarship (not based on financial need) ranging from $16,000 to $22,000 annually, the stronger the academic record, the larger the scholarship. The merit scholarships were renewable, based on continued full-time enrollment and satisfactory academic progress. Students with financial need as documented on their FAFSA could also receive federal financial aid. Additionally, those students who were Virginia residents were eligible for the Virginia Tuition Assistance Grant, estimated at $5,000 per year. Because of the combination of merit and need-based aid, the average student was estimated to have to pay about $24,000 per year, not the $50,450 sticker price.[27]

Still, the high acceptance rate of 96 percent (virtually all applicants were being admitted) indicated that the demand for what Lynchburg was offering was lagging.[28] The strategic plan that was launched in 2022 by President Alison Morrison-Shetlar spoke to the need to expand enrollment and "work toward 'programs of distinction' that draw new students to us and enhance the value and reputation of the Lynchburg experience."[29] On May 30, 2024, a press release was issued announcing "University of Lynchburg Takes Bold Steps to Secure a Bright Future." There would be a restructuring—downsizing—that would close twelve undergraduate programs and five graduate programs, immediately eliminate forty staff positions (described as less than 10 percent of university staff), and over the next three years realign forty faculty positions. As was explained in the press release, it was a necessary response to a perfect storm of un-precedented challenges: "steadily declining birth rates that mean fewer college-aged students nationwide, the Federal Application for Student Aid (FAFSA) crisis impacting student financing, and the lingering effects of the COVID-19 pandemic that will likely shape the state of education for the next several years."[30]

As painful as such reductions are, the message ended with an expression of optimism for the future: "The changes announced today will allow the university to provide a richer, more valuable experience for students and position it to thrive in a fast-changing and extremely challenging academic climate that is affecting colleges and universities across the country."[31] Meanwhile, the cliff still loomed.

FARTHER FROM THE EDGE

In his 2018 predictive HEDI analysis, Nathan Grawe observed that not all institutions would feel the threat of declining enrollments to the same degree. Since most students attend a college or university less than fifty miles from their home, geographic location would be an important distinguishing factor. For those students attending a public four-year institution, the median distance they live from home is eighteen miles. For students at private, nonprofit four-year colleges, the median number is forty-six miles. That number drops to eight miles for students attending public two-year colleges.[32] In fact, location is the factor cited most often in a student's choice of institution, ahead of affordability, school reputation and fit, and preparation for a good job or career. More than 80 percent will choose to attend a higher ed institution in their home state.[33] Population shifts within the United States have favored the South and the West (net growth areas), with the Northeast and the Midwest showing net losses in the number of children (future college students) living there.[34] Simply by virtue of their location, higher ed institutions in the Northeast and Midwest are most at risk for enrollment declines. Not surprisingly then, the enrollment declines during the pandemic were indeed more pronounced in the Midwest and Northeast than in other regions.[35]

But even within the same geographic regions, not all institutions suffered or will suffer the same fate. In his HEDI analysis, Grawe divided institutions into four categories: two-year institutions; "regional institutions" (defined as four-year institutions not included by US News & World Report among its lists of top one hundred national universities or top one hundred national liberal arts colleges); "national institutions" (the fifty national liberal arts colleges and fifty national universities that make up the bottom half of the two top-hundred lists—that is, nos. 51 to 100); and "elite institutions" (those ranked by US News & World Report among the top fifty national liberal arts colleges and the top fifty national universities). Grawe projected that while two-year and regional four-year schools would experience a modest rise in enrollment through 2025, the decade that followed would see a decline approaching 10 percent, resulting in a net loss of about 5 to 6 percent over that entire period. National institutions would see a significant post-2025 enrollment decline of more than 8 percent but would eventually recover to current levels. However, he projected that elite institutions, after a modest decline in the late 2020s, would see "a persistent rise" in demand of 13 percent or higher. His demographic explanations for this more optimistic projection for elite institutions are related to increasing student diversity, specifically the growth of the Asian American student population and the increase in college-educated parents.[36]

The demographic shift in the United States is not just one of size; it is also a shift of race and ethnicity. In 2022, 49 percent of US children (age seventeen and below) were White, non-Hispanic; 26 percent were Hispanic; 14 percent were Black, non-Hispanic; 6 percent were Asian, non-Hispanic; and 6 percent were non-Hispanic "all other races," a category that includes American Indian or Alaska Native, Native Hawaiian or other Pacific Islander, and those who are classified by the Census as "two or more races." By 2050, it is projected that 39 percent of all children will be White, non-Hispanic; 31 percent will be Hispanic; 14 percent will be Black, non-Hispanic; 7 percent will be Asian, non-Hispanic; and 9 percent will be non-Hispanic "all other races."[37] Immigration patterns are shifting as well. From 2010 to 2017, more immigrants came from Asian countries than from Central America, so while differential birth rates have led to an increase in Hispanic/Latinx children, the Asian population has grown more quickly because of immigration.[38]

Asian youth have the highest rates of college attendance of any racial or ethnic group in the US. In 2022, the college enrollment rate for eighteen- to twenty-four-year-olds was higher for those who were Asian (61 percent) than for those of all other racial/ethnic groups. The enrollment rate was 41 percent for White students, 36 percent for Black students as well as mul- tiracial students ("two or more races"), 33 percent for Hispanic students, 27 percent for Pacific Islanders, and 26 percent for American Indian/ Alaska Natives.[39] In fact, the college enrollment rate for those who were Asian was higher than the rates for those who were White, those of two or more races, and for Black, Hispanic, and American Indian/Alaska Native students in every year from 2012 through 2022. Given the higher rates of college attendance, Grawe suggests that the projected growth in the young Asian population could offset the population decline in the White college- going population. As a group, Asian college-going students have shown a strong interest in attending elite colleges. Grawe found that Asian Ameri- cans are more than eleven times as likely to attend an elite school as Black students are.[40]

It is worth noting here that there is considerable variation within the Asian American population regarding college attendance. Among adults over the age of twenty-five, some groups have extremely high lev- els of education attainment, well above the national average. For example, approximately 45 percent of all Taiwanese Americans in that age group have an advanced degree (master's, professional, or PhD degree), and almost 79 percent have at least a bachelor's degree. Seventy-six percent of (South Asian) Indian Americans have a college degree. By contrast, other Asian American groups have educational attainment levels significantly below the US national average. For example, approximately 17 percent of Laotians have a college degree. Among the most highly educated groups, foreign-born individuals have typically come to the US as already educated, high-skilled workers or as international students, while among the least educated Asian groups are immigrants such as Vietnamese, Hmong, Cambodian, and Laotian who came to the US as refugees escaping war. Among the refugee groups, their US-born children are steadily increasing their college-going rates, surpassing the educational attainment of their parents and grandparents.[41]

Another demographic factor that favors elite institutions is the overall rise in educational attainment. More young people than ever before have two parents who earned undergraduate degrees. Grawe wrote, "Higher education's success in expanding access pays an intergenerational dividend as the children of our former students reach college age." Despite a falling population, the percentage of dual-degree families is expected to grow in absolute numbers over the next fifteen years. Because of the high rates of college attendance among many Asian families, the share of dual-degree families in this group is expected to increase significantly from 40 percent in 2018–2019 to almost 55 percent in 2033–2034. By comparison, the percentage of dual-degree White families is expected to grow from 25 percent to slightly less than one-third during the same time frame. Dual-degree families among Hispanics and non-Hispanic Blacks are only expected to grow two or three percentage points. The economic advantage that comes with two college-educated parents is significant, increasing the likelihood that growing numbers of Asian students from dual-degree families will have higher family incomes and will seek out elite institutions in the coming decade.[42]

While the future enrollment news is better for elite institutions than for others, it is important to remember that *most* college students don't attend such institutions. Approximately seven hundred thousand students attend the universities ranked by *US News & World Report* as in the top fifty, and about one hundred thousand attend the top fifty national liberal arts colleges. Just slightly more than 5 percent of the fifteen million undergraduates in 2023 attended one of these institutions.[43]

The enrollment pressures of community colleges and public and private regional colleges are more similar to those of the University of Lynchburg than to the national or elite institutions—places like the University of Michigan or Harvard and Yale. While the elite institutions are accepting just a tiny percentage of those who apply from across the nation and around the world, the two-year schools and the regional institutions are welcoming almost all their applicants, drawing most of their students from nearby communities. If they happen to be in regions where the college-age population is shrinking, their ability to fill their seats is also dwindling. The days of being choosy are over.

BACK FROM THE BRINK:
THE CASE OF SWEET BRIAR COLLEGE

When I was in high school in Massachusetts preparing to apply to colleges in the fall of 1970, my guidance counselor encouraged me to consider attending a women's college. She was particularly keen on Mount Holyoke College. I was not interested. I only applied to coed schools and was delighted when I was accepted at Wesleyan University in Middletown, Connecticut. When I enrolled there in the fall of 1971, I was in the second class of women to be admitted to what had previously been an all-male institution. It was the beginning of a trend. As more historically male colleges began accepting women, the enrollment at women's colleges began to suffer. Later, as a faculty member at Mount Holyoke and then as president of Spelman College, the oldest historically Black college for women, I understood clearly and regularly spoke to prospective students about the distinct benefits offered by a college specifically designed with women's empowerment in mind. Yet, for many teenage applicants, a women's college can be a hard sell. That is especially true if it is a very small liberal arts college located in a rural area, as many of them were. Though women represented almost 60 percent of the US undergraduate population in 2024, fewer than 5 percent were enrolled at women's colleges.[44]

A sector of higher education that was once more than two hundred strong in the 1960s had dwindled to fewer than forty in 2024.[45] Some, like Vassar College in New York and Wheaton College in Massachusetts, began accepting men, in 1969 and 1988 respectively, and after a period of adjustment continued to thrive as coed institutions.[46] Others merged with neighboring men's colleges—Radcliffe College and Harvard University completed a full merger in 1999—or with larger coed universities.[47] In 2022, Mills College in Oakland, California, merged with Boston-based Northeastern University to become the coed Mills College at Northeastern University, the West Coast anchor for Northeastern's global operations.[48] Many just went out of business.

When in March 2015 the Sweet Briar College board of trustees announced that the college would close that summer owing to "insurmountable financial difficulties," it looked like Sweet Briar, located in the foothills of the Blue Ridge Mountains in Virginia, would join the ranks of other small, rural women's colleges that slid off the cliff. The announcement came as a shock to many. The president, James F. Jones Jr., had been in place less than a year. As one news outlet reported, "The move is unusual in that Sweet Briar still has a meaningful endowment, regional accreditation and some well-respected programs," including one of only two women's college engineering programs in the nation. President Jones said that there were intersecting challenges that he and the board felt just could not be overcome: declining interest from young women in attending a small women's college like Sweet Briar, declining interest in liberal arts colleges, and declining interest in attending colleges in rural areas. In recent years college administrators had quietly explored the possibility of a merger without success and considered the possibility of attracting male students to the Sweet Briar campus, but that also seemed unlikely to be successful, without a major investment in athletic facilities, housing, and probably a name change. Even then, being in a rural location would still be a disadvantage. So the decision was made to close before it was too late to do it in an orderly fashion. Paul G. Rice, the board chair, declared, "We have moral and legal obligations to our students and faculties and to our staff and to our alumnae. If you take up this decision too late, you won't be able to meet those obligations. People will carve up what's left—it will not be orderly, nor fair."[49]

Was it a courageous decision or a premature one? Higher education experts were divided in their opinions. Judith Shapiro, president of the Teagle Foundation and former president of Barnard College, said, "I happen to think that what Sweet Briar did was gutsy and principled. They decided that they could not continue to provide the kind of education that accorded with their mission and values. And they wanted to face the fact— and that was responsible." Vassar College President Catherine Bond Hill, an economist who studies higher education, commented, "I wish they had experimented and innovated to address the challenges, demonstrating to others how to productively make education available at a lower cost."[50]

The Sweet Briar alumnae were united in their view—their college could not close! Using social media to mobilize, they quickly began raising money, formed a nonprofit called Saving Sweet Briar Inc., and went to court to block the closure. By early June 2015, the alumnae group had raised $16 million in pledges and had a court injunction. Faculty members and a group of students had also filed lawsuits to prevent closure. By June 22, 2015, a mediated agreement had been reached with all the parties involved. Lawyers from all sides presented a signed settlement agreement, which the Bedford County Circuit Judge James W. Updike Jr. quickly accepted. Saving Sweet Briar Inc. would provide $12 million to keep the school operating for at least one more year. President Jones and at least thirteen members of the board would resign, eighteen new board members would be selected, and a new president would be appointed. That person would be the past president of nearby Bridgewater College, Phillip Stone.[51]

During his sixteen-year tenure at that small liberal arts college, Stone had successfully doubled the enrollment and was well thought of in the region. He brought a great sense of optimism to the Sweet Briar task, saying in a statement, "After seeing the extraordinary passion, courage and strength of the Sweet Briar alumnae, I feel privileged to be asked to join their heroic efforts to save this great college....My commitment is not merely to keep the college open for the coming school year but to help it embark on a path for its next 100 years!"[52] Notwithstanding his enthusiasm and optimism, President Stone had to start virtually from scratch. Everyone had been sent home—there were no students, no faculty, no staff. He rehired any of the previous faculty and staff who would come back. Within six weeks, he had an administrative team in place, restored key programs, and had hired enough faculty to teach the 240 students who showed up in the fall. Most of them were returning students who were glad to be back, but total enrollment was still less than half that of the year before (561). Only twenty-four of them were first-year students.[53]

It would have been impossible to keep the college financially solvent with so few entering students, but continuing alumnae donations kept the college going. Their passion helped inspire a new generation of young women to enroll. One young woman explained that she chose Sweet Briar because of the strong sense of community, the beautiful campus, the engineering program where she wouldn't be "the only girl in a class full of boys," and the alumnae. "I saw what the alumnae did....That made me want to be connected with them, also. I couldn't imagine going somewhere else."[54] The alums not only gave money; they volunteered their labor—doing recruiting and fundraising, organizing campus cleanups, providing pro bono consulting services, and more.

During that first year under Phillip Stone's leadership, the college received thirteen hundred applications—the highest number in fifty years. "In just one year, the women's college has gone from doomed to resurrected but on life support, to something that is still fragile. But the school is strong enough that its leaders talk confidently about long-range plans and successes that they feel could become a national model for sustaining both liberal arts and women's education."[55] After two years, having set the college on a path to recovery, Stone stepped down, and in the summer of 2017 Sweet Briar welcomed its new president, Meredith Woo, a former dean of the College of Arts and Sciences at the University of Virginia.

Within three months, President Woo was ready to unveil a two-part strategy for Sweet Briar—a new curricular approach designed by the college's faculty, and a significant tuition reduction. The curricular plan eliminated traditional academic departments and instead created three curricular clusters designed to focus on women's leadership and showcase the college's strengths: its existing engineering program; its thirty-two-hundred-acre campus, ideal for environmental studies; and its connection to the Virginia Center for the Creative Arts and artists' colony, which leases land from the college. The three curricular clusters would be (1) engineering, science, and technology, (2) environment and sustainability, and (3) creativity and the arts. A core curriculum highlighting leadership would include ten to twelve "integrated courses" such as design thinking, leadership, and persuasion and making decisions in a data-driven world. A new academic calendar would pair with the curricular changes. Instead of two fifteen-week semesters, the new plan would be a three-week term, a pair of twelve-week terms, followed by another three-week term, designed to give more flexibility for internships, research, and study-abroad experiences. The tuition reduction would shift from a high sticker price that was deeply discounted to a much lower price, equivalent to in-state tuition at the University of Virginia. The cost for tuition, room and board, and fees would go from $50,000 in 2017–2018 to $34,000, still with the promise of need-based aid for those who qualified.[56]

About the new plan, Woo said, "We decided to double down on the liberal arts.... The context in which learning takes place could be much more relevant and contemporary.... It's difficult to prepare students for the 21st century when you're insisting on a curriculum that dates back to the medieval period." Regarding the pricing change, "Our intention is to make it very transparent to American families that we are as affordable as some of the flagship public universities in the commonwealth."[57] It was the fall of 2017, and they were up to 335 students. By March 2018, the third anniversary of the announced closing, $44 million had been raised.[58]

Higher ed institutions are notoriously slow to make changes, particularly relating to the curriculum. Faculty seldom are quick to agree, particularly if the elimination of departments or programs is involved. But a near-death experience is motivating. "We now have a campus where everybody's kind of united and ready to roll up their sleeves," Woo said.[59] As the plan was implemented, however, tough choices had to be made by the administration. In mid-December 2017, approximately a dozen faculty members (among a full-time faculty of sixty-eight) were notified that their positions were being eliminated as of June 2018 because of the restructuring. Given the still low enrollment, the student-faculty ratio was 4 to 1, completely unsustainable.[60] The reductions were difficult but necessary. Looking back on that time, Woo said, "We were in a situation where we had no choice. Either we do this, or we weren't going to be viable."[61]

Then the pandemic hit. For many schools in Sweet Briar's enrollment position, the impact of the pandemic would be the last straw. But Sweet Briar was able to leverage its huge campus as a safe place to be in school. There were lots of extra dorm rooms—everyone could have a room of her own, no sharing required. The small classes and wide-open spaces meant social distancing would be easy. As the *Washington Post* headline read in the summer of 2020, "This college is tiny and isolated. For some students during the pandemic, that sounds perfect." At a time when COVID-19 was driving down enrollments at other schools, Sweet Briar hit its target of 150 new students and opened to in-person instruction in the fall of 2020.[62]

After seven years of innovative leadership (2017–2024), President Woo decided she was ready to pass the leadership baton to someone else. Enrollment had grown to almost five hundred, with the expectation that they would keep inching toward six hundred or more. Reflecting on her experience, Woo said,

> Joining Sweet Briar, deciding to lead it, was an act of faith. Sweet Briar is not just a very fine college, but it has served for a very long time as a significant cultural, social and economic pillar for Central Virginia.... There is a role to be fulfilled by all-women's institutions, which provide truly empowering education for that small segment of women that could really benefit from it. And so, for me, it was a belief that this institution has the right backbone, right building blocks, and that with some creativity and imagination, we can make it work.[63]

Woo passed her baton to Mary Pope Maybank Hutson, the fourteenth president of Sweet Briar and the first alumna to serve in the role. A professional fundraiser, President Hutson was one of the alums who spearheaded the fundraising effort that saved the college from the brink in 2015. She had been leading the development effort at Sweet Briar ever since. It was a smooth handoff.[64]

The story of Sweet Briar College is an inspiring one. With enrollment not yet at its optimal level, the college is still a vulnerable institution, but for a decade its backers have defied the odds they were given by the college leaders who said in 2015 they could not continue. What made the difference? Yes, the alumnae raised the money needed. But new leadership brought new optimism and new vision, a reimagining of what the college could be in the twenty-first century. In the words of Nathan Grawe, they proved themselves to be an "agile college," one with a new sense of possibility. Grawe writes, "With student-centered, mission-focused reform, institutions may emerge, not untouched by demographic change but reshaped into better, if sometimes leaner, versions of themselves, prepared to serve students for generations to come."[65] That is what Sweet Briar intends to be.

Saving Sweet Briar required some reinvention. It also required courageous, committed, and persistent leadership. We will see another dramatic example of dynamic leadership and reinvention in response to enrollment challenges and changing societal pressures in Chapter 10. Dealing with changing demographics and federal policy snafus at a time when costs are rising and questions of affordability grow more urgent is difficult for every leader, causing problems that are sometimes insurmountable. But as these examples attest, hard does not always mean impossible.

Chapter Eight

College Finances 101

It's easy to understand why college leaders would worry about declining enrollments. For most institutions, the tuition and fees the students pay are essential to the college's operating budget. But many people, even those who work at the institution, don't really understand college financing. During my thirteen years as president of Spelman College, I gave a "State of the College" presentation to the faculty and staff at least once a year, often once a semester, to make sure everyone was well informed about the financial health of the institution and understood what we all needed to do collectively to ensure the college's continuing strength. Particularly during the years of the Great Recession, when salary increases were frozen or slow in coming, it was important to me that everyone understood our budget.

Where was our money coming from? How was it being spent? What were the sources of our budgetary pressures? And the opportunities for budgetary solutions? Such questions are fundamental to every organizational enterprise, yet the funding of colleges and universities has unique elements that everyone should understand. That is the purpose of this chapter—to pull back the curtain on how higher education is financed and provide a primer for readers of all backgrounds on how colleges are funded and what that means for students and their families.

The typical college or university budget is made up of three or four main sources of revenue: what students pay, what donors give, what the endowment earns (if there is one), and what the state or federal government provides (if the school is eligible for such funds). Whether an institution is public or private, the most important of these sources is what students pay—tuition and fees, and, if students live on campus, room and board. Institutions that rely on what students pay to provide more than 60 percent of their total revenue are referred to as "tuition-dependent."[1] Every institution needs that revenue, but those tuition-dependent institutions are especially vulnerable when there are significant drops in enrollment, because that revenue makes up such a large proportion of the budget.

WHAT STUDENTS *REALLY* PAY

It is important to note that the number that matters most to the institution's budget is not what the "sticker price" is but what students on average are actually paying. As we saw with the University of Lynchburg, discussed in Chapter 7, the 2023–2024 sticker price was $50,450, but the average student was only paying $24,000, representing a discount of approximately 52 percent. According to a recent survey of 325 private, nonprofit colleges conducted by the National Association of College and University Business Officers (NACUBO), the University of Lynchburg's discount was right in line with what many other private colleges were doing. NACUBO found the average tuition discount rate among its survey respondents in the 2023–2024 school year was approximately 56 percent for first-year students and averaged 52 percent for all undergraduate students, noting that these are the highest discount rates since they started keeping track in

1994. To state it differently, "for every dollar of undergraduate tuition and fees colleges could have charged in 2023–2024, schools awarded roughly 56 cents of aid to freshmen and 52 cents to all undergraduates who received institutional grant aid."[2] What students actually pay after all the institutional aid has been accounted for is called "net tuition revenue." Even if the enrollment number stays the same or even increases, if the net tuition revenue *declines* because the tuition is being so heavily discounted, the outcome is the same—financial trouble—particularly if the institution does not have other significant sources of income to offset the loss of tuition revenue.

While tuition discounting is common, not every college or university distributes its institutional aid in the same way. The wealthiest and most selective institutions admit students without consideration of their ability to pay, known as "need-blind" admissions, promising to meet the full demonstrated financial need (as shown on the FAFSA) to make attendance possible. Those students whose families are wealthy enough that they don't have any demonstrated financial need will be expected to pay the full price, or something very close to it. Other less selective schools, in an effort to draw more students, will offer non-need-based aid (called "merit" aid) as the University of Lynchburg did, providing scholarships to some or all of their students, independent of financial need, thereby incentivizing their enrollment. Many schools have a hybrid approach, as Spelman College did—prioritizing need-based financial aid for the students with demonstrated financial need, but also providing merit aid to a subset of students with especially strong academic profiles or other special characteristics. As was the case at Spelman, merit awards may come from scholarship funds established by donors with very specific criteria (e.g., for students majoring in a particular subject, from a particular region, or with a demonstrated interest in community service). Such criteria limit how and to whom the funds can be awarded. Recipients of these specially designated scholarships might also have demonstrated need, but the specific scholarship criteria determine their eligibility. No matter how an institution chooses to award its aid, the NACUBO study found that, on average, nine out of ten first-year students received some level of financial aid in 2023–2024.[3]

WHAT DONORS GIVE

Another revenue source is what donors give each year for current expenses—often called the annual fund—though how much institutions can raise each year varies widely from institution to institution. Institutions with many wealthy graduates will likely raise more money each year than schools with a smaller, less affluent donor base, for example. In general, fiscal year 2023 was an especially good fundraising year for higher education—more than $58 billion was given to support colleges and universities across the nation. Approximately 65 percent of that amount came from entities such as foundations, corporations, and donor-advised funds. Gifts from individuals declined.[4] Annual alumni giving has traditionally been the bedrock of an institution's fundraising efforts, but alum support has been part of the individual gift decline. One recent survey of alumni donors indicated that 24 percent made a recent gift of less than $100, while only 3 percent had made a gift of $10,000 or more. At 46 percent, Princeton University had the highest percentage of alumni giving for the 2022–2023 academic year. The national average of alumni giving across all institutions was only 8 percent.[5] During my tenure as president of Spelman College, I found a concerted and consistent focus on increasing alum support could yield great results. We saw our annual alumnae giving rise steadily, from a low of 13 percent at the start of my presidency in 2002 to a high of 41 percent in 2014. "Every woman, every year!" became our slogan for encouraging alums to make a yearly gift to the college, not just during their reunion years. Those annual gifts—large or small—made a meaningful difference.

Some of the gifts that donors provide are not intended for current use but instead are expected to be invested and preserved for future use, for generations to come. Some portion of the interest earned from those investments can be used each year in accordance with the donor's instructions, but the bulk of the invested funds are left unspent so they can continue to grow over time. Those invested funds are joined with other similar gifts to become part of what is known as an institution's endowment.

WHAT THE ENDOWMENT EARNS

What the endowment earns—if there is one—is another major source of revenue. An endowment can be thought of as a large cash reserve made up of many individual funds—those large gifts that were made by donors to the institution, often designated for particular purposes such as scholarships, or to support faculty positions, innovative academic programs, the campus library, or the art museum, with the promise of the institution to invest the donations in such a way as to preserve, and ideally increase, the gift's useful value in perpetuity. These many gifts have been aggregated and invested over generations, in some cases growing into endowments valued in billions of dollars. To keep the promise of preserving the principal, only a portion of the endowment total (usually between 4 and 5 percent) will be spent annually. If the investments earned more than 5 percent in a given year (a minimum of 8 percent is the usual target), the additional earnings are retained in the fund, increasing its size. If the investments take a loss and the endowment decreases in value, the institution can still take the usual percentage draw, with the expectation that careful investing will yield more years of gains than losses. Most institutions have spending policies designed to smooth out the investment ups and downs and ensure consistent levels of funding from year to year, as well as the growth of the fund needed to stay ahead of inflation and maintain intergenerational purchasing power for the future. Monitoring the investment professionals who manage the endowment is one of the important fiduciary tasks of the institution's board of trustees.[6]

Though many state flagship universities, such as the University of Michigan or the University of Virginia, have multibillion-dollar endowments, small public regional institutions are likely to have very small endowments (under $50 million), if they have any at all.[7] Endowments are more often associated with private nonprofit colleges and universities like Harvard University. Harvard is the wealthiest university in the world, with an endowment valued in 2024 at almost $51 billion.[8] A 5 percent draw of an endowment that size is approximately $2.5 billion, one of the reasons that Harvard can afford, among other things, a very generous financial aid program. In 2023–2024, the cost of attendance at Harvard was $80,263, but the average cost for a student with need-based aid was $15,210.[9] Families with incomes below $85,000 are not expected to pay anything toward the cost of their child's education. In 2024, roughly 24 percent of Harvard students came from families that had total incomes less than $85,000.[10] The deep tuition discount is affordable for Harvard because of its extraordinarily large endowment.

Of course, the typical endowment is much lower than the one Harvard has. According to an annual study conducted by NACUBO in partnership with the Commonfund Institute, in fiscal year 2023 (July 1, 2022, to June 30, 2023), the 688 institutions that participated in the study represented a total of $839.1 billion in endowment assets. The institutions ranged from those with endowments under $50 million to those with assets over $5 billion. The median endowment size was $209.1 million. Almost one-third of the institutions had endowments of $100 million or less.[11] In 2024 there were eighty-two private nonprofit colleges or universities and fifty-three public universities with endowments of $1 billion or more. Among the fifteen richest institutions, the endowment average was close to $22 billion.[12] For most institutions, the endowments generated about 11 percent of the institutions' annual expenses. However, the institutions with $1 billion or more relied on their endowments to cover 17 percent or more of their annual operating costs.[13] Having that additional income, even though there may be donor restrictions on how it is used, can be very helpful during periods of enrollment uncertainty.

There is one caveat: If an institution is endowment-dependent and there is an unusual event like the collapse of the financial markets in 2008, the sudden drop in endowment value could wreak havoc on even the wealthiest institution's budgets. In December 2008, Harvard's president Drew Faust notified the deans that the endowment had lost 22 percent of its value since September and further losses were expected, perhaps a decline of as much as 30 percent by the end of the fiscal year. Harvard uses its endowment to cover about 35 percent of its operating budget, and some of its schools rely on endowment income to cover more than 50 percent of their operating costs. A 30 percent loss in value would mean budgets would have to be cut.[14] In an unusual turn of events, those schools with small or no endowments may have been less disrupted by the financial turbulence.

Another concern for highly endowed institutions is the threat of taxation. During the first Trump presidential term, the Tax Reform Act of 2014 included a provision to tax the endowment earnings of those institutions that enrolled at least five hundred students and had at least $500,000 in endowment assets per full-time student. The wealthiest institutions far exceed that. For example, as of June 30, 2023, Princeton University's endowment was valued at $33.4 billion, equivalent to $4 million per enrolled student.[15] Though the tax rate was only 1.4 percent, and in 2023 only fifty-six institutions were required to pay the tax, it set a precedent of taxation that was a departure from the long-standing principle that nonprofit organizations should be exempt from such taxation because they provide valuable benefits to society. In the case of colleges and universities, not only do endowment funds support the operations of the institution, but, on average, at least half the endowment income is used to support student financial aid.[16]

At the time of the bill's passing, many higher education leaders expressed concern that the idea of endowment taxation might spread. Republican Representative Bradley Byrne of Alabama, a former chancellor of a community college system, wrote in opposition to the bill, "While the impact of the excise tax on college endowments may be small today, I worry about future growth and expansion of this misguided tax on higher education.... We should all be looking for ways to increase access to higher education, and endowments play a very important role in funding scholarships, student aid, and important research initiatives."[17]

Representative Byrne's comment about the future was prescient, as at this writing the idea of a much larger tax is being discussed by the second Trump administration. In 2024, while serving as the Republican senator from Ohio, J. D. Vance proposed a bill to increase the endowment tax to a whopping 35 percent. A tax of that magnitude could cost each of the wealthiest institutions as much as $250 million per year. It is not yet known if Trump will embrace an increase of that size, but he has expressed support for raising the tax. Other proposals have included tax rates between 14 and 21 percent.[18] The impact could be devastating for college budgets while yielding only a small benefit to federal revenues. The large annual tax that institutions would be required to pay "would drain their endowments over time and result in massive cuts in their operating budgets. The enormous financial hit would deteriorate the educational opportunities they offer. Yet the tax collected would still only reflect 0.13 percent of the federal budget."[19]

Despite the particular risks associated with large endowments, every institution wants to see its endowment grow, particularly so the school can increase scholarship support for its students. That is especially true at institutions that enroll significant numbers of low-income students. Those institutions are *not* the ones with the biggest endowments. Though Pell Grant recipients make up approximately 30 percent of the total undergraduate population, they are not evenly distributed across the higher education landscape. They are most likely to attend community colleges or regional public universities, as well as for-profit colleges. At these types of institutions, more than 50 percent of the students are Pell Grant recipients. Ironically, among the most selective (and typically best-endowed) colleges and universities, Pell-eligible students represent less than 20 percent of the student body. In a report on the enrollment of Pell Grant recipients at selective colleges, scholars Anthony P. Carnevale and Martin Van Der Werf of the Georgetown University Center on Education and the Workforce noted, "Just as colleges are stratified by race, they are stratified by class.... [For example], 38 elite colleges had more students from the families in the top 1 percent of incomes (more than $630,000 per year) than from families in the bottom 60 percent of incomes (less than $65,000 per year)."[20]

The limited access that low-income students have to the best-resourced institutions has implications for educational outcomes. As reported by Carnevale and Van Der Werf, "the open-access colleges that low-income students are most likely to attend have the lowest graduation rates (49%), while the selective colleges that wealthy students are most likely to attend have the highest graduation rates (82%)." Pell Grant recipients are most likely to start their college journey at a two-year community college, yet only 12 percent of students who start at a community college will complete a bachelor's degree within six years. However, more than half (57 percent) of those who start at a four-year college or university will earn a bachelor's degree within six years.[21]

Where students enroll first matters. For Black Pell Grant recipients, choosing a four-year HBCU rather than a two-year college significantly increases the likelihood of degree completion. Although they make up less than 3 percent of all postsecondary institutions, HBCUs account for 8 percent of Black undergraduate enrollment and 13 percent of all bachelor's degrees earned by Black students and nearly one-fourth of all bachelor's degrees earned by Black students in science, technology, engineering, and mathematics (STEM). "Recent research indicates that HBCUs provide more access to higher education for lower-income students than other institutions and foster greater upward mobility than most U.S. colleges: about 30% of HBCU students will move up at least two income quintiles from their parents by age 30 . . . nearly double that of non-HBCUs, where only 18% will do so."[22]

On average, 70 percent of the students attending HBCUs are Pell-eligible. Unfortunately, most HBCUs have endowments too small to meet the financial aid needs of their students, the consequence of inequities in both public and private funding experienced since their founding in the nineteenth and early twentieth centuries. As of 2022, only two had surpassed the $500 million mark—Howard University, founded in 1867, and Spelman College, founded in 1881.[23] Most HBCU endowments are below $100 million, which puts the institutions in a very challenging financial position, particularly if they are private (approximately half are), as private institutions typically receive little if any funding from state governments.[24] As noted in the research report *Investing in Change: A Call to Action for Strengthening Private HBCU Endowments*, private HBCUs have a multipronged financial challenge—they charge lower tuition rates, receive fewer philanthropic gifts, and enroll a higher percentage of students with significant need for financial aid, yet they operate without state funding and, in most cases, with small endowments.[25]

The combination of small endowments and a large pool of students with a high need for financial aid creates a real dilemma for both the students and the institutions. On the one hand, as noted earlier, research shows that students who graduate from HBCUs often experience more favorable life outcomes than their peers who do not. On the other hand, the limited availability of institutional aid means they or their families must take on more debt to achieve their educational goals. According to a 2021 report of the Century Fund, "High student and parent borrowing for attending HBCUs has been one of the unfortunate impacts of the underfunding of Black colleges combined with the low wealth of Black families and communities." The Century Fund estimated that to solve the problem—creating HBCU endowments large enough to offer sufficient financial aid to eliminate the need for student and parent debt—would require an investment of $53 billion.[26]

The encouraging news for HBCU leaders and their students is that philanthropic interest in HBCUs grew in response to the wave of antiracist sentiment that followed the 2020 death of George Floyd, an African American man whose callous murder by a White police officer was captured on cell phone video, sparking civil rights protests around the world.[27] The most striking example is that of multibillionaire MacKenzie Scott, who donated $560 million, distributed to twenty-three HBCUs in the year following Floyd's murder. She also funded twenty-two community colleges with donations totaling $429 million, noting that she was eager to support those institutions "successfully educating students who come from communities that have been chronically underserved."[28] Her multimillion-dollar donations were unusual in that they came with no strings attached, allowing the college leaders to determine what the best use of the funds would be. A majority used a large portion of the funding to increase their endowments.[29] Other eight- and nine-figure gifts from donors such as Reed Hastings, cofounder of Netflix, and his wife, Patty Quillin, made headlines, though the gifts were not as widely distributed across multiple institutions as Scott's donations were.[30] A historic HBCU gift came to Spelman College in January 2024 when longtime member of the Spelman board of trustees Ronda Stryker and her husband William Johnston made a $100 million gift, $75 million of which was designated for endowed scholarships. It was noted to be the largest ever single gift to an HBCU.[31] Despite these record-setting gifts, HBCUs are still far behind in the accumulation of institutional wealth and support, reflecting generations of underinvestment. As one commentator observed, "It will take decades of Scott-style giving for HBCUs to recover what has been lost in time, compound interest, and impact over generations."[32]

THE LAND GRANT INSTITUTIONS

Approximately half (fifty) of HBCUs are public institutions, and as with all public higher ed institutions, state funding provides another important source of revenue. But for generations the pattern of funding between the traditionally White public institutions and public HBCUs was highly inequitable, as the history of land grant state institutions clearly illustrates. The Morrill Act, named after Senator Justin Morrill of Vermont, was passed in 1862 for the purpose of expanding educational opportunity to working people in largely rural communities, establishing state institutions to "focus on the agricultural and mechanical arts, without excluding other scientific and classical studies," in contrast to the more narrowly focused classical curriculum of private colleges of that time.[33] Morrill proposed that the federal government give states large tracts of federal land (most of which had been taken from Indigenous tribes), which states could then sell to others, using the proceeds for the "perpetual endowment" of at least one college in each state. Known as "land grant" institutions, many well-known state universities today were founded as the result of the 1862 Morrill Act. The list includes Penn State, Michigan State, Purdue, Rutgers, Ohio State, Texas A&M, the University of Florida, the University of Georgia, Auburn University, Clemson University, and many others. In total, there are fifty-seven "1862" universities.[34]

By 1890, the success of such colleges was evident; they were "enrolling more students than non-land-grant colleges were and expanding the college-going population."[35] However, most states excluded Black students, though that was not Morrill's intent. In the face of growing demand for expansion of the program, the Second Morrill Act was passed in 1890, with the specific condition that the federal funds could not be used to support an institution that discriminated based on race or sex. However, states could, if they chose, satisfy the government's condition of nondiscrimination by establishing "separate but equal" land grant colleges for Black students. Some states, like Iowa, chose to admit Black students (George Washington Carver was the first admitted in 1891). However, the former Confederate and border states made the segregated choice, establishing what are known as the "1890" land grant HBCUs, of which there are nineteen today.[36]

Though distinctly separate, the funding was never equal. While the law mandated states to establish a "just and equitable division" of monies between the 1862 and 1890 universities, ambiguity in the legislative language created a loophole that states would use to send a much greater share of appropriations to the White land grant institutions, leaving Black land grant institutions barely enough to function.[37] The disparities were extreme. In 1914 Senator Wesley Jones, representing the state of Washington, brought the funding differences to the attention of his Senate colleagues, using the state of Georgia as his most telling example. At that time, the Whites-only University of Georgia (UGA) had 423 students, and the HBCU land grant institution, Savannah State College, had 568 students.[38] Though Savannah State had more students, it received *far* less in state support. In total, Savannah State received $24,667, with $8,000 of that from the federal land grant program, while UGA received more than ten times as much—$249,656, including more than $50,000 from the federal program. In response, Sen. Albert B. Cummins of Iowa asked Jones with astonishment, "Does that mean that they were trying to teach 500 colored students on $24,000 and 400 white students on $240,000, in round numbers? That seems to me a very startling disparity."[39]

It *was* a startling disparity, and Senator Jones argued that states should be required to report how they spent the land grant funding, thereby allowing the federal government to see if the states had complied with the "equal" requirement that was legally mandated. Southern senators objected, and the 1914 bill aimed at addressing the inequity did not pass.

It was not until the passage of the 2018 Farm Bill, more than one hundred years later, that states would be required to report their land grant spending.[40]

In 1887, Congress determined that land grant universities needed a steady flow of federal funds to support the nation's need for agricultural research. The Hatch Act of 1887 provided those federal appropriations, with the requirement that funds had to be matched dollar for dollar from a nonfederal source—typically the state. All states provided the matching funds to the 1862 (White) land grant institutions, but the 1890 schools were not included. A program for the 1890 schools to receive regular federal funding was not established until 1967, *eighty* years later. More federal funding for land grant institutions was authorized by the Smith-Lever Act in 1914, again requiring 100 percent matching funds from the states. To date, all states provide the matching funds for the 1862 institutions, but again the 1890 institutions were excluded and did not gain access to routine federal funding for extension programs (or any matching state funds) until 1977 under the National Agricultural Research, Extension, and Teaching Policy Act.[41]

Not surprisingly, the differential state and federal support over many decades has created a significant wealth gap between the 1862 and the 1890 institutions. According to a 2020 analysis conducted by *Forbes*, the average endowment of the eighteen 1862 land grant institutions located in the same southern states as 1890 institutions was $1.9 billion. At the HBCU land grant institutions, the average endowment was $34 million. In Georgia the comparison is especially stark. Fort Valley State University (designated Georgia's land grant HBCU in 1947) had an endowment of $6.6 million, as compared to the University of Georgia's 2020 endowment total of $1.3 billion.[42]

In 2023, the Biden administration did an assessment of the state land grant funding disparities, just for the thirty-three-year period from 1987 (the earliest year for which comprehensive data were available) through

2020. It was the first time the federal government had attempted to quantify the degree to which the nineteen historically Black land grant institutions had been underfunded by their state legislatures. Only two states—Ohio and Delaware—were found to have equitably funded their three HBCU land grant institutions during that period (two in Ohio, one in Delaware). (The research did not address potential funding disparities prior to 1987.) The remaining sixteen historically Black land grant universities—one in each of sixteen states—had been underfunded by their states by almost $13 billion collectively. Individual states had funding gaps ranging from $172 million in Kentucky to approximately $2 billion or more (i.e., Florida, North Carolina, and Tennessee).[43] One of the most egregious examples was not in the distant past but took place in 2020 with the severe underfunding of North Carolina Agricultural and Technical State University (known as North Carolina A&T) in Greensboro. With 11,700 students, it is one of the largest HBCUs in the country. According to the analysis done by Forbes, "the single worst instance of annual underfunding for any school was in 2020, when the North Carolina legislature appropriated A&T $95 million, *$8,200 less per student* than the $16,400 per student it gave to NC State."[44]

On September 18, 2023, Education Secretary Miguel Cardona and Agriculture Secretary Tom Vilsack sent joint letters to the governors of Alabama, Arkansas, Florida, Georgia, Kentucky, Louisiana, Maryland, Mississippi, Missouri, North Carolina, Oklahoma, South Carolina, Tennessee, Texas, Virginia, and West Virginia, highlighting just how much the Black land grant institutions in their state were owed because of the underpayments from 1987 to 2020 and exhorting the governors to take steps to fix the problem.[45] Beyond "naming and shaming" the states that had been most discriminatory in their funding, it was unclear what enforcement powers the secretaries of education and agriculture had to enact change at the state level. But there had already been successful lawsuits brought against states for their history of underfunding HBCUs, the governors were reminded. For example, in 2021, after nearly fifteen years of litigation in a lawsuit brought by the Coalition for Equity and Excellence in Maryland Higher Education (a group of Maryland HBCU graduates who sued the state in 2006), the state of Maryland agreed to a $577 million settlement for inequitable funding of its HBCU land-grant, the University of Maryland Eastern Shore, as well as three other HBCUs in the state—Morgan State University, Coppin State University, and Bowie State University.[46] In their joint letter, Cardona and Vilsack reminded the governors of the risk of similar "burdensome and costly litigation" and invited their cooperation in developing "a plan of action to make [their state's] institution whole after decades of being underfunded."[47]

As of 2020–2021, the historically White 1862 land grant institutions enrolled approximately 1.8 million students, but only 6 percent were Black, and only 22 percent were Pell Grant recipients. Relative to their size, the historically Black 1890 institutions were providing much more access to educational opportunity. Of the more than 117,000 students enrolled, 75 percent were Black and 57 percent were Pell Grant recipients.[48] The 1862 and 1890 institutions have a shared mission of teaching, research, and service on behalf of their states but clearly have not received anything resembling an "equal" investment to help them do it, to the detriment of some of their states' most disadvantaged students.

No discussion of land grant institutions would be complete without mentioning the third category of such institutions—the 1994 land-grants. Ironically it was the sale of previously held Indigenous lands that fueled the land grant movement in 1862, but it was not until 1994 that Congress authorized the creation of twenty-nine land grant tribal colleges and universities (TCUs), established by the Equity in Educational Land-Grant Status Act of 1994, introduced by Senator Jeff Bingaman of New Mexico. As of 2024, thirty-five tribal colleges had been chartered to "meet the immediate and unique needs of Indian Country."[49] TCUs enroll nearly twenty-eight thousand full- and part-time students, but they also serve as a hub for community education, with more than one hundred thousand community members participating on a yearly basis. The TCUs are clearly still in an early stage of development relative to the 1862 and 1890 institutions, and like the HBCUs their progress has been hampered by inadequate funding, almost all of which comes from the federal government. Unlike the 1862 and 1890 institutions, TCUs, which were founded and chartered by their respective American Indian tribes, receive little or no support from the states where they are located, primarily because of the complex history and special legal relationship between the tribes and the federal government. That unique government-to-government relationship entails "more than 400 treaties, several Supreme Court decisions, prior congressional action, and the ceding of more than 1 billion acres of land to the federal government."[50] Consequently, even though there are non–Native American students attending TCUs, the states typically do not provide any enrollment-based funding.

As of 2024, the thirty-five accredited TCUs, serving students from more than 250 federally recognized Indian tribes, operated more than ninety campuses and sites in fifteen states, mostly located on or near reservations in the Southwest or Great Plains region of the United States. American Indian and Alaska Natives have the lowest college enrollment rate of any racial group (26 percent) and a high poverty rate.[51] One-third of Native American families are living in poverty, with a median income of $23,000 a year.[52] Like many HBCUs, TCUs are constrained to keep tuition costs as low as possible to meet the needs of their target population, a challenging task with limited tuition revenue, few if any endowment resources, and little or no access to state funding.

THE IMPACT OF STATE AND FEDERAL FUNDING

As we can see in the case of land grant institutions, state funding has been an important revenue source for many public institutions, but not equitably so. Even at the predominantly White public institutions that have been advantaged over the decades by discriminatory state allocations, state funding has ebbed and flowed with the economic and political tide. When a college education is perceived as a public good, benefiting the local community and the larger society in which graduates live, work, and vote, that perception translates into larger state investments. When it is perceived as a private good—primarily benefiting the recipient, not the community—the expectation is that the individual should bear the cost burden rather than the state. In *The Agile College: How Institutions Successfully Navigate Demographic Change*, Nathan Grawe summarized the thirty-year pattern of this ebb and flow:

> In the 1990 and early 2000s, families paid for only 30% of a public higher education. Then, in the wake of recession, public support pulled back and the family share rose to 36%. After economic recovery, equilibrium at this higher level was established until the Great Recession, when state appropriations fell again and the family share rose to 47% in 2012. Since that time, the families' share has once again been stable, but the pattern is established: in times of financial hardship, higher education is treated less and less like a public good.[53]

The post-pandemic years from 2022 to 2024 were good ones for state university funding, with public higher ed funding growing in most states. State support for higher education in fiscal year 2024 reached $126.5 billion, a 10.2 percent increase over 2023. It was the third year in a row that state spending for higher education exceeded $100 billion and represented an average 36.5 percent increase over the previous five years.[54] That growth in funding helped reduce the cost share for families. In 2024, however, there were still twenty-one states where public university students bore more than half the share of college cost. Despite the good news of recent increases in state funding of higher education, there is still a looming threat. Net tuition revenue at public institutions declined by 3.3 percent in 2023, the steepest decline since 1980. Full-time enrollment fell in 2023 by 0.5 percent from 2022, and was 12 percent below its peak in 2011. In those states where the size of the appropriation is calculated on a per-student basis, a drop in enrollment represents a double whammy—a loss in tuition revenue and a loss in state funding.[55]

According to data from the Organization for Economic Cooperation and Development (OECD), which tracks educational attainment among its thirty-eight member countries, the percentage of twenty-five to thirty-four-year-olds with a postsecondary degree increased in the United States by 13 percentage points between 2000 and 2022, reaching 51 percent, placing the US above the OECD average of 47 percent, but not by much. While the United States once had the most highly educated population in the world, by 2022 the US trailed behind eleven countries: South Korea (70 percent with a postsecondary degree), Canada (67 percent), Japan (66 percent), Ireland (63 percent), Luxembourg (60 percent), Lithuania (58 percent), the United Kingdom (58 percent), Norway (56 percent), the Netherlands (56 percent), Australia (56 percent), and Sweden (52 percent).[56] Kevin Reilly, former president of the University of Wisconsin system, warned, "[This decline] is not a trend we can tolerate if we're going to continue to be competitive in a global knowledge economy. More and more of our people are going to have to be competent at higher and higher levels of knowledge and skills. We're really damaging the future of our competitiveness, and I would argue, even our security."[57]

Clearly it is in the national interest for the federal government to invest in the higher education of its citizenry, and to some extent it does. However, unlike the states that direct most of their higher education appropriations to support the general operations of public colleges and universities, the federal government mainly supports higher education by providing financial assistance to individuals (i.e., Pell Grants, education benefits for veterans, work-study subsidies, and various federal loan programs) *and* by funding research projects at higher education institutions. The federal government is the largest funder of scientific research and development in the United States.[58]

The partnership between the federal government and the nation's leading research universities dates back to the end of World War II. Vannever Bush, a physicist and electrical engineer, served as head of the Office of Scientific Research and Development and adviser to President Harry Truman during the war. In 1945, as the war came to a close, he wrote a very influential report, *Science, the Endless Frontier*, which called for significant federal investment in basic scientific research through universities. Bush argued that the pioneering American spirit associated with the frontier and westward expansion of the nineteenth century could be reinvigorated in the twentieth century with a national focus on scientific exploration. As his report title implied, "science was the appropriate and endless frontier."[59]

The implementation of this idea of federally funded scientific research was the development of the system we know today, one of competitive grants awarded to university researchers who submitted proposals for peer review and were then selected to carry out government-funded projects. In the late nineteenth century, the federal government had been building its own research infrastructure—its own labs, agencies, and researchers. But partnering with universities that had already made the investment in the scientists and the research facilities would not only be an efficient use of resources; a university-based research enterprise would also create teaching opportunities for the next generation of scientists. As education historian John Thelin explained, "The competitive research grants advocated by Bush... were the genesis of what became the permanent support mechanism for a small number of powerful, well-funded research universities. These were the program and policy structures that would define large-scale academic scientific research for decades to come."[60] The research partnership between the federal government and universities that grew from

Bush's manifesto became the foundation for virtually every major scientific and technological advancement—from space travel to the internet to medical breakthroughs—that the United States has produced since that time.[61]

Fast forward to 2022, when academic institutions spent approximately $98 billion on research and development. In keeping with the research partnership Bush envisioned, federal funding paid for 55 percent of that cost—about $54 billion. The rest came from varied sources: the institutions' own funds (largely from endowment earnings) covered 25 percent, companies (biomedical corporations, for example) supported 6 percent, foundation grants funded 6 percent, state appropriations funded 5 percent, and 3 percent came from other miscellaneous sources. But a lot of those federal dollars were concentrated in just a few universities. Thirty universities accounted for 42 percent of the higher education total spent on research and development, with Johns Hopkins University leading the pack with a research investment of $3.4 billion. Sixteen of the top thirty were public (e.g., the University of California San Francisco, the University of Michigan, the University of Washington), and fourteen were private (e.g., the University of Pennsylvania, Duke University, Stanford, and Harvard).[62] Not surprisingly, these are also well-endowed institutions. Having resources to invest in research infrastructure makes an institution more competitive in seeking federal grants, which in turn creates more revenue for the institution.

Exactly how does that work? When a grant is awarded to an institution, the institution receives the "direct costs" of doing the project (money for the researcher's salary, stipends for graduate students, the equipment and supplies, and any necessary travel). It also receives "facilities and administrative costs," often referred to as "indirect costs," the purpose of which is to reimburse the institution for the cost of things that are not specific to any particular project but are a necessary part of the research environment (e.g., constructing and maintaining research facilities, the cost of utilities, technology infrastructure, accounting staff, and hazardous waste removal). These are things that the university has already spent money on; the indirect cost reimbursement rate helps offset the expense that the university has incurred and is incurring to maintain a strong research infrastructure. Institutions negotiate with a designated federal agency what the reimbursement rate should be, based on the particulars of their campus and an analysis of their actual cost history. Consequently, not every campus has the same rate. Once negotiated, the agreement is usually good for three years, and the same rate is applied to every federal grant the university has.[63]

Among the thirty institutions with the most research funding, the indirect rate ranges from 52 percent to as high as 69 percent; the average is 59 percent.[64] As an example, at an indirect cost rate of 59 percent, if the direct costs of the grant add up to $100,000, added to the grant request would be 59 percent of that, or $59,000. The total grant request would then be the direct and indirect cost added together—$159,000. If the grant is awarded, $100,000 would go to the researcher to cover the specific costs of the project, and the $59,000 would be used by the institution to help pay for the research infrastructure. Those institutions that invest in building research capacity but are not successful in obtaining federal grants must bear the financial burden of their investment without the benefit of indirect cost reimbursement.

The research partnership between the federal government and research-intensive universities (often referred to as R-1 institutions) was for many years a relatively smooth and predictable one. However, new uncertainties threatened to rupture the relationship when in January 2025, on the second day of his new term as president, Donald Trump ordered federal health agencies under the administration of the Department of Health and Human Services (HHS), including the National Institutes of Health (NIH), to cease all external communications and to suspend all travel, meetings, and hiring until further notice (but for at least a minimum of ten days—until February 1). The announcement came just as the January grant-review panels were scheduled to meet to discuss funding proposals.[65] This peer review process is a well-established step in determining the distribution of the billions of dollars—$60 billion in 2022—that the federal government invests in scientific research done on university campuses.[66] In 2023, more than half that amount—$33 billion—came through HHS, and NIH in particular.[67] Interrupting the review process effectively meant interrupting the flow of funding for an unknown period of time.

Even a short delay could prove quite disruptive to researchers doing time-sensitive clinical research. NIH money funds basic and applied research in medicine and many other disciplines, "with grants for work in biology, chemistry, physics, engineering, social sciences, and social work, among other fields. Take that all away, all at once, and a mess of different kinds of researchers are left uncertain as to whether and how long their labs, personnel, and experiments can be sustained."[68] As discussed earlier, the indirect costs associated with these grants also help pay for the university infrastructure; those funds literally keep universities running.

Perhaps most unsettling for university personnel was the unexpected nature of the interruption, without explanation. If it happened once, could it happen again? As journalist Ian Bogost observed, "The fact that this support has been switched off so haphazardly, for reasons that remain unclear, and despite the scope of troubles it creates, suggests that higher ed will be profoundly vulnerable during the second Trump era."

That vulnerability was made even clearer when in the second week of his presidency Trump attempted to stop the distribution of trillions of dollars in federal grants and loans (not including payments to individuals such as Social Security, Medicare, food stamps, and student loans) until his staff could ensure that the recipients were in compliance with his executive orders, such as removing protections from transgender people and ending DEI efforts. In this instance, higher education was not alone in its confusion and dismay. Local governments, K–12 public schools, and nonprofit organizations of all kinds were left struggling to figure out what programs would be affected by the pause, which even if brief could lead to layoffs and interruption of public services. Just before the order was to take effect, a federal judge blocked it temporarily. The legality of Trump's action was in question because the funds had already been authorized by Congress and approved by the previous administration and therefore presumably could not be withheld by presidential fiat.[69] At this writing, the legal question had not yet been adjudicated. However, the incident revealed Trump's willingness to disrupt business as usual, underscoring the higher education community's feelings of uncertainty about the security of federal funding.

Particularly vulnerable to such funding interruptions are underfunded HBCUs. A small percentage of federal higher education funding is provided for the support of "special mission" institutions such as military academies and land grant institutions (as previously discussed). The Higher Education Act of 1965 authorized funding for HBCUs to help "strengthen their academic, administrative, and fiscal capabilities." While the funding level is based on enrollment size, in 2023 ninety-eight HBCUs received discretionary grants, for which they must apply annually, of approximately $4 million and mandatory awards of approximately $800,000 each.[70] In the 1980s, recognition was given to a category of institutions known as Hispanic-serving institutions (HSIs), defined by the federal government as "non-profit degree-granting institutions with full-time equivalent (FTE) undergraduate Hispanic student enrollment of at least 25%." In 2023, there were approximately six hundred institutions that met that definition and were eligible to compete for federal grants intended to strengthen their capacity to meet the educational needs of Hispanic students.[71] That year approximately one hundred of them received grants ranging in size from $400,000 to $600,000.[72] Similar grant programs intended to improve academic programs and resources exist for other nonprofit higher education institutions that serve at least 50 percent low-income students (as measured by Pell Grant eligibility), have lower core operational expenses than average for institutions of their type, and serve a significant number of underrepresented students of color from one or more of the following groups: Asian and Pacific Islander (10 percent or more), Alaska Native (20 percent or more), Native Hawaiian (10 percent or more), Native American (nontribal, 10 percent or more), and non-HBCU predominantly Black institutions (40 percent or more).[73]

WHERE DOES ALL THE MONEY GO?
A PRESIDENT'S VIEW

What students pay, what donors give, what the endowment earns, what states and the federal government provide—together it all adds up to a lot! Clearly it takes a lot of money to run a college or university. Where does all that money go? Whether it concerns a large, complex university with graduate and professional schools in a major city or a small liberal arts college in a rural community, most of the money pays for two things: people and places. The people are the employees: faculty, staff, and administrators. The places are the buildings and grounds—the classrooms, offices, research labs, art studios and performance spaces, the library, residence halls, and playing fields, and all the equipment and technology infrastructure needed to make them usable. When I was president of Spelman College, 66 percent of our budget covered the cost of employee salaries and benefits. When I served as interim president of Mount Holyoke College, the percentage was about the same. It's typical. Because employee compensation is such a big chunk of the budget, it is very difficult to make any increases in compensation without also increasing revenue.

How can you increase revenue? You can either increase tuition, increase philanthropic giving, grow your endowment through investing, and/or, if eligible, get more money from the state or the federal government, or find some new unrelated revenue source—sell some land or lease some property, perhaps. Ideally, you would be able to do enough of a few of those things that it would not be necessary to increase the cost to students, but the one source that is most readily within your control is what students pay. If your employees expect salaries to keep up with the cost of living, it is no wonder that tuition costs rise each year.

Is the need for more revenue the result of wasteful spending, inefficiencies, or bad fiscal management? Maybe sometimes. But in their book, *Why Does College Cost So Much?*, economists Robert Archibald and David H. Feldman make a convincing argument that the main driver of college costs is the fact that in the current US economy, "all industries that use highly educated labor have had to pay more for their major service providers: college professors, physicians, dentists, lawyers"; and the technology that those highly educated professionals need to do their work has increased the cost of the service they provide as well. Just as patients expect their doctors to use up-to-date diagnostic machines, students expect to learn in modern labs and to have access to cutting-edge technology.[74] If these costs rise, and the number of students in each classroom increases, the cost can be spread across more people. But if the student population stays approximately the same year after year or gets smaller to provide more engagement with the professor, the cost to each student must go up. When prices rise but productivity does not (the number of students being taught did not increase), economists call it "cost disease."[75] Archibald and Feldman conclude that "technological change and innovation itself are major forces behind rising education costs. Costs rise rapidly in higher education and in other related industries because of the kind of industries they are and because of the economic environment in which they operate."[76] Archibald and Feldman's explanation resonates with my experience as the person trying to make the numbers work year after year as president.

For the thirteen years I served as president of Spelman College, the vice president for business and administration (the CFO) and I agreed on one very important thing: Our budget would always be balanced. We would present a balanced budget to the board for its approval, and we would make whatever adjustments we needed to make during the year to ensure the budget was indeed balanced when the year ended. A budget surplus could be a nice year-end surprise, but we would do whatever was needed to be sure we did not end the year in the hole. Deficit spending is the road to ruin for so many institutions. We were not going down that road. But balancing a college budget is not an easy task.

Like many families sitting at their kitchen tables trying to pay the bills, most colleges always have more needs and wants than there is money to pay for them. So, the leader must decide what is most needed to deliver the high-quality educational experience the students expect and that they have been promised. Just as anyone's personal record of spending is a reflection of their priorities and values, so is the institutional budget. Are we investing in the classroom experience? Faculty development? The research labs? Financial aid? Student academic support? Athletics? Managing the deferred maintenance on century-old buildings?

Over the years I have read opinion pieces that suggest that colleges and university leaders cavalierly raise their prices "because they can," but that was not my experience. We knew that any price increase would mean some students might not be able to return to school the next semester, unless we could also offset the increase with additional financial aid. Any tuition increase was a calculated risk for student retention. In November of each year, department heads were asked to prepare their budgets for the next academic year, usually with the instruction not to expect any routine budget increases. Any budget increase requests would have to be vetted with the appropriate division head (usually the provost or an administrative vice president), who would then bring the request to a president-led budget meeting for review. New budget requests were always received with skepticism. Do we *really* need...? A yes to one request would inevitably mean a no to something else considered at least as important by the person requesting it.

Some people, faculty members among them, point to the rise in high-priced administrative staff as the cause for rising costs, pointing to a newly created dean position or someone with a new vice president title. There is no doubt that such positions, if they have been created, are likely to cost more than a new faculty member would. But sometimes those new people are necessary to support the work of the faculty. A vice president for development—the chief fundraising officer—is an expensive position to fill, but a good one will raise many multiples of that salary on behalf of the institution, providing support for faculty salaries and research infrastructure. A vice president of enrollment management can transform the effective recruitment and retention of the students you want to generate the tuition revenue you need.

Imagine a slew of faculty complaints about sluggish internet speeds and long waits for technology assistance. The problem can be solved with a greater investment in the IT infrastructure, but every new hire means an increase in the administrative budget. The federal government has created new sets of regulations, and managing compliance is becoming a full-time job. Another staff position needed? The wait list at the counseling center is way too long—can we hire another counselor? Is that what they meant when they said there was administrative bloat?

The cost of health insurance has risen exponentially. Can we maintain the same level of benefits for our employees at the higher cost? Yes, we must to remain competitive in the job market, but how will we pay for it? The cost of utilities has risen. The steam plant is aging; when will we be able to replace it? The psychology department has more majors than ever. Students are having trouble getting in to the classes they need. We should hire another professor. Yes, we should, but what about biology? They have a lot of majors, too. Can we afford to hire both? Enrollments are declining in the English department. A faculty member in that department just retired. The department wants to hire a replacement to maintain the curriculum. Should you make that investment if enrollments are declining? Or hire an adjunct lecturer to fill in? Adjuncts are much less expensive than a full-time tenure-track professor, but they are also less likely to have a long-term commitment to the department and its students. Will they even still be here when students need letters of reference or someone to advise a thesis? But can you make the long-term commitment that a tenure-track position represents when you are unsure about future enrollment needs? And what about the risk management committee that says we need to invest in an all-campus alert system? That makes sense, but how much will it cost? What is urgent? What can wait?

And what about the president's compensation? If that president wasn't making so much money, we could hire a whole bunch of people—or so some faculty (in particular) might say. How much is too much for the president to be paid? It is not unreasonable to benchmark salaries and offer fair compensation to the institutional leader, just as we benchmark salaries for faculty and staff and make improvements in compensation when we are too far off the mark. Adequate compensation for a job that we all can agree is very difficult is necessary.

That said, when the *Chronicle of Higher Education* publishes its periodic review of presidential salaries, no one in my circle of presidential friends wants to be the person at the top of the list—nor do you want to be at the bottom of it. In a world where gender pay equity has not yet been achieved, as a woman I did not want to see male colleagues at peer institutions being paid more than I was, especially when I knew I was outperforming them in measurable ways. Savvy boards of trustees will pay attention to those kinds of situations and correct them as needed. Leadership matters, and presidential transitions are always disruptive. Retaining an effective leader is one of a board's most important responsibilities, and wise boards will protect the investment they have made in selecting the right leader for their institution. Money, however, is not always the best reward for mission-driven leaders, and when such leaders decide it is time to pass the presidential baton, money will not keep them.

Are some campuses spending money unnecessarily on luxury items like fancy rock-climbing walls and "lazy rivers" winding through the campus in an effort to attract more students? Not as many as you might think. The 2024 closing of Birmingham-Southern College, founded in 1856 and long considered one of the best liberal arts colleges in Alabama, is a cautionary tale about that kind of spending. Years of deficit spending and millions of dollars of debt incurred to enhance the campus, including the construction of a man-made lake, doomed the school.[77] Most public and private institutional leaders are striving to remain as affordable as they can, because they know there is a limit to what students and their families can pay. And there is a real enrollment cliff waiting if they can't make their numbers work.

The funding of higher education is complex, but what should be clear now is that schools rely on more than just tuition and fees to cover the cost of delivering the education they provide. What students pay is just one piece of the funding puzzle. It is common to hear enrollment professionals (and college presidents) talk about the importance of recruiting more "full pay" students. The term "full pay" is used to refer to the student whose family can pay the sticker price without financial assistance. But actually, there is no such thing as a "full pay" student. *Every* student's education is subsidized by the institution to some degree. The tuition and fees, room and board do not cover the full cost of the education—the revenue from the endowment, the fundraising, the state or the federal government fills the gap.

If you earned a college degree, no matter where or when you went to school, no matter how hard you struggled to pay the bills, I can assure you that you did not pay for it all by yourself. Whether you had a partial scholarship, or a full scholarship, or no scholarship at all, you were *still* the recipient of an investment made possible by so many people who came before you—women and men who made contributions to the school, who invested in the faculty, who helped pay for the buildings, who paid state and federal taxes, and who gave every year to the annual fund to keep the institution strong. *Everyone's* degree has been subsidized to some extent by the generosity and investment of people, past and present, who wanted to ensure the continued availability of educational opportunity. They believed it was an investment worth making, and that the societal return on investment has been and would continue to be undeniable.

At Spelman, to illustrate the return on investment, I often shared the story of Dovey Johnson Roundtree, a member of the Spelman class of 1938. In her autobiography, *Justice Older Than the Law*, she recounted her struggle to finish her college degree during the years of the Great Depression. In her senior year, she needed $300 to stay in school, an amount way beyond her grasp. Without family members who could help her, or a bank to give her a loan, her dream of completing her Spelman education was slipping away. Just when she was about to give up hope, something wonderful happened. In a tremendous act of generosity, one of her professors, a woman with resources, stepped forward to pay her tuition bill. Her benefactor asked for only one thing in return—that Dovey pay it forward. That act of kindness changed Dovey's life, but it also changed ours. Because of that gift, Dovey was able to graduate and went on to become one of the first Black women to serve in the US armed forces, paving the way for others, and later became a prominent civil rights attorney. Her work laid the legal foundation for the successful challenge to school segregation in the Supreme Court case *Brown v. Board of Education*, expanding opportunity for Black children across the nation.[78]

Who is the next Dovey Johnson Roundtree? The next student ready to break down barriers and change the course of history? As a nation, we cannot afford to let the next generation's talent and leadership go undeveloped. A college education is undoubtedly a private benefit to the recipient, but it is also immeasurably a public good. We need public policy to help address the problem of educational access and affordability. In the meantime, for those of us who have already benefited from the generosity of others, our obligation should be clear. *Pay it forward!* The future we save may truly be our own.

CHAPTER NINE

"THE TIME HAS NOW COME"

The End of Affirmative Action

On June 29, 2023, the Supreme Court issued its ruling in two cases: *Students for Fair Admissions, Inc. v. President and Fellows of Harvard College*, and *Students for Fair Admissions, Inc. v. the University of North Carolina*, effectively eliminating race-based affirmative action programs across the higher education landscape. In doing so, the court reversed forty-five years of legal precedent and undermined more than sixty years of effort to diversify the classrooms of the most elite colleges and universities.

Since the 1960s, most predominantly White higher education institutions have sought to increase the racial diversity of their student population, and slowly but surely, most have. Particularly at elite, highly selective institutions, affirmative action programs have been an important strategic tool. In the late 1990s, two former Ivy League presidents, William Bowen (Princeton) and Derek Bok (Harvard), conducted a groundbreaking study of the academic, employment, and personal histories of more than forty-five thousand students of all racial backgrounds who attended twenty-eight of the most academically selective institutions in America, in order to understand the impact of those admissions decisions not only on the individuals but on the communities they entered after graduation, measuring professional success as well as civic engagement. They published their findings in the 1998 landmark book *The Shape of the River: Long-Term Consequences of Considering Race in College and University Admissions.*

Their research questions were rooted in the understanding that "American colleges and universities have long prided themselves on educating individuals—who will be good citizens—effective participants and respected leaders in civic as well as commercial activities."[1] Serving as a pipeline of leadership talent for the nation is a core part of the educational mission of these elite institutions. Bowen and Bok acknowledged that the active recruitment of students of color, particularly Black students, that began in the 1960s was not only because of the educational benefits associated with diverse learning environments, but "it was also inspired by the recognition that the country had a pressing need for well-educated black and Hispanic men and women who could assume leadership roles in their communities and in every facet of national life."[2]

Their massive dataset provided a wealth of empirical evidence that the decades of affirmative action outreach efforts beginning in the 1960s had been an unqualified success in terms of graduation outcomes and the achievement of high levels of both professional success and civic engagement among recipients of that outreach. "If, at the end of the day," they wrote, "the question is whether the most selective colleges and universities have succeeded in educating sizable numbers of minority students who have achieved considerable success and seem likely in time to occupy positions of leadership throughout society, we have no problem in answering the question. Absolutely."[3] In the closing paragraph of their data-rich book, they concluded that "academically selective colleges and universities have been highly successful in using race-sensitive admissions policies to advance educational goals important to them and societal goals important to everyone."[4]

Yet, twenty-five years later, the political winds had shifted enough to raise the question of whether those societal goals were still as important to everyone as Bowen and Bok might have thought. For some, the 2008 election of Barack Obama—the first Black president of the United States and a graduate of two elite institutions, Columbia University (1983) and Harvard Law School (1991)—was the embodiment of the success Bowen and Bok predicted. For some people, it signaled (falsely) that America had overcome its history of racial discrimination and thus affirmative action programs were no longer warranted.[5] In 2023, with a conservative majority on the Supreme Court, the decision declaring race-conscious affirmative action programs unconstitutional was not unanticipated, but disturbing nonetheless. What could institutional leaders do to continue to achieve their stated diversity goals? Now that the court's action had effectively ended race-conscious admissions, what would the educational and societal impact be?

To understand the full meaning and impact of the 2023 Supreme Court decision, it is important to know something of its historical roots. When President Lyndon B. Johnson gave the commencement speech at Howard University on June 4, 1965, he made the case for what came to be known as affirmative action. "You do not take a person who, for years, has been hobbled by chains and liberate him, bring him up to the starting line of a race and then say, 'you are free to compete with all the others,' and still justly believe that you have been completely fair," Johnson said.[6] Three months later, Johnson signed Executive Order 11246, requiring federal contractors to "take affirmative action to ensure that applicants are employed, and that employees are treated during employment without regard to their race, color, religion, sex, or national origin." By law, contractors were obligated to make a "good faith effort" to use procedures that would result in equal employment opportunity for historically disadvantaged groups. The groups initially targeted for this "affirmative action" were White women, and men and women of color (specifically defined by the federal government as American Indian / Alaska Natives, Asian or Pacific Islanders, Blacks, and Hispanics).[7] The executive order had as its goal equal employment opportunity, but in practice, because of continuing patterns of discrimination, that goal could not be reached without positive steps—affirmative action—to create that equality of opportunity.[8] Though focused on employment, the executive order laid the groundwork for selective colleges and universities to take their own positive steps—affirmative action—to begin to admit more students of color.

Jerome Karabel, author of *The Chosen: The Hidden History of Admission and Exclusion at Harvard, Yale, and Princeton*, wrote in a *New York Times* guest essay,

The need for change was undeniable: As late as 1960, just 15 students (0.5 percent) of the combined entering classes at Harvard, Yale and Princeton were Black. At the UCLA School of Medicine, which, like other University of California institutions, followed an official policy of colorblindness, not a single Black person was among the 764 students who received M.D.s from 1955 to 1968. Among people in the legal profession as a whole, including graduates of the five historically Black law schools, fewer than 1 percent were Black in 1968. Affirmative action offered a way to take into account far-reaching differences in personal circumstances and to begin to right a historic wrong.[9]

The 1968 assassination of Rev. Dr. Martin Luther King Jr. proved to be a catalytic moment for change, followed as it was by uprisings in cities across the nation and student protests.[10] Civil rights leaders pressed colleges to admit more Black students, and four weeks after King's assassination, the dean of admissions at Harvard announced a commitment to increase the number of Black students there. Indeed, the following year the number of Black freshmen increased by 76 percent, from 51 in 1968 to 90 in 1969. In an entering class of 1,202 students, those 90 represented 7 percent of the incoming freshmen.[11] Other elite colleges also began increasing their Black enrollments, though on average it was a slow process. For example, a sample of twenty-five selective public and private universities whose Black enrollments averaged 1 percent or less in 1951 had only increased their share of Black undergraduates to approximately 7 percent by 1998, forty-seven years later.[12]

As affirmative action programs spread and became institutionalized in higher education, legal challenges arose, brought by White applicants who alleged they had been denied admission because less qualified students of color had been given preference over them. Though not the first affirmative action case to come before the Supreme Court, the *Regents of the University of California v. Bakke* Supreme Court decision on June 26, 1978, was the case that set the terms of affirmative action programs for the next forty-five years.[13] After being rejected twice by the medical school at the University of California, Davis, Alan Bakke, a White applicant, argued that the school's policy of reserving sixteen out of one hundred available spaces in the entering class for qualified students of color was unfair and violated the Civil Rights Act of 1964. The Supreme Court agreed, ruling that a racial quota system was a violation of the Civil Rights Act and that Alan Bakke had to be admitted. However, Justice Lewis Powell wrote in his opinion that there was a "compelling state interest" in considering the race of applicants, "for diversity adds an essential ingredient to the educational process." Though racial quotas were not permissible, race could be used as a "narrowly tailored factor" in the admissions process.[14] In the *Bakke* case, the court asserted that "the foundational reason for considering race in college admissions— as a remedy for a centuries-long history of racial oppression—had no legal standing" but simultaneously affirmed the educational benefits of diversity as a justification for race-conscious admissions policies.[15]

By the late 1990s, the idea of affirmative action had become in the minds of many White people a symbol of "White disadvantage," or "reverse discrimination," even though all data regarding racial disparities in education, employment, criminal justice, health, wealth, and other measures of well-being showed no evidence of such disadvantage.[16] Still, there were Black people who were critical of affirmative action programs as well, pointing out the stigmatizing nature of being seen as an "affirmative action" admit, routinely having their achievements diminished as a result. In fact, it was Ward Connerly, a successful Black businessman in California, who led the campaign to pass Proposition 209, a ballot initiative to ban state and local governments from using racial and sexual preferences in hiring, contracting, and college admissions. The measure passed with 55 percent of the vote and inspired similar changes in several other states.[17]

On June 23, 2003, twenty-five years after the *Bakke* ruling, two cases involving the University of Michigan were decided by the Supreme Court: *Grutter v. Bollinger* and *Gratz v. Bollinger*. In the *Grutter* case, Barbara Grutter, a White woman who was denied admission to the University of Michigan Law School, argued that race had been used as "a predominant factor" in its admissions process. In a 5–4 ruling, the Supreme Court, consistent with the *Bakke* decision, ruled that diversity on campus was indeed a compelling state interest and race could be considered as one of multiple factors in the admissions decisions. The *Gratz* case involved two White undergraduates who were denied admission to the University of Michigan. The university had been using a point system, automatically assigning twenty points (toward the required one hundred points needed for admission) to underrepresented applicants of color, and the plaintiffs argued the system was unconstitutional. The justices agreed (6–3) that while race could be a factor for consideration, the point system went beyond what was permissible. Together the two cases further refined how race-conscious admissions policies could be implemented.[18]

Justice Sandra Day O'Connor wrote the majority opinion for the *Grutter* case. One oft-quoted sentence stood out: "We expect that 25 years from now, the use of racial preferences will no longer be necessary to further the interest approved today."[19] Her message was clear. Race-conscious admissions policies should be a temporary strategy, not a permanent solution—but O'Connor would later say that her reference to twenty-five years was an estimation, not a deadline.[20]

The *Fisher v. University of Texas* cases, decided on June 23, 2016, involved the admission policy known as the Top Ten Percent Plan used by the state to diversify its student body. Because of a high degree of racial and ethnic school segregation in Texas, the state could admit the top 10 percent of every Texas high school and be reasonably certain that the incoming student population would reflect the state's racial and ethnic diversity. If there were still available spaces, several factors, including race, would be considered for additional admits. Abigail Fisher was not in the top 10 percent and was not admitted during the second part of that process. She argued that any consideration of race was unconstitutional. Once again, the Supreme Court ruled that the University of Texas met the standard set by previous rulings and allowed it to continue its practice.[21]

The 2023 cases against Harvard University and the University of North Carolina at Chapel Hill were different from previous affirmative action cases, which all involved White plaintiffs, as these two cases were focused on Asian American applicants. To quickly summarize, Harvard University was accused of discriminating against Asian Americans in its admissions process. Similarly, the University of North Carolina at Chapel Hill was accused of giving preference to Black, Hispanic, and Native American applicants to the detriment of White and Asian applicants. Both cases were filed by Students for Fair Admissions (SFFA), an organization led by Edward Blum, an activist best known for his efforts to use legal challenges to eliminate affirmative action policies.[22] The majority of the Supreme Court justices agreed with SFFA that the schools had discriminated against Asian American students who had stronger academic records (higher grades and SAT scores) than any other racial group, including White students. Even though Asian students were almost a third (29 percent) of the entering class at Harvard, more than three times their representation in the US population (7 percent), SFFA argued that more of them should have been admitted, given the strength of their academics. Harvard used several criteria for rating students in its admissions process—academic, extracurricular, athletic, personal, and overall. SFFA argued that Harvard consistently rated Asian American applicants lower than applicants from other racial/ethnic groups in the more subjective "personal characteristics" criteria in an effort to lower their admissions rates, not unlike how such criteria had been used in the 1920s and 1930s to impose quotas on Jewish applicants.[23]

Harvard argued that its holistic approach to evaluating applicants, looking at not only grade point averages and test scores but also extracurricular activities, personal essays, letters of recommendation, and interviews to get a full picture of who the student was and what unique qualities they might contribute, was not being used in a discriminatory way. Unlike so many higher education institutions worried about the enrollment cliff, Harvard and elite schools like it *can* be choosy. In its defense, Harvard noted that each entering class has approximately sixteen hundred spaces, and it receives thousands of applicants who have similar academic profiles. For example, for the class of 2019 (the cohort under review in the court case), it had thirty-five thousand applications, and thirty-seven hundred of them had perfect math SAT scores, twenty-seven hundred had perfect verbal SAT scores, and more than eight thousand had perfect grade point averages.[24] If Harvard wanted to fill every seat with a student with perfect SATs and a perfect GPA, it could—but it didn't want to.

One could argue that creating a dynamic mix of incoming students who will learn from one another as well as their professors is like building an orchestra. You don't want sixteen hundred flute players; you need all kinds of instrumentalists—percussionists, horn players, string musicians, keyboardists—and maybe some singers for your chorale, and others with a talent for conducting, maybe some composers, and others who just like to hang out with musicians and be part of the audience. Every orchestra needs an audience—and some folks managing the behind-the-scenes operations. Can bias creep in when selecting an orchestra? Yes, it can. But an individual's rejection by itself is not evidence that it has. As higher education researcher Julie Park succinctly stated, "Just because students have great grades, test scores, accomplishments, and experiences doesn't mean that anyone is guaranteed admission into Harvard or any other highly selective institution."[25] Any student who is denied admission and points to someone they think was "less qualified" as having taken "their spot" rarely knows enough about the other person and their talents to make that claim.

Lower courts (the district court and the court of appeals) had concluded, based on detailed findings of fact entered after a three-week trial, that Harvard had not violated the law, was not overemphasizing race in its admissions decisions, and was not discriminating against Asian American applicants.[26] Nevertheless, the conservative majority of the Supreme Court sided with SFFA and ruled that the race-conscious admissions policies that had been allowed in previous high court rulings had expired in the eyes of the court and were no longer permissible.[27] Wrote Chief Justice John Roberts, "We have permitted race-based admissions only within the confines of narrow restrictions.... University programs must comply with strict scrutiny, they may never use race as a stereotype or negative, and—at some point—they must end.... College admissions are zero-sum. A benefit provided to some applicants but not to others necessarily advantages the former group at the expense of the latter."[28] Referring back to Justice O'Connor's 2003 comment that race-conscious admissions programs would eventually have to end, "That time has now come," Justice Roberts said.[29] Time was up.

Justice Sonia Sotomayor, joined by Justices Elena Kagan and Ketanji Brown Jackson, was fierce in her critique of the ruling. She wrote,

> Today, this Court stands in the way and rolls back decades of precedent and momentous progress. It holds that race can no longer be used in a limited way in college admissions to achieve such critical benefits. In so holding, the Court cements a superficial rule of colorblindness as a constitutional principle in an endemically segregated society where race has always mattered and continues to matter. The Court subverts the constitutional guarantee of equal protection by further entrenching racial inequality in education, the very foundation of our democratic government and pluralistic society. Because the Court's opinion is not grounded in law or fact and contravenes the vision of equality embodied in the Fourteenth Amendment, I dissent.[30]

Though the ruling disallowed the systematic consideration of race in the admissions process, Chief Justice Roberts did leave open the opportunity for individual students to reference their racial group membership as part of their personal essays if they chose. He wrote, "Nothing in this opinion should be construed as prohibiting universities from considering an applicant's discussion of how race affected his or her life, be it through discrimination, inspiration, or otherwise."[31]

As noted by the dissenting judges, the Supreme Court ruling was momentous in its symbolic importance, claiming an era of colorblindness that does not yet exist. Just as President Johnson's 1965 executive order had ripple effects across society, not just in federal contracts, so would this ruling. What kind of ripple effects would it have beyond the borders of college admissions? Edward Blum, the anti-affirmative-action activist, indicated that similar lawsuits in more areas of American life would be coming. In an interview with the *New York Times*, he said, "I think employment is one area that will garner greater attention....I also think some of the things that we associate with higher education—internships, scholarships, certain research grants—those need to be revisited if they have been race-exclusive."[32] Harvard law professor Randall Kennedy predicted, "We're going to be fighting about this for the next 30 years."[33] But, as it related to student access, how much difference did it really make?

One surprising answer might be "not that much." A 2017 study found that there had been a significant decline in affirmative action in the two decades between 1994 and 2014. In 1994 60 percent of selective colleges indicated that they had a race-conscious admissions process. By 2014 only 35 percent did. The change was most dramatic among the less selective schools in that cohort—in that subsector, the percentage dropped from 46 percent to 18 percent. Among the subset of most-selective schools the change was much smaller, from 93 percent in 1994 to 88 percent in 2014. In effect, "affirmative action went from being a common policy across all sorts of campuses to more of a niche practice particular to brand-name, wealthy colleges."[34]

To be clear, the Supreme Court case was not about access to community colleges, the regionals, or even some of those national institutions. The majority of Black, Latinx, and White students attend schools that are not selective—where 75 percent or more of all applicants are admitted.[35] The case was about access to elite institutions and what they represent—lifelong access to the influential social networks that lead to money, power, and other rarefied opportunities.

Leadership positions in the United States are held disproportionately by graduates of a group of 12 highly selective, private "Ivy-Plus" colleges—the eight colleges in the Ivy League, the University of Chicago, Duke, MIT, and Stanford. Less than one percent of Americans attend these 12 colleges, yet they account for 13.4% of those in the top 0.1% of the income distribution, a quarter of U.S.

Senators, half of all Rhodes scholars, and three-fourths of Supreme Court justices appointed in the last half-century.[36]

A 2023 study by Opportunity Insights, a group of economists based at Harvard who study inequality, found that attending an "Ivy-Plus" college not only increased a student's predicted chances of earning in the top 1 percent by 60 percent (as compared to attending a highly selective public institution), it also doubled the likelihood of attending a top graduate school, and tripled the likelihood of working for "prestigious employers in medicine, research, law, finance and other fields."[37] It is easy to see why so many students want to be admitted. Yet the two Supreme Court cases brought by Students for Fair Admissions seemed to be "framing the issue as a zero-sum competition between Asian Americans and other students of color... [which] obscures *the largest beneficiaries of preferential treatment in admissions: wealthy and connected white students.*"[38]

In fact, a team of researchers, using data publicly released about Harvard's admissions, examined the preferences Harvard gave for a group they call ALDCs—athletes, legacies (family members of alumni), those on the dean's interest list (children of donors or potential donors), and children of faculty and staff. Most ALDC applicants are White and from higher-income households. Among White students admitted to Harvard, over 43 percent were ALDCs. Among admits who were African American, Asian American, or Hispanic, fewer than 16 percent of each group were ALDCs. The researchers found that admission preferences for ALDC applicants were quite significant. For example, they reported that "a white non-ALDC with a 10 percent chance of admission would see a five-fold increase in admissions likelihood if they were a legacy; more than a seven-fold increase if they were on the dean's interest list; and that they would be admitted with near certainty if they were a recruited athlete."[39] Stating it differently, as *New York Times* editor Spencer Bokat-Lindell does, without the special treatment, three-quarters of White ALDCs would have been rejected, more than the number of Black and Latinx admits combined.[40]

The Opportunity Insights study, even more far-reaching in its data analysis, asked this two-part research question: "Do highly selective colleges perpetuate privilege across generations and, conversely, could these colleges diversify America's leaders by changing their admissions policies?" Focusing their analysis on the twelve Ivy-Plus schools, the answer to both parts was a resounding YES.[41] Using a "big data" approach, researchers Raj Chetty, David Deming, and John Friedman did their analysis with amazing and completely unprecedented access to enormous amounts of information about income and college attendance from 1999 to 2015. "The researchers could see, for nearly all college students in the United States from 1999 to 2015, where they applied and attended, the SAT or ACT scores and whether they received a federal Pell grant, as well as their parents' income tax records, allowing them to analyze attendance by earnings in more detail than any previous research."[42] They also gained access to internal admissions data at some elite colleges (with the promise of anonymity), allowing them to see how applicants had been rated by admissions staff, focusing on the years 2011–2015. In all cases, the data were anonymized.

Echoing the Harvard ALDC study, their analysis found that students from the top 1 percent of the income distribution were nearly twice as likely to be admitted as students from low- or middle-income families with comparable SAT/ACT scores. The preference for wealthy students was amplified by legacy admission policies. A high-income legacy applicant was five times more likely to be admitted to an Ivy-Plus college than similarly qualified peers without a legacy connection to the institution, with the notable exception of MIT, which did not (and still does not) give preferences to legacy applicants.[43] As previously noted, nonacademic ratings are part of the admissions criteria, including factors such as extracurricular

activities, leadership qualities, and other personal traits. The researchers also found that students who attended private high schools (a factor
also correlating with family income) received much higher nonacademic
ratings than peers with similar academic qualifications from public high
schools.

Being a recruited athlete also correlated with being from a high-
income family. That may come as a surprise to some readers, because
the popular public image is of a low-income basketball or football player
making it to a selective college with an athletic scholarship. However, according to data from the National Center for Health Statistics, participation in organized sports increases with family income. Only 31 percent of
children at or below the federal poverty level are involved, as compared to
70 percent of children with a family income at 400 percent or more above
the federal poverty level.[44] University of Michigan professor of education
Michael Bastedo, who studies college admissions, observed, "The enrollment leaders know athletes tend to be wealthier, so it's a win-win." Nearly
13 percent of the admitted students from the top 1 percent were recruited
athletes.[45] By contrast, at highly selective public colleges, wealth was not a
factor in the recruitment of athletes. There was no difference in the share
of recruited athletes across the income distribution.[46]

Even among students of color, the scale is tipped toward affluence.
Richard Kahlenberg, a longtime advocate for a class-conscious approach
to college admissions, noted that "71% of Black, Latinx and Indigenous /
Native American students at Harvard come from college-educated families with incomes above the national median; such students are in roughly
the most advantaged fifth of families of their own race."[47]

So, do highly selective colleges perpetuate privilege across generations? Without a doubt. Could these colleges diversify America's leaders
by changing their admissions policies? Absolutely. The Opportunity Insight researchers wrote, "We conclude that even though they educate a
small share of students overall and therefore cannot change rates of social

mobility by themselves, Ivy-Plus colleges could meaningfully diversify the socioeconomic origins of society's leaders by changing their admission practices." What would they need to do? "Eliminating or adjusting admissions policies that benefit high-income applicants—even stopping short of class-based affirmative action policies that favor lower-income applicants—would increase socioeconomic diversity by a magnitude comparable to the effect of racial preferences on racial diversity."[48] The first place to start would be to eliminate legacy preferences.

Certainly, since the US Supreme Court ruling eliminating race-conscious affirmative action policies in higher education, the glare of a spotlight has been focused on those elite schools with legacy preferences. In July 2023, the US Department of Education opened an investigation to examine allegations that Harvard's practice of giving preference to legacy applicants and relatives of donors discriminates against Black, Latinx, and Asian applicants in favor of less qualified wealthy White applicants.[49] In 2018 a survey of admissions officers indicated that 42 percent of private universities and 6 percent of public colleges said legacy status was a factor in their admissions decisions.[50] However, in 2021, Amherst College became one of the first highly selective schools to abandon the policy, joining MIT, Johns Hopkins University, and the California Institute of Technology along with a few other highly selective schools that long ago opted not to use legacy preferences. Shortly after the 2023 Supreme Court decision, Wesleyan University, Occidental College, Carnegie Mellon University, and the University of Minnesota announced that they would no longer give preferential treatment to legacies. State legislatures in Colorado and Virginia passed laws banning legacy preference at public institutions in those states; Maryland eliminated the practice in both private and public institutions in Maryland. As of this writing, a similar bill was making its way through the California legislative process. Public colleges and universities in California already ban legacy preferences; the new bill would add private institutions in the state to that restriction.

WHAT'S NEXT?

One year after the *Students for Fair Admissions v. Harvard* June 2023 Supreme Court decision, there was considerable curiosity about what the impact of the decision would be on the demographics of the class of 2028, those students who received their admission letters in the spring of 2024. Beginning August 1, 2023, Common App, the organization that administers a universal application used by many students to apply to the colleges of their choice, gave colleges the ability to conceal information about the applicant's racial/ethnic identification. The admissions reviewers would not know which box a student had checked. "Masking the race boxes on the Common App could give universities a measure of plausible deniability—and perhaps some protection from lawsuits," legal experts said.[51]

Of course, as Justice Roberts said, there is nothing that prohibits applicants from discussing their racial/ethnic background as part of an admissions essay. In fact, in the post–Supreme Court decision environment, many colleges have fashioned essay question prompts that might encourage such disclosures. For example, Babson College, a small, selective business-focused undergraduate institution in Wellesley, Massachusetts, introduced a new supplemental essay question that reads, "A defining element of the Babson experience is learning and thriving in an equitable and inclusive community with a wide range of perspectives and interests. Please share something about your background, lived experiences, or viewpoint(s) that speaks to how you will contribute to and learn from Babson's collaborative community." Sarah Lawrence College, a moderately selective national liberal arts college, created an essay prompt by quoting directly from Justice Roberts's decision, asking applicants to discuss how the ruling would affect their college experience.[52]

During the *Students for Fair Admissions v. Harvard* court case, experts were called on to make projections about what would happen to Black and Latinx enrollment if race-conscious admissions practices were discontinued. They all expected it to drop precipitously. David Card, a prominent economist hired as an expert witness for Harvard, developed simulations demonstrating that without consideration of race, Black students would have made up 6 percent of the class of 2019 rather than the 14 percent they were, more than a 50 percent decline. Others projected a decline to about 7 percent of the entering class, the same percentage of Black students that entered Harvard in 1969.[53]

Indeed, drops of that magnitude and greater occurred in California and Michigan after those states banned affirmative action programs in 1998 and 2006, respectively. Black and Latinx enrollment plummeted, and decades later still had not fully recovered. "Despite incredibly valiant, sustained efforts to navigate the realities of a post–affirmative action world, the flagship campuses in California and Michigan have been unsuccessful in enrolling members of marginalized racial groups" to the levels that they had achieved previously. Those Black and Latinx students who are on the campuses talk about their sense of isolation because their numbers are so few, one reason it has been difficult to get students of color to attend.[54]

While history does suggest a drop is likely, what if the numbers don't drop as expected? Or rise as expected? The number of admitted Asian students was expected to go up by as much as 10 percent. Is it possible to imagine that without racial or ethnic identifying information to guide reviewers, they might evaluate a student's portfolio differently, consciously or unconsciously? If the percentages don't change as predicted, will some assume the institution is not in compliance with the law? One expert, Mitchell Chang of UCLA, anticipated that "Harvard will face heightened scrutiny if the racial composition of its admitted class—especially the number of Black students—does not change."[55]

What did happen with the Harvard class of 2028? Harvard received applications from 54,008 students and offered admission to 1,937 of them, an acceptance rate of 3.59 percent.[56] On June 18, 2024, the *Harvard Gazette* announced that 84 percent of them accepted those offers of admission. The class of 2028 was made up of approximately 20 percent first-generation college students, 20 percent Pell Grant recipients, 53 percent women, 47 percent men, thirteen transfer students, nineteen veterans, and twenty-three students on ROTC scholarships. They were from all fifty states and the US territories, with the largest percentage (20 percent) from the Mid-Atlantic region. Just under 17 percent were international citizens, representing ninety-four countries. What Harvard did not announce, breaking with its previous practice, was any information about the racial and ethnic makeup of the class of 2028.[57]

However, once the academic year was underway, Harvard and other elite colleges such as Yale, Princeton, Duke, and MIT released the demographic data for the entering class of 2028, the first to be admitted in the new post–affirmative action context. The results were mixed. In one case, MIT reported a 15 percent drop in the enrollment of Black and Latinx students, as compared to the class of 2027, and a 7 percent increase for Asian Americans, who made up almost 50 percent of entering students.[58] At Harvard the changes were less dramatic. The population of African American students at Harvard dropped from 18 percent to 14 percent, the Asian American percentage remained unchanged at 37 percent, and the Latinx population rose from 14 percent in the class of 2027 to 16 percent in the class of 2028. The Native American student population declined from 2 percent to 1 percent, and the Native Hawaiian / Pacific Islander population remained unchanged at less than 1 percent.[59] At Princeton, Black enrollment dropped very slightly, from 9 percent to 8.9 percent, stayed the same at Yale (14 percent), and went up at Duke, from 12 percent to 13 percent. Conversely, Asian American enrollment dropped from 26 percent to 23.8 percent at Princeton, from 30 percent to 24 percent at Yale, and from 35 percent to 29 percent at Duke. These results clearly took Edward Blum by surprise, and his organization, Students for Fair Admissions, threatened legal action against Yale, Princeton, and Duke. "Based on S.F.F.A.'s extensive experience, your racial numbers are not possible under true neutrality.... You are now on notice. Preserve all potentially relevant documents and communications."[60]

Their suspicions may be unwarranted, experts say. Yale, Duke, and Princeton compete against other schools. Maybe some of their Asian American applicants simply chose to go elsewhere—perhaps among the 7 percent increase at MIT, for example. Or perhaps they are among the growing number of students who declined to identify their race or ethnicity. Among Asian American applicants, there was a 13 percent drop in those who chose to "check the box" identifying their racial category. Those students may well be on the campus but remain uncounted because their box went unchecked.[61] In addition, while the Supreme Court disallowed using race as a categorical screen for applicants, it did allow institutions to consider essays in which applicants might discuss race-related experiences as part of their life story. SFFA implied that they would be looking at the use of those essays as they investigated the schools whose percentages didn't change in the way SFFA predicted.[62]

In their 1998 book, *The Shape of the River*, Bowen and Bok cautioned against a court decision that would interfere with one of a college's fundamental freedoms—to choose its own students. They wrote, "Once prohibitions are put in place, someone has to determine whether they are being respected."[63] Edward Blum and SFFA seem to have claimed that role. One wonders what set of statistics might satisfy Blum. Ironically, it looks like the colorblind advocate is demanding quota-like counting of students. Wrote University of Chicago law professor Sonja Starr, "It's striking that colorblindness advocates, who have long decried a focus on demographic breakdowns, are now the ones watching those breakdowns like hawks. One wonders what diminution of racial diversity they would think sufficient."[64] For his part, Blum said shortly after the Supreme Court decision was rendered, "It is now up to the world of higher education to create fair and equitable admissions policies that do not discriminate on the basis of race.... Each of them now has an institutional responsibility and an individual responsibility. They have their work cut out for them."[65]

Blum's cause has been taken up by the second Trump administration as well. In Section 5 of his executive order "Ending Illegal Discrimination and Restoring Merit-Based Opportunity," Trump instructed the attorney general and the secretary of education to "jointly issue guidance to...all institutions of higher education that receive Federal grants or participate in the Federal student loan assistance program under Title IV of the Higher Education Act...regarding the measures and practices required to comply with Students for Fair Admissions, Inc. v. President and Fellows of Harvard College."[66] At this writing, the "measures and practices" had not yet been identified. Again, one wonders what evidence will satisfy federal watchdogs. However, within the first week of his administration, Trump had certainly made clear his intent to withhold funds from any organization perceived to be noncompliant with his executive orders.

As campus leaders navigate the current political landscape, what *can* they do to ensure forty-five years or more of progress is not lost—to ensure that the environment they create is one that provides the broadly diverse setting needed for a twenty-first-century education and the diverse pipeline of leaders our society needs? They can do what Michael Roth of Wesleyan University did—end legacy preferences. Explaining his decision, President Roth said that legacy status had played a "negligible role" in Wesleyan's admissions process, but the existence of the practice was "a sign of unfairness to the outside world."[67] Some leaders hesitate to take such action, afraid of offending big donors who expected their children or grandchildren to be given preferential status. Roth was making a bet on the egalitarian values of his alumni: "I'm wagering, I guess, that Wesleyan alumni will be proud of that, and they want it to be a place that doesn't give unearned privileges to applicants."[68]

Campus leaders could also reimagine their admissions criteria and how they are measured. Conventional wisdom says that the best predictor of future performance is past performance. Understanding a student's previous academic performance as demonstrated by school grades and performance on a high-stakes exam is not the only way to predict performance. The Posse Foundation has found another way. Founded in 1989, the Posse Foundation has become known as a pipeline of exceptional talent, sending students in groups of ten ("a posse") to selective institutions across the country with whom the foundation has established partnerships. The schools agree to provide a full scholarship and a faculty mentor for each Posse student who enrolls. Posse recruits are selected for their demonstrated leadership strength, and those qualities are in abundant evidence on the campuses where they enroll.

Deborah Bial, the founder of Posse, tells the story of a conversation she had with a young first-generation student of color who struggled with feelings of isolation at his college, where he was one of few who shared his background. He lamented, "I never would have dropped out of college if I had my posse with me." From that conversation, the idea of Posse was born. Don't send just one, send ten—a cohort of students who can support one another on their undergraduate journey, with the financial support and mentoring they need to not just succeed, but excel on campus and beyond.

Posse began in New York City with five students and one partner school, Vanderbilt University. Today Posse recruits students from more than twenty cities across the United States, with program offices in ten recruitment cities: Atlanta, the Bay Area, Boston, Chicago, Houston, Los Angeles, Miami, New Orleans, New York, and Washington. Posse recruits in other cities through its virtual program. Posse also recruits post-9/11 US veterans nationwide for three partner colleges and universities through its veterans program. As of 2024, Posse has identified, trained, and supported more than thirteen thousand students. These students have won over $2 billion in full-tuition four-year scholarships from Posse's partner institutions, which in 2024 numbered sixty-seven.[69]

Potential Posse scholars must be nominated by someone from their school or community organization. Nominees participate in a unique three-part assessment process that includes large-group and individual interviews designed to give students "an opportunity to demonstrate their intrinsic leadership abilities, their skill at working in a team setting, and their motivation and desire to succeed." Called the Dynamic Assessment Process, it has proven to be an extremely effective tool for identifying outstanding young leaders who might be overlooked by traditional admissions criteria but who can excel at selective colleges and universities. Through the interactive process, Posse staff and partner college and university administrators ultimately select a diverse group of ten students— the posse—for each institution. Those nominated students who are not ultimately selected to be part of a posse still have an opportunity to be recruited by one or more of the partner colleges and universities that through their partnership with the Posse Foundation have access to the application profiles of hundreds of Posse finalists. The partner schools benefit from Posse's identification of a diverse pool of exceptional applicants that the schools might not have identified through their traditional recruitment methods.

The Posse approach to talent identification is labor-intensive and expensive, but it works. Posse students graduate at a rate of 90 percent, much higher than the national graduation rate of 64 percent, and typically emerge as leaders on their campuses. Posse scholar cohorts are multiracial in their composition. Fifty-seven percent have been the first in their families to go to college. Robert A. Oden Jr., president emeritus of Carleton College, spoke from his experience as the past president of a partner institution when he said, "I was a professor for most of two decades at Dartmouth College and then the president of Kenyon College and the president of Carleton College. So, I speak with some fair experience about higher education when I say that I think one of the best ideas in higher education in the last quarter of a century is the Posse Program."[70]

The Posse Foundation asserts, "Together with the nation's top institutions of higher education, Posse is building a powerful new leadership network—one that better represents the voices of all Americans."[71] As of this writing, however, the most elite institutions—the Ivy-Plus schools—had not partnered with Posse. What if they chose to do so? Or adapted Posse's interactive assessment process as an innovative way of identifying talent to yield a greater diversity of results? If elite institutions wanted to scale up a Posse approach, they certainly have the resources to do it.

What does it take to interrupt the inequities of the status quo? Courage and imagination. What is the personal cost of doing so? When I was a professor teaching my course on the psychology of racism at Mount Holyoke College, each semester I invited a special guest speaker to my class—Rev. Andrea Ayvazian, a White woman and pastor who had spent decades working against racism in her personal and professional life. My students, most of them White, often wanted to know how her antiracist activism had impacted her personal relationships. Their most frequently asked question was "Did you lose friends?" Her answer was "My friendships changed." She grew away from some people who did not support her in her commitment to living an antiracist life, but connected with many new people who shared her values and became her companions on her learning journey. She felt her life and her friendships had been enriched, not diminished.

When I think of the policy choices leaders of elite institutions need to make to meet the diversity challenge posed by the Opportunity Insight researchers—"Could these colleges diversify America's leaders by changing their admissions policies?"—and operate within the constraints created by the 2023 Supreme Court decision, a question similar to the one my students asked seems relevant: "Will you lose friends (donors)?" The answer might be a version of the one that my guest speaker gave: "My friendships (donors) changed." There will still be donors, but maybe they will be ones who share the meritocratic values the institution wants to model and that the nation needs. Now is the time to find out.

CHAPTER TEN

DISRUPTION AT THE DOOR?

According to a series of Gallup polls, since 2015 there has been a steady decline in the confidence people in the US have in higher education institutions. In 2015, 57 percent of Americans polled expressed a "great deal" or "quite a lot" of confidence in US higher education, and only 10 percent had little or no confidence. By 2024, the number who had a great deal or quite a lot of confidence had dropped to 36 percent, and those with little or no confidence had risen to 32 percent. The greatest loss of confidence occurred among those poll respondents who identified themselves as Republicans. In 2015, 56 percent of Republicans expressed a great deal or quite a lot of confidence, and 11 percent had little or no confidence. In 2024, the numbers had nearly reversed, with only 20 percent feeling confident, and 50 percent having little or no confidence. However, Democrats and independents had also lost confidence by double-digit percentages, down from 68 percent to 56 percent and 48 percent to 35 percent, respectively. Disaggregating the data by other categories—level of education, racial group membership, gender, and age—the results were similar.[1] What is driving this season of discontent?

And what does the loss of confidence mean for the future of higher education? Is higher education an industry ripe for disruption?

For the 36 percent who said they had a great deal or quite a lot of confidence in higher education, it was because they valued education, considered it important to have an educated society, and recognized the job opportunities that come with a college degree. For the 32 percent with little or no confidence, many felt colleges had become too politicized, indoctrinating students and not teaching relevant skills for the job market, as well as being too costly and debt-inducing. In considering the future of higher education, only 31 percent said it was headed in the right direction, and 68 percent believed it was headed in the wrong direction. The Gallup pollsters sounded a warning, concluding, "to the extent these views are held by parents and young adults, it could lead to drops in college applications and enrollment."[2]

What is it that we as a nation want from higher education? In the mid-twentieth century, the answer was multifaceted and focused on the common good. In fact, on July 13, 1946, with the nation still reeling from the carnage of World War II, President Harry Truman created a twenty-eight-member Commission on Higher Education with the charge to examine the purpose of higher education in a democracy and how that purpose might best be fulfilled.[3] The commission identified three paramount goals for higher education: "Education for a fuller realization of democracy in every phase of living; Education directly and explicitly for international understanding and cooperation; and Education for the application of creative imagination and trained intelligence to the solution of social problems."[4] A college education was conceived by the commission as much more than just a ticket to a good job; it was seen as the underpinning of a thriving democratic society. Today the public discourse about the value of a college education seems much more unidimensional.[5] The earlier broad understanding of college as a public good has become greatly overshadowed by the focus on college as a private economic benefit, and it is from that limited perspective that today's consumers often express disappointment.

To be clear, despite the changing public perception, the economic value of a bachelor's degree (as compared to a high school diploma) is still significant. According to the Georgetown University Center for Education and the Workforce, graduates of a four-year college will, on average, earn approximately $1 million more over their lifetime than will high school graduates without a college degree. Though the educational benefit varies by race and gender, "no matter how you cut it, more education pays." Indeed, the difference in earnings between those who go to college and those who don't is increasing, making the completion of a postsecondary degree more valuable than ever.[6]

Independent of college major, completing the degree signals to employers the likelihood that the graduate has desirable traits such as persistence, industriousness, and an aptitude for learning new skills, all of which will contribute to career success. College graduates often have greater access to job opportunities than non–college grads because of participation in job fairs, career services, and student and alumnae social networks. According to the US Bureau of Labor, approximately two-thirds of the thirty fastest-growing occupations in the US through 2032 require a bachelor's degree, giving college graduates continued benefits in the job market. Lower rates of unemployment even during recessions, higher rates of volunteerism in the communities, higher rates of homeownership, higher rates of marriage, lower divorce rates, healthier habits (e.g., not smoking, exercising regularly, wearing seatbelts, visiting the doctor regularly, keeping a healthier weight), and longer life spans are all associated with being a college graduate.[7]

However, these benefits are associated with those who actually do graduate. Those with some college but no degree completion do not reap the same level of benefits and may be at risk for the worst outcome—student debt and no degree. The combination of student debt and no degree is a personal disaster, leaving students worse off than if they had not entered college. The economic benefit that could help repay the debt is not usually forthcoming without the degree in hand. At some institutions, completion rates are disastrously low, fueling the discontent.

College completion rates vary by type of institution. Among four-year institutions, on average, the highest completion rates can be found at private, nonprofit institutions (78 percent), followed by four-year public institutions (69 percent), and the lowest at private, for-profit institutions (46 percent). The low graduation rates at for-profit institutions, along with the high cost and high student debt associated with them, make this option a particularly risky one for low-income students. Researchers at Cornell University have found that attending for-profit colleges causes students to take on more debt and to default at higher rates, on average, compared with similarly selective (low selectivity) public institutions in their communities. It is not because for-profits tend to enroll students from more disadvantaged backgrounds, they concluded. The problem is that "more expensive for-profits lead students to take out more loans, which they then struggle to repay because they're less likely to find jobs, and the jobs they get tend to pay lower wages."[8] Though two-year community colleges also have similar graduation rates (42 percent), the relatively low cost of attendance and the possibility of eventually transferring credits to a four-year institution make them a better, less debt-ridden option for many students who might otherwise consider a for-profit institution.[9]

A 2023 survey conducted by the *Chronicle of Higher Education* echoed some of the themes of the Gallup poll, noting the more negative sentiments of Republicans toward higher education as compared to Democrats. However, in general, they found that Americans still believe in the value of a college degree and would recommend attending college to other people. Yet they were unsure of the quality of the education being provided and skeptical about the positive difference colleges make to the local community and the larger society. College was seen as a benefit to individuals but not necessarily contributing to the greater good.

Even though college was considered a benefit by most respondents, a particularly alarming finding concerned the public's assessment of how well colleges delivered on their core mission of educating students. Only 40 percent said colleges did that work very well, while almost 20 percent said they were below par on that measure. "Most surprisingly, those with *more* education had less-positive views on this question. Ratings were higher among people who hadn't gone beyond high school, and lower among those with some college or a bachelor's degree."[10]

However, when asked, "Considering the costs of getting your degree versus the benefits to you personally, was getting your degree worth it or not worth it?," 79 percent of all the college-degree-holding respondents said it was worth it. Respondents with above-average incomes were the most enthusiastic about the benefits of a college degree. Eighty-eight percent of people with household incomes above $100,000 said the cost of college was worth it. Only 63 percent of graduates whose household income was less than $50,000 agreed. Similarly, 86 percent of those without student loan debt said the cost of their degree was worth it, while that number dropped to 64 percent among those burdened with debt. Still, 78 percent of respondents would encourage a close friend or relative to pursue a bachelor's degree. Among college graduates, that number rose to 85 percent. Among the most mentioned reasons for endorsing the pursuit of postsecondary education was to improve career options and, perhaps harking back to that earlier understanding of college, to broaden one's worldview. "Bachelor's degrees are almost mandatory for higher-paying jobs," one said. "College also exposes you to people different from where you grew up.... It helps you figure out who you are and who you want to be."[11]

Among the 20 percent who would not recommend pursuing a bachelor's degree, the reasons were linked to the cost—in time and money—and the risk of accumulating too much debt with insufficient financial reward. "Degrees have become expensive pieces of paper that trap people into an unfair amount of loans for little or no return on investment. The higher education system in the U.S. feels like a scam," one respondent wrote. "You can gain the same if not better experience from online courses for free," said another.[12]

In fact, most of the respondents, even if supportive of college-going, indicated that there were educational alternatives that were the same or better than a bachelor's degree in providing a path for a successful livelihood. When specifically asked to rate five alternatives for achieving a successful livelihood as "better," "about the same," or "not as good" as getting a bachelor's degree, most respondents said each one was better or about the same as a college degree. Specifically, 86 percent said attending trade school was similar to or a better choice than going to college. The same percentage indicated "other professional or technical training" was a similar or better choice. Eighty percent considered a work apprenticeship as a similar or better choice, 66 percent endorsed military service as a similar or better option, and 60 percent indicated union membership as a similar or better choice.[13] The growing perception that there are desirable alternatives to a traditional four-year college degree is a signal that the door to disruption is now wide open.

It is a door whose opening has been predicted for more than a decade. In 2011, Clayton Christensen and his coauthor, Henry J. Eyring, published *The Innovative University: Changing the DNA of Higher Education from the Inside Out*, a book many university leaders read with great interest, including me. Christensen was known for his theory of disruptive innovation, which differentiated between two types of innovation—sustaining innovation and disruptive innovation. Sustaining innovation was the kind that makes a product or service "bigger or better"—batteries that last longer or universities that offer more majors and have new campus centers, for example. Disruptive innovation sneaks up on you. Instead of offering a product or service that is "bigger and better," the disrupter offers a product or service that is "more affordable and easier to use"—online learning, for example.

As the disruptive theory explains, the quality of the new product is clearly seen as inferior to the traditional one (in this case, face-to-face classroom instruction), and the traditional providers don't consider it to be their competition. Only people who have no access to the traditional provider's service will show interest in the new one. But, over time, the new product quality improves, and some of the traditional customers begin to take interest in it because it costs less and is more convenient, eventually threatening the traditional provider. Applying the theory of disruptive innovation to higher education specifically, Christensen and Eyring asserted that as the quality of online learning improved it would challenge the traditional higher education model, threatening all but the most prestigious and well-endowed institutions. They predicted, "For the vast majority of universities change is inevitable. The main questions are when it will occur and what forces will bring it about."[14]

Not everyone agreed with their disruptive assessment. Education leaders like Lawrence Bacow and Henry Rosovsky, both of Harvard University, expressed faith in higher education's ability to adapt and reform itself in a more incremental way, a view perhaps specific to Harvard's highly endowed capacity for resilience.[15] But there was trouble afoot.

The COVID-19 pandemic accelerated the spread of online learning and virtual interaction via Zoom and other platforms. As Arthur Levine and Scott Van Pelt observed in their book, *The Great Upheaval: Higher Education's Past, Present, and Uncertain Future*, while "one in three students had taken an online course before COVID-19, in a matter of days the number jumped to nearly 100 percent."[16] As the pandemic waned, many students wanted to continue the convenience of the virtual classroom, sometimes even while living on a college campus.[17] The increased acceptance of online learning, together with widespread concerns about the steadily rising cost of higher education, is a disruptive combination.

What happens if institutional leaders ignore what Christensen and Eyring called the inevitability of change? The entertainment industry offers a cautionary tale, an example of what disruptive innovation looks like in the twenty-first century. Carnegie Mellon University professor Michael D. Smith, author of *The Abundant University: Remaking Higher Education for a Digital World*, succinctly summarized what happened: "Throughout the twentieth century, the entertainment industry was remarkably stable, despite technological innovations that regularly altered the way books, music, movies, and television shows were created, distributed, and consumed. That stability convinced executives that their model was not only the right one but maybe even the only viable one.... Trouble arrived early in the twenty-first century when upstart companies powered by new digital technologies began to challenge the status quo."[18]

In the case of music, for example, for most of the twentieth century, record labels controlled the artists, production, promotion, and distribution of the music consumers purchased, whether in the form of vinyl albums, cassettes, or compact discs (CDs). In 2001, when an MP3 player like the iPod became widely available, music in digital form could be downloaded, stored, and carried around in a pocket. It was no longer necessary to buy whole albums or CDs. You could just pick the songs you liked, buy them from Apple's iTunes Music Store for ninety-nine cents, and listen to them anytime, anywhere, "making music mobile, individualized, around the clock, and consumer driven."[19] The development of streaming services took individualization, convenience, and choice to another level. "In 2020, that same consumer—for roughly the same price as a single CD each month—could subscribe to a service like Spotify or Apple Music for on-demand access to a universe of music."[20] Music consumers were no longer locked into what they could find at the local record store (if there still was one) or what was playing on the radio. They could choose exactly what they wanted to hear—from a myriad of musical choices— and could listen to it anytime, anywhere, and avoid what they didn't want to hear. New technologies gave artists the freedom to create their music independently in their own home studios, promote it independently via new digital channels like Spotify and YouTube, and distribute it digitally as well. Within a ten-year span, 1999 to 2009, the record companies lost 50 percent of their sales.

A similar process disrupted movies and television. Entertainment executives initially dismissed the threat of the upstart companies as inconsequential. Netflix and Amazon Studios were nothing to worry about, they thought. "In 2013, the chief operating officer of Fox told investors, 'People will give up food and a roof over their head before they give up TV.'"[21] He was wrong. By 2019, approximately sixteen million cable customers in the US had canceled their subscriptions. The new alternatives got better and better, and customers drifted away from the traditional providers to the new, less expensive, more convenient, digital on-demand versions.

Why didn't the entertainment executives see the threat to their business model coming? It wasn't just overconfidence. Smith's answer to that question is, "They failed to understand that scarce resources were critical to their market power, and that new digital technologies were about to make those scarce resources abundantly available."[22] The new technologies changed the mode of delivery but did not change the basic goal of the entertainment—the mission remained. People still consume the content—books, movies, and music—but do it in new, more abundant and convenient ways.

Smith argued that traditional higher education, like the entertainment industry of the twentieth century, is operating from a scarcity model. There is scarcity of access (limits on class size and selectivity of admissions), scarcity of instruction (limits on the number of faculty), and scarcity of credentials (university degrees as the only way to certify knowledge). But, he asked, what if new digital technologies made those scarce resources abundantly available? How would institutions need to change? What would that look like?[23]

THE CASE OF SOUTHERN
NEW HAMPSHIRE UNIVERSITY

It might look like Southern New Hampshire University, under the leadership of President Paul LeBlanc. In 2003, when LeBlanc took the helm, SNHU (pronounced "snew") was a small, private residential institution in Manchester, New Hampshire—on the leading edge of the demographic decline in the Northeast. With its enrollment plummeting and its endowment shrinking, it was an institution headed for the cliff. But twenty years later, in December 2023, when LeBlanc announced his decision to retire from the presidency at the end of that school year, SNHU was not just surviving—it was thriving as the largest accredited university in the United States, with an enrollment of 185,000, routinely recognized as one of the most innovative institutions in the country, "one of the first of a new breed of nonprofit 'mega-universities' now beginning to transform the higher education landscape."[24] What happened?

LeBlanc proposed to the SNHU board of trustees that they should approve the investment needed to create an online program that would serve the needs of nontraditional adult learners. There was no shortage of those potential students. While still maintaining a traditional residential campus, which today enrolls about twenty-six hundred undergraduate students, SNHU began offering classes and degrees online at a very affordable cost, well below that of residential classes and degrees, open to anyone with a high school diploma or GED. The courses, designed centrally by subject-matter experts, were taught by a large cadre of faculty, some full-time, but most part-time adjunct instructors. Then and now, the classes consist of a mix of readings, short video segments, practice problems and other assignments, and online discussion boards and email interactions with the instructors, who today number more than six thousand.[25] And, of particular importance to its success, SNHU targeted working adults with an aggressive marketing campaign, including spending millions on television ads, a strategy rarely used by nonprofit colleges.[26]

In 2011, online tuition was set at $320 per credit hour, making it possible to complete a 120-credit, four-year bachelor's degree for less than $10,000 a year.[27] Thirteen years later, in 2024, the cost had risen just $10— to $330 per online credit hour.[28] The ability to increase employee compensation *and* increase the size of the online enrollment means the "cost disease" problem (discussed in Chapter 8) has been solved. Meanwhile, the revenue generated by the online programs helped to offset the costs of the residential program, allowing SNHU to reduce the price of that offering as well. In 2020, the school reported a $60 million surplus. A surplus of that magnitude made it possible for SNHU to announce in 2021 that it was lowering residential tuition rates by more than 50 percent, from $31,000 to $15,000 for in-person instruction and to $10,000 for a hybrid mix of in-person and online instruction.[29]

In an interview shortly after he announced his intention to step down as president, LeBlanc reflected on the twenty-year journey of transformation at SNHU.[30] It was evident in that conversation that his passion for its mission of providing access and opportunity to its students was rooted in his own growing-up experience in a low-income French Canadian immigrant family in Massachusetts. Driven by the encouragement of teachers and the dreams of his mother, he became the first in his extended family and neighborhood to go to college. Access to an affordable, high-quality college education transformed his life. His goal was to make similar opportunities possible for a new generation of immigrants and "to the 45% of Americans who today say they would struggle to come up with $400 for an unexpected car repair."

When, under President LeBlanc's leadership, SNHU launched its online program, it was reaching beyond recent high school graduates to nontraditional students: veterans, college dropouts, workers stuck in dead-end jobs—all who needed a college degree to advance economically. They were people who had jobs and family responsibilities, and often unpredictable work schedules. LeBlanc observed, "For big swaths of the American work-force…you may not even know what your [work] schedule is next week. So how do you commit to being on campus at a certain time?" A convenient solution was paramount: online asynchronous courses, available on demand.

Convenience was the first of what Leblanc called the four Cs that fueled SNHU's transformational growth. He explained:

> The second [C] was cost.…Can you make it affordable? And in the American context, that's a big question mark. We saddle our students with $1.7 trillion of student loan debt in America, second only to home mortgage debt. The third one was credential. Can you give me a credential that actually makes a difference? Does it tie to workforce demands and needs? Will it allow me to better my life? And then the last C is completion time. In other words, I'm doing this because I feel urgency. So, do you have transfer-credit-friendly policies? Will you take more of my credits from my previous schools than this other provider will?…We grew because we got really focused on what people actually needed.[31]

The timing was right for LeBlanc's innovation. When SNHU launched its online degree program, there was limited competition. Other institutions were "still looking down their noses [at online education]." LeBlanc told his board that eventually online education would start to be accepted, but until then there was a chance to grow unimpeded by competition from other nonprofit institutions. He showed the board a picture of a window with shutters, and said, "The shutters are open, they will be closed some-day.… For now we've got a chance to really grow."

With the support of the board, LeBlanc invested in the necessary technology and got very aggressive with the marketing of the online programs.

LeBlanc was ready to run with the new initiative, but faculty governance required him to slow the process down. He recalled, "We were still having to take every program we wanted to bring online and bring it back to the faculty for approval." Worried about creating competition with the residential programs, the faculty expressed reluctance about the online effort and were slow to make decisions. But then the impact of the Great Recession of 2008 hit the campus. Residential enrollments were down, there was a budget shortfall, and layoffs were on the horizon. New revenue was urgently needed. With financial pressures mounting, LeBlanc was able to "renegotiate our governance" and expedite decision-making. He explained:

> What we were able to do is say to the faculty we will never take a program online without talking to you first…. You get to raise your hand and tell us your concerns and we will address those. And if [necessary]…we'll adjudicate it. But it won't drag on, it's 30 days and then the provost will decide. We never had a case go to the provost. We were able to address concerns, that allowed us to grow really fast…. So in 2012, in the list of 50 largest non-profit providers of higher ed online, we were number 50. Three years later, we were number four. Those three years were a rocket ride.[32]

The meteoric rise of SNHU to become what was in 2024 the largest accredited university in the country was truly astonishing. More than 90 percent of current students and alums indicate high levels of satisfaction, a point of pride for LeBlanc. He attributed their satisfaction to the use of SNHU's "advising-centric model," built on a foundation of data analytics. Over the course of the degree, students will meet many faculty members online but may not have a sustained relationship with any of them. But the assigned academic adviser is there with the student from beginning to end. Taking courses asynchronously means when you log on you may not be on at the same time as your classmates, which can feel isolating. The relationship with the adviser is designed to combat that sense of isolation and encourage persistence in the face of personal and academic challenges as well as celebrate successes along the way. It is the adviser's readiness to intervene with timely additional academic (or sometimes financial) resources that is often the difference between a student dropping out or making it to graduation.

President LeBlanc's passion for meeting students' needs for convenience, affordable cost, meaningful credentials, and efficient completion times led to another innovation—competency-based education (CBE). The school's CBE program was the first of its kind in the nation. The course material was completely "untethered from time." Progress toward degree was measured by mastery of the required competencies, irrespective of how long it takes to acquire that mastery. With CBE, students can work at their own pace to achieve mastery. LeBlanc illustrated the power of CBE through the example of Mariam, an African American woman from a very low-income community in Boston. Mariam was a single mother with a seven-year-old daughter with a chronic respiratory illness. Whenever her daughter got sick, Mariam would miss several days of class, would fall behind on assignments, perform poorly on exams, and ultimately fail her courses. LeBlanc explained, "If you looked at her transcript, you'd say, 'God, this Mariam's just not ready for college. She's not right for college.'" Yet when Mariam was able to join the CBE program, she thrived, clearly demonstrating her ability to do college-level work. Whenever she needed to pause to care for her daughter, she could stop without penalty, resuming her studies when the crisis had passed. "We didn't have a student who wasn't right for higher ed. We had a higher ed that wasn't right for the student. So, our innovation is always about [getting] right models for the right students in the right place.... When you see the impact, it's hard not to be excited about what's possible."[33]

SNHU transformed scarcity of access to abundance.[34] There are plenty of spaces for students in their online model at an affordable price, no selective admission process required, and enough online faculty and advisers for everyone, putting an affordable degree in reach for thousands and thousands of people. But SNHU is also exploring "microcredentials," educational options that are "shorter targeted solutions" focusing on specific job skills. LeBlanc elaborated: "Education that comes as stackable blocks is a win-win product.... It provides an immediate payoff both to employers who are willing to pay for courses and employees who want to step toward a broader education that might help them in the future."[35]

Of course, SNHU is not the only nonprofit online university servicing thousands of students. Institutions like Western Governors University and Arizona State University are among the industry leaders. Nor is it the only school using data analytics to inform "just in time" advising to help keep students on track and progressing to degree completion. Georgia State University is a large urban campus in the heart of downtown Atlanta that has become known for its data-informed interventions with students, resulting in greatly improved graduation rates, particularly for first-generation, Pell-eligible students.[36] The use of technology to facilitate student success is at the heart of these innovations.

THE ARRIVAL OF ARTIFICIAL INTELLIGENCE

Will all technological advancements facilitate student success? Or will some advancements undermine student learning? On November 30, 2022, during my year as interim president at Mount Holyoke College, the tech company OpenAI introduced ChatGPT, an artificial intelligence (AI) chatbot, built on the foundation of OpenAI's "large language models" and able to engage with users in their own language, answering questions and generating text at lightning speed.[37] News of ChatGPT's capabilities spread quickly on social media, and almost instantly college students began exploring how it could help them with their course assignments. Faculty members were scrambling to catch up, eager to discuss with each other how to apply the rules regarding academic integrity. If students use

ChatGPT to write entire papers, and then they submit the work as their own, the cheating seems clear. If students use ChatGPT to provide source material (like a virtual research assistant) but then write the text for their papers without ChatGPT assistance, have they violated the academic honor code? In the spring of 2023, these were the questions under discussion. Headlines like this one were quick to follow: "ChatGPT is making universities rethink plagiarism. Students and professors can't decide whether the AI chatbot is a research tool—or a cheating engine."[38]

Fast forward two years to the fall of 2024 and the conversation had shifted. Generative AI (GAI) is defined as "AI models that can create ('generate') original content (e.g. text, images, code), for example, ChatGPT, Midjourney, Google Bard, etc."[39] Just as there was once a time when calculators were not allowed in a math class but then became essential tools, GAI was being embraced by some instructors as an instructional tool that students should learn to use. For example, two professors at Rollins College, Dan Myers and Ann Murdaugh, began by requiring their students to use GAI as a collaboration partner to complete their semester-long research projects. As the students generated their research topics, identified and reviewed the relevant literature, and developed the thesis and initial outline, first drafts, and subsequent revisions, they were expected to track their use of the chatbot in a logbook, noting where it had been helpful and where it was not. The professors found that the students were highly engaged in their projects and learned not only the content of their research topic but also the fundamental skills of how best to work with generative AI, skills that will certainly be needed in their future. Myers and Murdaugh asserted that "the skills that students use to engage thoughtfully with AI are the same ones that colleges are good at teaching. Namely, knowing how to obtain and use information, thinking critically and analytically, and understanding what and how you're trying to communicate."[40]

The challenge for institutional leaders is how to ensure that the faculty have the AI skills they need to facilitate such learning. In most cases, students are far ahead of their instructors in AI literacy. The Digital Education Council Global AI Student Survey gathered nearly four thousand responses across sixteen countries from both graduate and undergraduate students about their attitudes toward and their experience using AI in higher education.[41] Eighty-six percent of the students surveyed indicated they used AI tools at least weekly. Most (69 percent) used AI as a search engine for information, 42 percent to check their written work for grammatical errors, and 33 percent to summarize documents. Almost one in four (24 percent) used AI to create the first draft of a writing assignment. Fewer than half (48 percent) feel prepared for an AI-using workplace, and 59 percent expect their universities to help them get ready by increasing the use of AI in teaching and learning. They recognize that their faculty aren't ready either; 73 percent want their universities to provide training for faculty on the effective use of AI tools. Many students (63 percent) of those surveyed were especially interested in the use of chatbots to answer questions, to be available to provide 24/7 assistance with any questions they might have.[42]

Faculty were indeed further behind. In February 2024, a little more than a year after the release of ChatGPT, Ithaka S+R, a nonprofit research organization, conducted the largest survey to date of faculty in the United States about the use of generative AI for teaching purposes. With more than five thousand respondents, they found that most had gained some familiarity with GAI tools, but about half indicated a lack of confidence in their abilities to use them in their teaching. Only 19 percent agreed that using generative AI would benefit their teaching. Most (56 percent) were quite uncertain about whether the impact of GAI would be positive or negative. In general, younger faculty were both more familiar and more comfortable with the use of GAI. A broad cross-section of faculty expressed interest in assistance from their institutions to help them learn how to use GAI to support their teaching—for example, for creating tutorials and study guides for students, creating images for classroom use, and using GAI to design syllabi and other course materials. However, a significant number (42 percent) did not want their students to use GAI in their coursework, completely prohibiting their students from using GAI. That was particularly true of humanities faculty (53 percent) as compared to 45 percent in the sciences and 40 percent in the social sciences.[43]

The reluctance of many faculty to bring student use of GAI into the classroom (or even allow it) is in direct conflict with student desire for faculty guidance in the use of GAI, but it is likely that faculty reluctance will change (perhaps quickly) as institutions invest in faculty development. The Ithaka S+R researchers rightly observed,

> Provosts and presidents will spend the coming years grappling with equipping students with AI skills and literacies and assessing the most appropriate and ethical ways to harness this technology to promote teaching and learning. CIOs and IT directors are beginning to make financial commitments to specific generative AI platforms. Centers for teaching and learning, libraries, and other university offices are developing service models and articulating best practices. The success of all these initiatives will hinge on the instructional practices of individual instructors.[44]

While some individual instructors drag their feet, others are charging ahead, aided by an institutional investment in studying the impact of GAI. For example, Carnegie Mellon University provided support for teaching experiments designed to answer important pedagogical questions like these: "Does using AI while brainstorming generate more or fewer distinct ideas? Can a generative AI tool give less-experienced students a better chance to be successful in technical courses? To what extent does using AI help or hinder writing skills?"[45]

A particularly exciting (or disrupting) development is the creation of AI tutors. At Harvard, physics instructor Greg Kestin created an AI tutor for his physics class, trained exclusively with materials from his class and designed to give guided responses and feedback to students in a manner that was consistent with best pedagogical practice. He then created an experiment with the two hundred students in his course, with half the class receiving standard in-class instruction and taking quizzes on the material covered that day in class, while the other half studied the same material at home with the assistance of the AI tutor. Later the groups were switched. Kestin found that the students did better when using the AI tutor, learning the material more quickly and scoring higher on the quizzes. Students liked using the AI tutor because "they could go at their own pace and could have unfettered access to a nonjudgmental instructor who would not get frustrated or annoyed no matter how many times they asked" their questions. For Kestin, the experiment demonstrated that the AI tutor could help students understand the basic concepts at home, preserving class time for the discussion and review of more complex problems.[46]

In his book *Brave New Words*, Salman Khan, creator of Khan Academy, gives many examples of how GAI tutors can be effective teaching partners for human instructors and their students. For example, for professors worried about students using GAI to avoid doing their own work, Khan has a solution. "What if we could go one step further and have the AI actually support the student while making the process transparent to the professor?" he asked. Using GAI called Khanmigo, he explained, "we are developing the ability for a professor to create both an assignment and a grading rubric with the AI and then prompt students to complete tasks through the application. The professor can decide how much support the AI should provide." It could include basic proctoring, in which the application takes screenshots of the paper as the student is writing it, allowing the professor to see that students are doing the work on their own, or Khanmigo could serve as a writing coach, brainstorming topics with the student, giving feedback on an initial outline and on early drafts of writing assignments.

Then Khanmigo can give the professor a report on the student's efforts. Here is a sample of such a report:

Khanmigo: Sal and I worked on the essay for about five hours total. He had a little trouble deciding on a thesis statement, but I helped nudge him to pick one. I gave some light feedback on the outline, asking him to make his argument...stronger....Based on the rubric we created, I'd give the paper a B+ in its current form. If you agree with that assessment, I can work with him to improve it further. Click on the following link to view the entire transcript of our interaction. Overall, I am confident that he did this paper with me and didn't cheat. Not only did the action seem authentic, but Sal's writing style and level seemed consistent with the writing he has been doing inside the classroom.[47]

In the case of a student who did cheat, the report might say something like this one:

Khanmigo: We worked together on this paper for five minutes. For the most part, the paper just seemed to be prewritten somewhere else and pasted in. The writing level is also significantly more advanced that what Sal has done in his classwork.[48]

Another important benefit of Khanmigo for the student is timely feedback. It is difficult for a writing instructor to read and evaluate a classroom's worth of student assignments very quickly. Khan observed, "Before generative AI came on the scene, it could take days or weeks before students got feedback on their papers....Contrast this to the vision in which students receive immediate feedback on every dimension of their writing from the AI. They will have the chance to practice, iterate, and improve much faster."[49]

While such sophisticated uses of GAI may not eliminate the need for the primary classroom instructor, it certainly could reduce the need for instructional support positions like teaching assistants and subject matter tutors. Can AI reduce the cost of education *and* improve instruction in meaningful ways? What are the unintended consequences of the widespread use of GAI in higher education—and the society at large? Higher education has a role to play in answering that latter question as well. Jennifer Frederick, associate provost for academic initiatives at Yale and executive director of the Poorvu Center for Teaching and Learning, cautioned, "Universities really need to be the counterpoint to the big tech companies and their development of AI. . . . We need to be the ones who slow down and really think through all the implications for society and humanity and ethics."[50]

But slowing down may not be possible. Generative AI is evolving rapidly. In September 2024, OpenAI released a new version of GAI called o1-preview that has the capacity to "think" about a problem, planning and testing ideas before committing to a solution. It can now outperform PhD experts in solving very difficult physics problems.[51] For many institutional leaders, the speed of the changes and the struggle to keep up with the technology to meet the needs of both faculty and students can make their heads spin and their budgets explode. *But wait, there's more.*

LOSING THE MONOPOLY?

In an interview in 2018, SNHU President Paul LeBlanc predicted that in the future, "higher education will surrender its monopoly on credentials, transcripts, and delivery of education."[52] That disruptive future is on the horizon, if not already here. While the development of AI tutors has implications for the delivery of education, other innovations challenge the monopoly on credentialing and transcripts. For example, when an employer recruits a college graduate, that employer is relying in large part on the institutional reputation and the signal that a college degree sends about the graduate's readiness for employment.[53] But what if there was another way to learn about a candidate's skills and readiness for the job that was less inferential, that provided more direct evidence? In the world of technology, there now is.

In *The Abundant University*, Michael Smith describes the world of Kaggle, a website that hosts machine learning and data science competitions among an online community of about half a million data scientists.[54] Companies can post datasets and problems in need of solutions on the site, and interested community members can work on the problems as they choose. There are courses in coding and machine learning offered on the site at no cost, and competitions for beginners as well as for those more advanced.[55] Some competitions offer prize money, ranging from $10,000 to over $1,000,000. Doing well in a Kaggle competition, or similar events hosted on other sites such as CrowdAI or HackerRank, is proving to be more meaningful to tech employers than a college degree.

Google, for one, found that a potential hire's GPA or college test scores were not very predictive of whether the person would be a successful employee. Now they rely on "a series of practical tests and behavioral interviews" and are hiring more non–college graduates as a result. LinkedIn, too, is focusing on "skills, not degrees," in its hiring.[56]

Some companies have gone a step further and decided to do employee education themselves. Google launched an online eight-month IT support certificate program in early 2018. By June 2019, nearly seventy-five thousand people had enrolled in the program, preparing for entry-level IT support staff roles. For the low price of $49 per month (for those who don't qualify for financial aid), certificate completers could become job ready.[57] In the summer of 2019, Amazon announced its intention to spend $700 million to "upskill" one hundred thousand of its employees by 2025 for jobs within the company "and beyond." *Inside Higher Ed* reported, "The retail giant's decision to expand its own postsecondary training and credential programs, largely outside traditional higher education, also is a shot across the bow for colleges and universities."[58] Was the behemoth organization moving into the higher education business too?

The companies are developing their own curricula, setting competency standards, and recruiting and enrolling the students (their employees)—looking very university-like in the process. Amazon's programs have names like Amazon Technical Academy, Associate2Tech, and Machine Learning University. The latter program, MLU, was described in an Amazon press release as "help[ing] employees learn core skills to propel their career growth—skills that are often taught only in higher education."[59] Eyebrows were raised by the choice of language, and experts questioned if Amazon would repeat its pattern of "successfully developing a service for itself, then selling it on the open market—in this case to potential students."[60] What Amazon will do remains to be seen, but corporations as potential providers of useful postsecondary credentials is not a future possibility, but a present reality.

In the conversation about disruptive innovation, the long-established value of research universities that are the source of scientific discovery and the liberal arts colleges that foster the habits of mind that have been the launching pad of civic and corporate leadership seems to get lost. Education as a pillar of democracy and civic engagement, as espoused by the Truman Commission in 1946, is missing from the conversation. The Association of American Colleges and Universities (AAC&U) has long been a champion of the importance of a liberal arts education to prepare students broadly for careers and civic life. In a 2023 AAC&U-sponsored study, researchers found that most employers (80 percent) agreed that higher education is preparing graduates with the skills needed to succeed in the workforce and that getting a college degree was a worthwhile investment. In particular, employers expressed strong support for learning experiences "that engage students in the hands-on application of ideas, encourage them to think for themselves, engage them in independent inquiry, expose them to a wide variety of topics and disciplines, and enable them to participate in community-based experiences."[61] In addition, 75 percent of the employers surveyed indicated their expectation that strong job candidates would show evidence of these "very important" skills: "oral and written communication, critical and creative thinking, complex problem-solving, teamwork and the ability to work with diverse others, and digital literacy and data analysis."[62]

Those "very important" skills are the hallmark of a traditional liberal arts education. Is there a way to preserve the best of the residential liberal arts college experience and maintain affordability? That is the challenge facing those campus leaders committed to that model. When Vanderbilt University announced its cost of attendance for 2024–2025 had nearly hit the $100,000 mark, it underscored just how critical the question of affordability had become.[63] Even acknowledging that most students will not pay that sticker price, due to generous financial aid awards, many families will undoubtedly be asking, "Is it worth it?"

In *The Innovative University*, Christensen and Eyring acknowledged the indispensable role of the traditional university, still providing young people an environment to stretch themselves, broaden their horizons, and mature intellectually and interpersonally, under the guidance of talented and inspiring professors. They argued for the continuation of the traditional model—if it can be made affordable. They wrote, "If [traditional universities] cannot find innovative, less costly ways of performing their uniquely valuable functions, they are doomed to decline....Fortunately such innovation is within their power."[64]

We will have to use our imaginations. Creativity is required. Institutional leaders don't have to do what they have always done. Paul LeBlanc saw the need his constituents had for the four Cs—convenience, cost, credential, and completion—and found a way to meet those needs. SNHU still has a traditional campus with twenty-six hundred students. The revenue from its online programs helps keep the residential program affordable. That is a win-win solution. We need more of them.

ANOTHER WIN-WIN SOLUTION—
THE WELLNESS REVOLUTION

When I least expected it, I found myself disrupted by external circumstances and in need of a win-win solution. It was December 2011, and our athletic director informed me that our NCAA Division III athletic conference was falling apart. Each conference must have a minimum of seven institutions as members, and our conference, known as the Great South Athletic Conference, had exactly seven—four women's colleges and three coed institutions. The three coed schools all had football teams and had decided to join another conference that offered more football competition. With only four members left, our conference would be dissolved in May 2013.

Our challenge was to find another conference. It was possible to do so, but only at great expense and investment in our athletics infrastructure. The four remaining women's college presidents met to discuss our conference options. We decided to apply to the same conference the three coed schools had joined, but each of our schools was rejected, probably because we did not have football teams. We discussed creating our own women's college conference, assuming we could find at least three other women's colleges willing to leave their current conferences to join us. Even if we were successful in that endeavor, all the possible candidate schools were geographically quite distant from the four of us. The cost of traveling to competitions would increase significantly.

What should Spelman do? To be a member of NCAA Division III, we were required to field at least seven teams—ours were soccer, volleyball, basketball, softball, golf, tennis, and cross-country. Unlike NCAA Division I and Division II, within Division III athletic scholarships are prohibited. Students play for the love of the sport; there is no financial incentive for the players. The cost of the program is largely related to the coaches, equipment, facilities, and travel expenses. I asked the athletic director for some data. What were we currently spending on our intercollegiate athletics program? What would the likely increase be if we had to travel farther for competitions? How many students were participating?

What surprised me the most was how few of our students were playing on teams. Our student population at the time was approximately 2,100. Each entering class ranged from 525 to 550 students. Only eighty students total were participating in intercollegiate sports—approximately twenty in each class year. The cost of our program was more than $10,000 per student. I had questions: Why were so few of our students participating? Was our spending sufficient to support our program? Or was our spending misplaced?

I knew our facilities were not designed to support our intercollegiate participation. The gym had been built in 1950, when the Spelman College student population totaled five hundred. In the Jim Crow South, there was no real opportunity for an HBCU for women to send teams away from campus for intercollegiate competition. The 1950s gym had not been designed with a separate locker room for visiting teams. Our compact urban campus had tennis courts but no soccer field, softball field, or golf course. Our teams played on a community golf course, and on fields borrowed from other colleges or high schools in our area. The basketball court in our gym was not regulation size—we had been allowed a waiver to use it in competitions. The inadequacy of our facilities was just one of the impediments to finding another conference to join. What would it take to really support our intercollegiate participation with the quality of facilities our students deserved and expected? How much more would our athletic program cost?

I was pondering what to do about our problem late one afternoon while sitting in the stands watching our basketball team compete. There were five Spelmanites on the court, and another five or so on the bench. There were just a handful of Spelman students and family members in the stands with me watching the game. As I watched, I wondered if any of our students would be playing basketball recreationally after they graduated. Maybe. But the career women I knew did different things—Zumba classes, Pilates, yoga, fitness classes at the local Y, or walking or jogging in the neighborhood. We offered some fitness classes in the gym, which were popular, but the teams took priority in use of the space. Fitness classes could only be scheduled when our teams weren't using the gym for practice or their games.

As I sat there, I thought about an article I had been reading about the sedentary lives of young Black women. About four out of five African American women are overweight or obese, and among all children, Black girls are most likely to report they engaged in no physical activity in the past week. A National Institutes of Health study found that by the age of seventeen, more than half of Black girls were reporting no leisure-time physical activity at all.[65] Whether it is diabetes, high blood pressure, heart disease, breast cancer, or stroke, Black women are more likely to suffer from these ailments and die from them—early.[66] All those illnesses are linked to obesity and lack of physical activity. I thought about the funerals of Spelman alums I had recently attended, young women whose lives had been cut too short by such diseases.

As I continued to watch the game, an idea came to me: "Flip it!" Flip the flow of resources from the small number of student athletes (eighty) to the whole campus of twenty-one hundred. I realized we could change the life trajectory of our students by reallocating our resources—from intercollegiate athletics for a few to a campus-wide wellness initiative for all. We could launch a wellness revolution!

In the spring of 2012, we let all our players and their coaches know that we would discontinue our NCAA participation in May 2013 when our conference disbanded. Of course, there was disappointment among the athletes, but seniors graduating that year would not be affected by the decision. Students in the class of 2013 would also still be able to play on a team until they graduated. But first-year students (class of 2015) and sophomores (class of 2014)—forty in total—were very upset. Some threatened to transfer, though to my knowledge no one did. When the news became public, I got some letters of protest from alumnae, but mostly the idea gained support.

The key to what turned out to be a win-win solution was the framing of our decision in the context of our mission and in keeping with our history. Christensen and Eyring wrote, "Today the traditional university's challenge is to change in ways that decrease its price premium and increase its contributions to students and society."[67] When we decided to discontinue our participation in intercollegiate athletics, that is exactly what we were doing. We were not rejecting sports, or competition, just the limited benefit that our NCAA participation offered a few student athletes—and the increased cost associated with it—in favor of a program of activity that would support the lifelong fitness for all our students. Why did we call that a "revolution"? We at Spelman College, the leading educator of Black women, intended to launch a movement for the improvement of Black women's health.

Our institutional history was revolutionary. When Sophia Packard and Harriet Giles, the founders of Spelman College, traveled through the South after the end of the Civil War, they found an illiterate community of formerly enslaved people in desperate need of education. Recognizing that a community of educated women could be transformational, they set a literacy revolution in motion when they opened their school in 1881. One hundred thirty-one years later, in 2012, another literacy revolution was needed in the African American community—wellness literacy—and a community of educated women could again be transformational.

The need was urgent. It was our students—young Black women—who were and still are among the most at risk for negative health outcomes. Committed to educating the whole person—mind, body, and spirit—we had an opportunity to change this epidemic. Ending intercollegiate participation might have seemed to some counterintuitive, given our focus on physical activity, but instead of spending hundreds of thousands of dollars transporting a small number of athletes to intercollegiate events, we would be investing those dollars in intramural programs and wellness activities that could be sustained for a lifetime. Our wellness program intended to transition our students from high school sports to lifelong fitness. Just as we developed the habits of the mind—critical thinking skills that will be used for a lifetime—we wanted to develop habits of the body that would support healthy living for a lifetime.

We expanded what had been a fledgling wellness program with activities like aqua aerobics, Zumba, kickboxing, fitness walking, and yoga, to name just a few. A chapter of "Black Girls Run" began meeting weekly on our campus, and as the health and wellness program expanded, it was incorporated into our mandatory physical education curriculum, so it would touch every student.

Still, there was a barrier to our progress. Our physical education building, Read Hall, built in 1950 when our student population was just five hundred, no longer met the needs of a campus of twenty-one hundred students. We could do without a lot of practice fields, but we needed a twenty-first-century facility that would accommodate our larger student population and support our wellness initiatives. We set out to raise funds to renovate and expand Read Hall, an $18 million project, to house a state-of-the-art fitness education program that would benefit all our students, not only improving their health outcomes but also preparing them to be wellness champions in communities beyond our gates. It would even have a demonstration kitchen to allow for hands-on nutrition sessions. The trustees approved the project on the condition that the money would be fully raised before we began the construction. We would not take on debt to do it. Amazingly, the money for the project poured in quickly. Donors were excited to be part of our wellness revolution. One large foundation expressed appreciation in particular for the fact that we were making a strategic and cost-effective choice to *stop* doing something instead of just adding on new costs. In June 2015, just days before my retirement from Spelman, the building was completed, and I was thrilled to cut the ribbon.

An unanticipated benefit for Spelman was all the positive publicity we received when we announced that we were leaving the NCAA voluntarily. Only one other school had done so in recent memory. The *New York Times* wrote two articles about Spelman's decision that year—including a Sunday *Times* front-page story featuring photos of our first "Founders Day 5k"—and other colleges from across the country called to inquire about what we were doing and how.[68] Two years after our announcement, *Inside Higher Ed* did a follow-up story.[69] In 2017, two years after my retirement and five years after our decision, ESPN did a follow-up story, too. I was thrilled to read in the ESPN article about how many students were using the new facility and embracing our wellness slogan, "Eat better, move more, sleep well!" The ESPN journalist, Cecelia Townes, wrote, "Spelman's Wellness Center, which partners with the college's Counseling Center and Dining Services... offers yoga, guided meditation, self-care consultations and vibrational sound massage therapy in addition to the more traditional exercise activities like weight lifting, water aerobics, boot camp and spin. What is apparent is that students are doing more than attending group sessions and working out from time to time. Their minds and bodies are truly being transformed."[70]

Cited in the ESPN article was the story of Shanice Alexander, who was in her junior year at the time of the interview. Shanice had suffered an accident just before entering college that had made it hard for her to be as active as she wanted to be. With the support of the course instructors, personal trainers, and intramural coaches who staff the Wellness Center (at no additional cost to students), Shanice found just what she needed on a life-changing journey to better health. She said, "I have lost about 50 to 60 pounds since coming to the Wellness Center. The coaches and programs they offer are the best. They are helpful and we talk on a personal level. I'm here almost every day." Another student, senior Taylor Parnell, said, "When I was in high school, I played basketball, soccer and volley-ball. So, I was used to being competitively active every day. It was defi-nitely a shock to not have any sports, but our intramural offerings really give me the opportunity to fill that competitive void."[71]

The Spelman wellness approach offers effective and affordable health and wellness education that could be a model for many colleges and uni-versities. Just as the Spelman founders forged a new educational path for Black women, we were forging a new wellness path, one that could lead the way to better health for this generation of students and for those whose lives they will touch. Just as literacy spread in 1881 as the result of edu-cated Spelman women, this generation of "wellness-literate" women can make a long-term impact on the quality of health among African Ameri-can women and their families in the years to come.

I know that the decision to leave behind the NCAA and intercollegiate athletics would not be the right choice for every institution. Having sports teams is important to the cocurricular life of many residential campuses, both for the scholar athletes and for the cheering fans. For some NCAA Division I institutions with name-brand football and basketball teams, the revenue generated from athletic proceeds and the donors the teams inspire is substantial. But for many schools, athletics is a big money-losing expense and getting bigger. As student athletes push for revenue-sharing rights, contemplate unionization (as Dartmouth basketball players did successfully in 2024), and the rules change for how student athletes can use their name, image, and likeness for their own financial gain, some campus leaders might consider what their other options might be.[72] Could it be that it's time to rethink the role of athletics?

What is clear is change of some kind is coming for every institution. Disruption seems inevitable. Even the elite institutions, though buffered by their wealth and prestige, will confront the challenge of change—whether the result of congressional hearings, the emergence of artificial intelli-gence, global conflicts, changing student expectations, or something else.

Christensen and Eyring offer these closing words: "The universities that survive near-term challenges will be those that recognize and honor their strengths while innovating with optimism"—words of encouragement that every campus leader can use.[73]

As institutions innovate, one challenge for many leaders is the response of their constituents, particularly previous generations of graduates. Alumni often remember with great affection the college as it was when they were students, and sometimes express dismay—even anger— when changes are made. I, like most college presidents, encountered this phenomenon occasionally, receiving unhappy letters, emails, and phone calls from disappointed constituents when a new policy was introduced or a tough budget decision was made.

To those readers who have been tempted to make such a call, or to send a letter or email, I invite you to pause and consider if how you read books, listen to music, or watch movies has changed since you graduated. Have you made any difficult financial decisions in your life? Disruption is everywhere, and the school you love may have to change, too, to continue to thrive. In the face of critical challenges, the leader needs support. Offer your ideas—your time, your talent, your treasure—but keep in mind that armchair quarterbacking is easy. It's hard to see the complexity of the challenges from a distance. And, really, do *you* want that job?

CHAPTER ELEVEN

REASONS FOR JOY

During the years that I was dean of the college at Mount Holyoke, I was also a part-time student at Hartford Seminary.[1] I came across a small book in the seminary bookstore titled *Always We Begin Again: The Benedictine Way of Living*, by John McQuiston II. It was a contemporary interpretation of the Rule of Saint Benedict, a set of instructions for a community of monks written by Benedict of Nursia in the sixth century in Italy. The Rule of Benedict became the foundation for Benedictine monastic life across Europe during the Middle Ages. In the book's introduction, McQuiston observes,

> Almost none of us want to, or could, retire to a monastery. Nevertheless, at the heart of the Rule is a core of truth about the human condition. It contains a series of brilliant insights concerning how one may make ordinary life into something deeply fulfilling.... The Rule teaches that if we take control of our lives, if we are intentional and careful how we spend the hours of each irreplaceable day, if we discipline ourselves to live in a balanced and thankful way, we

will create from our experiences, whatever they may be, the best possible life.[2]

Among the insights that I gained from reading the book, this one truly resonated and has remained with me: *"Life will always provide matters for concern. Yet each day brings with it reasons for joy."*[3]

In the daily life of a college president, it is easy to stay focused on the matters of concern: the enrollment cliff and the need for more financial aid for deserving students, the importance of recruiting and retaining excellent faculty, the cost of rapidly increasing demands for technology, the inevitable aging and expensive repair of facilities, the impact of politics on campus climate, and the challenge of maintaining the health and safety of the community, to name just a few. But truly each day does bring with it reasons for joy. For me, finding reasons for joy has become a daily practice. For the beleaguered campus leader, finding reasons for daily joy is one of the best ways to preserve your own mental health and carry the weight of your institution lightly on your shoulders. When people ask me how it was that I was able to serve as president for thirteen years, at a time when the average tenure was approximately six years, I often think of the sustaining power of finding daily reasons for joy (and well-timed vacations).

During those years, there were indeed many matters for concern, as there are now, but indeed each day did bring reasons for joy. I have categorized the most frequent sources of joy I experienced—and that other presidents have told me they experienced—as the big three: people, problem-solving, and purpose.

THE PEOPLE YOU MEET

Being a college president gives you the opportunity to meet amazing people. Every student and faculty or staff member has a story, and presidents get to hear a lot of them. The lifelong connections that alums have with the institution bring many of them back to campus again and again, and some you get to know well. One of the first people I met when I arrived in Atlanta was an elderly Spelman alumna, Mignon Lackey Lewis of the class of 1951, who made it a point to come to the office and meet me. Mignon was quick to correct me if she felt the college was failing to meet its own standards, but was also willing to work tirelessly to champion the college everywhere she went. I came to appreciate her correction and deeply valued her obvious love for the college—and for me as its representative in the world. I knew she had my back. When she passed away, it was a privilege to speak at her funeral, to honor her and her love for the college. Though that might seem sad, it was a joy to be part of the celebration of her well-lived life. She was one of the many extraordinary ordinary people I never would have met had I not assumed the role of president.

I also met a lot of extraordinary famous people who made their way to Spelman College. Every campus occasionally invites dynamic speakers. At Spelman we were lucky that our institutional reputation and our location (twenty minutes from the busiest airport in the world, Hartsfield-Jackson International Airport in Atlanta) made it easy to attract special visitors to campus, and I was honored to be able to sit and talk with many of them, Oprah-style, in front of an audience of students, or host them for a special lunch or dinner at the president's campus residence.

On November 6, 2014, one reason for joy was the campus visit of Misty Copeland, the brilliant ballerina soloist of the American Ballet Theatre, one of only three African American women to achieve that prized status in its sixty-year history, and the first Black woman in history to play the Firebird for a major ballet company. As a result of her boundary-breaking career, this young Black woman has sometimes been described as "the Jackie Robinson of ballet." I had the privilege of hosting a conversation with her in front of an audience packed with talented young Spelman students, all eager to learn from her experiences. Her story of hard work and perseverance in the face of adversity, and her ability to push past racial barriers using an art form—classical ballet—that she described as "the province of the white and the wealthy," was a source of inspiration to all.

Perhaps the most meaningful part of the conversation for me occurred at the beginning when we took our seats on the stage. Misty looked out at the sea of beautiful brown faces beaming at her, and her eyes filled with tears. She quickly explained that living her life in the world of ballet, where so often she was the only Black woman in the rehearsal studio or on the stage, she often felt isolated. In Sisters Chapel she instantly felt the warmth and love radiating from the Spelman sisterhood and felt at home. That feeling of welcome moved her to tears.

In our conversation she reminded us of the importance of mentoring, the need to find your voice and make it heard, and to live your life with a sense of purpose. Quoting from her book *Life in Motion: An Unlikely Ballerina*, Misty read, "When I soar across the stage, I feel that I am carrying every little brown girl with me, those with broken wings and those who are just about to take flight."[4] As students lined up to ask their questions, the power of the Spelman experience was evident—the power of a convocation where you can speak directly with a childhood idol; the power of a community that places Black women at the center of the experience, not on the margins; the power of the arts to enrich our lives and inspire us to greatness in whatever field of study we choose.

I had so many wonderful conversations over the years—with musical genius Stevie Wonder, historian and author Howard Zinn, US Speaker of the House Nancy Pelosi, television journalist Katie Couric, Howard Schultz (longtime CEO of Starbucks), Judith Jamieson (of Alvin Ailey Dance Theater fame), Ursula Burns (first Black woman CEO of a Fortune 500 company), even Oprah Winfrey herself. My husband enjoyed taking photographs of these special conversations. Looking back at the photos, one thing is consistent—I am beaming. Those close encounters with such interesting people who generously gave of their time to share their lives with our students were pure joy.

In the same way, talking with donors was delightful. Many people think fundraising is a chore, and I would have been one of them when I was a faculty member. As a child, I never liked selling my Girl Scout cookies, and as an adult, I imagined fundraising to be not too far removed from that dreaded task. But I was wrong. Fundraising is really just telling the story of your institution and sharing a compelling vision of what you hope to accomplish. When a potential donor listened attentively and then asked with sincerity, "How can I help you?" I was well on my way to a meaningful philanthropic partnership. That is not only exciting, it's fun. I learned that when you can invite someone to participate in something meaningful through their giving, you have actually given them a gift, and they are grateful. That is a reason for joy.

I also took joy in thanking people. That may sound odd, but the link between gratitude and happiness is widely recognized by psychologists and spiritual practitioners alike.[5] In the book *Braiding Sweetgrass: Indigenous Wisdom, Scientific Knowledge, and the Teachings of Plants*, by Robin Wall Kimmerer, one of the central themes is the importance of expressing gratitude for all that we are given by the Earth and each other. "It's such a simple thing, but we all know the power of gratitude to incite a cycle of reciprocity," she writes.[6] When we express our appreciation and gratitude to someone for their gifts, whatever they may be, it makes them happy, *and* it also makes us happy. Saying "thank you" is important, but how you do it has to be authentic.

I was confronted with a "thank you" dilemma early on as the new president of Spelman College. I walked into my office one October day, and my assistant Yvonne greeted me with this news: "It's time to order the turkeys and hams." "Turkeys and hams?" I asked quizzically. "Yes, apparently the president is supposed to give turkeys at Thanksgiving and hams at Christmas to the physical plant staff and to the public safety officers," she said. "I don't want to do that," I replied. "Why not?" she asked. "It feels too much like being on a plantation. The lady in the big house giving turkeys and hams to the field hands for the holidays. I don't like it. And what about everybody else?" I said. "Maybe it's because they make the least," she suggested. "Well, what about administrative assistants? They probably make less than the public safety officers, or any of the skilled craftsmen," I countered. "How do we decide who gets a turkey and who doesn't? And besides that, I'm a vegetarian. Why would I give *anyone* a turkey or a ham?" "I don't know, Bev," she sighed. "What are you going to do? Everyone will be expecting it." "Well, I know one thing: If I do it once, I will have to keep doing it. If I don't want to continue this practice, now is the time to make a change." It was my first semester as president of Spelman College, and here we were, two women from Massachusetts, preparing for the holidays in Atlanta.

The workers in question fell under the auspices of the vice president for business and financial affairs, so I asked him about the history of the practice. He couldn't remember which president had started the giving of the turkeys and hams, but he was clear about one thing—there was no line item in my budget to support the purchase. I was sure it was intended to show appreciation for the staff, but I couldn't do it that way. He offered to tell the staff not to expect the turkeys and hams this year on my behalf. But I insisted that it was a message I would need to deliver myself. I had only been in my job a few months, and of course I wanted the staff to like me and see me as someone who cared about them. But surely I had to be true to myself in the process.

The VP and I agreed that I would speak to the employees at one of their regularly scheduled staff meetings. He would make sure that all the buildings and grounds and public safety officers would be there with their direct supervisors. What would I say? It was Friday, payday, and the dimly lit auditorium was full of dark-skinned men and women in blue uniforms. I couldn't help but notice the contrast with my own light-skinned complexion, so often associated with class privilege and status in the Black community, and I again thought of plantations, and the history of enslaved domestic workers who sometimes had access to education when enslaved field hands did not. Was it just a coincidence that the supervisors in the room were light-skinned men, and there I stood as the leader, the lightest one of all? Was I the only one thinking about that history in that moment? I didn't know, and I wasn't going to bring it up, but I felt that history hanging in the room like a ghost. The supervisor stepped forward to greet me and turned to his staff to introduce me. Many were meeting me up close for the first time, and they looked at me with curious but tired Friday faces. What had I come to say?

It took no more than five minutes. My effort to break the ice with a warm greeting, my earnest expression of my desire to honor and appreciate all our employees, and my concise explanation of my discomfort with the "turkeys and hams" practice because it did not include everyone, and of course, because I was a vegetarian. I kept my thoughts about race and class and plantations to myself. I acknowledged that I knew this might be disappointing news but said that I hoped I would be able to find another way to express my genuine thanks to all of them for their service. I paused, and the silence in the room was agonizing. It seemed to go on forever, as I looked out and saw blank faces staring back at me. Finally, one young man stood up in the back of the auditorium. After stating his name, he said, "Dr. Tatum, I am new here. I just started a few months ago, so I haven't ever received a turkey or anything else, but I just want to say that I'm OK with it." Kinder words had never been spoken, or so I thought. Then an older man in the front stood, and in a voice that clearly commanded the respect of his peers, he said, "I just want to say that I really appreciate that you came here and told us yourself. You didn't have to do that, and I want to thank you for it."

Relieved by the graciousness of these two men, I wondered for a moment what should happen next. The silence had returned. One of the supervisors invited the staff to take advantage of this opportunity to introduce themselves to the new president, and one by one each stood to say their name and job title. The process went quickly but not without commentary. As one of the housekeepers stood, I suspect she spoke for more than just herself when she said, "I'm going to miss my turkey."

Though delivering my message at that meeting was among the most awkward moments of my time at Spelman, I look back on it without regret. Doing anything else would not have been authentic for me. As the leader, I wanted to create a culture that was more collegial than hierarchical, more inclusive than exclusive, and instinctively I knew that meant doing some things differently from the beginning. Raising salaries for the lowest-paid employees (so they could buy their own turkeys and hams) was an important place to start, signaling that everyone in the organization was valued, and over time, we did that significantly. But thanking them was important too.

How was I going to do that? I decided to write them all thank-you notes. Every year the communications team created a beautiful holiday card, mass-produced with the president's signature. I used those cards to send each of the six hundred employees—faculty, staff, and administrators—one of those cards with a handwritten message of thanks for the work they did and why it mattered to the success of the college. While of course I did not know every individual personally, I knew what their job titles were, and I could imagine the work they did each day. I knew that each person, whether a housekeeper or a vice president, contributed something unique and valuable throughout the year, and I thanked them for it. In writing those notes—a project that took many weeks to complete (I started in October to be finished by early December)—I was able to celebrate all equally, regardless of their status in the institution. And over the years, as I did get to know individual employees, I could be ever more specific in my expression of gratitude. Thirteen years later, when I retired from Spelman, employees told me that they had saved every card they received from me, and that they displayed my handwritten messages at home with pride. In the end, a heartfelt thank-you was more long-lasting than any turkey or ham.

When I arrived back at Mount Holyoke as interim president for the year, I explained to my assistant that I would need to have the holiday cards ready in October so I could begin writing my thank-you notes. She asked, did I really intend to send everyone a card? The employee base, including part-timers, was about one thousand. Yes, I did. Coming out of two long pandemic years, so many people felt exhausted and worn down by the toll the pandemic had taken. Surely it was a community in need of some appreciation.

Of course, personalized thank-you notes are not always practical, perhaps because the employee population is just too large. Still, a heartfelt thank-you conveyed collectively can go a long way. At Spelman I also learned the power of a well-crafted email thank-you, a message that could be sent after the opening of school, at the end of a semester, following commencement. Anytime we had a collective "win," I learned to write a community message in which every division of the college was mentioned for its unique contribution to the success of that particular accomplishment. I repeated that practice at Mount Holyoke. The appreciative responses I received to those community messages from COVID-weary colleagues were gratifying. But nothing was better than the notes I received after sending the personalized holiday cards. Here are just a few:

- I just want to wish you a Happy New Year and thank you for the lift your holiday card gave me. I was not expecting that, and then to see your nice note—it gave me such a sense of being appreciated and valued!
- Thank you so very much for your note in my holiday card. I cannot tell you how much it means to me!
- A belated thanks for the kind note on your Christmas card. I was genuinely speechless when I read it.... [With one

exception] it is the only time in the last decade that I have felt genuinely appreciated by the administration at this college. (My wife was so surprised by your note, I think she told everyone she knew about it.)

Another wrote, "I can't imagine how you found the time for that, but it sent a strong signal that we are valued." I could tell the effort had cheered people up and boosted morale. And just as the happiness experts attest, thinking about each of the employees, the work they did every day, and why I was grateful for their service as I wrote each card made me happier, too.

THE PROBLEMS YOU SOLVE

When I retired from Spelman, I was often asked if I missed it. My short answer was no. I loved my job, but thirteen years was enough. I was exhausted and grateful for the break at a time when I really needed one. My longer answer was, "I don't miss the work. I do miss the people." The people I worked with every day were truly a source of joy. I worked with a close team of smart, talented problem-solvers who shared a commitment to our mission. My favorite part of the week was our staff meetings, because of the camaraderie I felt when we were focused on solving a problem. Problem-solving can be fun, especially when you have a great team to help you. There is deep satisfaction in finding a creative solution to a vexing problem.

When President LeBlanc reflected in an interview on an intense three-year period when he and his team were working hard to scale up the SNHU online program, he described that time as a "rocket ride." It was thrilling! He said, "Honestly, in some ways it was the three most fun years of my career....It was just fun. It was blowing up and it was like, Holy cow, every day was another problem we had to solve. But students were really well served, and they came to us in droves, and then we never looked back."[7]

Similarly, when Meredith Woo took the helm of Sweet Briar College just after the previous president had attempted to close its doors, she was facing many urgent issues. But she said, in the fall of 2015, just two months into her role, that Sweet Briar's recent struggles made it "really ripe for doing something bold and fundamental." She said, "We now have a campus where everybody's kind of united and ready to roll up their sleeves....Because we did this over the summer, it could not include 100 percent of the faculty, but the vast majority took part. It was actually a fairly joyful process—it was incredibly gratifying to work with a faculty eager for change."[8] To paraphrase Saint Benedict, there were many matters for concern, but Woo had found some reasons for joy. As senior *Chronicle of Higher Education* editor Alexander Kafka wrote in *Trouble at the Top*, a 2023 special report on the college presidency, "Problems let problem-solvers shine."[9] Problem-solvers can find daily joy in solving problems—and the role of campus leader provides a never-ending supply to work on!

THE PURPOSE YOU FULFILL

While I was a student at Hartford Seminary I eventually earned a master's degree in religious studies, and I had the great fortune to have as my adviser the president of the seminary, Barbara Brown Zikmund (known to many by her nickname, BBZ). During one of our last meetings together, BBZ asked me if I had considered becoming a college president. "I don't know if I would want that job," I said. Her question was followed by these words of wisdom: "*Well, a lot of people think you can just go out and find a presidency. It doesn't work that way; presidencies find you.* [Search consultants will come looking for you.] *And you can't be president of just any institution. The job is too demanding. It must be someplace you truly love. After all, you will do a lot for your lover.*" Those were words to remember.

What makes an institution a place you can truly love? The people, maybe even its problems, but most especially its mission—its purpose for existing. When I was contacted by a search consultant to inform me that I had been nominated as a potential candidate for the presidency of Spelman College, I wasn't sure I wanted the job. I liked what I was doing in Massachusetts. But I was intrigued enough by the idea to take a trip to Spelman, a campus I had never visited previously, to get the vibe of the place and see if I could imagine myself there. I flew to Atlanta just for the day and toured the campus with a friend, unannounced and unescorted by anyone from the college. We were a pair of anonymous campus visitors on a Friday afternoon in late January. The campus was alive with student activity, it was a balmy seventy-five degrees, and spring was already in the air. My friend and I stopped at the admissions office, and I asked for a brochure. The defining moment for me came when I read this paragraph on the back of that 2001–2002 admissions brochure:

> When you are inducted into the Spelman sisterhood in a candle-light ceremony, you are given the power to change your life and to light the world. When you graduate, you walk into the Oval and through the Arch, the same path past graduates have taken. For 120 years now, Spelman has sought to develop the total person: to instill in our students a sense of responsibility for bringing about positive change in the world. This is our heritage and our calling.

"To instill in our students a sense of responsibility for bringing about positive change in the world. This is our heritage and our calling." When I read those words, that felt like purpose to me. I was being called. Back at home that evening, I shared the brochure with my husband, who responded by saying, "This sounds like you wrote it. If you don't pursue it, you will always regret it." I knew that he was right. The Spelman mission statement sealed the deal.

Spelman College, a historically Black college and a global leader in the education of women of African descent, is dedicated to academic excellence in the liberal arts and sciences and the intellectual, creative, ethical and leadership development of its students. Through diverse learning modalities, Spelman empowers the whole person to engage the many cultures of the world and inspires a commitment to positive social change.

It spoke of excellence, leadership, empowerment, appreciation and respect for others, social change—values that have been at the core of my personal and professional work for my entire career. During my years of study at Hartford Seminary, I had been asking myself, "Where could I make the most meaningful impact?" What I learned on that first visit to Spelman College convinced me that I could make a unique and meaningful contribution to higher education and the world by leading that institution, which had (and still has) such a powerful mission. I was falling in love. Three months later I was announced as the incoming ninth president of Spelman College.

Spelman College flourished, and so did I, despite the challenge of navigating the hazards posed by the years of the Great Recession. Upon my arrival in 2002, I told the campus community that I wanted Spelman College to be recognized as one of the finest liberal arts colleges in the country—a place where young women of African descent could say, "This place was built for me *and* it is nothing less than the best!" Thirteen years later, when I retired from the role in the summer of 2015, it was indeed widely recognized not only as the best HBCU in the nation, but more broadly as one of the leading liberal arts colleges in the United States. Spelman graduates truly are positive agents of change in the world, empowered by the unique learning environment students find there. Articulating a bold vision and working collaboratively with an entire campus community to bring that vision to fruition were a tremendous privilege. The presidential burden of responsibility was offset by the joy of shared accomplishment and the knowledge that Spelman College was, and still is, shining brightly as a strong beacon of opportunity for the next generation of powerful women. That is *still* a reason for joy!

In 2013, I received the Carnegie Academic Leadership Award in the company of my three fellow honorees, one of whom was Michael Crow, president since 2002 of Arizona State University. Under his leadership, ASU has been repeatedly recognized as the number one university in the nation for innovation.[10] Crow's vision for ASU has become known as the "New American University," described succinctly by its new charter, adopted in 2014: "ASU is a comprehensive **public research university**, measured not by whom it excludes, but by **whom it includes** and **how they succeed**; advancing **research and discovery** of public value; and assuming **fundamental responsibility** for the economic, social, cultural and overall health of the **communities it serves**."[11] Along with the new charter is a new objective, to prepare "master learners," defined as those who have been trained to think critically and are ready to learn anything in a world where knowledge is advancing rapidly:

> Though their expertise may lie in certain areas, the way they learn and apply information will be radically different from past generations, allowing them to move seamlessly between disciplines and to work collaboratively with others in innovative ways.
>
> The reconceptualization of ASU as a comprehensive knowledge enterprise has evolved precisely to prepare this type of broadly proficient thought-leader, focused on deriving purpose-driven solutions and improving the quality of life for all mankind.[12]

In 2023, with more than twenty years at the helm, President Crow reflected on one source of the tremendous energy he has brought to the task of leadership, honing and delivering on the Arizona State mission.

He said, "For me, it is impossible to imagine burning out.... [Each new wave of students] is so awe-inspiring to me...their new ideas about society, their ambitions about the future....My energy, my drive, my hopes, they only accelerate....You only get this little life. But you get to live it *here*, man. It's unbelievable."[13] That is the sound of joy that comes from fulfilling one's sense of purpose.

As I was working to complete this book, I had a conversation with another presidential colleague who has been dealing with very difficult enrollment challenges. The cliff is looming. I asked her what gave her joy. She said, "I want to show you a photo I have on my phone." It was a photo taken at commencement of a mother and the president standing together in a hallway, both women crying. She explained that the mother had seen her in the hallway and rushed over to tell her how grateful she was for all the college had done for her daughter, the first in their family to graduate from college. The family had made a lot of financial sacrifices to get to the finish line, and it had not been easy for either the mom or her daughter. But they had made it. As the mother told her story, both women started to cry, the moment captured on a cell phone. "This is why I do this work," she told me. "This is what keeps me going."

Who in their right mind would want that job? It is a fair question. It is undoubtedly a very challenging time to be a college president. There are understandable reasons why there is so much turnover at the top, the length of presidential service getting steadily shorter and shorter. But each day there are indeed reasons for joy. To the reader wondering about assuming a leadership role, I say if you can find the joy, you just might be able to do the job. To everyone else, please know that joyful leadership relies on the support of others.

We live in a time when we are quick to criticize missteps, to publicize and amplify failures. Yet if we are to cultivate and keep good leaders, we must be intentional about lending support, calling them in when necessary rather than calling them out. At a worship service celebrating my

Spelman inauguration, my dear friend Rev. Ed Harding told the story of geese flying in formation. The lead goose, he explained, takes the brunt of the wind and sets the course for the flock. As the lead goose gets tired, it drops back in the formation and another goose comes forward to take the lead. What are the other geese doing as they follow behind? They honk! Their honking encourages the lead goose to keep going, and lets the leader know that they're still there, following. He told the audience that it was their job to keep honking, to support a tired leader, to offer encouragement and counsel.

Every generation has its unique challenges, and there is no question that the twenty-first century is proving to be an especially difficult time for institutional leaders. What our nineteenth- and twentieth-century predecessors accomplished transformed lives—and society—for the better. Despite the hardships, they persisted. Today's college leaders are still in the same business. The challenges are real, but so are the reasons for joy, as we renew education's promise of transformation for the generations to come.

ACKNOWLEDGMENTS

No one writes a book alone. What I know about higher education I have learned from many people. There are always helpers, seen and unseen, past and present. My parents are both now deceased, but I would not be writing this book without all that they invested in me. Travis Tatum, my beloved husband, is my biggest fan, and most important critic. He reads every sentence and gives me his honest opinion before anyone else gets to see what I have written. Our longtime friend and retired provost, Joan Rasool, was another reader who gave me great feedback, especially as I navigated writing about the complicated campus politics surrounding the Israel-Hamas war. My walking buddy and fellow college trustee, Molly Burke, was a patient listener as I outlined my writing plans and the arguments I was making. Two dear friends in New England, Andrea Ayvazian and Rita McDougald-Campbell, each helped me over the finish line, sending emoji prayers and encouraging email messages throughout the months of my writing.

My siblings and I live at great distances from one another, but we started meeting up over Zoom in 2020 and have been doing so every couple of weeks since then. To Eric, Patti, Kevin—and partners, Angela, Matt, and Melissa—I really appreciated our Zoom conversations and your encouragement as I leaned into getting this book done. Writing a book always feels to me like birthing a baby—at the end, you just want it out of your body and into the world! Our two real babies, our sons David and Ajíṣafé, have grown up to be fine men who make us proud. I trust they will read this book with pride.

We moved to Atlanta in 2002, and more than two decades later it is now the place we have lived the longest. As president of Spelman, I was surrounded by the support of so many people, on campus and off, whom I now count as friends and fellow community members working to make our city the best place it can be for all of us. There are too many of you to name, but I trust you know who you are. Thank you!

Sadly, some of my closest colleagues have passed on, while others have retired or moved on to new positions; all are appreciated! I especially want to lift up the names of the deceased: Jane Smith, the dynamic builder of our Leadership Center; Cathy Daniels, whose legal skills and calm presence as board secretary were invaluable; and Robert "Danny" Flanigan, who was the best CFO I could have ever imagined, a true "partner in progress," as my colleague Eloise Alexis liked to say. A special shout-out to the rest of my team—Delores Barton, Myra Burnett, Tomika DePriest, Ingrid Hayes, Kassandra Jolley, Darnita Killian, and most especially the dynamic duo that traveled with me from Massachusetts to Atlanta, Yvonne Skillings and Sherry Turner. Consultants can be very helpful—and over the years I relied on three: Patricia Romney, Karin George, and Michelle Matthews. Thank you all! Thirteen years would not have been possible without your help and support!

Every president needs the support of faculty. Candid feedback is sometimes hard to come by. I want to especially thank Cynthia Spence for her wisdom and friendship, and Beverly Guy-Sheftall for always being willing to give honest feedback.

I had the privilege of working with wonderful trustees at Spelman, again too many to name. But I want to especially thank Yvonne Jackson, who chaired the presidential search committee that brought me to Spelman and who taught me so much about what good governance looks like. A special thank-you to Ronda Stryker for her extraordinary generosity for all the years that I have known her.

My administrative leadership journey began at Mount Holyoke College under the leadership of President Joanne Creighton. Thank you, Joanne, for opening that door! When I returned to Mount Holyoke as interim president, I was in desperate need of an interim CFO—Mary Jo Maydew came to my rescue. It made that year so much better! Thank you, Mary Jo, and to the rest of the team at MHC—it was a privilege to continue learning with you.

I also want to thank the Academic Leadership Institute (ALI) co-founders, Earl Lewis and Dwight McBride, as well as my ALI faculty colleagues and the 2024 summer cohort in particular. Our timely conversations about topics related to my book helped me get the manuscript over the finish line.

Over the forty-plus years of my higher ed career, I have had great teachers and fabulous students. My undergraduate mentor, the late Mrs. Fay Boulware, introduced me to ideas in psychology I have used throughout my career. My University of Michigan doctoral dissertation adviser, Eric Bermann, passed away in 2023. I will always be grateful for his support at such a critical stage in my early career. To my MHC and Spelman mentees who are now out in the world doing great things, you keep hope alive! Thank you.

Throughout my leadership journey, I often turned to my friend and spiritual mentor Rev. Ed Harding Jr., who taught me so much about listening to one's inner voice. Ed passed away in 2024 while I was working on this book. I will always be grateful for his friendship and wisdom. I am still listening.

To my agent Faith Childs and my publisher Lara Heimert, thanks for helping me see that I should write a more ambitious book than the one that I had originally planned. This one is the right one for such a time as this.

NOTES

Introduction: For Such a Time as This

1. Daniel Drexner, "You Could Not Pay Me Enough to Be a College President," *Chronicle of Higher Education*, December 14, 2023; Alan Blinder and Stephanie Saul, "Anyone Want to Be a College President? There Are (Many) Openings," *New York Times*, May 22, 2024; Gabriel Sanchez, Katia Riddle, and Ari Shapiro, "Campus Protests Prompt the Question: Who Wants to Be a College President?," *NPR: All Things Considered*, August 15, 2024.

2. Chronicle of Higher Education, "The College Presidency Is Broken. Here's How to Fix It," *Chronicle of Higher Education*, October 8, 2024.

3. Adam Harris, "Who Wants to Be a College President?," *Atlantic*, January 24, 2019.

4. Adam Liptak, "In 6-to-3 Ruling, Supreme Court Ends Nearly 50 Years of Abortion Rights," *New York Times*, June 24, 2022.

5. Nina Totenberg, "Supreme Court Guts Affirmative Action, Effectively Ending Race-Conscious Admissions," NPR, June 29, 2023.

6. Only five remain as women's colleges today: Mount Holyoke, Smith, Wellesley, Barnard, and Bryn Mawr. Vassar College now admits men. Radcliffe College merged with Harvard University and is now the Radcliffe Institute for Advanced Study.

7. The focus throughout this book is on the undergraduate experience.

8. V. Irwin, K. Wang, T. Tezil, J. Zhang, A. Filbey, J. Jung, F. Bullock Mann, R. Dilig, and S. Parker, *Report on the Condition of Education 2023*, NCES 2023-144rev (Washington, DC: National Center for Education Statistics, 2023), https://nces.ed.gov/pubsearch/pubsinfo.asp?pubid=2023144rev.

9. National Center for Education Statistics, Digest of Education Statistics, "Total Fall Enrollment in Degree-Granting Postsecondary Institutions, by Level and Control of Institution and Race/Ethnicity or Nonresident Status of Student:

Selected Years, 1976 Through 2022," Table 306.20, https://nces.ed.gov/programs/digest/index.asp.

10. Lyss Welding, "College Enrollment Statistics in the U.S.," *Best Colleges*, February 7, 2024.

11. V. Irwin, K. Wang, J. Jung, E. Kessler, T. Tezil, S. Alhassani, A. Filbey, R. Dilig, and F. Bullock Mann, *Report on the Condition of Education 2024*, NCES 2024-144 (Washington, DC: National Center for Education Statistics, 2024), https://nces.ed.gov/pubsearch/pubsinfo.asp?pubid=2024144.

12. Best Colleges, "What Is a For-Profit College?," www.bestcolleges.com/blog/what-is-a-for-profit-college/.

13. Stephanie Riegg Cellini, "The Alarming Rise in For-Profit College Enrollment," Brookings, November 2, 2020. Italics in original.

14. Chris Quintana, "Are For-Profit Colleges Worth the Cost? Graduates Are Split on the Value of Their Degrees," *USA Today*, January 31, 2023.

15. V. Irwin et al., *Report on the Condition of Education 2024*, 30.

16. American Council on Education, *The American College President: 2023 Edition—Pathways to the Presidency* (Washington, DC: American Council on Education, 2023).

17. Mary Dana Hinton, *Leading from the Margins: College Leadership from Unexpected Places* (Baltimore: Johns Hopkins University Press, 2024), 3.

18. White House, "Ending Illegal Discrimination and Restoring Merit-Based Opportunity: Executive Order," January 21, 2025, www.whitehouse.gov/presidential-actions/2025/01/ending-illegal-discrimination-and-restoring-merit-based-opportunity/.

19. Katherine Mangan, "How a Trump Executive Order Could Upend Colleges' Hiring Practices," *Chronicle of Higher Education*, January 22, 2025.

20. White House, "Defending Women from Gender Ideology Extremism and Restoring Biological Truth to the Federal Government: Executive Order," January 20, 2025, www.whitehouse.gov/presidential-actions/2025/01/defending-women-from-gender-ideology-extremism-and-restoring-biological-truth-to-the-federal-government/.

21. Geoff Mulvihill, "6 Ways Trump's Executive Orders Are Targeting Transgender People," *PBS News*, February 1, 2025, www.pbs.org/newshour/politics/6-ways-trumps-executive-orders-are-targeting-transgender-people.

22. Kate Hidalgo Bellows and Sarah Brown, "Colleges, the Title IX Changes Are Finally Here. What's in Them?," *Chronicle of Higher Education*, April 19, 2024.

23. Kate Hidalgo Bellows, "Biden's Title IX Rule Is Now Blocked Nationwide. Here's What That Means," *Chronicle of Higher Education*, January 9, 2025.

24. Maddie Khaw, "4 Years Later, Trump's Title IX Rule Is Back. It's Whiplash for Colleges," *Chronicle of Higher Education*, January 31, 2025.

25. US Department of Education Office of Civil Rights, "Dear Colleague" letter, February 4, 2025, www.ed.gov/media/document/title-ix-enforcement -directive-dcl.

26. Khaw, "4 Years Later."

27. Zolan Kanno-Youngs, Michael D. Shear, and Noah Weiland, "Trump's Executive Orders: Reversing Biden's Policies and Attacking the 'Deep State,'" *New York Times*, January 20, 2025.

28. Maya Stahl, "What Some Colleges Say They'll Do If Immigration Authorities Come to Campus," *Chronicle of Higher Education*, January 27, 2025.

29. Phillip Levine, "What Trump Means for College Budgets," *Chronicle of Higher Education*, January 22, 2025.

30. Stephanie M. Lee, "Here's How Science Funding Could Change Under Trump," *Chronicle of Higher Education*, January 23, 2025.

31. See Ian Bogost, "The Chaos in Higher Ed Is Only Getting Started," *Atlantic*, January 24. 2025. Bogost was quoting UCLA Professor Lindsay Wiley.

32. Phillip Levine, "How Trump Could Devastate Our Top Colleges' Finances," *Chronicle of Higher Education*, January 13, 2025.

Chapter One: The Dean with the ABC Agenda

1. Beverly Daniel Tatum, "Talking About Race, Learning About Racism: The Application of Racial Identity Development Theory in the Classroom," *Harvard Educational Review* 62, no. 1 (Spring 1992): 1–24.

2. Beverly Daniel Tatum, *Why Are All the Black Kids Sitting Together in the Cafeteria? And Other Conversations About Race*, 20th anniversary rev. ed. (New York: Basic Books, 2017).

3. National Center for Education Statistics, "Full-Time Faculty in Degree-Granting Postsecondary Institutions, by Race/Ethnicity, Sex, and Academic Rank: Fall 2020, Fall 2021, and Fall 2022," Table 315.20.

4. William J. Clinton, "Commencement Address at the University of California San Diego in La Jolla, California," June 14, 1997, American Presidency Project, September 23, 2024.

5. The other two authors were David Shipler and Abigail Thernstrom.

6. "About The Program on Intergroup Relations," http://igr.umich.edu/about.

7. Jean Baker Miller, "Connections, Disconnections and Violations," *Work in Progress*, no. 33 (Wellesley, MA: Stone Center Working Paper Series, 1988).

8. Beverly Daniel Tatum, "Who Am I?," chap. 2 in *Why Are All the Black Kids Sitting Together in the Cafeteria?*

9. Eric Jensen, Nicholas Jones, Megan Rabe, Beverly Pratt, Lauren Medina, Kimberly Orozco, and Lindsay Spell, "2020 U.S. Population More Racially, Ethnically Diverse Than in 2010," United States Census Bureau, August 12, 2021.

10. Sandy Dietrich and Erik Hernandez, "What Languages Do We Speak in the United States?," United States Census Bureau, December 6, 2022.

11. PRRI Staff, *2023 PRRI Census of American Religion: County-Level Data on Religious Identity and Diversity*, August 29, 2024.

12. See Geoffrey L. Cohen, "Belonging in School," chap. 9 in *Belonging: The Science of Creating Connection and Bridging Divides* (New York: W. W. Norton, 2022).

13. Herbert Kohl, "I Won't Learn from You: Confronting Student Resistance," in *Rethinking Our Classrooms: Teaching for Equity and Justice*, rev. ed., vol. 1, ed. Wayne Au, Bill Bigelow, and Stan Karp (Milwaukee: Rethinking Our Schools, 2007), 165–166.

14. Gathering with those who have shared experiences of marginalization for mutual support should not be equated with true segregation, the state-mandated, legalized enforcement of rigid controls regarding access to public goods and services and other civil rights.

15. Julie J. Park, *Race on Campus: Debunking Myths with Data* (Cambridge, MA: Harvard Education Press, 2018), 24–25.

16. Gordon W. Allport, *The Nature of Prejudice* (Boston: Addison-Wesley, 1954).

17. US Government Accountability Office, "K–12 Education: Student Population Has Significantly Diversified, but Many Schools Remain Divided Along Racial, Ethnic, and Economic Lines," GAO-22-104737, June 16, 2022.

18. Henry A. Giroux, "Resisting Difference: Cultural Studies and the Discourse of Critical Pedagogy," in *Cultural Studies*, ed. Lawrence Grossberg, Cary Nelson, and Paula Treichler (New York: Routledge, 1992), 209.

19. The terminology "from the center to the margin" is attributable to bell hooks, *Feminist Theory: From Margin to Center* (Boston: South End, 1984), xvii–xviii.

20. Heather McGhee, *The Sum of Us: What Racism Costs Everyone and How We Can Prosper Together* (New York: One World, 2022).

21. "College Makes Regular-Admission Offers to 1,220, as University Changes Family-Income Threshold for Second Year," *Harvard Gazette*, March 30, 2023.

22. Nolan L. Cabrera, *White Guys on Campus: Racism, White Immunity, and the Myth of "Post-racial" Higher Education* (New Brunswick, NJ: Rutgers University Press, 2019).

23. For a comprehensive summary of this social science research see Geoffrey Cohen, *Belonging: The Science of Creating Connection and Bridging Divides* (New York: W. W. Norton, 2022).

24. "Day of Dialogue Welcome Ceremony," Franklin and Marshall College, October 5, 2016, www.youtube.com/watch?v=-azgbWIWFjk.

25. For more information about Audre Lorde and her relationship to Spelman College see Johnnetta Betsch Cole and Beverly Guy-Sheftall, "Audre Lorde and Spelman College," *Feminist Wire*, February 27, 2014.

Chapter Two: Who's Afraid of DEI—and Why?

1. Robert H. Terte, "New College Due in Florida in '64; Privately Endowed School to Be Open to All Races," *New York Times*, July 24, 1961.

2. New College of Florida, History Highlights, www.ncf.edu/about/history/#.

3. Steven Walker, "New College of Florida Sees Record Enrollment After DeSantis Shakeup, but at Academic Cost," *USA Today*, July 27, 2023.

4. Derek Black changed his name in 2013 to Roland Derek Black and has written his own book: R. Derek Black, *The Klansman's Son: My Journey from White Nationalism to Antiracism* (New York: Abrams, 2024).

5. Eli Saslow, *Rising out of Hatred: The Awakening of a Former White Nationalist* (New York: Doubleday, 2018), 6.

6. Saslow, *Rising out of Hatred*, 22.

7. Saslow, 48.

8. Bill Woodson, "We Didn't Get It Then, but We Get It Now," New College of Florida, January 31, 2021, www.ncf.edu/news/we-didnt-get-it-then-but-we-get-it-now/.

9. Saslow, *Rising out of Hatred*, 218–219.

10. Saslow, 225.

11. Silvia Hurtado, "Reaffirming Educators' Judgment: Educational Value of Diversity," *Liberal Education* 85, no. 2 (1999): 24–31.

12. Patricia Gurin, Eric L. Dey, Sylvia Hurtado, and Gerald Gurin, "Diversity and Higher Education: Theory and Impact on Educational Outcomes," *Harvard Educational Review* 72, no. 3 (2002): 330–366.

13. Cleveland Clinic, "Stockholm Syndrome: What It Is, Symptoms and How to Treat," February 14, 2022.

14. Merriam-Webster Wordplay, "Stay Woke: The New Sense of 'Woke' Is Gaining Popularity," www.merriam-webster.com/wordplay/woke-meaning-origin.

15. Josh Moody, "DeSantis Aims to Turn Public College into 'Hillsdale of the South,'" *Inside Higher Ed*, January 10, 2023.

16. Benjamin Wallace-Wells, "How a Conservative Activist Invented the Conflict over Critical Race Theory," *New Yorker*, June 18, 2021.

17. Moody, "DeSantis Aims to Turn Public College into 'Hillsdale of the South.'"

18. Johanna Alonso, "Chaos at New College of Florida," *Inside Higher Ed*, August 16, 2023.

19. Susan Dominus, "Recruited to Play Sports, and Win a Culture War," *New York Times Magazine*, January 31, 2024.

20. Walker, "New College of Florida Sees Record Enrollment."

21. Dominus, "Recruited to Play Sports."

22. Anemona Hartocollis, "Florida Eliminates Sociology as a Core Course at Its Universities," *New York Times*, January 24, 2024.

23. Josh Moody, "DEI Spending Banned, Sociology Scrapped in Florida," *Inside Higher Ed*, January 18, 2024.

24. Hartocollis, "Florida Eliminates Sociology."

25. Ryan Quinn, "New College of Florida Is Dumping Books—and Losing Professors," *Inside Higher Ed*, August 20, 2024.

26. Patricia Okker, "I Was President of Florida's New College. Then I Was Fired," *Chronicle of Higher Education*, July 19, 2023.

27. Karen Fischer, "Why Hungary Inspired Trump's Vision for Higher Ed," *Chronicle of Higher Education*, January 15, 2025.

28. Fischer, "Why Hungary Inspired Trump's Vision."

29. *Eyes on the Prize: America's Civil Rights Years, 1954–1965*, directed by Henry Hampton (Blackside Production, 1987).

30. Beverly Daniel Tatum, "Talking About Race, Learning About Racism: The Application of Racial Identity Development Theory in the Classroom," *Harvard Educational Review* 62, no. 1 (Spring 1992): 1–24.

31. "DEI Legislation Tracker," *Chronicle of Higher Education*, August 30, 2024.

32. Kelly Field, "What's in a Name? After Texas Banned DEI, a Campus Space for LGBTQ Students Got an Overhaul," *Chronicle of Higher Education*, February 12, 2024.

33. Field, "What's in a Name?"

34. Daarel Burnette II, "Race on Campus: Some Observations About the Evolution of Anti-DEI Legislation," *Chronicle of Higher Education*, February 20, 2024.

35. *Educational Gag Orders: Legislative Restrictions on the Freedom to Read, Learn, and Teach*, Pen America Report, November 8, 2021.

36. *Educational Gag Orders*, 12–13.

37. Marguerite Ward, "Top CEOs in the US Unveil Plan to Advance Racial Equity," *Business Insider*, October 15, 2020.

38. Marguerite Ward, "Over 160 Business Groups Ask President Trump to Withdraw Executive Order Banning Diversity Training," *Business Insider*, October 16, 2020.

39. *Educational Gag Orders*, 22.

40. Martin Luther King Jr., *Where Do We Go from Here: Chaos or Community?* (Boston: Beacon, 1968), 12.

41. Juliana Menasce Horowitz and Ruth Igielnik, "A Century After Women Gained the Right to Vote, Majority of Americans See Work to Do on Gender Equality," Pew Research Center, July 2020.

42. Hannah Hartig, Andrew Daniller, Scott Keeter, and Ted Van Green, "Voter Turnout, 2018–2022," Pew Research Center, July 12, 2023; Will Wilder and Stuart Baum, "5 Egregious Voter Suppression Laws from 2021," Brennan Center for Justice, January 31, 2022.

43. Kim Parker, Juliana Menasce Horowitz, and Anna Brown, "Americans' Complex Views on Gender Identity and Transgender Issues," Pew Research Center, June 28, 2022.

44. Luona Lin, Juliana Menasce Horowitz, Kiley Hurst, and Dana Braga, "Race and LGBTQ Issues in K–12 Schools," Pew Research Center, February 22, 2024.

45. White House, "The Inaugural Address," January 20, 2025.

46. NPR News, "Historian Discusses the Politics That Shape U.S. History in Schools," *All Things Considered*, January 24, 2021.

47. Tatum, "Talking About Race," 1–24.

48. Ximena Zúñiga, B. A. Nagda, Mark Chesler, and Adena Cytron-Walker, "Intergroup Dialogue in Higher Education: Meaningful Learning About Social Justice," *ASHE Higher Education Report* 32, no. 4 (2007).

49. Patricia Gurin, Biren (Ratnesh) A. Nagda, and Ximena Zúñiga, *Dialogue Across Difference: Practice, Theory, and Research on Intergroup Dialogue* (New York: Russell Sage Foundation, 2013), chap. 2.

50. Kristie A. Ford, ed., *Facilitating Change Through Intergroup Dialogue: Social Justice Advocacy in Practice* (New York: Routledge, 2017).

51. Lasya Priya Rao Jarugumilli, Mount Holyoke College 2021 fall convocation speech, August 29, 2021, personal communication.

52. Ford, *Facilitating Change*, chap. 1.

53. Gurin, Nagda, and Zúñiga, *Dialogue Across Difference*, 165.

54. Gurin, Nagda, and Zúñiga, 166.

55. Rani Varghese et al., "Higher Learning and Future of Intergroup Dialogue: The Importance of Community Partnerships," presentation given at Mount Holyoke College Intergroup Dialogue Symposium, November 18, 2023; George D. Kuh, *High Impact Educational Practices: What They Are, Who Has Access to Them, and Why They Matter* (Washington, DC: AAC&U, 2008).

56. Beverly Daniel Tatum, *Why Are All the Black Kids Sitting Together in the Cafeteria? And Other Conversations About Race*, 20th anniversary rev. ed. (New York: Basic Books, 2017), 202.

57. Tatum, epilogue.

58. Everyday Democracy, accessed March 1, 2024, https://everyday-democracy .org/.

59. Essential Partners, accessed March 1, 2024, https://whatisessential.org/.

60. Kristie Ford and Marcella Runell, "Intergroup Dialogue: Learning from Its Past and Mapping Its Future," unpublished video, screened at the Mount Holyoke College Intergroup Dialogue Symposium, November 18, 2023.

61. Kristie Ford and Marcella Runell video, David Schoem interview, November 18, 2023.

62. Okker, "I Was President of Florida's New College."

63. Eric Kelderman, "College Presidents Are Quietly Organizing to Support DEI," *Chronicle of Higher Education*, January 29, 2024.

64. Kelderman, "College Presidents Are Quietly Organizing."

65. Robert Hart, "Georgia House Passes Bill Stripping Delta of a Multimillion Tax Break After It Slammed the State's New Voting Restrictions," *Forbes*, April 1, 2021.

66. Gabriella Borter and David Morgan, "Exclusive: U.S. Lawmakers Demand Harvard, MIT, Penn Remove Presidents After Antisemitism Hearing," Reuters, December 8, 2023.

67. Chris Otts, "University of Louisville President Affirms Support for DEI," WDRB.com, February 19, 2024.

68. Sarah Brown, "Trump Singled Out These 130 Colleges as Possible Targets for Investigation. Is Yours on the List?," *Chronicle of Higher Education*, January 24, 2025.

69. "Dear Colleague Letter," US Department of Education Office for Civil Rights, February 14, 2025, www.ed.gov/media/document/dear-colleague-letter-sffa-v-harvard-109506.pdf.

70. Liam Knox, "Ed Department: DEI Violates Civil Rights Law," *Inside Higher Ed*, February 15, 2025.

71. Liliana Garces, "Hitting Pause on the 'Dear Colleague' Letter," *Chronicle of Higher Education*, February 18, 2025.

72. Eli Capilouto, "Important Legislative Update," University of Kentucky, Office of the President, February 14, 2024.

Chapter Three: Free Speech in the Time of War

1. Erwin Chemerinsky and Howard Gillman, *Free Speech on Campus* (New Haven, CT: Yale University Press, 2018), preface.

2. Chemerinsky and Gillman, 14.

3. Chemerinsky and Gillman, 11.

4. Chemerinsky and Gillman, preface.

5. Michael S. Roth and Jeffrey Sonnenfeld, "For College Leaders, Silence on Israel-Hamas Is Not Golden," *Time*, November 22, 2023; Josh Moody, "College Leaders' Mideast Statements Spark Controversy on Both Sides," *Inside Higher Ed*, October 18, 2023.

6. Tanner Stening, "How the Israel-Hamas War Turned Language into a Battleground," *Northeastern Global News*, October 2, 2024.

7. Sharon Otterman, "Columbia Symbolized Campus Strife over the Israel-Hamas War. What Changed?," *New York Times*, December 29, 2023.

8. Anna Betts and Jenna Russell, "For Palestinian Students Shot in Vermont, Two Worlds Collapsed into One," *New York Times*, December 3, 2023; Vimal

Patel and Anna Betts, "How Campuses Are Clamping Down on Pro-Palestinian Speech," *New York Times*, December 17, 2023.

9. Stephanie Saul and Anemona Hartocollis, "College Presidents Under Fire After Dodging Questions About Antisemitism," *New York Times*, December 6, 2023.

10. Michelle Goldberg, "At a Hearing on Israel, University Presidents Walked into a Trap," Opinion, *New York Times*, December 7, 2023.

11. Jenna Russell, "So Far, No Major Fallout for M.I.T. President After Contentious Testimony," *New York Times*, December 13, 2023.

12. Claudine Gay, "Claudine Gay: What Just Happened at Harvard Is Bigger Than Me," Opinion, *New York Times*, January 3, 2024.

13. Nicholas Confessore, "How a Proxy Fight over Campus Politics Brought Down Harvard's President," *New York Times*, January 3, 2024; Alia Wong, "Claudine Gay Was Just the Start: US College Presidents Feel a Chilling Effect," *USA Today*, January 4, 2024.

14. Liz Mineo, "On Campus and Beyond, Rise of 'Natural Leader' Cause for Celebration," *Harvard Gazette*, December 15, 2022.

15. Stephanie Saul, "Stanford President Will Resign After Report Found Flaws in His Research," *New York Times*, July 19, 2023.

16. Lisa M. Rasmussen, "Stanford President Marc Tessier-Lavigne and the New Standards of Scientific Conduct," *STAT*, July 21, 2023.

17. *The State of Black Women in Corporate America: 2020*, LeanIn.org, August 13, 2020.

18. Ryan Quinn, "Black Scholars Face Anonymous Accusations in Anti-DEI Crusade," *Inside Higher Ed*, April 1, 2024.

19. Robert A. Pape, *Understanding Campus Fears After October 7 and How to Reduce Them*, Chicago Project on Security and Threats (CPOST), University of Chicago, March 7, 2024, iii.

20. Pape, 9.

21. Sheri Walsh, "Former Cornell Student Pleads Guilty to Posting Anti-Semitic Threats," UPI, April 10, 2024.

22. Pape, *Understanding Campus Fears*, 3.

23. Pape, 10.

24. Brian Bushard, "'Doxxing Truck' Takes Columbia—Here's What to Know About the Trucks That Post Names of Students," *Forbes*, October 26, 2023.

25. Pape, *Understanding Campus Fears*, 33.

26. Pape, 12–13.

27. Pape, 12–13.

28. Pape, 16.

29. Pape, iv–v.

30. Columbia University, "Our Values," accessed March 1, 2024, https://cufo .columbia.edu/content/mission-vision-values.

31. Sharon Otterman, "How Columbia's President Has Avoided Fallout over Israel-Gaza Protests," *New York Times*, December 29, 2023.

32. Columbia University, "Deans' Message on Columbia and Community," December 20, 2023.

33. Columbia University, "Deans' Message."

34. Christopher L. Eisgruber, *President's Annual "State of the University" Letter 2024: Excellence, Inclusivity, and Free Speech*, Princeton University, January 18, 2024.

35. Eisgruber, *President's Annual "State of the University" Letter 2024*.

36. Pape, *Understanding Campus Fears*, 35.

37. Len Gutkin, "A Decade of Ideological Transformation Comes Undone," *Chronicle of Higher Education*, December 22, 2023.

38. Erin Gretzinger, "Can Colleges Foster Civil Discourse?," *Chronicle of Higher Education*, March 22, 2024.

39. Gretzinger, "Can Colleges Foster Civil Discourse?"

40. Beverly Daniel Tatum, "Talking About Race, Learning About Racism: The Application of Racial Identity Development Theory in the Classroom," *Harvard Educational Review* 62, no. 1 (Spring 1992): 1–24.

41. Gretzinger, "Can Colleges Foster Civil Discourse?"

42. Maud S. Mandel, "Campus Vigil on Israel and Gaza, and the College President's Role in the Wake of World Crises," Office of the President, Williams College, October 12, 2023.

43. "What We Know About the Colorado Springs Shooting," *New York Times*, November 22, 2022.

44. Derrick Bryson Taylor, "What We Know About the Michigan State University Shooting," *New York Times*, February 14, 2022.

45. Mandel, "Campus Vigil on Israel and Gaza, and the College President's Role in the Wake of World Crises."

46. Harry Kalven Jr. et al., *Kalven Committee: Report on the University's Role in Political and Social Action*, University of Chicago, November 11, 1967.

47. Kalven et al., *Kalven Committee: Report*.

48. Pape, *Understanding Campus Fears*, 38.

49. Sally Kornbluth, "Letter from the President: New Steps for a New Year," Office of the President, Massachusetts Institute of Technology, January 3, 2024.

50. Carrie N. Baker, "For Equality, Loretta Ross Argues We 'Call In,' Not 'Call Out': 'There's Too Much Infighting in the Feminist Movement,'" *Ms. Magazine*, May 20, 2021.

51. Claudine Gay, "Installation Address: Courage to Be Harvard," *Harvard Magazine*, November–December 2023.

52. Alan Blinder, "4 Takeaways from Today's Hearing on Antisemitism at Columbia University," *New York Times*, April 17, 2024.

53. Nicholas Fandos, Stephanie Saul, and Sharon Otterman, "Columbia Leaders Grilled at Antisemitism Hearing over Faculty Comments," *New York Times*, April 17, 2024.

54. Stephanie Saul, "Who Are the Columbia Professors Mentioned in the House Hearing?," *New York Times*, April 17, 2024.

55. Joseph Massad, "Just Another Battle or the Palestinian War of Liberation?," *Electronic Intifada*, October 8, 2023.

56. Noah Bernstein, "Petition Calling for Removal of MESAAS Professor Joseph Massad Garners over 47,000 Signatures," *Columbia Daily Spectator*, October 17, 2023.

57. Sarah Brown, Sonel Cutler, and Alecia Taylor, "How Faculty Discipline Played a Key Role in the Congressional Hearing on Columbia U.," *Chronicle of Higher Education*, April 17, 2024.

58. Fandos, Saul, and Otterman, "Columbia Leaders Grilled."

59. Katherine Knott and Jessica Blake, "Columbia President Grilled over Campus Antisemitism," *Inside Higher Ed*, April 18, 2024.

60. Len Gutkin, "The Antisemitism Hearing Forgot About Academic Freedom," *Chronicle of Higher Education*, April 22, 2024.

61. Gutkin, "Antisemitism Hearing Forgot."

62. Chemerinsky and Gillman, *Free Speech on Campus*, 47.

63. Kalven et al., *Kalven Committee: Report*.

64. I have paraphrased Audre Lorde from the title of her posthumously published book. See Audre Lorde, *Your Silence Will Not Protect You* (London: Silver, 2017).

Chapter Four: Who's in Charge, Really? Understanding Shared Governance

1. Ryan Quinn, "Columbia President Accused of Throwing Profs 'Under the Bus,'" *Inside Higher Ed*, April 19, 2024.

2. Quinn, "Columbia President Accused."

3. Association of Governing Boards, "AGB Board of Directors' Statement on Shared Governance," 2017.

4. Spelman College Board of Trustees, "Trustee Responsibilities," accessed April 18, 2024, https://dev4.spelman.edu/about-us/president's-office-revised/board-of-trustees.

5. John R. Thelin, *A History of American Higher Education*, 3rd ed. (Baltimore: Johns Hopkins University Press, 2019), 393.

6. Thelin, 393.

7. Thelin, 394.

8. Gary A. Olson, "Exactly What Is Shared Governance?," *Chronicle of Higher Education*, July 23, 2009.

9. Scott S. Cowen, "Shared Governance Does Not Mean Shared Decision Making," *Chronicle of Higher Education*, August 13, 2018.

10. Maya Weilundemo Ott and Kiernan Mathews, *Effective Academic Governance: Five Ingredients for CAOs and Faculty* (Cambridge, MA: Collaborative on Academic Careers in Higher Education, 2015), 3.

11. In 2023, Spelman College was ranked no. 39 on the list of National Liberal Arts Colleges and the no. 1 HBCU, a position it has held continuously since 2007.

12. Susan Resneck Pierce, *On Being Presidential: A Guide for College and University Leaders* (San Francisco: Jossey-Bass, 2012), 69.

13. Megan Zahneis, "Why Higher Ed Is Seeing a Spate of High-Profile No-Confidence Votes," *Chronicle of Higher Education*, September 29, 2023.

Chapter Five: Presidents, Protests, Police, and Politics

1. Alecia Taylor, "Students Are Voting to Support Boycotts of Israel. How Are Colleges Responding?," *Chronicle of Higher Education*, April 5, 2024.

2. Kayla Jimenez, "US Has Long History of College Protests: What Happened in the Past?," *USA Today*, April 28, 2024.

3. Joanne Creighton, *The Educational Odyssey of a Woman College President* (Amherst: University of Massachusetts Press, 2018).

4. Johanna Alonso, "Smith College Students Protest for Divestment, Occupy Hall," *Inside Higher Ed*, April 2, 2024.

5. James Pentland, "Smith College Students End Sit-In over Divestment, but Vow to Expand Their Protest Movement," *Daily Hampshire Gazette*, Northampton, MA, April 9, 2024.

6. Mick Rhodes and Andrew Alonzo, "20 Pomona College Protesters Arrested After Occupying President's Office," *Claremont (CA) Courier*, April 5, 2024.

7. Gabrielle Starr, "Statement of the President: Campus Harassment and Disruption," Pomona College, April 5, 2024.

8. *Claremont (CA) Independent*, "Pomona Faculty Condemn Use of Police and Punishment of Protester," April 11, 2024.

9. Ben Lauren, Elena Townsend-Lerdo, and Ansley Washburn, "7C and National Organizations Denounce Pomona College's Response to Student Arrests," *Student Life*, April 6, 2024.

10. Susanne Rust, "20 Pomona College Protesters Arrested After Storming, Occupying President's Office," *Los Angeles Times*, April 6, 2024.

11. Jenny Gold, "Pomona College Moves Graduation Ceremony to L.A. After Protesters Occupy Stage," *Los Angeles Times*, May 11, 2024.

12. Sarah Willie-LeBreton, email communication with author, May 10, 2024.

13. Ginia Bellafante, "What Columbia University Should Have Learned from the Protests of 1968," *New York Times*, April 25, 2024.

14. Thomas J. Sugrue, "College Presidents Behaving Badly," *Chronicle of Higher Education*, May 6, 2024.

15. Stephanie Saul, "Columbia's University Senate Is Said to Consider Less Severe Action Against Its President," *New York Times*, April 25, 2024.

16. Bellafante, "What Columbia University Should Have Learned."

17. Sharon Otterman and Alan Blinder, "Over 100 Arrested at Columbia After Pro-Palestinian Protest," *New York Times*, April 18, 2024.

18. Josh Moody, "Divest? Call the Cops? Presidents Grapple with How to Respond," *Inside Higher Ed*, April 29, 2024.

19. Sonel Cutler, Alecia Taylor, and Amelia Benavides-Colón, "Here's Where Student Protesters Have Demanded Divestment from Israel," *Chronicle of Higher Education*, April 23, 2024.

20. "Where Protesters on U.S. Campuses Have Been Arrested or Detained," *New York Times*, July 22, 2024.

21. Stephanie Saul and Anna Betts, "Columbia's University Senate Calls for an Investigation into the Administration," *New York Times*, April 26, 2024.

22. Eric Kelderman, "Daily Briefing: As Protests Grow, Presidents Struggle to Manage," *Chronicle of Higher Education*, May 2, 2024. Italics are mine.

23. Minouche Shafik, "A Message from President Minouche Shafik," Office of the President, Columbia University, May 1, 2024.

24. Sharon Otterman, "Columbia Faculty Group Passes No-Confidence Resolution Against President," *New York Times*, May 16, 2024.

25. Timothy Pratt, "'Like a War Zone': Emory University Grapples with Fallout from Police Response to Protest," *Guardian*, April 27, 2024.

26. Josh Fiallo, "Emory University's Philosophy Chair Arrested at Campus Gaza Protest," *Daily Beast*, April 25, 2024.

27. WSB-TV News staff, "Emory Faculty Votes They Have 'No Confidence' in University President," May 3, 2024.

28. Erin Gretzinger, "Unrest Has Gripped Campuses Across the Country. These 3 Colleges Struck Deals with Their Protesters," *Chronicle of Higher Education*, May 1, 2024.

29. Michael Loria, "Northwestern, Brown University Reach Deals with Student Demonstrators to Curb Protests," *USA Today*, May 7, 2024.

30. Loria, "Northwestern, Brown University Reach Deals."

31. Christina H. Paxson, "Regarding the Encampment and Freedom of Expression," Office of the President, Brown University, April 24, 2024.

32. Jacey Fortin, "At Brown, a Rare Agreement Between Administrators and Protestors," *New York Times*, April 30, 2024.

33. Jacey Fortin et al., "Campus Protests: Republicans Accuse University Leaders of 'Giving In' to Antisemitism," *New York Times*, May 23, 2024.

34. Rob Copeland, "Billionaire Donor Barry Sternlicht Assails Brown's Deal with Protesters," *New York Times*, May 3, 2024.

35. Erin Gretzinger, "Yet Another Congressional Hearing Came for Higher Ed.; College Presidents Tried to Fight Back," *Chronicle of Higher Education*, May 23, 2024.

36. Blake Ellis, Melanie Hicken, Allison Gordon, et al., "Unmasking Counterprotesters Who Attacked UCLA's Pro-Palestine Encampment," *CNN*, May 16, 2024.

37. Gretzinger, "Unrest Has Gripped Campuses."

38. Alvaro Huerta, email communication with author, April 24, 2024.

39. Annie Karni, "Johnson Calls to End Pro-Palestinian Protests, Including by Military Means," *New York Times*, April 24, 2024.

40. Bellafante, "What Columbia University Should Have Learned."

41. Kayla Jimenez, "US Has Long History of College Protests: Here's What Happened in the Past," *USA Today*, April 28, 2024.

42. Keeanga-Yamahtta Taylor, "The Kids Are Not All Right. They Want to Be Heard," *New Yorker*, May 8, 2024.

43. Taylor, "Kids Are Not All Right."

44. Minouche Shafik, "Universities Must Engage in Serious Soul Searching on Protests," *Financial Times*, May 10, 2024.

45. Alecia Taylor, "Actually, HBCUs Have a Lot to Say About Gaza," *Chronicle of Higher Education*, May 20, 2024.

46. Taylor, "Kids Are Not All Right."

47. Catherine E. Lhamon, "Dear Colleague Letter: Protecting Students from Discrimination, Such as Harassment, Based on Race, Color, or National Origin, Including Shared Ancestry or Ethnic Characteristics," United States Department of Education, Office of Civil Rights, May 7, 2024.

48. Gretzinger, "Unrest Has Gripped Campuses."

49. Sammy Feldblum, " 'If You're Suppressing Speech in the Name of Safety, You're Doing the Wrong Thing.' An Interview with Irene Mulvey, President of the AAUP," *Chronicle of Higher Education*, May 8, 2024.

50. Michael S. Roth, "On Protests, Encampments, Freedom of Expression," Office of the President, Wesleyan University, April 30, 2024.

51. Michael S. Roth, "Wesleyan Ends Encampment," Office of the President, Wesleyan University, May 18, 2024.

52. Beth McMurtrie, "Debating Israel's Future, One Week at a Time," *Chronicle of Higher Education*, April 30, 2024.

53. Aleyna Rentz, "Johns Hopkins Professor, Students Debate Israel's Future," *Hub*, Johns Hopkins University, May 16, 2024.

54. McMurtrie, "Debating Israel's Future."

55. McMurtrie, "Debating Israel's Future."

56. Erin Gretzinger, "These Arab and Jewish Students Want to Talk About the War," *Chronicle of Higher Education*, May 22, 2024.

57. Atidna International, accessed May 25, 2024, www.atidnainternational .com/.

58. Gretzinger, "These Arab and Jewish Students Want to Talk."

59. Atidna International, "Atidna International Joint Vigil to Honor Innocent Israelis and Palestinians," YouTube video, November 15, 2023, www.youtube.com /watch?v=flA7mDrcktU.

60. Atidna International, "Atidna International Joint Vigil."

61. "Student Group Brings Palestinians, Jews Together in Dialogue," *ABC News* video, April 27, 2024.

62. Robert A. Pape, *Understanding Campus Fears After October 7 and How to Reduce Them*, Chicago Project on Security and Threats (CPOST), University of Chicago, 2024.

63. Feldblum, " 'If You're Suppressing Speech.' "

64. Bellafante, "What Columbia University Should Have Learned."

65. Alan Blinder and Sharon Otterman, "Columbia President Resigns After Months of Turmoil on Campus," *New York Times*, August 14, 2024.

66. White House, "Fact Sheet: President Donald J. Trump Takes Forceful and Unprecedented Steps to Combat Anti-Semitism," January 30, 2025, www .whitehouse.gov/fact-sheets/2025/01/fact-sheet-president-donald-j-trump-takes -forceful-and-unprecedented-steps-to-combat-anti-semitism/.

67. Jessica Blake, "Trump's Antisemitism Order Leaves Many Questions Unanswered," *Inside Higher Ed*, February 4, 2025.

68. Blake, "Trump's Antisemitism Order."

69. "Working Definition of Antisemitism," International Holocaust Remembrance Alliance, 2025, https://holocaustremembrance.com/resources /working-definition-antisemitism.

70. Sarah McLaughlin, "Trump's Threat to Deport Anti-Israel Protesters Is an Attack on Free Speech," Foundation for International Rights and Expression, January 31, 2025, www.thefire.org/news/trumps-threat-deport-anti-israel-protesters -attack-free-speech.

Chapter Six: Managing Risks: Campus Safety and Mental Health

1. Out of respect for family privacy, I am using initials rather than student names in this chapter.

2. Violence Prevention Project Research Center, "Key Findings—Comprehensive Mass Shooter Data," Hamline University, https://hamline.edu/violence-prevention -project-research-center.

3. Chronicle of Higher Education, *The Future of Campus Safety: Managing Risk, Promoting Welfare* (Washington, DC, 2023), 8.

4. Chronicle of Higher Education, *Future of Campus Safety*, 8.

5. Julie Bosman and Jesus Jiménez, "Three Booms. A Masked, Armed Man. How Horror Unfolded in a Michigan State Classroom," *New York Times*, February 16, 2023.

6. Derrick Bryson Taylor, "What We Know About the Michigan State University Shooting," *New York Times*, February 14, 2023.

7. Chronicle of Higher Education, *Future of Campus Safety*, 17–18.

8. Orlando Mayorquin and John Yoon, "5 People Injured in Shooting at Morgan State University in Baltimore," *New York Times*, October 3, 2023.

9. Chronicle of Higher Education, *Future of Campus Safety*, 18.

10. Amy Rock, "An Updated List of States That Allow Campus Carry," *Campus Safety*, April 26, 2024, www.campussafetymagazine.com/news/list-of-states-that-allow-concealed-carry-guns-on-campus/.

11. Thomas H. Benton, "Fearing Our Students," *Chronicle of Higher Education*, December 14, 2007.

12. Vanessa Romo, "We're Seeing a Spike in Workplace Shootings. Here's Why," NPR, May 27, 2021.

13. John Gramlich, "What the Data Says About Gun Deaths in the U.S.," Pew Research Center, April 26, 2023.

14. Walter Berry, "Former Arizona Grad Student Convicted of First-Degree Murder in 2022 Shooting of Professor," *AP News*, May 21, 2024.

15. Michael Levenson, "U.N.C. Graduate Student Is Charged in Fatal Shooting of Professor," *New York Times*, August 29, 2023.

16. Meg Bernhard and Nicholas Bogel-Burroughs, "Gunman Who Killed 3 in UNLV Shooting Had Pursued College Jobs, Official Says," *New York Times*, December 7, 2023.

17. N'dea Yancey-Bragg, "Hate Crimes Reached Record Levels in 2023. Why 'a Perfect Storm' Could Push Them Higher," *USA Today*, January 5, 2024.

18. UCLA Luskin Center for History and Policy, *All Is Not Well in the Golden State: The Scourge of White Nationalism in Southern California*, 2020.

19. Brian Levin with Kiana Perst, Analissa Venolia, and Gabriel Levin, *Report to the Nation: 2020s—Dawn of a Decade of Rising Hate*, Center for the Study of Hate and Extremism, California State University San Bernardino, August 4, 2022.

20. Associated Press, "After Jacksonville Shootings, Historically Black Colleges Address Security Concerns," *NBC News*, August 31, 2023.

21. "Fast Facts: Historically Black Colleges and Universities," National Center for Education Statistics, accessed October 24, 2024.

22. "Addressing Bomb Threats at Historically Black Colleges and Universities," US Department of Homeland Security, August 30, 2022.

23. "FBI Statement on Investigation into Bomb Threats to Historically Black Colleges and Universities and Houses of Worship," FBI News, February 2, 2022.

24. Hope Ford, "Spelman Students React to Third Bomb Threat," 11 Alive, February 8, 2022.

25. Esther Schrader, "HBCU Student, Leaders 'Lean into History' amid Bomb Threats," SPLC, February 9, 2022.

26. Margaret Huang, "The Rise in Violence Against Minority Institutions," testimony given before the House Judiciary Subcommittee on Crime, Terrorism, and Homeland Security, February 17, 2022, SPLC Action Fund.

27. Perry Stein and Danielle Douglas-Gabriel, "Most Threats Against HBCUs This Year Linked to One Minor, FBI Says," Washington Post, November 14, 2022.

28. Sara Weissman, "Suspect Identified in Bomb Threats Against HBCUs," Inside Higher Ed, November 16, 2022.

29. Yancey-Bragg, "Hate Crimes Reached Record Levels in 2023."

30. "CISA's Critical Resources for Handling Bomb Threats," YouTube, accessed April 5, 2022.

31. US Department of Homeland Security, "Addressing Bomb Threats at Historically Black Colleges and Universities," August 30, 2022.

32. Huang, "Rise in Violence Against Minority Institutions."

33. Huang, "Rise in Violence Against Minority Institutions."

34. Cynthia Miller-Idriss and Susan Corke, "How Parents Can Learn to Recognize Online Radicalization and Prevent Tragedy—in 7 Minutes," USA Today, May 8, 2021.

35. Miller-Idriss and Corke, "How Parents Can Learn to Recognize Online Radicalization."

36. Southern Poverty Law Center, Building Resilience and Confronting Risk: A Parents and Caregivers Guide to Online Radicalization, January 31, 2022.

37. Miller-Idriss and Corke, "How Parents Can Learn to Recognize Online Radicalization."

38. Karen Gaffney, "Countering the Rise of White Nationalism," Inside Higher Ed, February 15, 2023.

39. Shelly Tochluk and Christine Saxman, Being White Today: A Roadmap for a Positive Antiracist Life (Lanham, MD: Rowman & Littlefield, 2023).

40. Huang, "Rise in Violence Against Minority Institutions."

41. Michael H. Gavin, "Presidents Must Speak Out Against White Nationalism," Inside Higher Ed, January 5, 2023.

42. Gaffney, "Countering the Rise of White Nationalism."

43. Gaffney, "Countering the Rise of White Nationalism."

44. US Department of Health and Human Services, *Our Epidemic of Loneliness and Isolation: The U.S. Surgeon General's Advisory on the Healing Effects of Social Connection and Community*, 2023.

45. Jeremy Noble, *Project UnLonely: Healing Our Crisis of Disconnection* (New York: Avery/Penguin Random House, 2023), 5, Kindle.

46. Chronicle of Higher Education, *Overcoming Student Loneliness: Strategies for Connection*, 2024.

47. Ellyn Maese, "Almost a Quarter of the World Feels Lonely," *Gallup Blog*, October 24, 2023.

48. Noble, *Project UnLonely*, 37–44.

49. Noble, 44.

50. Richard Weissbourd, Milena Batanova, Joseph McIntyre, and Eric Torres, with Shanae Irving, Sawsan Eskander, and Kiran Bhai, *On Edge: Understanding and Preventing Young Adults' Mental Health Challenges*, Making Caring Common Project, Harvard Graduate School of Education, October 2023.

51. Chronicle of Higher Education, *Overcoming Student Loneliness*, 15.

52. Noble, *Project UnLonely*, 3.

53. Chronicle of Higher Education, *Overcoming Student Loneliness*, 62.

54. Gramlich, "What the Data Says About Gun Deaths in the U.S."

55. Emily Baumgaertner, "U.S. Rate of Suicide by Firearm Reaches Record Level," *New York Times*, November 30, 2023.

56. Means Matter, "Firearm Access Is a Risk Factor for Suicide," Harvard T. H. Chan School of Public Health, https://means-matter.hsph.harvard.edu/means-matter/risk/.

57. Daniel Eisenberg, Sarah Ketchen Lipson, Justin Heinze, and Sasha Zhou, *The Healthy Minds Study: 2022–2023 Data Report*, Healthy Minds Network, https://healthyminds network.org/wp-content/uploads/2023/08/HMS_National-Report-2022-2023_full.pdf.

58. White House, "Defending Women from Gender Ideology Extremism and Restoring Biological Truth to the Federal Government: Executive Order," January 20, 2025, www.whitehouse.gov/presidential-actions/2025/01/defending-women-from-gender-ideology-extremism-and-restoring-biological-truth-to-the-federal-government/; Geoff Mulvihill, "6 Ways Trump's Executive Orders Are Targeting Transgender People," *PBS News Hour*, February 1, 2025, www.pbs.org/newshour/politics/6-ways-trumps-executive-orders-are-targeting-transgender-people.

59. Chronicle of Higher Education, *Future of Campus Safety*, 29.

60. Chronicle of Higher Education, *Overcoming Student Loneliness*, 66.

61. Kate Hidalgo Bellows, "The S-Word: After a Suicide, What Information Does a College Owe Its Campus?," *Chronicle of Higher Education*, May 31, 2024.

62. Jed Foundation, *Youth Suicide: Current Trends and the Path to Prevention*, 2023.

63. Zara Abrams, "Student Mental Health Is in Crisis. Campuses Are Rethinking Their Approach," *Monitor on Psychology* 53, no. 7 (2022): 60.

64. Abrams, "Student Mental Health Is in Crisis."

65. Jed Foundation, https://jedfoundation.org.

66. Alison Badgett, "Promoting a Culture of Caring in Education," *Stanford Social Innovation Review* 22, no. 3 (2024): 18–27.

67. Jed Foundation, *A Decade of Improving College Mental Health Systems: 2024 JED Campus Impact Report*, 2024, 8.

68. Jed Foundation, *Decade of Improving College Mental Health Systems*.

69. Chronicle of Higher Education, *Overcoming Student Loneliness*, 45.

70. Abrams, "Student Mental Health Is in Crisis."

71. Katie Rose Guest Pryal, "2 Ways to Support Student Mental Health," in *Overcoming Student Loneliness*, Chronicle of Higher Education, 55.

72. Chronicle of Higher Education, *Future of Campus Safety*, 15.

73. Jed Foundation, *Decade of Improving College Mental Health Systems*, 19.

74. NABITA, www.nabita.org.

75. Badgett, "Promoting a Culture of Caring in Education," 25.

76. Jed Foundation, *Decade of Improving College Mental Health Systems*, 3, 8. See also https://jedfoundation.org/jed-campuses.

77. Jean M. Twenge, *iGen: The Ten Trends Shaping Today's Young People—and the Nation* (New York: Simon & Schuster, 2017).

78. Jean M. Twenge, "Have Smartphones Destroyed a Generation?," *Atlantic*, September 2017.

79. Twenge, "Have Smartphones Destroyed a Generation?" Italics are mine.

80. Vivek H. Murthy, "Surgeon General: Why I'm Calling for a Warning Label on Social Media Platforms," *New York Times*, June 17, 2024.

81. Murthy, "Why I'm Calling for a Warning Label."

82. Joanna Slater, "How a Connecticut Middle School Won the Battle Against Cellphones," *Washington Post*, May 1, 2024.

83. Melissa G. Hunt, Rachel Marx, Courtney Lipson, and Jordyn Young, "No More FOMO: Limiting Social Media Decreases Loneliness and Depression," *Journal of Social and Clinical Psychology* 37, no. 10 (2018): 751–768, https://doi.org/10.1521/jscp.2018.37.10.751.

84. Kasley Killam, *The Art and Science of Connection* (New York: HarperCollins, 2024), 85, Kindle.

85. Chronicle of Higher Education, *Future of Campus Safety*, 29.

86. Killam, *Art and Science of Connection*, 85.

87. Naz Beheshti, "Is It Truly Lonely at the Top?," *Forbes*, September 26, 2018.

88. Jim Loehr and Tony Schwartz, *The Power of Full Engagement: Managing Energy, Not Time Is the Key to High Performance and Personal Renewal* (New York: Free Press, 2003), 12.

Chapter Seven: Walking on the Edge of a Cliff

1. Sara Lipka, "Demographic Data Let Colleges Peer into the Future," *Chronicle of Higher Education*, January 19, 2014. Italics are mine.
2. Gretchen Livingston, "In a Down Economy, Fewer Births," Pew Research Center, October 12, 2011.
3. Mike Stobbe, "US Births Fell Last Year, Marking an End to the Late Pandemic Rebound, Experts Say," *AP News*, April 25, 2024.
4. Nathan D. Grawe, *Demographics and the Demand for Higher Education* (Baltimore: Johns Hopkins University Press, 2018), 68–69, Kindle.
5. Grawe, 69. Italics are mine.
6. Andrew Smalley, "Higher Education Responses to Coronavirus (COVID-19)," NCSL, March 22, 2021.
7. Smalley, "Higher Education Responses to Coronavirus."
8. Stephanie Saul, "U.S. College Enrollment Dropped Again in the Fall of 2021, Despite the Arrival of Vaccines," *New York Times*, January 13, 2022.
9. "Trends in College Pricing 2023," November 2023, https://research.collegeboard.org/media/pdf/Trends%20Report%202023%20Updated.pdf.
10. Elissa Nadworny, "More Than 1 Million Fewer Students Are in College. Here's How That Impacts the Economy," NPR, January 13, 2022.
11. "A Look at the Year Ahead with Research Center Executive Director Doug Shapiro," National Student Clearinghouse, NSC Blog, January 26, 2023.
12. Olivia Sanchez, "Experts Predicted Dozens of Colleges Would Close in 2023—and They Were Right," *Hechinger Report*, January 12, 2024.
13. Lincoln College—Home, accessed May 15, 2024, https://lincolncollege.edu/home.
14. Bill Chappell, "Lincoln College Closes After 157 Years, Blaming COVID-19 and Cyberattack Disruptions," NPR, May 10, 2022.
15. US Department of Education, "U.S. Department of Education Releases New Data Highlighting How the Simplified, Streamlined, and Redesigned Better FAFSA Form Will Help Deliver Maximum Pell Grants to 1.5 Million More Students," press release, November 15, 2023.
16. Emma Kerr and Sarah Wood, "Everything You Need to Know About the Federal Pell Grant," *US News & World Report*, March 23, 2023.
17. Lyss Welding, "Who Receives Pell Grants? Full Statistics," *Best Colleges*, December 19, 2022.

18. US Department of Education, "U.S. Department of Education Releases New Data Highlighting How the Simplified, Streamlined, and Redesigned Better FAFSA Form Will Help Deliver Maximum Pell Grants," November 15, 2023.

19. National Center for Education Statistics, tables, "Trends in Pell Grant Receipt and the Characteristics of Pell Grant Recipients: Selected Years, 2003–04 to 2015–16," September 2019, https://nces.ed.gov/pubsearch/pubsinfo.asp?pubid=2019487.

20. US Department of Education, "U.S. Department of Education Releases New Data Highlighting How the Simplified, Streamlined, and Redesigned Better FAFSA Form Will Help Deliver Maximum Pell Grants."

21. Katherine Knott and Liam Knox, "Waiting for FAFSA," *Inside Higher Ed*, October 6, 2023.

22. A Director of Financial Aid, "The FAFSA Broke Me," *Inside Higher Ed*, June 24, 2024.

23. Matthew Arrojas, "Ongoing FAFSA Issues Threaten to Derail Financial Aid Awards," *Best Colleges*, June 28, 2024.

24. Liam Knox, "FAFSA Fiasco Forces Cuts at Small Colleges," *Inside Higher Ed*, June 28, 2024.

25. University of Lynchburg, accessed July 26, 2024, www.lynchburg.edu/.

26. University of Lynchburg.

27. Financial Aid—University of Lynchburg, www.lynchburg.edu/.

28. *US News & World Report*, "University of Lynchburg Admissions," www.usnews.com/best-colleges/university-of-lynchburg-3720/applying#.

29. Strategic Plan—University of Lynchburg, www.lynchburg.edu/.

30. University of Lynchburg, "University of Lynchburg Takes Bold Steps to Secure a Bright Future," May 30, 2024, www.lynchburg.edu/news/2024/05/.

31. University of Lynchburg, "University of Lynchburg Takes Bold Steps."

32. Ellen Wexler, "Geography Matters," *Inside Higher Ed*, February 2, 2016.

33. Grawe, *Demographics*, 31.

34. Grawe, 22.

35. Stephanie Saul, "College Enrollment Drops, Even as the Pandemic's Effects Ebb," *New York Times*, May 26, 2022.

36. Grawe, *Demographics*, 28–29.

37. ChildStats Forum on Child and Family Statistics, *America's Children: Key National Indicators of Well-Being, 2023*, accessed July 26, 2024, www.childstats.gov/americaschildren/.

38. Grawe, *Demographics*, 67.

39. National Center for Education Statistics, "College Enrollment Rates," in *Condition of Education 2024*, US Department of Education, Institute of Education Sciences, https://nces.ed.gov/programs/coe/indicator/cpb/college-enrollment-rate.

40. Grawe, *Demographics*, 71.

41. New American Economy Research Fund, "Examining Educational, Workforce, and Earning Divides in the Asian American and Pacific Islander Community," May 13, 2021, https://research.newamericaneconomy.org/report /aapi-examine-educational-workforce-earning-divides/.

42. New American Economy Research Fund, "Examining Educational, Workforce, and Earning Divides," 72.

43. Grawe, *Demographics*, 177.

44. Women's College Coalition, "Our History," accessed July 26, 2024, www .womenscolleges.org/history.

45. Women's College Coalition, "Our History."

46. Vassar, "A History of Vassar College," accessed July 26, 2024, www .vassar.edu/about/history; Wheaton College, "History and Traditions," https:// wheatoncollege.edu/about-wheaton-college/history-and-traditions/.

47. Harvard Radcliffe Institute, "Presidents of Radcliffe College," accessed July 26, 2024, www.radcliffe.harvard.edu/about-the-institute/history/presidents -of-radcliffe-college.

48. Emma Whitford, "Northeastern Acquires Mills College," *Inside Higher Ed*, September 15, 2021.

49. Scott Jaschik, "Shocking Decision at Sweet Briar," *Inside Higher Ed*, March 3, 2015.

50. Jaschik, "Shocking Decision."

51. Susan Svrluga, "Sweet Briar Survives: Judge Approves Settlement Deal to Keep the College Open," *Washington Post*, June 22, 2015.

52. Svrluga, "Sweet Briar Survives."

53. Susan Svrluga, "Alumnae Vowed to Save Sweet Briar from Closing Last Year. And They Did," *Washington Post*, March 3, 2016.

54. Svrluga, "Alumnae Vowed to Save Sweet Briar."

55. Svrluga, "Alumnae Vowed to Save Sweet Briar."

56. Lawrence Biemiller, "After All but Closing, Sweet Briar Will Shift Curriculum and Pricing," *Chronicle of Higher Education*, September 6, 2017.

57. Biemiller, "After All but Closing."

58. Drew Lindsay, "The $44-Million Rescue," *Chronicle of Higher Education*, March 13, 2018.

59. Biemiller, "After All but Closing."

60. Rick Seltzer, "Sweet Briar Eliminating Tenured Faculty Positions as It Puts New Curriculum in Place," *Inside Higher Ed*, December 18, 2017.

61. Lilah Burke, "Sweet Briar College's President Looks Back on What It Was Like to Take Over a College on the Brink of Closing," *Higher Ed Dive*, February 10, 2023.

62. Susan Svrluga, "This College Is Tiny and Isolated. For Some Students During the Pandemic, That Sounds Perfect," *Washington Post*, June 28, 2020.

63. Burke, "Sweet Briar College's President Looks Back."

64. Susan Svrluga, "Alumnae Saved Sweet Briar College. Now One of Them Will Lead the School," *Washington Post*, November 30, 2023.

65. Nathan D. Grawe, *The Agile College: How Institutions Successfully Navigate Demographic Changes* (Baltimore: Johns Hopkins University Press, 2021), 211.

Chapter Eight: College Finances 101

1. James Shewey, "Tuition Dependency and the Impacts of Declining Enrollments," RCM&D, July 10, 2019.

2. Kaitlin Mulhere, "The Average Tuition Discount at Private Colleges Hits 52%, a Record High," Money.com/Nasdaq, May 17, 2024.

3. Mulhere, "Average Tuition Discount at Private Colleges Hits 52%."

4. CASE, "Giving to U.S. College and Universities at $58 Billion in Fiscal Year 2023," February 21, 2024, www.case.org/resources/giving-us-college-and -universities-58-billion-fiscal-year-2023.

5. Sarah Wood, "15 Colleges Where the Most Alumni Donate," Best Colleges / The Short List: Colleges, *U.S. News & World Report*, December 29, 2023.

6. American Council on Education, *Understanding College and University Endowments*, 2014, www.acenet.edu/Documents/Understanding-College-and-University -Endowments.pdf.

7. American Council on Education, *Understanding College and University Endowments*.

8. Aimee Picchi, "How Rich Is Harvard? It's Bigger Than the Economies of 120 Nations," Money Watch / CBS News, December 12, 2023.

9. *US News & World Report*, "Harvard University Tuition and Financial Aid," 2024, www.usnews.com/best-colleges/harvard-university-2155/paying#.

10. Harvard College, "Financial Aid Fact Sheet," 2024, https://college.harvard.edu /guides/financial-aid-fact-sheet.

11. Natalie Schwartz, "Endowment Returns Averaged 7.7% in Fiscal 2023," *Higher Ed Dive*, February 15, 2024.

12. Wikipedia, "List of Colleges and Universities in the United States by Endowment," last modified September 10, 2024.

13. Schwartz, "Endowment Returns."

14. Geraldine Fabrikant, "Harvard Endowment Loses 22%," *New York Times*, December 3, 2008.

15. Sarah Brown, "Trump Singled Out These 130 Colleges as Possible Targets for Investigation. Is Yours on the List?," *Chronicle of Higher Education*, January 24, 2025; Phillip Levine, "How Trump Could Devastate Our Top Colleges' Finances," *Chronicle of Higher Education*, January 13, 2025.

16. Levine, "How Trump Could Devastate Our Top Colleges' Finances."

17. Adam Harris, "A Tax on Endowments Became Law. But Congressmen and Colleges Are Still Fighting It," *Chronicle of Higher Education*, March 8, 2018.

18. Phillip Levine, "What Trump Means for College Budgets," *Chronicle of Higher Education*, January 22, 2025.

19. Levine, "How Trump Could Devastate Our Top Colleges' Finances."

20. Anthony P. Carnevale and Martin Van Der Werf, *The 20-Percent Solution: Selective Colleges Can Afford to Admit More Pell Grant Recipients*, Georgetown University Center on Education and the Workforce, 2017, 2.

21. Carnevale and Van Der Werf, *20-Percent Solution*, 2.

22. White House Council of Economic Advisors, "The Economics of HBCUs," May 16, 2024.

23. Mirtha Donastorg, "HBCU Endowments Grew by More Than One Billion Dollars in 2021," *Plug*, December 22, 2022.

24. "HBCU Money's 2022 Top 10 HBCU Endowments," HBCU Money, February 21, 2023.

25. PGIM-UNCF, *Investing in Change: A Call to Action for Strengthening HBCU Endowments*, 2023, www.pgim.com/hbcu.

26. Denise A. Smith, *Achieving Financial Equity and Justice for HBCUs*, Century Foundation, September 14, 2021.

27. Zamira Rahim and Rob Picheta, "Thousands Around the World Protest George Floyd's Death in Global Display of Solidarity," *CNN*, June 1, 2020.

28. Goldie Blumenstyk, "The Edge: How Does MacKenzie Scott Pick Which Colleges Get Donations?," *Chronicle of Higher Education*, July 21, 2021.

29. Oyin Adedoyin, "MacKenzie Scott Donated $560 Million to 23 HBCUs. These Are the Other Things They Have in Common," *Chronicle of Higher Education*, August 6, 2021.

30. Stephanie Saul, "Historically Black Colleges Finally Get the Spotlight," *New York Times*, October 20, 2021.

31. Stephanie Saul, "Spelman, a Historically Black Women's College, Receives $100 Million Gift," *New York Times*, January 18, 2024.

32. Tyrone McKinley Freeman, "MacKenzie Scott's No-Strings Giving to HBCUs Sets High Bar for Other Donors," *Chronicle of Philanthropy*, August 2, 2021.

33. Genevieve K. Croft, "The U.S. Land-Grant University System: An Overview," Congressional Research Service, August 29, 2019.

34. Denise A. Smith, "Nourishing the Nation While Starving: The Underfunding of Black Land-Grant Colleges and Universities," Century Foundation, July 24, 2023.

35. Adam Harris, "The Government Finally Puts a Number on the Discrimination Against Black Colleges," *Atlantic*, September 20, 2023.

36. Harris, "Government Finally Puts a Number."

37. Smith, "Nourishing the Nation While Starving."

38. Note that the state of Georgia transferred land grant status from Savannah State College (now University) to Fort Valley State College (now University) in 1947. Fort Valley State is also an HBCU.

39. Harris, "Government Finally Puts a Number."

40. Harris, "Government Finally Puts a Number."

41. Smith, "Nourishing the Nation While Starving."

42. Susan Adams and Hank Tucker, "How America Cheated Its Black Colleges," *Forbes*, September 22, 2022.

43. Katherine Knott, "States Underfunded Historically Black Land Grants by $13 Billion over 3 Decades," *Inside Higher Ed*, September 20, 2023.

44. Adams and Tucker, "How America Cheated Its Black Colleges." Italics are mine.

45. Knott, "States Underfunded Historically Black Land Grants."

46. Danielle Douglas-Gabriel and Ovetta Wiggins, "Hogan Signs Off on $577 Million for Maryland's Historically Black Colleges and Universities," *Washington Post*, March 24, 2021.

47. Letters to state governors, *Washington Post*, September 18, 2023.

48. Smith, "Nourishing the Nation While Starving."

49. Christine A. Nelson and Joanna R. Frye, "Tribal College and University Funding: Tribal Sovereignty at the Intersection of Federal, State, and Local Funding," American Council on Education, May 2016.

50. Nelson and Frye, "Tribal College and University Funding."

51. National Center for Education Statistics, "College Enrollment Rates," in *Condition of Education 2024*, US Department of Education, Institute of Education Sciences, https://nces.ed.gov/programs/coe/indicator/cpb/college-enrollment-rate.

52. Beth Redbird, "What Drives Native American Poverty?," Institute for Policy Research, Northwestern University, February 24, 2020.

53. Nathan D. Grawe, *The Agile College: How Institutions Successfully Navigate Demographic Changes* (Baltimore: Johns Hopkins University Press, 2021), 187.

54. State Higher Education Executive Officers Association (SHEEO), "Annual Grapevine Data Show Initial 10.2% Increase in State Support for Higher Education," February 1, 2024.

55. Liam Knox, "State Higher Ed Funding Is Still Rising—for Now," *Inside Higher Ed*, May 8, 2024.

56. "Education at a Glance 2023: Putting U.S. Data in a Global Context," National Center for Education Statistics, *NCES Blog*, November 15, 2023.

57. Jon Marcus, "Most Americans Don't Realize State Funding for Higher Ed Fell by Billions," *PBS News Hour*, February 26, 2019.

58. Pew Charitable Trusts, "Two Decades of Change in Federal and State Higher Education Funding," Issue Brief, October 15, 2019.

59. John R. Thelin, *A History of American Higher Education* (Baltimore: Johns Hopkins University Press, 2019), 271–272.

60. Thelin, 272.

61. Association of American Universities, "Reinvigorate the Government-University Partnership That Fosters Innovation."

62. Michael T. Gibbons, "R&D Expenditures at U.S. Universities Increased by $8 Billion in FY 2022," InfoBrief, National Center for Science and Engineering Statistics, National Science Foundation, NSF 24-307, November 30, 2023.

63. Association of American Universities and the Association of Public and Land-Grant Universities, "2017 Frequently Asked Questions About Facilities and Administrative (F&A) Costs of Federally Sponsored University Research," May 2017.

64. Most universities post their indirect cost rate on their websites. I was able to obtain the rates from the websites and calculated the average.

65. Kathryn Palmer, "Scientists Worried After Trump Halts NIH Grant Reviews," *Inside Higher Ed*, January 24, 2025.

66. Levine, "What Trump Means for College Budgets."

67. Ian Bogost, "The Chaos in Higher Ed Is Only Getting Started," *Atlantic*, January 24, 2025.

68. Bogost, "Chaos in Higher Ed."

69. Mattathias Schwartz and Benjamin Oreskes, "Federal Judge Blocks Trump's Freeze of Federal Grant Funds," *New York Times*, January 28, 2025.

70. US Department of Education, "Title III Part B, Strengthening Historically Black Colleges and Universities Program," September 18, 2024.

71. Hispanic Association of Colleges and Universities (HACU), "HACU List of Hispanic Serving Institutions (HSIs), 2022–2023," www.hacu.net/hacu/hsis.asp.

72. White House Initiative on Advancing Educational Equity, Excellence, and Economic Opportunity for Hispanics, Hispanic-Serving Institutions Fast Facts, US Department of Education, October 17, 2024, https://sites.ed.gov/hispanic -initiative/hispanic-serving-institutions-hsis/.

73. US Department of Education, Eligibility for Titles III & V Grant Programs, accessed October 29, 2024, www.ed.gov/media/document/eligibility -infographicpdf.

74. Robert B. Archibald and David H. Feldman, *Why Does College Cost So Much?* (New York: Oxford University Press, 2011), 16.

75. Michael D. Smith, *The Abundant University: Remaking Higher Education for a Digital World* (Cambridge, MA: MIT Press, 2023), 15.

76. Archibald and Feldman, *Why Does College Cost So Much?*, 16.

77. Emily Cochrane, "A Private Liberal Arts College Is Drowning in Debt. Should Alabama Rescue It?," *New York Times*, December 27, 2023.

78. Katie McCabe and Dovey Johnson Roundtree, *Justice Older Than the Law: The Life of Dovey Johnson Roundtree* (Jackson: University Press of Mississippi, 2009).

Chapter Nine: "The Time Has Now Come": The End of Affirmative Action

1. William G. Bowen and Derek Bok, *The Shape of the River: Long-Term Consequences of Considering Race in College and University Admissions* (Princeton, NJ: Princeton University Press, 1998), 155.

2. Bowen and Bok, 156.

3. Bowen and Bok, 284.

4. Bowen and Bok, 290.

5. Beverly Daniel Tatum, *Why Are All the Black Kids Sitting Together in the Cafeteria? And Other Conversations About Race*, 20th anniversary rev. ed. (New York: Basic Books, 2017), 209.

6. Lyndon B. Johnson, Howard University Commencement Address, June 4, 1965, American Yawp Reader.

7. In the 1970s, legislation broadened the protected groups to include persons with disabilities and Vietnam veterans.

8. Office of Federal Contract Compliance Programs, "History of Executive Order 11246," US Department of Labor, www.dol.gov/agencies/ofccp/about/executive-order-11246-history.

9. Jerome Karabel, "This Moment Is the Culmination of a Decades-Long Backlash Against Affirmative Action," Opinion, *New York Times*, June 29, 2023.

10. Anemona Hartocollis, "50 Years of Affirmative Action: What Went Right, and What It Got Wrong," *New York Times*, March 30, 2019.

11. Anemona Hartocollis, "What Is the History Behind Affirmative Action?," *New York Times*, October 31, 2022.

12. Charles T. Clotfelter, *After Brown: The Rise and Retreat of School Desegregation* (Princeton, NJ: Princeton University Press, 2004), 159.

13. The first case was *Marco DeFunis Jr. v. Odegaard*, involving his denied admission to the University of Washington Law School. He sued and was eventually admitted. By the time the case made its way to the Supreme Court, he was already a third-year law student at the University of Washington, and the court ruled that the case was moot.

14. Margaret Kramer, "A Timeline of Key Supreme Court Cases on Affirmative Action," *New York Times*, March 30, 2019.

15. Karabel, "This Moment Is the Culmination."

16. Victoria M. Massie, "Americans Are Split on 'Reverse Racism.' That Still Doesn't Mean It Exists," *Vox*, June 29, 2016.

17. Kevin Carey, "A Detailed Look at the Downside of California's Ban on Affirmative Action," *New York Times*, August 21, 2020; nine states in the United States have banned race-based affirmative action: California (1996), Washington (1998), Florida (1999), Michigan (2006), Nebraska (2008), Arizona (2010), New Hampshire (2012), Oklahoma (2012), and Idaho (2020). Antonia Leonard, "How Many States Have Banned Affirmative Action?," CLI (https://communityliteracy .org), accessed August 1, 2024.

18. Leonard, "How Many States Have Banned Affirmative Action?"

19. Peter Schmidt, "Sandra Day O'Connor Revisits and Revives Affirmative-Action Controversy," *Chronicle of Higher Education*, January 14, 2010.

20. Schmidt, "Sandra Day O'Connor Revisits."

21. Kramer, "Timeline of Key Supreme Court Cases."

22. Olivia B. Waxman, "Supreme Court Rules Against Affirmative Action," *Time*, June 29, 2023.

23. Anemona Hartocollis, "Harvard Rated Asian-American Applicants Lower on Personality Traits, Suit Says," *New York Times*, June 15, 2018.

24. Nina Totenberg, "Supreme Court Reverses Affirmative Action, Effectively Ending Race-Conscious Admissions," NPR, June 29, 2023.

25. Julie J. Park, *Race on Campus: Debunking Myths with Data* (Cambridge, MA: Harvard University Press, 2018), 73.

26. Supreme Court of the United States, *Students for Fair Admissions, Inc. v. President and Fellows of Harvard College* (20-1199), and *Students for Fair Admissions, Inc. v. University of North Carolina* (21-707), www.supremecourt.gov/opinions /22pdf/20-1199_hgdj.pdf.

27. The conservative majority in this case were Chief Justice John G. Roberts Jr., Clarence Thomas, Samuel Alito, Neil M. Gorsuch, Brett M. Kavanaugh, and Amy Coney Barrett.

28. Totenberg, "Supreme Court Reverses Affirmative Action."

29. Totenberg, "Supreme Court Reverses Affirmative Action."

30. Supreme Court of the United States, *Students for Fair Admissions, Inc. v. President and Fellows of Harvard College* (20-1199), and *Students for Fair Admissions, Inc. v. University of North Carolina* (21-707).

31. Supreme Court of the United States, *Students for Fair Admissions, Inc. v. President and Fellows of Harvard College* (20-1199), and *Students for Fair Admissions, Inc. v. University of North Carolina* (21-707).

32. Lulu Garcia-Navarro, "Edward Blum Worked for Years to Overturn Affirmative Action. He's Not Done," *New York Times*, July 8, 2023.

33. Totenberg, "Supreme Court Reverses Affirmative Action."

34. Jordan Weissmann, "Outside of Elite Colleges, Affirmative Action Is Already Disappearing," *Slate*, August 3, 2017.

35. Richard Arum and Mitchell L. Stevens, "For Most College Students, Affirmative Action Was Never Enough," *New York Times*, July 3, 2023.

36. Raj Chetty, David J. Deming, and John N. Friedman, "Diversifying Society's Leaders? The Determinants and Consequences of Admission to Highly Selective Colleges (Non-Technical Research Summary)," Opportunity Insights, 2023.

37. Chetty, Deming, and Friedman, "Diversifying Society's Leaders?"

38. Spencer Bokat-Lindell, "Has America Outgrown Affirmative Action?," Opinion, *New York Times*, November 2, 2022. Italics are mine.

39. Peter Arcidiacono, Josh Kinsler, and Tyler Ransom, "Legacy and Athlete Preferences at Harvard," Working Paper 26316, National Bureau of Economic Research, 2019.

40. Bokat-Lindell, "Has America Outgrown Affirmative Action?"

41. Chetty, Deming, and Friedman, "Diversifying Society's Leaders?"

42. Aatish Bhatia, Claire Cain Miller, and Josh Katz, "Study of Elite College Admissions Data Suggests Being Very Rich Is Its Own Qualification," *New York Times*, July 24, 2023.

43. Chris Peterson, "Just to Be Clear: We Don't Do Legacy," MIT Admissions, June 25, 2012.

44. Lindsey I. Black, Emily P. Terlizzi, and Anjel Vahratian, "Organized Sports Participation Among Children Aged 6–17 Years: United States, 2020," NCHS Data Brief no. 441, National Center for Health Statistics, August 2022, https://stacks.cdc.gov/view/cdc/119026.

45. Bhatia, Miller, and Katz, "Study of Elite College Admissions Data."

46. Chetty, Deming, and Friedman, "Diversifying Society's Leaders?," 20.

47. Richard D. Kahlenberg, "The Affirmative Action That Colleges Really Need," *Atlantic*, October 26, 2022.

48. Chetty, Deming, and Friedman, "Diversifying Society's Leaders?," 5.

49. Vimal Patel, "Why Legacy Admissions Are at the Center of a Dispute in Higher Education," *New York Times*, July 26, 2023.

50. "The 2018 Surveys of Admissions Leaders: The Pressure Grows," *Inside Higher Ed*, September 24, 2018.

51. Anemona Hartocollis, "Colleges Will Be Able to Hide a Student's Race on Admissions Applications," *New York Times*, May 26, 2023.

52. Liam Knox, "The Common App Enters an Uncommon Era," *Inside Higher Ed*, August 2, 2023.

53. Elyse C. Goncalves and Matan H. Josephy, "Class of 2028 Results Will Offer the First Clues About Harvard's Post-Affirmative Action Admissions," *Harvard Crimson*, March 27, 2024.

54. Stephanie Saul, "Affirmative Action Was Banned at Two Top Colleges. They Say They Need It," *New York Times*, August 26, 2022.

55. Goncalves and Josephy, "Class of 2028 Results Will Offer the First Clues."

56. Elyse C. Goncalves and Matan H. Josephy, "Harvard Accepts 3.59% of Applicants to Class of 2028," *Harvard Crimson*, March 29, 2024.

57. "College Sees Strong Yield for Students Accepted to Class of 2028," *Harvard Gazette*, June 18, 2024.

58. Liam Knox, "An Early Look at Diversity Post-Affirmative Action," *Inside Higher Ed*, September 9, 2024.

59. John S. Rosenberg, "Harvard Class of 2028 Demographics Disclosed," *Harvard Magazine*, September 11, 2024.

60. Anemona Hartocollis, "Yale, Princeton and Duke Are Questioned over Decline in Asian Students," *New York Times*, September 17, 2024.

61. Sonja B. Starr, "Critics of Affirmative Action Say This Year's Admissions Data Are Fishy. They're Not," *New York Times*, October 16, 2024.

62. Hartocollis, "Yale, Princeton and Duke Are Questioned."

63. Bowen and Bok, *Shape of the River*, 289.

64. Starr, "Critics of Affirmative Action."

65. Garcia-Navarro, "Edward Blum Worked for Years."

66. White House, "Ending Illegal Discrimination and Restoring Merit-Based Opportunity: Executive Order," January 21, 2025, www.whitehouse.gov/presidential-actions/2025/01/ending-illegal-discrimination-and-restoring-merit-based-opportunity/.

67. Vimal Patel, "Wesleyan University Ends Legacy Admissions," *New York Times*, July 19, 2023.

68. Patel, "Wesleyan University Ends Legacy Admissions."

69. Posse Foundation, "Posse Facts & Figures," 2024, www.possefoundation.org/posse-facts.

70. Posse Foundation, "Posse Facts & Figures."

71. Posse Foundation, "Shaping the Future," 2024, www.possefoundation.org/shaping-the-future.

Chapter Ten: Disruption at the Door?

1. Jeffrey M. Jones, "US Confidence in Higher Education Now Closely Divided," Gallup, July 8, 2024.

2. Jones, "US Confidence in Higher Education."

3. John R. Thelin, *A History of American Higher Education*, 3rd ed. (Baltimore: Johns Hopkins University Press, 2019), 268.

4. George F. Zook, ed., *Higher Education for American Democracy: A Report of the President's Commission on Higher Education*, vols. 1–6, 1947, 1:8.

5. Carol Geary Schneider, "All In? Or Just Some?," *Inside Higher Education*, January 9, 2022.

6. Anthony P. Carnevale, Ban Cheah, and Emma Wenzinger, *The College Payoff: More Education Doesn't Always Mean More Earnings* (Washington, DC: Georgetown University Center on Education and the Workforce, 2021).

7. Brent Orrell and David Veldran, *The Value of a Bachelor's Degree*, American Enterprise Institute, January 2024.

8. James Dean, "For-Profit Colleges Increase Students' Debt, Default Risk," *Cornell Chronicle*, April 6, 2022.

9. "Completing College: National and State Reports," National Student Clearinghouse Research Center, February 2022.

10. Eric Kelderman, "What the Public Really Thinks About Higher Education," *Chronicle of Higher Education*, September 5, 2023.

11. Kelderman, "What the Public Really Thinks."

12. Kelderman, "What the Public Really Thinks."

13. Kelderman, "What the Public Really Thinks."

14. Clayton M. Christensen and Henry J. Eyring, *The Innovative University: Changing the DNA of Higher Education from the Inside Out* (San Francisco: Jossey-Bass, 2011), 18–19.

15. Arthur Levine and Scott Van Pelt, *The Great Upheaval: Higher Education's Past, Present, and Uncertain Future* (Baltimore: Johns Hopkins University Press, 2021), 2.

16. Levine and Van Pelt, 5.

17. Rhea Kelly, "73 Percent of Students Prefer Some Courses Be Fully Online Post-Pandemic," *Campus Technology*, May 13, 2021.

18. Michael D. Smith, *The Abundant University: Remaking Higher Education for a Digital World* (Cambridge, MA: MIT Press, 2023), 95.

19. Levine and Van Pelt, *Great Upheaval*, 175.

20. Levine and Van Pelt, 178.

21. Smith, *Abundant University*, 95.

22. Smith, 95.

23. Smith, 98.

24. Goldie Blumenstyk, "Meet the New Mega-university," *Chronicle of Higher Education*, November 11, 2018.

25. Smith, *Abundant University*, 104.

26. Lee Gardner, "How One University Became Exhibit A of Marketing Success," *Chronicle of Higher Education*, September 29, 2014.

27. Smith, *Abundant University*, 105.

28. Southern New Hampshire University, www.snhu.edu/tuition-and-financial-aid/online.

29. Smith, *Abundant University*, 105.

30. "Transcript: Dr. Paul LeBlanc, President, Southern New Hampshire University (SNHU) on Reimagining HE," December 1, 2023, www.studiosity.com /blog/dr-paul-leblanc-president-snhu.

31. "Transcript: Dr. Paul LeBlanc."

32. "Transcript: Dr. Paul LeBlanc."

33. "Transcript: Dr. Paul LeBlanc."

34. Smith, *Abundant University*, 106.

35. Blumenstyk, "Meet the New Mega-university."

36. Andrew Gumbel, *Won't Lose This Dream: How an Upstart Urban University Rewrote the Rules of a Broken System* (New York: New Press, 2020).

37. Bernard Marr, "A Short History of ChatGPT: How We Got to Where We Are Today," *Forbes*, May 19, 2023.

38. Sofia Barnett, "ChatGPT Is Making Universities Rethink Plagiarism," *Wired*, January 30, 2023.

39. Dylan Ruediger, Melissa Blankstein, and Sage Love, *Generative AI and Postsecondary Instructional Practices: Findings from a National Survey of Instructors*, Ithaka S+R, June 20, 2024.

40. Beth McMurtrie, "The Future Is Hybrid: Colleges Begin to Reimagine Learning in an AI World," *Chronicle of Higher Education*, October 3, 2024.

41. Digital Education Council, *Digital Education Council Global AI Student Survey 2024*.

42. Digital Education Council, *Digital Education Council Global AI Student Survey 2024*.

43. Ruediger, Blankstein, and Love, *Generative AI and Postsecondary Instructional Practices*.

44. Ruediger, Blankstein, and Love, *Generative AI and Postsecondary Instructional Practices*, 1.

45. McMurtrie, "Future Is Hybrid."

46. McMurtrie, "Future Is Hybrid."

47. Salman Khan, *Brave New Words: How AI Will Revolutionize Education (and Why That's a Good Thing)* (New York: Viking, 2024), 162–163.

48. Khan, 163.

49. Khan, 164.

50. McMurtrie, "Future Is Hybrid."

51. Ethan Mollick, "Something New: On OpenAI's 'Strawberry' and Reasoning," *One Useful Thing*, September 12, 2024.

52. Blumenstyk, "Meet the New Mega-university."

53. Smith, *Abundant University*, 165.

54. Smith, 166.

55. Kaggle Competitions, www.kaggle.com/competitions, accessed August 1, 2024.

56. Smith, *Abundant University*, 170.

57. Lindsay McKenzie, "Google's Growing IT Certificate," *Inside Higher Ed*, June 13, 2019.

58. Paul Fain, "Employers as Educators," *Inside Higher Ed*, July 16, 2019.

59. Fain, "Employers as Educators."

60. Fain, "Employers as Educators."

61. Ashley P. Finley, *The Career-Ready Graduate: What Employers Say About the Difference College Makes*, Association of American Colleges and Universities, 2023.

62. Finley, *Career-Ready Graduate*, 1–2.

63. Ron Lieber, "Some Colleges Will Soon Charge $100,000 a Year. How Did This Happen?," *New York Times*, April 5, 2024.

64. Christensen and Eyring, *Innovative University*, xxiii.

65. Taunya English, "For Black Girls, Lack of Exercise Heightens Obesity Risk," WHYY/NPR, December 29, 2011.

66. Jillian McKoy, "Racism, Sexism, and the Crisis of Black Women's Health," *Brink*, October 31, 2023.

67. Christensen and Eyring, *Innovative University*, 396.

68. Richard Pérez-Peña, "Spelman Drops Sports to Turn Focus on Fitness," *New York Times*, November 2, 2012; Mike Tierney, "At a College, Dropping Sports in Favor of Fitness," *New York Times*, April 13, 2013.

69. Jake New, "Fitness Without Athletics," *Inside Higher Ed*, October 14, 2014.

70. Cecelia Townes, "Life After Sports at Spelman College," ESPN, January 31, 2017.

71. Townes, "Life After Sports."

72. Billy Witz, " 'Scary and Daunting': Dartmouth Players Detail How Union Plan Came Together," *New York Times*, March 5, 2024; Nell Gluckman, "Colleges Have Agreed to Pay Athletes. What's Next?," *Chronicle of Higher Education*, May 24, 2024.

73. Christensen and Eyring, *Innovative University*, 401.

Chapter Eleven: Reasons for Joy

1. In 2023 the name of Hartford Seminary was changed to Hartford International University for Religion and Peace.

2. John McQuiston II, *Always We Begin Again: The Benedictine Way of Living*, rev. ed. (Harrisburg, PA: Morehouse, 2011), 17.

3. McQuiston, 2. Italics are mine.

4. Misty Copeland, *Life in Motion: An Unlikely Ballerina* (New York: Touchstone Books, 2014), 236.

5. Dalai Lama and Desmond Tutu, with Douglas Abrams, *The Book of Joy: Lasting Happiness in a Changing World* (New York: Avery, 2016), 241–249.

6. Robin Wall Kimmerer, *Braiding Sweetgrass: Indigenous Wisdom, Scientific Knowledge, and the Teachings of Plants* (Minneapolis: Milkweed, 2015), 115.

7. "Transcript: Dr. Paul LeBlanc, President, Southern New Hampshire University (SNHU) on Reimagining HE," December 1, 2023, www.studiosity.com/blog/dr-paul-leblanc-president-snhu.

8. Lawrence Biemiller, "After All but Closing, Sweet Briar Will Shift Curriculum and Pricing," *Chronicle of Higher Education*, September 6, 2017.

9. Alexander C. Kafka, "Trouble at the Top: Meeting the Daunting Challenges of Today's College Presidency," *Chronicle of Higher Education*, March 2023, 64.

10. Mary Beth Faller, "ASU Ranked No. 1 in Innovation for 9th Straight Year," Arizona State University, *ASU News*, September 17, 2023.

11. Arizona State University, "ASU Charter, Mission and Goals," accessed August 12, 2024, https://newamericanuniversity.asu.edu/about/asu-charter-mission-and-goals. Boldface in original.

12. Arizona State University, "A New Objective," accessed August 12, 2024, https://newamericanuniversity.asu.edu/about/new-objective.

13. Kafka, "Trouble at the Top," 65.

INDEX

ABCs agenda
   affirming identity, 25–31
   building community, 24, 31–36, 42
   cultivating leadership, 24, 37–41, 46
   DEI programs and, 42–43
academic freedom
   anti-DEI legislation and, 62
   as a core mission, 80
   disciplinary action and, 100
   free speech and, 98
   importance of, 91, 100–101
academic integrity, 281–282
adjuncts, 238–239
admissions
   ALDCs, 254–255
   athletes, 256
   essay questions, 258, 260
   income and, 255–257
   legacy preferences, 254–255, 257,
      261
   need-blind, 213
   race-conscious practices, 6,
      247–249, 251–252, 253
affinity groups, 29–30
affirmative action programs
   class-based, 257
   criticism of, 248
   decline in, 253
   enrollment and, 258–259
   Executive Order 11246, 245–246
   federal, 14, 245–246, 252–253
   hostility towards, 85
   legal challenges, 243, 245, 247–254,
      257–259
   race-based, 6, 243–257
   racial quotas, 247
   "reverse discrimination" claims,
      248
   success of, 244–245
affirming identity, 24, 25–31, 42–43
AI. See artificial intelligence
Allport, Gordon, 36
alumni giving, 214–215
Amazon, 288–289
American Association of University
      Professors (AAUP), 100–101, 132,
      145, 150
American College Presidents Study, 12
American Indian/Alaska Native
      students, 9, 195, 201, 227, 235, 260
American Sociological Association,
      57–58

Anti-Defamation League (ADL), 88,
138, 169
antisemitism
congressional hearings, 82–84,
97–101, 139, 142–144
executive order combatting, 151–152
free speech and, 90, 117
IHRA definition, 151
at Mount Holyoke College, 30–31
rise of, 166
types of, 88–89
antizionism, 89
anxiety, 174, 175, 181, 182
apartheid, 120, 133, 141–142
Arab students, 148–150
Archibald, Robert, 236
Arizona State University, 281,
312–313
artificial intelligence (AI), 8, 162,
281–287
Asian students, 9, 11, 120, 122, 195,
201, 235, 249–251, 259, 260–261
Association of American Colleges &
Universities (AAC&U), 8, 289–290
Atidna International, 148–150
authority, 21, 30, 44, 106, 109–110
Ayvazian, Andrea, 38–39, 265

Bakke, Alan, 247
belonging, sense of, 28–29, 171–172
Benedict of Nursia (St. Benedict), 299,
309
Bial, Deborah, 262
Biden, Joe, 64, 141, 143–144
Biden administration, 14–15, 151, 224
Birmingham-Southern College, 240
birth rates, declining, 6, 8, 190
Black, Derek, 50–54, 57, 59, 61, 78, 170
Black, Indigenous, people of color
(BIPOC), representation of, 27–28

Black Lives Matter movement, 55, 63
Black students, 9, 11, 29–30, 120,
164, 165–166, 195, 201, 219–220,
222–223, 244, 246–247, 254–255,
259, 260
Black women's health, 293–297
Block, Gene, 139, 140
Blum, Edward, 249, 252–253, 260–262
boards of trustees, 104–110, 216, 239
Bok, Derek, 243–245, 260
bomb threats, 166–167, 170–171
book bans, 62–63
"border crossing," 37–38, 45
Bowen, William, 243–245, 260
Brown University, 137–138, 145
Brown v. Board of Education, 47–48,
65, 241
budgets
administrative, 237–238
annual fund, 214–215
balancing, 236–237
donors, 214, 221
endowments, 215–222, 224
expenditures, 235
federal funding, 77, 144–145, 196,
224, 229–235, 261
increasing revenues, 235–236
research grants, 16–17, 230–235
revenue sources, 212
rising costs and, 235–241
state funding, 224–235
taxation, 217–218
tuition and fees, 5, 197–198,
212–214, 229, 235–236, 240, 277
building community, 24, 31–36, 42, 183
Bush, Vannever, 230–231

"call-in" culture, 98
campus safety
bomb threats, 166–168, 170–171

free speech and, 86–90
hate crimes, 164–172
risk mitigation, 158–159, 239
school shootings, 6, 95, 159–163
student support, 156–158
suicidal ideation and risk, 172,
    175–177
threat assessment, 180
"cancel culture," 98, 173
Capilouto, Eli, 76, 78
career colleges, 11–12
Carnegie Mellon University, 257, 284
Carnevale, Anthony P., 219
censorship, 62–63, 91
Center for the Study of Hate and
    Extremism (CSHE), 164
Center on Education and the
    Workforce, 219, 269
Century Fund, 220–221
certificate programs, 288–289
ChatGPT, 281–283
Chemerinsky, Erwin, 79–80, 102
Chetty, Raj, 255
Chicago Project on Security and
    Threats (CPOST), 86–90, 92,
    96–97, 150
Christensen, Clayton, 272–273, 290,
    294, 298
Christian students, 26–27, 32–34,
    38–41, 45
civil discourse, 92–102
Civil Rights Act (1964), 144, 247
civil rights movement, 50, 60, 79, 120,
    246
Clinton, Bill, 21–22
Club Q, 95
Coalition for Equity and Excellence in
    Maryland Higher Education, 226
college athletics, 56–57, 191–192, 256,
    291–297

college presidents
    average tenure, 103
    Black women, 83–85
    boards and, 108–110
    conflict management, 94–102
    congressional hearings, 82–84,
        97–101, 103–104, 139
    diversity, 12–13
    faculty and, 109–110
    finding joy, 300–314
    job challenges, 1–3
    mental health crisis, 185–186
    no-confidence votes against,
        117–118, 135
    role in hiring and firing decisions,
        104, 108–109
    role in promotion and tenure
        decisions, 104–105
    salaries, 239
    selection process, 106
    self-care, 186–187
    See also leadership
colleges and universities
    alternatives to, 272
    anti-DEI legislation, 61–65, 76–78, 81
    "anti-woke" agenda, 55–58
    author's experience in, 7–8
    completion rates, 269–272
    COVID-19 pandemic, 191–193
    "Dear Colleague" letter, 15, 77,
        144–145
    DEI programs, 77–78
    institutional neutrality, 96–97
    organizational structure, 100, 105–106
    segregated, 48–49, 223
    student demographics, 9–10, 16,
        42–43, 200–203, 247, 254–255,
        259–261
    types of, 10–12
    See also higher education

Columbia University, 82, 88, 90, 98–101, 105, 127–135, 141–142, 149, 151, 245

Commission on Higher Education, 268

communication
challenges at Spelman College, 110–111
dialogue, 44–45, 67–74, 98
effective, 96

community
building, 24, 31–36, 42, 183
sense of, 179
structured dialogue programs, 73

community colleges, 10–12, 75, 203, 219, 221, 270

competency-based education (CBE), 280

conflict management, 94–102

connection, cultivating, 185–186

Connerly, Ward, 248

Copeland, Misty, 301–302

Corcoran, Richard, 56–57

Cornell University, 87, 270

Council on American-Islamic Relations (CAIR), 88

COVID-19 pandemic, 2, 3, 307
community building following, 34–35
enrollment effects, 191–193, 209
FAFSA completions and, 197
mental health and, 177–178, 183–184
online learning, 273
online radicalization and, 169
student protests, 5, 123–127
workplace shootings, 163

CPOST. See Chicago Project on Security and Threats

credentialing, 287–290

Creighton, Joanne, 31, 120–122

critical race theory, 55

critical thinking, 54, 171

Cross, Cristina J., 86

Crow, Michael, 312–313

cultivating leadership, 24, 37–41, 46

cultural centers, 29–30, 38, 120–122

curriculum, BIPOC representation in, 27–28

Daniel, Robert, 48

Danube Institute, 59

data analytics, 280–281

David, Steven, 146–147

deans, 22–24, 104

"Dear Colleague" letter, 15, 77, 144–145

"Defending Women from Gender Ideology Extremism and Restoring Biological Truth to the Federal Government" executive order, 14

degree completion, 269–272

degree-granting institutions, 10

DEI. See diversity, equity, and inclusion programs

demographics
birth rates, 190
college students, 9–10, 16, 42–43, 200–203, 247, 254–255, 259–261
feelings of loneliness, 173
population shifts, 199–200
racial/ethnic shifts, 200–201
US population, 26–-27, 37

department chairs, 20–21, 104

Department of Education, 15, 17, 77, 144, 151, 194, 195–196, 257

Department of Health and Human Services (HHS), 16, 232–233

Department of Homeland Security, 167–168
Department of Justice, 151, 167
deportations, 16, 152–153
depression, 175, 177, 181, 182
DeSantis, Ron, 50, 54–58
dialogue, 44–45, 67–74, 98, 145–154
discrimination
  political, 88
  racial, 245
  state-sponsored, 79
  Title IX protections, 14–15
  workplace, 64
disruptive innovation, 272–275
diversity
  among student protesters, 143
  campus, 75
  in leadership, 12–13
  in learning environments, 23, 37, 53–54, 57, 244
  LGBTQ+ inclusion, 45–46
  racial/ethnic, 6, 10–13, 243–244
  religious, 34, 45
diversity, equity, and inclusion (DEI) programs
  ABCs agenda and, 42–43
  anti-DEI legislation, 61–65, 76–78, 81
  attacks on, 50, 75
  in business, 64
  concerns about, 65–66
  "Dear Colleague" letter, 15, 77 144–145
  executive orders against, 14, 17
  opposition to, 55
  "plagiarism hunt," 86
divestment demands, 127–131, 137–138, 141–142, 145–146
"divisive concepts," 63–64
donors, 214–215, 221, 303
Duke University, 231, 260–261

educational attainment, 202, 229, 244–245, 253–254
Education for All, 75
Edward Waters University, 164–165
Eisgruber, Christopher, 91
elite institutions, 200, 202–203, 219, 243–244, 253–257, 265
Emerson University, 93
Emory University, 135–136
employee education, 288–289
employee resource groups (ERGs), 29–30
"Ending Illegal Discrimination and Restoring Merit-Based Opportunity" executive order, 13–14, 261
endowments, 215–222, 224
enrollment
  cliff, 190–191, 240
  COVID-19 pandemic and, 191–193, 209
  declining, 5, 8, 189, 200, 211–212
  FAFSA and, 194–199
  geographic location and, 199–200
  international students, 191
  race-conscious admissions practices and, 258–259
  student demographics, 201–202
entertainment industry, 273–275
Equal Employment Opportunity executive order, 14
Equality in Educational Land-Grant Status Act (1994), 226
Essential Partners, 73
Everyday Democracy, 73
Executive Order 11246 (1965), 245–246, 252
"Executive Order on Combating Race and Sex Stereotypes," 63–64
executive orders, 14, 17, 63–64, 77, 151, 245–246, 261

extremist ideas, 168–172
Eyring, Henry J., 272–273, 290, 294, 298

faculty
  adjunct, 238–239
  AI literacy, 282–287
  Black, 20
  college presidents and, 109–110
  as first line of defense in mental health crisis, 179–181
  mental health crisis in, 183
  role in shared governance, 104–105, 109–110, 117–118
FAFSA, 194–199, 213
FAFSA Simplification Act, 194
Farm Bill (2018), 224
FBI Joint Terrorism Task Forces, 166
Federal Student Aid (FSA) office, 195–196
Feldman, David H., 236
Fenves, Greg, 135–136
financial aid, 10, 11, 17, 121, 144–145, 194–199, 213, 216, 220
FIRE. See Foundation for Individual Rights and Expression
firing decisions, 104
Fisher, Abigail, 249
Fisher v. University of Texas, 249
Florida A&M University, 48
Florida State Board of Education, 57–58
Florida State University (FSU), 48, 49
Floyd, George, 3, 63, 221
Ford, Kristie, 69
Fort Valley State University, 224
Foundation for Individual Rights and Expression (FIRE), 152–153
four-year institutions, 10–12, 191, 192, 199, 270

freedom of expression, 80, 96, 102
free speech
  academic freedom and, 98
  anti-DEI legislation and, 62
  "both sides" language, 81–82
  campus safety and, 86–90
  congressional hearings, 82–84
  defense of offensive language, 80–81
  importance of, 91, 102
  polarization and, 6
  Title VI violations, 145
  See also student protests
Friedman, John, 255
"full pay" students, 240
funding
  federal, 77, 144–145, 196, 224, 229–235, 261
  financial aid, 10, 11, 17, 121, 144–145, 194–199, 213, 216, 220
  land grant institutions, 222–227
  Pell Grants, 11, 194–195, 218–220
  private for-profit institutions, 11–12
  private nonprofit institutions, 11
  public institutions, 11
  research grants, 16–17, 230–235
  state, 224–235
  See also budgets
fundraising, 214–215, 303
FUTURE Act, 194

Gaffney, Karen, 171–172
GAI. See generative AI
gaming, radicalization and, 169
Gavin, Michael, 171
Gay, Claudine, 83–86, 98
Gaza, 81, 90, 117, 128, 142, 144, 147, 149
gender diversity, 14
gender fluidity, 6

gender identity, 14–15, 42, 61–62, 164, 176
gender studies, 58
generative AI (GAI), 282–287
genocide, 82–83, 89, 99, 150
Genovese, Eugene, 101
Georgetown University, 219, 269
Georgia State University, 281
Gillman, Howard, 79–80, 102
Giroux, Henry, 37
"The Good Idea Fund" (TGIF), 184–185
Google, 288
governance. *See* shared governance
gratitude, 303–308
Gratz v. Bollinger, 248
Grawe, Nathan, 190–191, 199–202, 210, 228
Great Migration, 48–49
Great Recession (2008), 190, 211, 217, 279, 311
"great replacement" theory, 168–169, 171
"Great Resignation," 184
Great South Atlantic Conference, 291
Greenwald, David, 98
Grutter, Barbara, 248
Grutter v. Bollinger, 248–249
gun violence, 5, 95, 156–163, 175
Gurin, Patricia, 53, 73–74

HackerRank, 288
happiness, 181–182, 303, 308
Harvard University, 43, 49, 76, 83–86, 88, 98, 149, 203, 204, 216, 217, 231, 243, 246–247, 249–253, 257–260, 273
Hashem, Jadd, 148–149
Hatch Act (1887), 224
hate crimes, 62, 164–172

HBCUs (historically Black colleges or universities), 8, 48, 143, 311
bomb threats, 166–167, 170–171
endowments, 220–222
founding of, 165
funding, 220–221, 222, 234–235
gun violence, 162
hate crimes, 164–165
land grant institutions, 222–227
Pell Grants, 219–220, 226
Healthy Minds Network, 175
Healthy Minds Study, 175
HEDI. *See* Higher Education Demand Index
Heritage Foundation, 59
higher education
anti-DEI legislation, 61–65, 76–78, 81
"anti-woke" agenda, 55–58
author's experience in, 7–8
benefits of, 269–272, 289–290
challenges facing, 5, 8
confidence in, 267–268
disruptive innovation, 272–275, 287–290, 297–298
extremist indoctrination risk reduction, 171–172
leadership diversity, 12–13
loss of confidence in, 6–7
purpose and goals of, 268–269
rise in educational attainment, 202, 229
See also colleges and universities
Higher Education Act (1965), 234
Higher Education Demand Index (HEDI), 190–191, 199–200
Higher Education Mental Health Alliance, 176
Hillsdale College, 56
Hindu students, 27, 34, 38, 41

Hinton, Mary Dana, 13
hiring decisions, 104, 108–109
Hispanic-serving institutions (HSIs), 234
Hispanic students, 9, 11, 195, 201, 244
Holley, Danielle R., 6, 69
Holloway, Jonathan, 139, 140, 141
House Committee on Education and the Workforce, 82, 98–99
House Judiciary Subcommittee on Crime, Terrorism, and Homeland Security, 168
Howard University, 48, 220, 245
Huang, Margaret, 168–169, 170–171
Hungary, 58–59
Hutson, Mary Pope Maybank, 209

identity
    affirming, 24, 25–31, 42–43
    marginalized, 74, 121
    privileged, 74
    social, 68
IHRA. *See* International Holocaust Remembrance Alliance
immigration, 16, 201
Immigration and Customs Enforcement (ICE), 16
inclusivity, 6, 32–33, 45–46, 50, 80–81
Indigenous students, 120
institutional neutrality, 96–97
intergroup dialogue programs, 23–24, 67–74
intergroup relations, 23
International Holocaust Remembrance Alliance (IHRA), 152
international students, 16, 191
invisibility, 25, 27
Islamophobia, 82, 87, 117, 150
isolation, 172

Israel-Hamas war, 1, 72, 81, 82, 86, 96, 98–99, 117, 127, 128, 137–138, 142, 144, 147, 149, 151, 164
Israeli-Palestinian conflict, 87–94, 129, 146–149
Ithaka S+R, 283–284
Ivy League, 10, 243–244, 253–257, 265

Jackson State University, 120
JED Campus program, 178–181
Jed Foundation, 178–179
Jeffries, Hasan Kwame, 65–66
Jewish students, 27, 38, 40–41, 45, 82–84, 87–90, 98, 137, 142–143, 147–148, 151
Jewish Voice for Peace, 90, 137–138
Jim Crow South, 49, 53, 292
Johns Hopkins University, 146–148, 231, 257
Johnson, Lyndon B., 14, 245, 252
Johnston, Angus, 119, 133
Jones, James F., Jr., 204, 206
joy, sources of
    people met, 300–308
    problems solved, 308–309
    purpose fulfilled, 309–314

Kaggle, 288
Kahlenberg, Elijah, 148–149
Kalven, Harry, Jr., 96
Kalven Report, 96, 102
Karabel, Jerome, 246
Kent State University, 120, 141
Kestin, Greg, 284–285
Khan, Salman, 285–286
Khan Academy, 285
Khanmigo, 285–286
Kimmerer, Robin Wall, 303
King, Martin Luther, Jr., 64, 246

Kirk, Grayson, 131–132
Kornbluth, Sally, 83, 84, 97

land grant institutions, 222–227
languages, spoken in US, 26
Latinx students, 29–30, 120, 164, 254–255, 259, 260
leadership
    authority, 30, 44
    Black women, 83–86
    civil discourse, 92–102
    coalition building, 74–78
    conflict management, 94–102
    cultivating, 24, 37–41, 46
    cultivating connection, 185–186
    deans, 22–24, 104
    department chairs, 20–21, 104
    diversity, 12–13
    importance of, 43–46
    societal, 64
    speaking out against anti-DEI legislation, 76–78
    Spelman College challenges, 111
    See also college presidents; shared governance
learning environments
    benefits of diverse, 23, 37, 53–54, 57, 244
    dialogue within, 146–154
    educational impacts, 71
    hostile, 86–87
    inclusive, 80–81
    intergroup dialogue programs, 23–24, 67–74
LeBlanc, Paul, 276–281, 287, 290, 308
legacy admissions, 254–255, 257, 261
legislation
    anti-DEI, 61–65, 76–78, 81
    educational gag orders, 62–63

executive orders, 14, 17, 63–64, 77, 151, 245–246, 261
Levine, Arthur, 273
LGBTQ+ rights, 5, 15, 65
LGBTQ+ students, 45–46, 57, 61–62, 120, 122, 164
Lincoln College, 193
Loehr, Jim, 187
loneliness, 172–181, 184, 186
Lorde, Audre, 46
Lyon, Mary, 2

Machine Learning University (MLU), 289
Magill, Elizabeth, 83, 84
Making Caring Common Project, 173
Mandel, Maud, 94, 95–96
marginalization, 27, 29, 31–32, 74, 173
Massad, Joseph, 99–101
mass shootings, 6, 95, 159–163, 173
McQuiston, John, II, 299–300
mental health crisis
    access to resources and counseling, 8, 177–181
    anxiety, 174, 175, 181, 182
    campus safety and, 5
    college presidents, 185–186
    COVID-19 pandemic and, 183–184
    depression, 175, 177, 182
    faculty and staff, 183
    impacts on, 173
    loneliness, 172–181
    smartphones and, 181–183
    suicide, 172, 175–177, 181
    threat assessment, 180
merit aid, 213
MHC COVID Safety Now Collective, 123–127
Michigan State University (MSU), 95, 159–161, 222
Miller-Idriss, Cynthia, 169–170

MIT, 83, 84, 97, 255, 257, 260
Morehouse College, 8, 143–144
Morgan State University, 162, 167, 225
Morrill Act (1862), 222
Morrill Act (1890), 222–223
Mount Holyoke College
  author's experience at,
    2–3, 4–7, 19–24, 30–31, 34–35,
    68–69, 94–95, 120–127, 155–156,
    159–161, 177–179, 183–185, 203,
    235, 265, 281, 307–308
  community-building, 34–36
  COVID-19 pandemic, 5, 34–35,
    123–127, 177–178, 183–185
  cultural centers, 38, 120–122
  founding of, 2–3
  "The Good Idea Fund," 184–185
  identity affirmation, 30–31
  Intergroup Dialogue Symposium,
    67, 69
  leadership cultivation, 38–41
  Multi-faith Council, 38–40
  Project Connect, 179
  Psychology of Racism course,
    19–20, 59–60, 69, 72, 265
  Religious Life Advisory Board, 38–40
  student protests, 120–127
multiracial identity, 26
Mulvey, Irene, 101, 145, 150
Murthy, Vivek, 172, 182
music industry, 274–275
Muslim students, 27, 38, 40, 45, 87–90,
  137

NACUBO. See National Association
  of College and University
  Business Officers
National Agricultural Research,
  Extension, and Teaching Policy
  Act (1977), 224

National Association of College and
  University Business Officers
  (NACUBO), 212, 214, 216
National Institutes of Health (NIH),
  16–17, 232–233, 293
national institutions, 200, 203
Native Americans, 226–227. See also
  American Indian/Alaska Native
  students
Native Hawaiian students, 235, 260
NCAA, 191–192, 291–294
need-blind admissions, 213
net tuition revenue, 213
New College of Florida
  "anti-woke" agenda, 55–58
  athletics program, 56–57
  author's experience with, 47, 50
  Corcoran's presidency, 56–57
  Derek Black's experience at,
    50–54, 57
  DeSantis and, 54–58
  founding of, 49–50
  Gender and Diversity Center, 58
  Okker's removal, 55–56, 58
  O'Shea's presidency, 47, 55
New York Police Department
  (NYPD), 131–134, 141
New York University, 141
NIH. See National Institutes of Health
Noble, Jeremy, 172–173, 174
nonbinary people, 14, 176
North Carolina Agricultural and
  Technical State University, 225
Northwestern University, 136–137,
  138, 139, 145, 151, 204

o1-preview, 287
O'Connor, Sandra Day, 249, 251
October 7 attack on Israel, 81, 82, 88,
  89, 99, 117, 149

Office of Civil Rights, 15, 77, 144–145
Okker, Patricia, 55–56, 58, 75
online learning, 272–273. *See also*
　Southern New Hampshire
　University
OpenAI, 281, 287
Opportunity Insights, 254–257, 265
Orbán, Viktor, 58–59
O'Shea, Donal, 47, 55

Pacific Islander students, 9, 195, 201,
　235, 260
Packard, Sophia, 2, 294
Palestinian students, 88, 148–150
Pape, Robert, 87, 89–90
parents, youth online radicalization
　and, 169–170
Paxson, Christina, 138, 141
Pell Grants, 11, 194–195, 218–220
PEN America, 62–63
phone-free schools, 182
plagiarism, 84–86, 282
polarization, 6, 44, 72, 73, 102
Pomona College, 127–131
population demographics, 26,
　199–201
Posse Foundation, 262–265
preferred pronouns, 6, 29
prejudicial antisemitism, 89
Princeton University, 91, 144, 214, 217,
　243, 260–261
private for-profit institutions, 10–12,
　270
private nonprofit institutions, 10–12,
　199, 216, 270
privilege, 74, 256–257
problem-solving, 74, 308–309
Program on Intergroup Relations
　(IGR), 23, 67–68, 73
pro-Israel counterprotests, 139–140

Project Connect, 179
promotion process, 104–105
pro-Palestinian protests, 81–84,
　87–88, 98, 101, 131–137, 142–151
proprietary institutions, 11–12
public institutions, 10–12, 191, 199,
　216, 222, 270

racism
　impacts of learning history of,
　　59–61, 65–66
　psychology of, 19–20, 59–60, 69
　public reckoning with, 63
　rise of, 166
radicalization, 168–172
*Regents of the University of California
　v. Bakke*, 247
regional institutions, 200, 203, 219
religious beliefs and practices
　accommodations for, 38–41
　celebrations of, 32–34
　demographics, 26–27
　representation of, 30–31, 45
representation, 27–28
research grants, 16–17, 230–235
research-intensive universities (R-1
　institutions), 232
Roberts, John, 251, 252, 258
Roe v. Wade, 4
Ross, Loretta, 98
Roth, Michael, 145, 261
Roundtree, Dovey Johnson, 241
Rufo, Christopher, 55, 56, 58–59,
　84–85, 86
Rule of Benedict, 299
Rutgers University, 101, 139, 140, 222

Schatzel, Kim, 76–77
Schill, Michael, 136–137, 138, 139, 140,
　141

scholarships, 213–214, 215, 218, 240
school shootings, 6, 95, 159–163
segregation
"1890" land grant HBCUs, 223–224
in Baltimore, 45
in Florida, 48–50
Jim Crow South, 49, 53
overcoming legacies of, 23, 50
in schools, 37, 47–50, 165
in Texas, 249
self-care, 186–187
Seven Sisters, 7, 8
sexual harassment, 15
sexual orientation, 45–46
Shafik, Nemat "Minouche," 82, 90,
98–101, 131–135, 143, 151
shared governance
author's experience with, 110–118
board's role, 104–110
delegation of authority, 106
faculty's role, 104–105, 109–110,
117–118
historically, 106–107
lack of understanding about,
103–104
as an organizing principle, 100, 103
president's role, 104–105, 106,
108–109
provost's role, 104–105
at Spelman College, 110–118
students' role, 119
smartphones, 181–183
Smith, Michael D., 274–275, 288
Smith College, 8, 127–131, 141
social identity, 68
social isolation, 172, 173
social justice, 60–61, 65
social media, 79–80, 176, 181–183
sociology, study of, 57–58
solidarity dividend, 40

Southern New Hampshire University
(SNHU), 276–281, 287, 290, 308
Southern Poverty Law Center, 52, 166,
168, 169–170
speech
limiting of, 79–80, 102
offensive, 91–92
protest, 81–84, 87–88, 89–90, 91,
101
punishing, 91–92
as violence, 87
See also free speech
Spelman College
alumnae giving, 214
athletics program, 291–297
Audre Lorde archive, 46
author's experience at, 2–3, 4,
6, 7–8, 30, 32–34, 45–46, 48,
110–118, 156–159, 176–177, 186,
203–204, 211–212, 214, 235,
236–237, 301–307, 309–312
bomb threats, 166–168
community-building, 32–34
endowments, 220, 221
Faculty Council, 113–117
financial aid, 213
founding of, 2–3, 33, 294
media impressions, 112
mission statement, 311
student protests, 143
wellness program, 293–297
Stanford University, 8, 85–86, 231
Starr, Gabrielle, 129
Stefanik, Elise, 83–84
Stone, Phillip, 206–207
student demographics, 9–10, 16,
42–43, 200–203, 247, 254–255,
259–261
student loans, 11, 195, 270
student protests

1960s/1970s social movements, 79–80, 96, 120, 131–132
building takeovers, 120–132
COVID-19 pandemic, 123–127
dialogue and, 145–154
divestment demands, 127–131, 137–138, 141–142, 145–146
encampments, 128–140, 145
history of, 119–120
institutional parameters, 101–102
negotiated resolution, 136–138
police involvement, 126, 127, 129–141
portrayal of by politicians, 140–141
pro-Israel counterprotests, 139–140
pro-Palestinian, 81–84, 87–88, 98, 101, 131–137, 142–151
in response to campus-based decisions, 120–122
Title VI violations, 145
Students for Fair Admissions (SFFA), 249–251, 254, 260–261
Students for Fair Admissions, Inc. v. President and Fellows of Harvard College, 6, 243, 249–253, 258–259
Students for Fair Admissions, Inc. v. the University of North Carolina, 243, 249
suicidal ideation and risk, 172, 175–177, 181
sustaining innovation, 272
Sweet Briar College, 204–210, 309

Tax Reform Act (2014), 217–218
Taylor, Keeanga-Yamahtta, 142–143, 144
technical schools, 10–12, 272
tenure decisions, 104–105
Tessier-Lavigne, Marc, 85–86
Texas A&M University, 62, 222

Texas Tech University, 62
Thelin, John R., 106–107, 230
Title IV, 10, 261
Title IX, 14–15
Title VI, 144–145
Tochluk, Shelly, 170
Top Ten Percent Plan, 249
trade schools, 272
Transgender Day of Remembrance, 94–95
transgender people, 14, 15, 164, 175–176
transphobia, 5
tribal colleges and universities (TCUs), 226–227
Truman, Harry, 230, 268
Truman Commission, 289
Trump, Donald, 13–17, 59, 63–64, 65, 77, 151–153, 217–218, 232–234, 261
trust-building, 71–72
tuition and fees, 5, 197–198, 212–214, 216, 229, 235–236, 240, 277
tuition-dependent institutions, 212
Turner, Sherry, 32–33
tutors, AI, 284–287
Twenge, Jean M., 181
two-year institutions, 10–12, 191, 192, 199, 200, 203, 270

uncertainty, 174, 187
undocumented immigrants, 16
University of California, Berkeley, 120, 151
University of California, Davis, 247
University of California, Los Angeles, 139–140, 259
University of Chicago, 86–87, 96, 149, 260
University of Georgia, 222, 223

University of Kentucky, 76
University of Louisville, 76
University of Lynchburg, 197–199,
    203, 212–213
University of Maryland Eastern Shore,
    225
University of Massachusetts, Amherst,
    68
University of Michigan, 7, 23, 53,
    67–68, 73–74, 203, 216, 231,
    248–249, 256
University of Michigan Law School,
    248
University of Minnesota, Twin Cities,
    151, 257
University of Nevada, Las Vegas, 163
University of North Carolina, 163,
    179–180
University of Pennsylvania, 76, 83, 84,
    102, 149, 150, 183, 231
University of Texas, Austin, 61,
    148–149, 249
University of Virginia, 216
US Congress, 76
    campus antisemitism hearings,
        82–84, 97–101, 103–104, 139,
        142–144
    House Committee on Education
        and the Workforce, 82, 98–99
    House Judiciary Subcommittee on
        Crime, Terrorism, and Homeland
        Security, 168
US Government Accountability
    Office, 37
US News & World Report, 112, 200, 203
US Supreme Court
    Brown v. Board of Education, 47–48,
        65, 241
    Dobbs v. Jackson Women's Health,
        4–5

Fisher v. University of Texas, 249
Gratz v. Bollinger, 248
Grutter v. Bollinger, 248–249
Regents of the University of
    California v. Bakke, 247
Roe v. Wade, 4
Students for Fair Admissions, Inc. v.
    President and Fellows of Harvard
    College, 6, 249–253, 258–259
Students for Fair Admissions, Inc. v.
    the University of North Carolina,
    243, 249
Students for Fair Admissions Inc. v.
    President and Fellows of Harvard
    College, 243

Vance, J. D., 59, 218
Vanderbilt University, 262, 290
Van Der Werf, Martin, 219
Van Pelt, Scott, 273
veterans, 75, 229, 260, 262
Vietnam War, 64, 79, 96, 120, 131–132
violence
    bomb threats, 166–168, 170–171
    extremist ideas and, 168–172
    gun, 5, 95, 156–163, 175
    hate crimes, 62, 164–172
    against LGBTQ+ community, 95
    political, 88–89, 96–97, 150
    speech as, 87
    student protests, 135–136,
        139–140
    workplace, 163
    See also campus safety
Virginia Tech, 161

Walberg, Tim, 99–100
Walmart, 64
Washington Post, 208–209
wellness programs, 293–297

Wesleyan University, 7, 8, 145–146, 203, 257, 261

Western Governors University, 281

White nationalism, 5, 51–53, 54, 59, 170–172

White students, 9, 11, 170, 195, 201, 254–255

Williams College, 94, 149

Willie-LeBreton, Sarah, 128, 131, 141

Wilson, David, 162

"woke," 54–55

women's colleges, 203–204. *See also* Sweet Briar College

Woo, Meredith, 207–209, 309

Yale University, 203, 260–261, 287

Yondr, 182

ZeroEyes, 162

Zúñiga, Ximena, 67, 68

BEVERLY DANIEL TATUM, PhD, is president emerita of Spelman College. She served as the ninth president of Spelman from 2002–2015. Her visionary leadership as president was recognized in 2013 with the Carnegie Academic Leadership Award. In 2014 she received the Award for Outstanding Lifetime Contribution to Psychology, the highest honor presented by the American Psychological Association. The author of four books, including the *New York Times*–bestselling *Why Are All the Black Kids Sitting Together in the Cafeteria?*, she lives in Atlanta, Georgia.

RAISING READERS
Books Build Bright Futures

Thank you for reading this book and for being a reader of books in general. As an author, I am so grateful to share being part of a community of readers with you, and I hope you will join me in passing our love of books on to the next generation of readers.

Did you know that reading for enjoyment is the single biggest predictor of a child's future happiness and success?

More than family circumstances, parents' educational background, or income, reading impacts a child's future academic performance, emotional well-being, communication skills, economic security, ambition, and happiness.

Studies show that kids reading for enjoyment in the US is in rapid decline:

- In 2012, 53% of 9-year-olds read almost every day. Just 10 years later, in 2022, the number had fallen to 39%.
- In 2012, 27% of 13-year-olds read for fun daily. By 2023, that number was just 14%.

Together, we can commit to **Raising Readers** and change this trend. How?

- Read to children in your life daily.
- Model reading as a fun activity.
- Reduce screen time.
- Start a family, school, or community book club.
- Visit bookstores and libraries regularly.
- Listen to audiobooks.
- Read the book before you see the movie.
- Encourage your child to read aloud to a pet or stuffed animal.
- Give books as gifts.
- Donate books to families and communities in need.

BOB1217

Books build bright futures, and **Raising Readers** is our shared responsibility.

For more information, visit **JoinRaisingReaders.com**

Sources: National Endowment for the Arts, National Assessment of Educational Progress, WorldBookDay.org, Nielsen BookData's 2023 "Understanding the Children's Book Consumer"